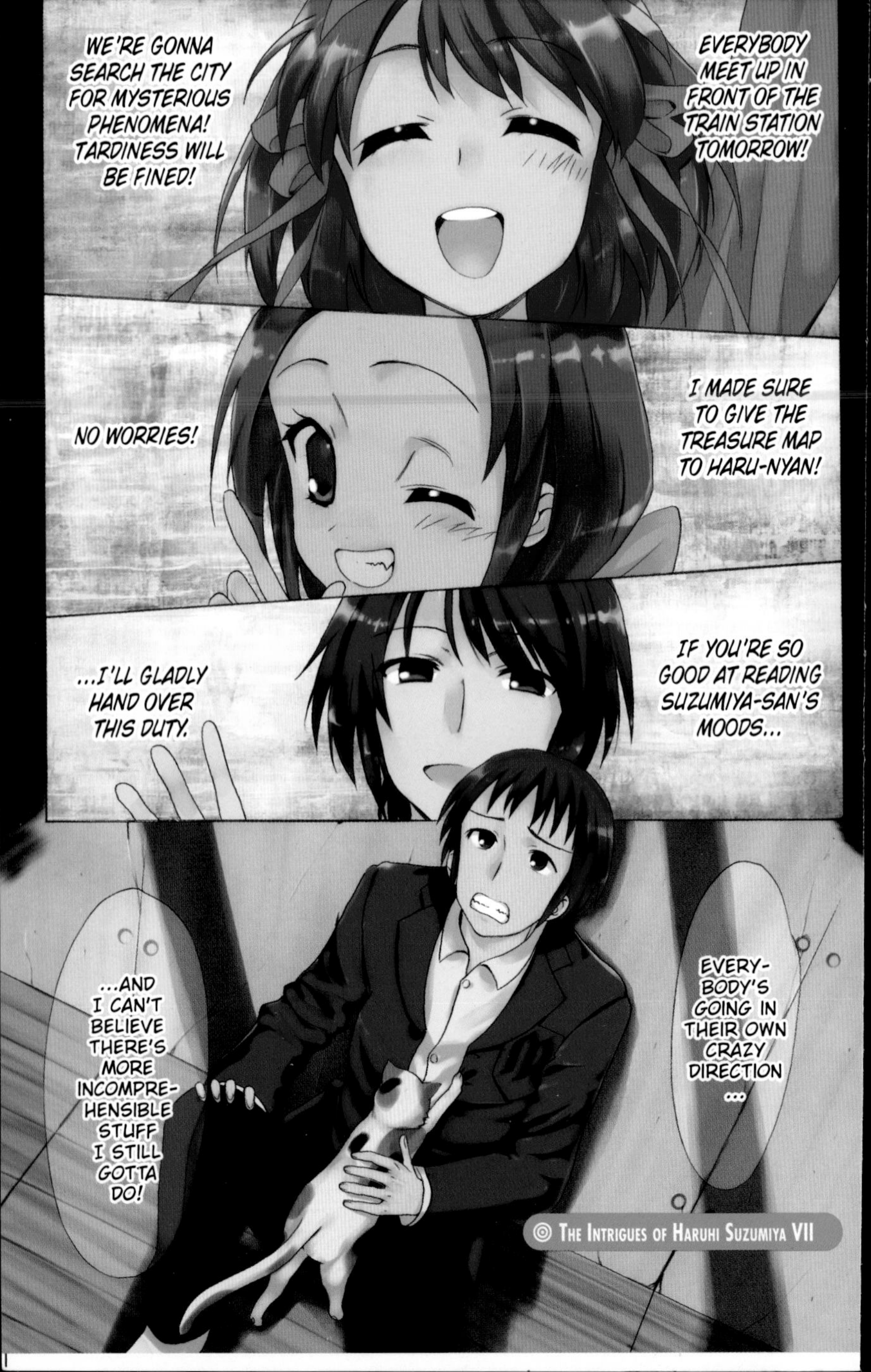
EVERYBODY MEET UP IN FRONT OF THE TRAIN STATION TOMORROW!
WE'RE GONNA SEARCH THE CITY FOR MYSTERIOUS PHENOMENA! TARDINESS WILL BE FINED!
I MADE SURE TO GIVE THE TREASURE MAP TO HARU-NYAN!
NO WORRIES!
IF YOU'RE SO GOOD AT READING SUZUMIYA-SAN'S MOODS...
...I'LL GLADLY HAND OVER THIS DUTY.
EVERY-BODY'S GOING IN THEIR OWN CRAZY DIRECTION...
...AND I CAN'T BELIEVE THERE'S MORE INCOMPRE-HENSIBLE STUFF I STILL GOTTA DO!
THE INTRIGUES OF HARUHI SUZUMIYA VII

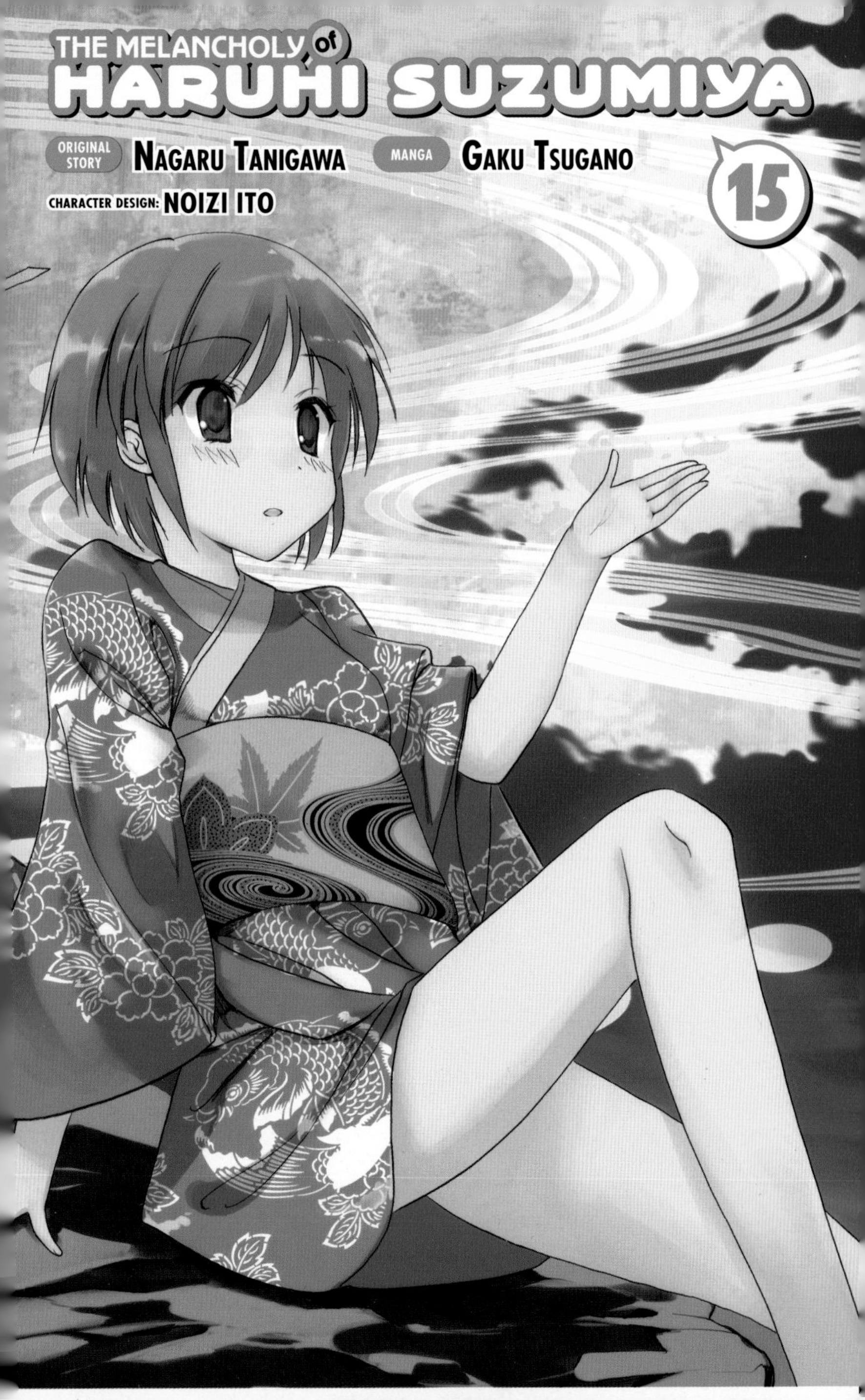
THE MELANCHOLY of
HARUHI SUZUMIYA
ORIGINAL STORY NAGARU TANIGAWA
MANGA GAKU TSUGANO
CHARACTER DESIGN: NOIZI ITO
15

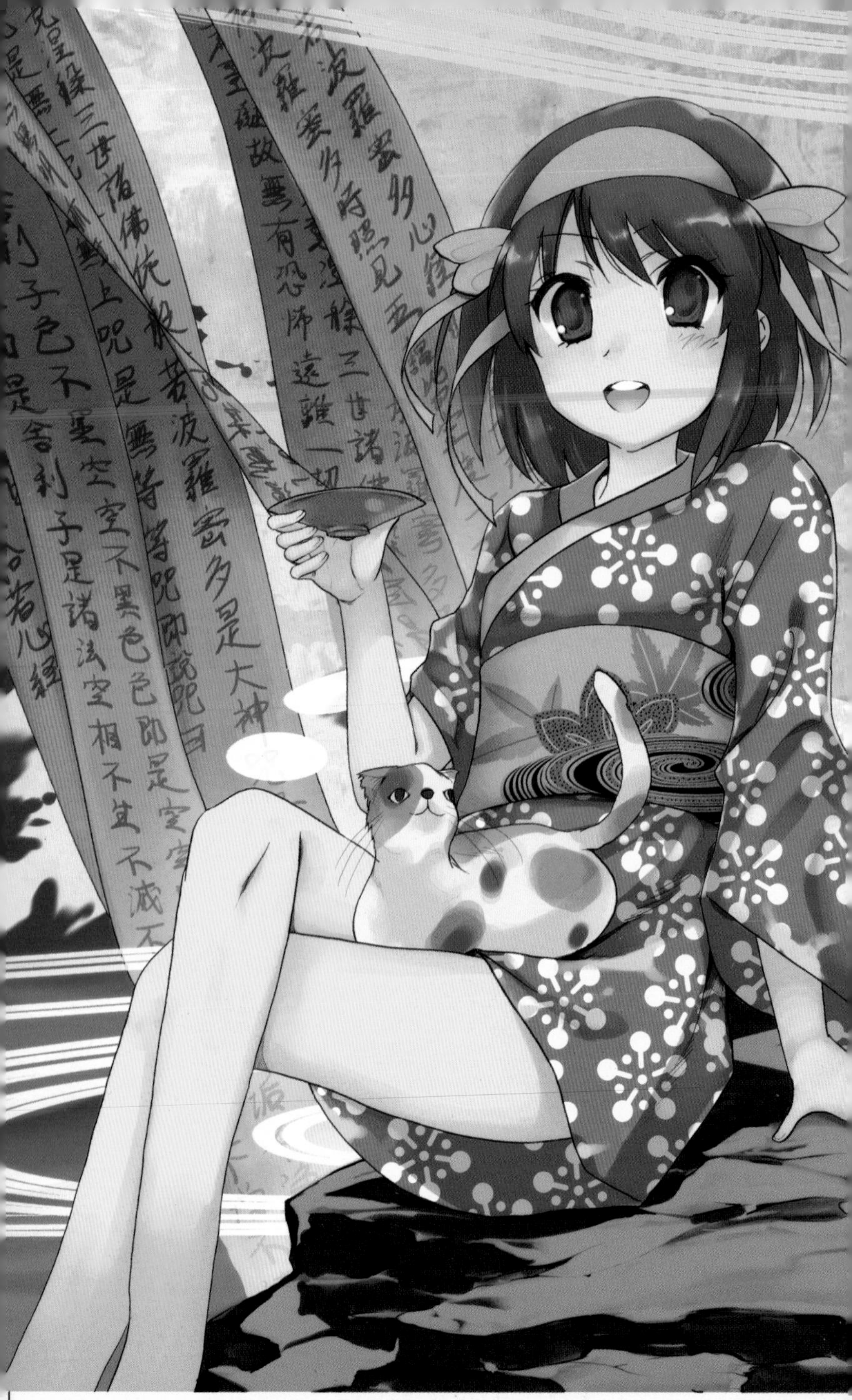

CONTENTS

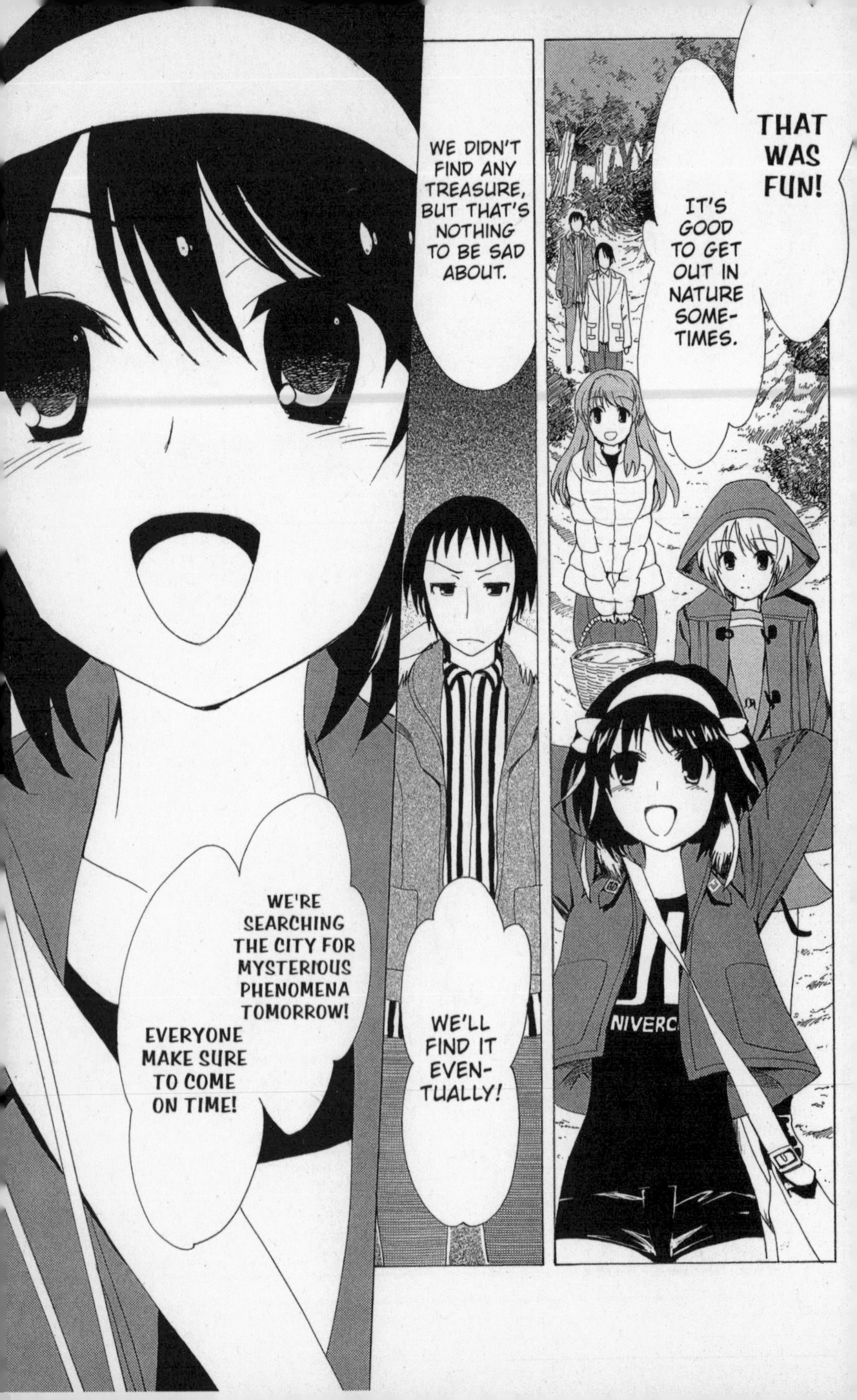
THAT WAS FUN!
IT'S GOOD TO GET OUT IN NATURE SOME-TIMES.
NIVERC
WE DIDN'T FIND ANY TREASURE, BUT THAT'S NOTHING TO BE SAD ABOUT.
WE'LL FIND IT EVEN-TUALLY!
WE'RE SEARCHING THE CITY FOR MYSTERIOUS PHENOMENA TOMORROW!
EVERYONE MAKE SURE TO COME ON TIME!

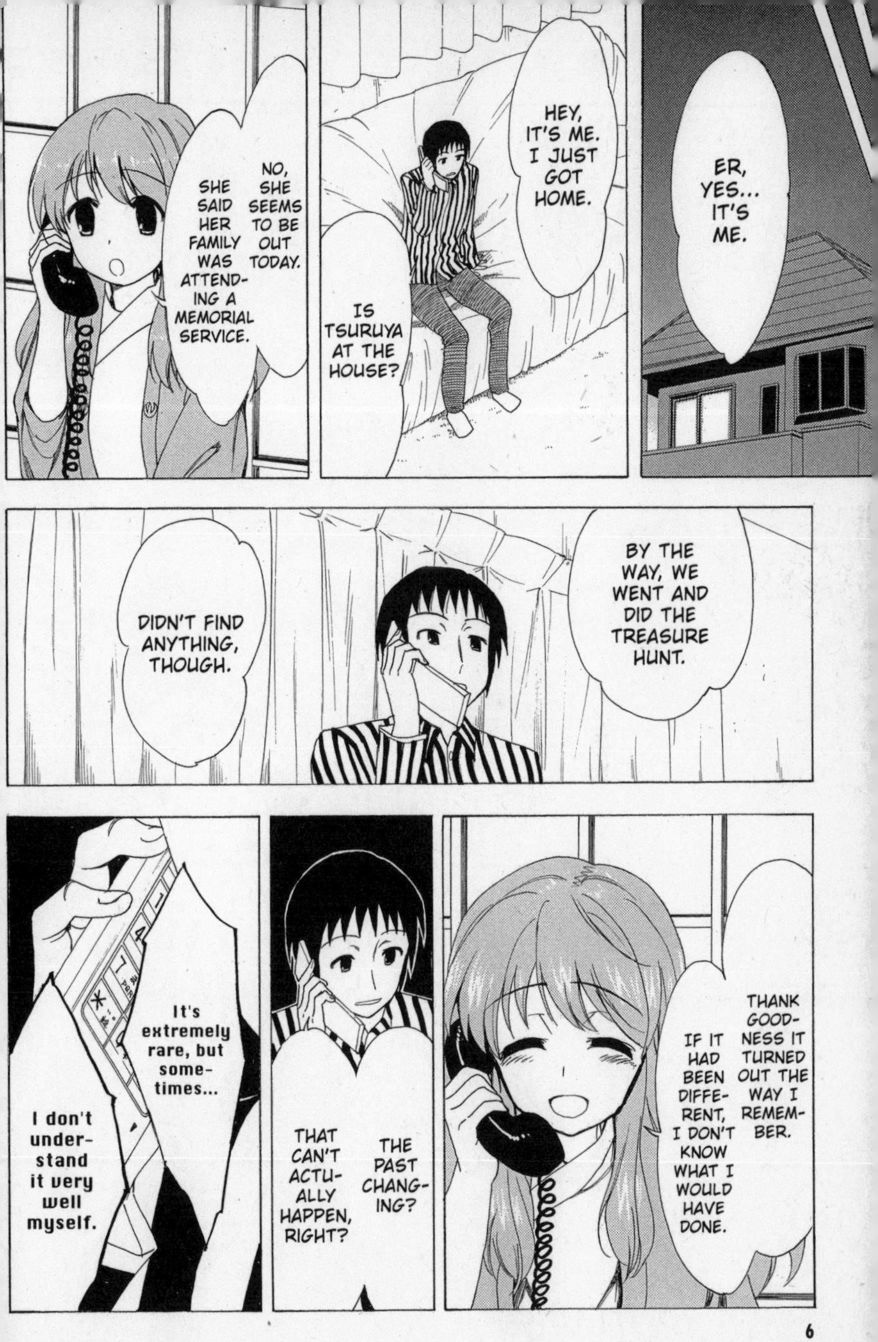
ER, YES... IT'S ME.
HEY, IT'S ME. I JUST GOT HOME.
IS TSURUYA AT THE HOUSE?
NO, SHE SEEMS TO BE OUT TODAY.
SHE SAID HER FAMILY WAS ATTENDING A MEMORIAL SERVICE.
BY THE WAY, WE WENT AND DID THE TREASURE HUNT.
DIDN'T FIND ANYTHING, THOUGH.
THANK GOODNESS IT TURNED OUT THE WAY I REMEMBER.
IF IT HAD BEEN DIFFERENT, I DON'T KNOW WHAT I WOULD HAVE DONE.
THE PAST CHANGING?
THAT CAN'T ACTUALLY HAPPEN, RIGHT?
It's extremely rare, but sometimes...
I don't understand it very well myself.

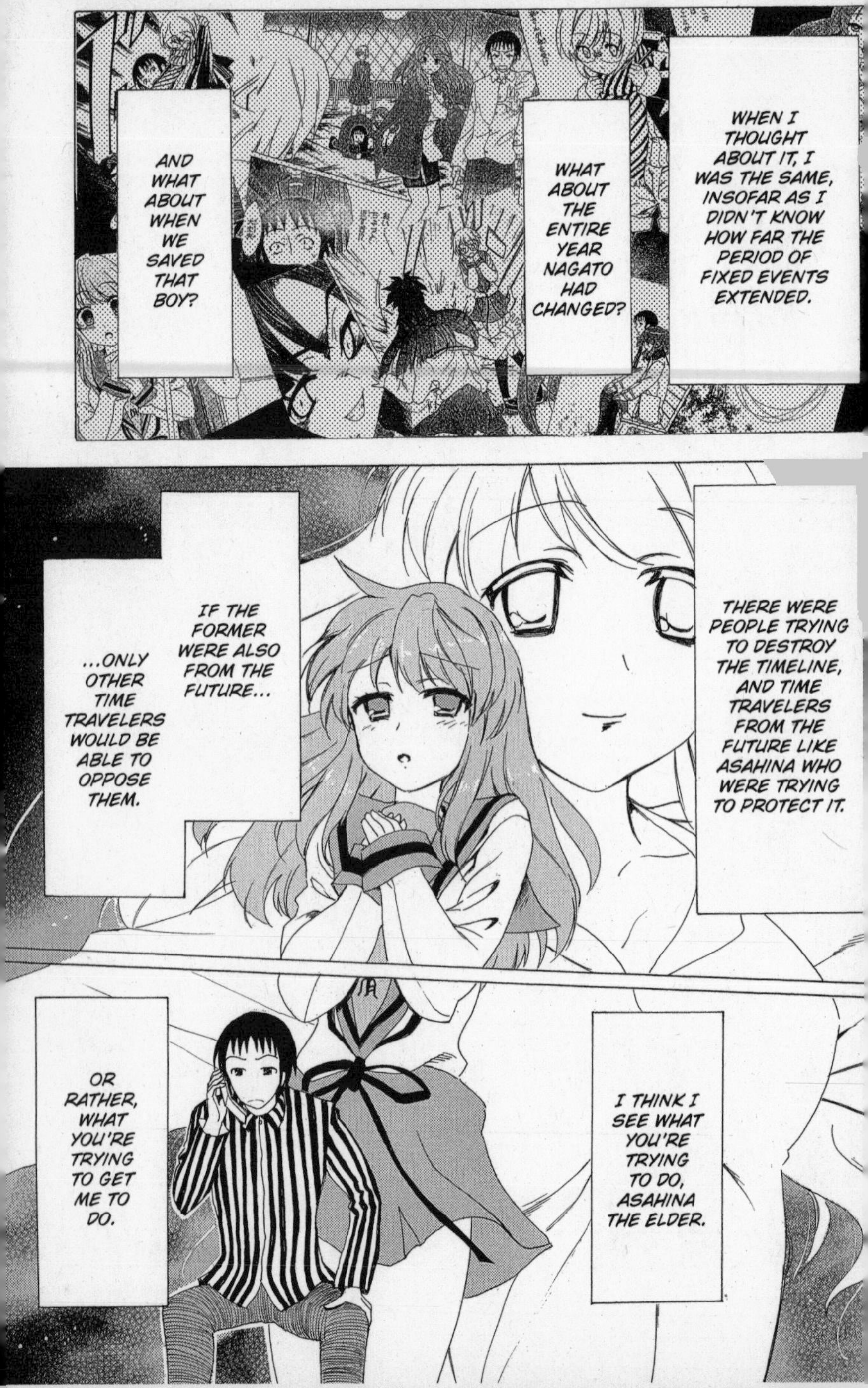
WHEN I THOUGHT ABOUT IT, I WAS THE SAME, INSOFAR AS I DIDN'T KNOW HOW FAR THE PERIOD OF FIXED EVENTS EXTENDED.
WHAT ABOUT THE ENTIRE YEAR NAGATO HAD CHANGED?
AND WHAT ABOUT WHEN WE SAVED THAT BOY?
THERE WERE PEOPLE TRYING TO DESTROY THE TIMELINE, AND TIME TRAVELERS FROM THE FUTURE LIKE ASAHINA WHO WERE TRYING TO PROTECT IT.
IF THE FORMER WERE ALSO FROM THE FUTURE...
...ONLY OTHER TIME TRAVELERS WOULD BE ABLE TO OPPOSE THEM.
I THINK I SEE WHAT YOU'RE TRYING TO DO, ASAHINA THE ELDER.
OR RATHER, WHAT YOU'RE TRYING TO GET ME TO DO.

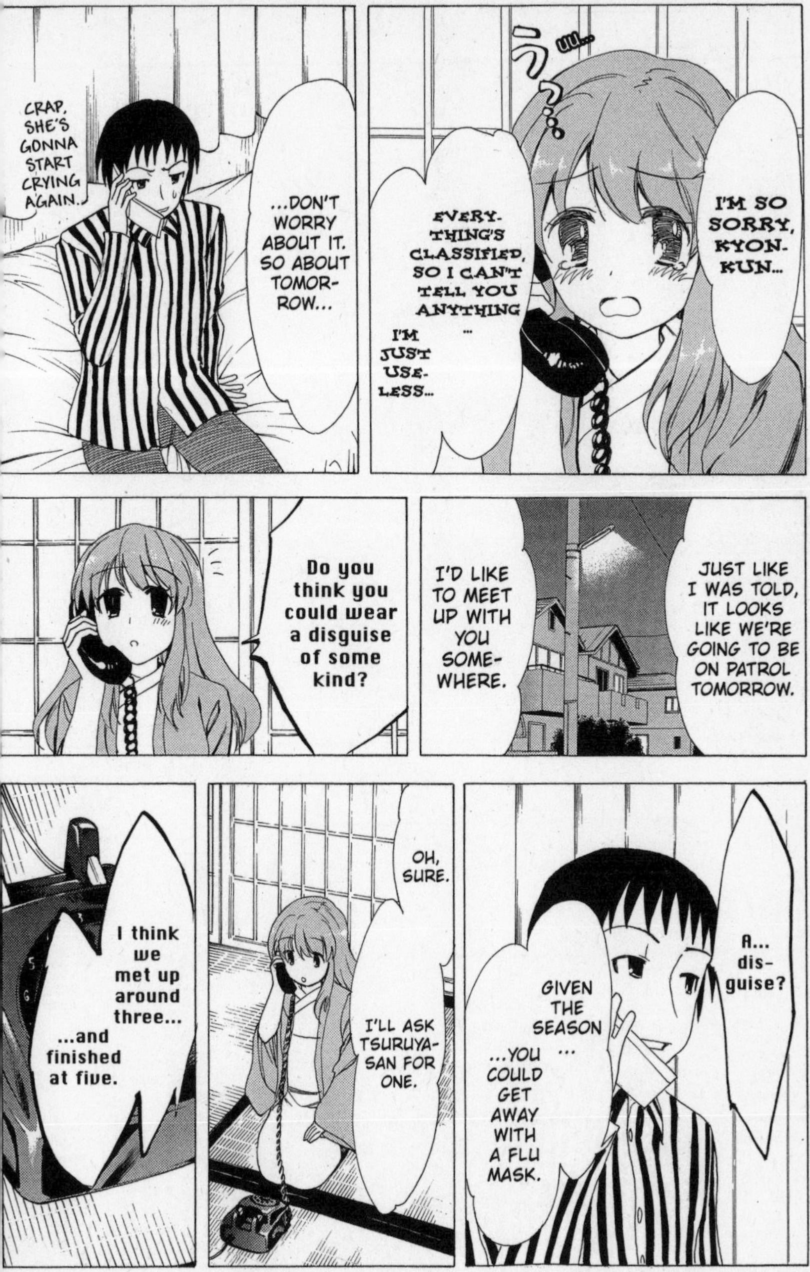
う uu...
I'M SO SORRY, KYON-KUN...
EVERYTHING'S CLASSIFIED, SO I CAN'T TELL YOU ANYTHING...
I'M JUST USELESS...
...DON'T WORRY ABOUT IT. SO ABOUT TOMORROW...
CRAP, SHE'S GONNA START CRYING AGAIN.
JUST LIKE I WAS TOLD, IT LOOKS LIKE WE'RE GOING TO BE ON PATROL TOMORROW.
I'D LIKE TO MEET UP WITH YOU SOMEWHERE.
Do you think you could wear a disguise of some kind?
A... disguise?
GIVEN THE SEASON...
...YOU COULD GET AWAY WITH A FLU MASK.
OH, SURE.
I'LL ASK TSURUYA-SAN FOR ONE.
I think we met up around three...
...and finished at five.

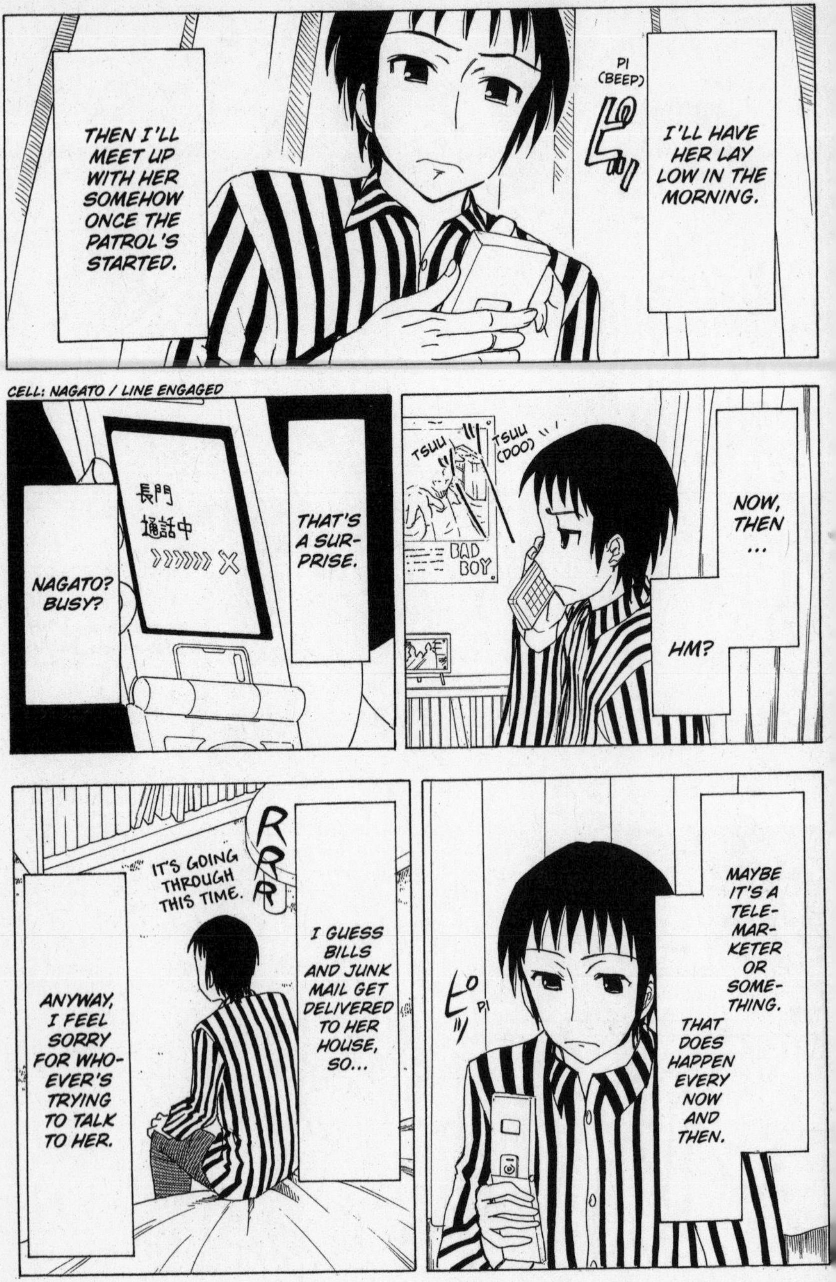
I'LL HAVE HER LAY LOW IN THE MORNING.
PI (BEEP)
THEN I'LL MEET UP WITH HER SOMEHOW ONCE THE PATROL'S STARTED.
NOW, THEN ...
TSUU (DOO)
TSUU
HM?
BAD BOY
CELL: NAGATO / LINE ENGAGED
THAT'S A SURPRISE.
長門
通話中
NAGATO? BUSY?
MAYBE IT'S A TELEMARKETER OR SOMETHING.
PI
THAT DOES HAPPEN EVERY NOW AND THEN.
RRR
I GUESS BILLS AND JUNK MAIL GET DELIVERED TO HER HOUSE, SO...
IT'S GOING THROUGH THIS TIME.
ANYWAY, I FEEL SORRY FOR WHO-EVER'S TRYING TO TALK TO HER.

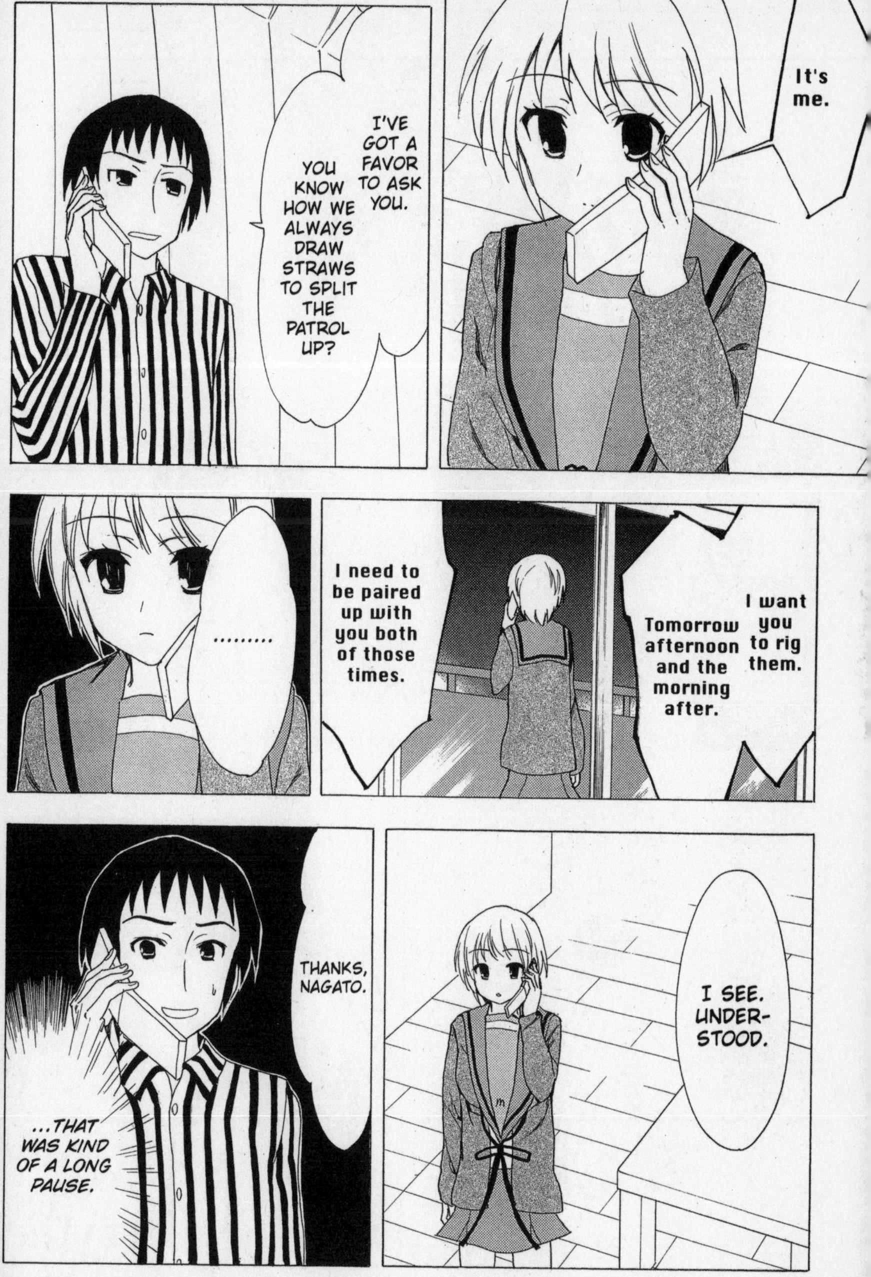
It's me.
I'VE GOT A FAVOR TO ASK YOU.
YOU KNOW HOW WE ALWAYS DRAW STRAWS TO SPLIT THE PATROL UP?
I want you to rig them.
Tomorrow afternoon and the morning after.
I need to be paired up with you both of those times.
....
I SEE. UNDERSTOOD.
THANKS, NAGATO.
...THAT WAS KIND OF A LONG PAUSE.

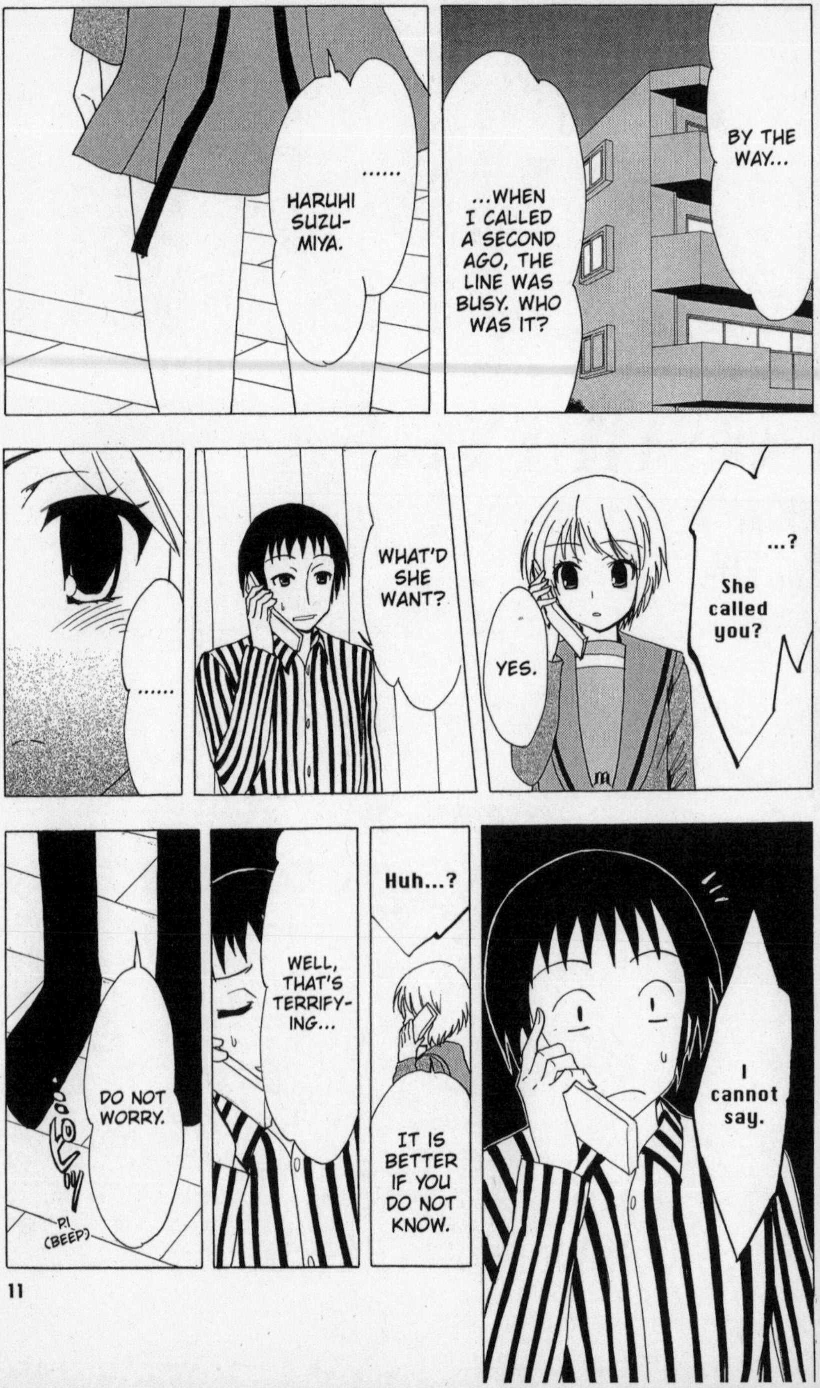
BY THE WAY...
...WHEN I CALLED A SECOND AGO, THE LINE WAS BUSY. WHO WAS IT?
......
HARUHI SUZU-MIYA.
...? She called you?
YES.
WHAT'D SHE WANT?
......
I cannot say.
Huh...?
IT IS BETTER IF YOU DO NOT KNOW.
WELL, THAT'S TERRIFY-ING...
DO NOT WORRY.
PI (BEEP)

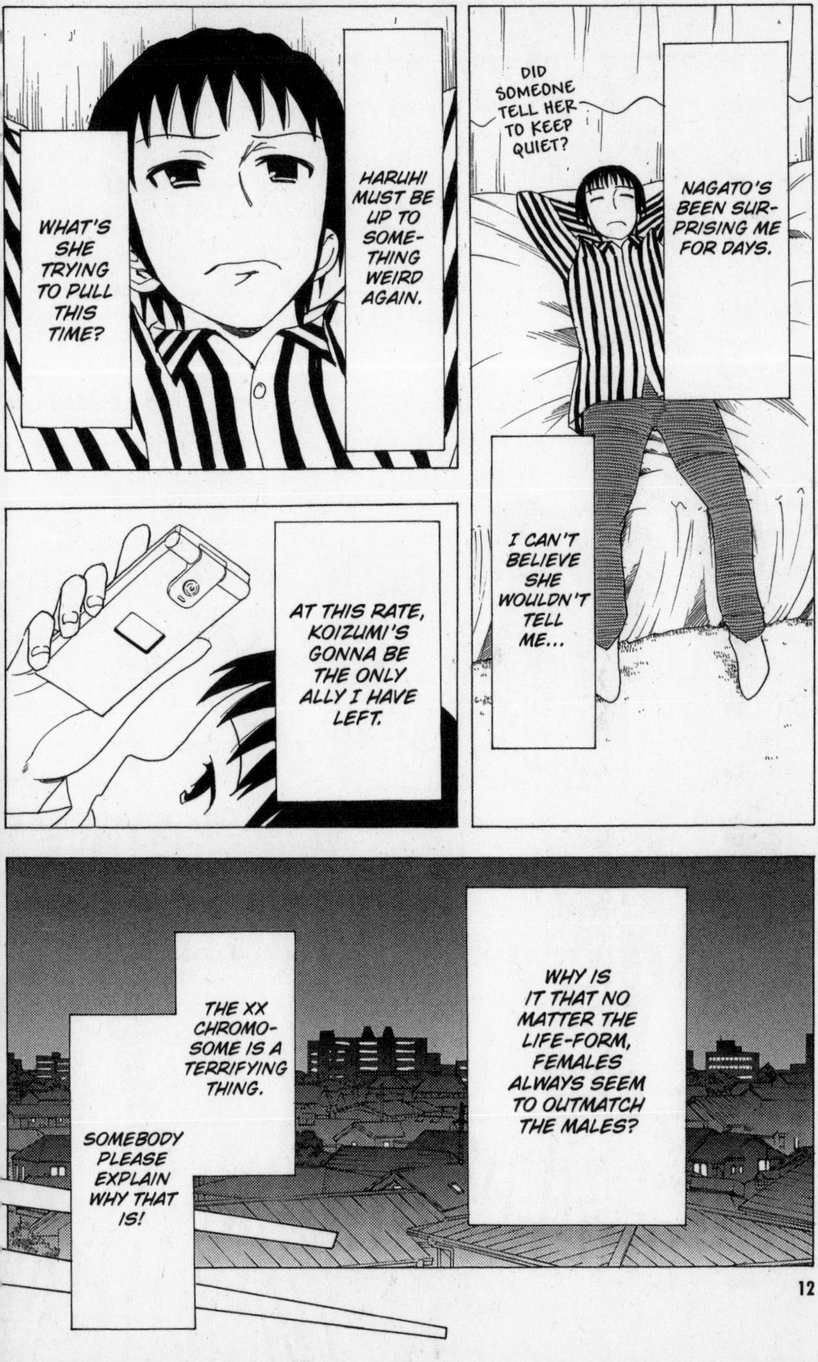
NAGATO'S BEEN SUR-PRISING ME FOR DAYS.
DID SOMEONE TELL HER TO KEEP QUIET?
I CAN'T BELIEVE SHE WOULDN'T TELL ME...
HARUHI MUST BE UP TO SOME-THING WEIRD AGAIN.
WHAT'S SHE TRYING TO PULL THIS TIME?
AT THIS RATE, KOIZUMI'S GONNA BE THE ONLY ALLY I HAVE LEFT.
WHY IS IT THAT NO MATTER THE LIFE-FORM, FEMALES ALWAYS SEEM TO OUTMATCH THE MALES?
THE XX CHROMO-SOME IS A TERRIFYING THING.
SOMEBODY PLEASE EXPLAIN WHY THAT IS!

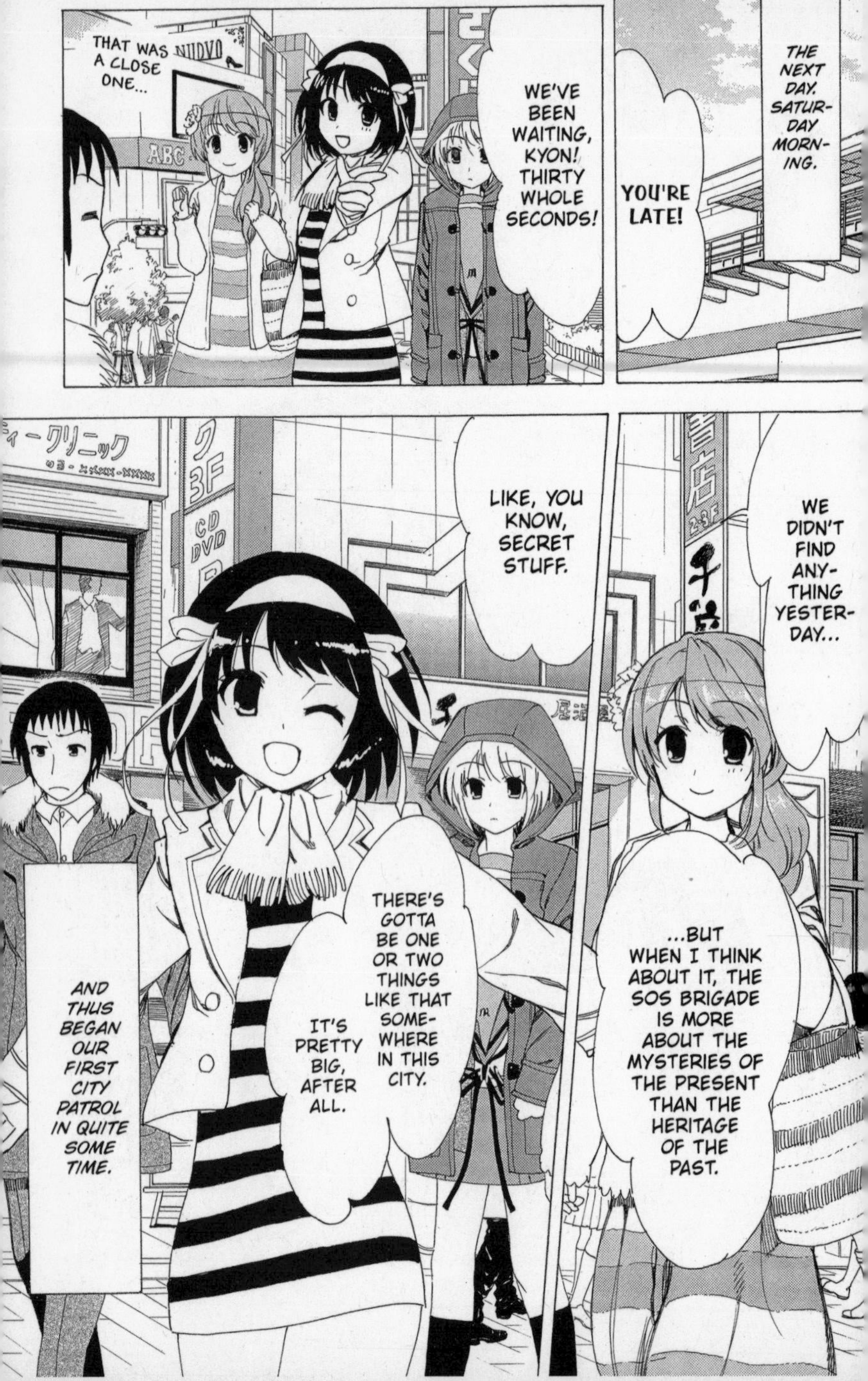
THE NEXT DAY. SATURDAY MORNING.
YOU'RE LATE!
WE'VE BEEN WAITING, KYON! THIRTY WHOLE SECONDS!
THAT WAS A CLOSE ONE...
WE DIDN'T FIND ANYTHING YESTERDAY...
...BUT WHEN I THINK ABOUT IT, THE SOS BRIGADE IS MORE ABOUT THE MYSTERIES OF THE PRESENT THAN THE HERITAGE OF THE PAST.
LIKE, YOU KNOW, SECRET STUFF.
THERE'S GOTTA BE ONE OR TWO THINGS LIKE THAT SOMEWHERE IN THIS CITY.
IT'S PRETTY BIG, AFTER ALL.
AND THUS BEGAN OUR FIRST CITY PATROL IN QUITE SOME TIME.

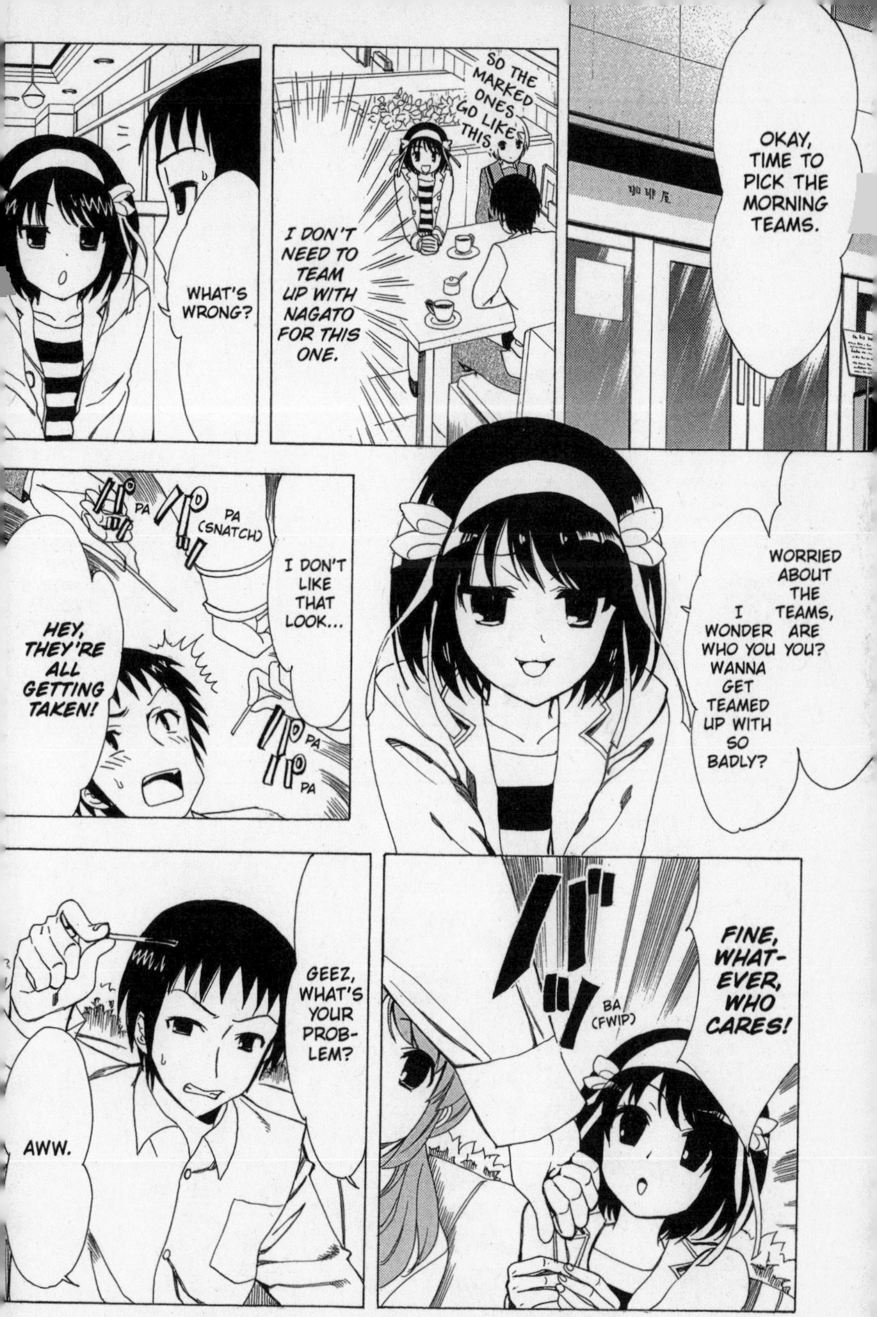
OKAY, TIME TO PICK THE MORNING TEAMS.
SO THE MARKED ONES GO LIKE THIS.
I DON'T NEED TO TEAM UP WITH NAGATO FOR THIS ONE.
WHAT'S WRONG?
WORRIED ABOUT THE TEAMS, ARE YOU?
I WONDER WHO YOU WANNA GET TEAMED UP WITH SO BADLY?
PA
PA (SNATCH)
I DON'T LIKE THAT LOOK...
HEY, THEY'RE ALL GETTING TAKEN!
PA
PA
FINE, WHAT-EVER, WHO CARES!
BA (FWIP)
GEEZ, WHAT'S YOUR PROB-LEM?
AWW.

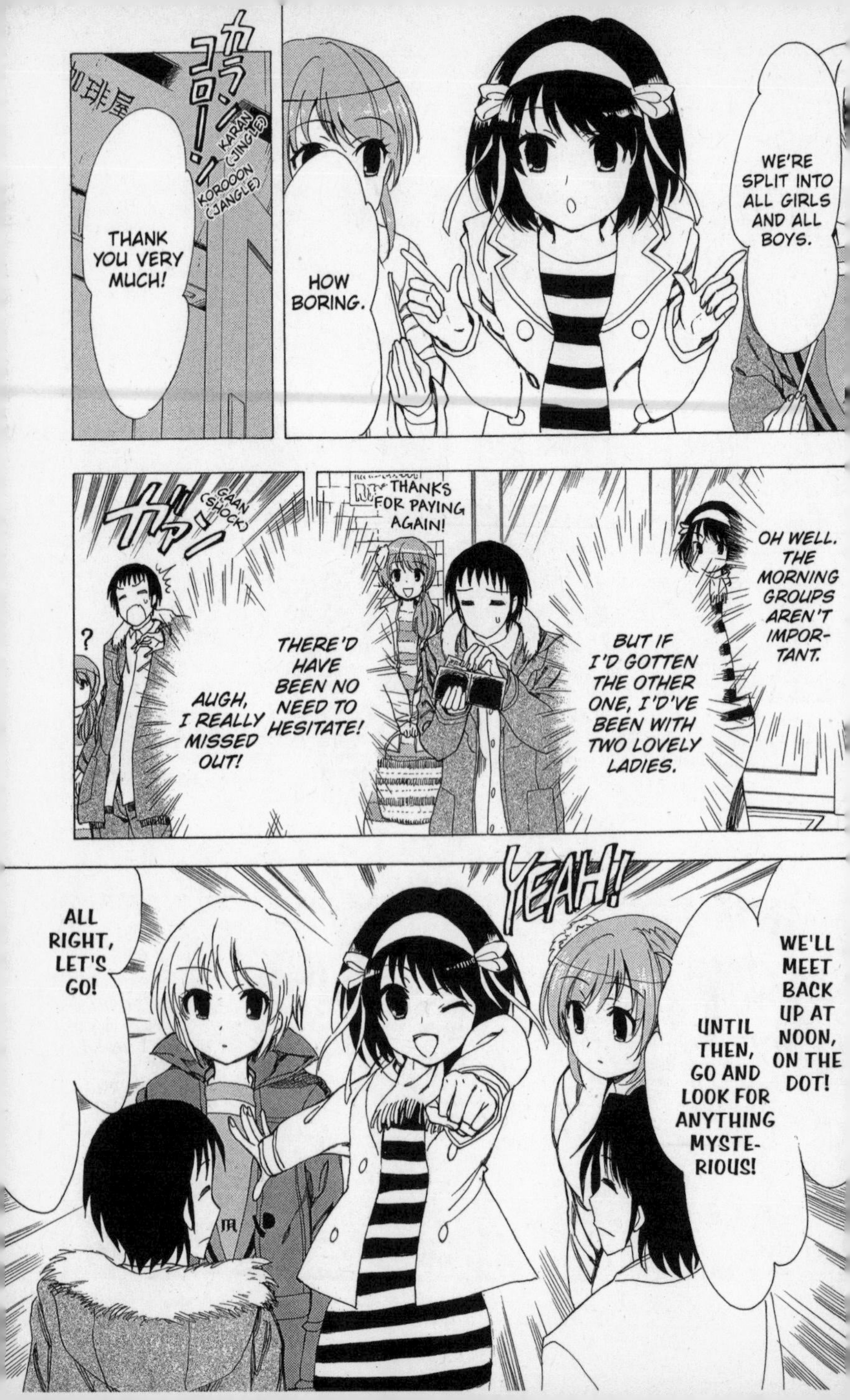
WE'RE SPLIT INTO ALL GIRLS AND ALL BOYS.
HOW BORING.
KARAN (JINGLE) KOROOON (JANGLE)
珈琲屋
THANK YOU VERY MUCH!
OH WELL. THE MORNING GROUPS AREN'T IMPORTANT.
THANKS FOR PAYING AGAIN!
BUT IF I'D GOTTEN THE OTHER ONE, I'D'VE BEEN WITH TWO LOVELY LADIES.
THERE'D HAVE BEEN NO NEED TO HESITATE!
AUGH, I REALLY MISSED OUT!
GAAN (SHOCK)
?
WE'LL MEET BACK UP AT NOON, ON THE DOT!
UNTIL THEN, GO AND LOOK FOR ANYTHING MYSTERIOUS!
YEAH!
ALL RIGHT, LET'S GO!

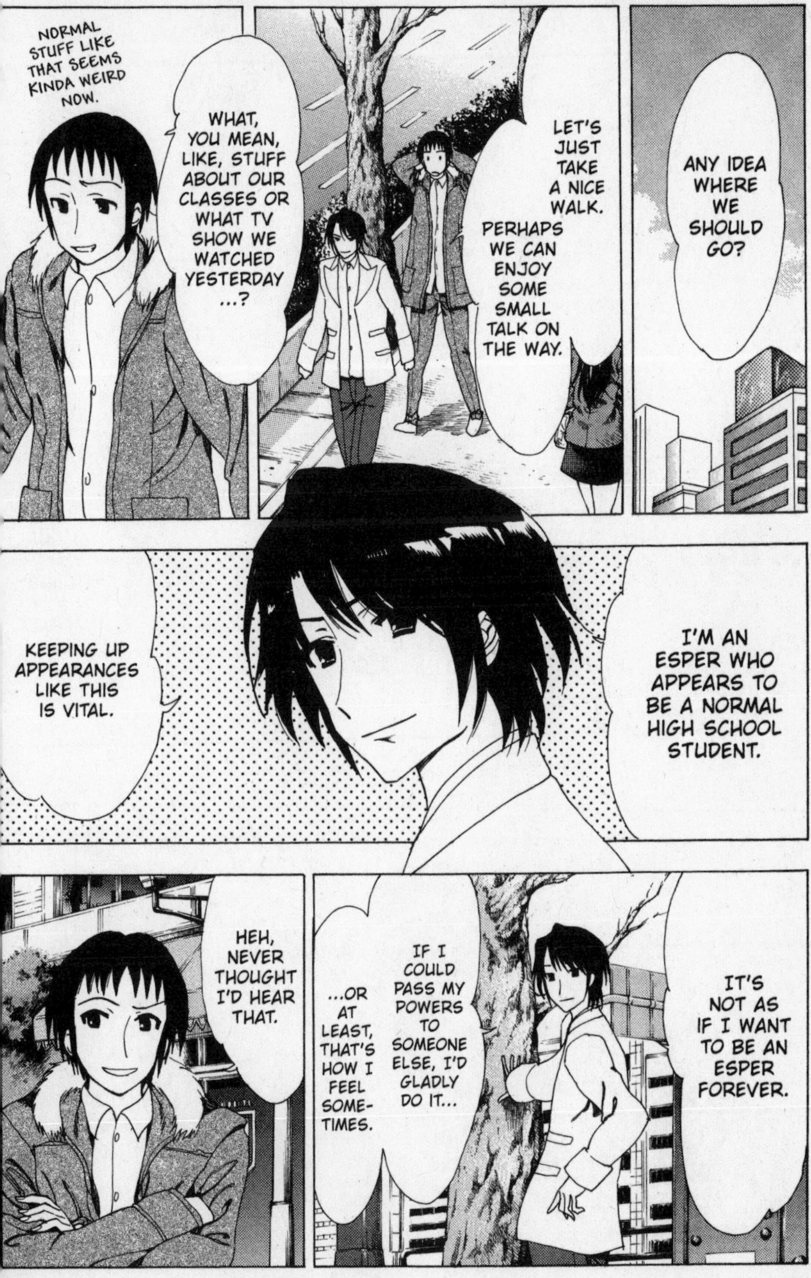
ANY IDEA WHERE WE SHOULD GO?
LET'S JUST TAKE A NICE WALK.
PERHAPS WE CAN ENJOY SOME SMALL TALK ON THE WAY.
WHAT, YOU MEAN, LIKE, STUFF ABOUT OUR CLASSES OR WHAT TV SHOW WE WATCHED YESTERDAY ...?
NORMAL STUFF LIKE THAT SEEMS KINDA WEIRD NOW.
I'M AN ESPER WHO APPEARS TO BE A NORMAL HIGH SCHOOL STUDENT.
KEEPING UP APPEARANCES LIKE THIS IS VITAL.
IT'S NOT AS IF I WANT TO BE AN ESPER FOREVER.
IF I COULD PASS MY POWERS TO SOMEONE ELSE, I'D GLADLY DO IT...
...OR AT LEAST, THAT'S HOW I FEEL SOME-TIMES.
HEH, NEVER THOUGHT I'D HEAR THAT.

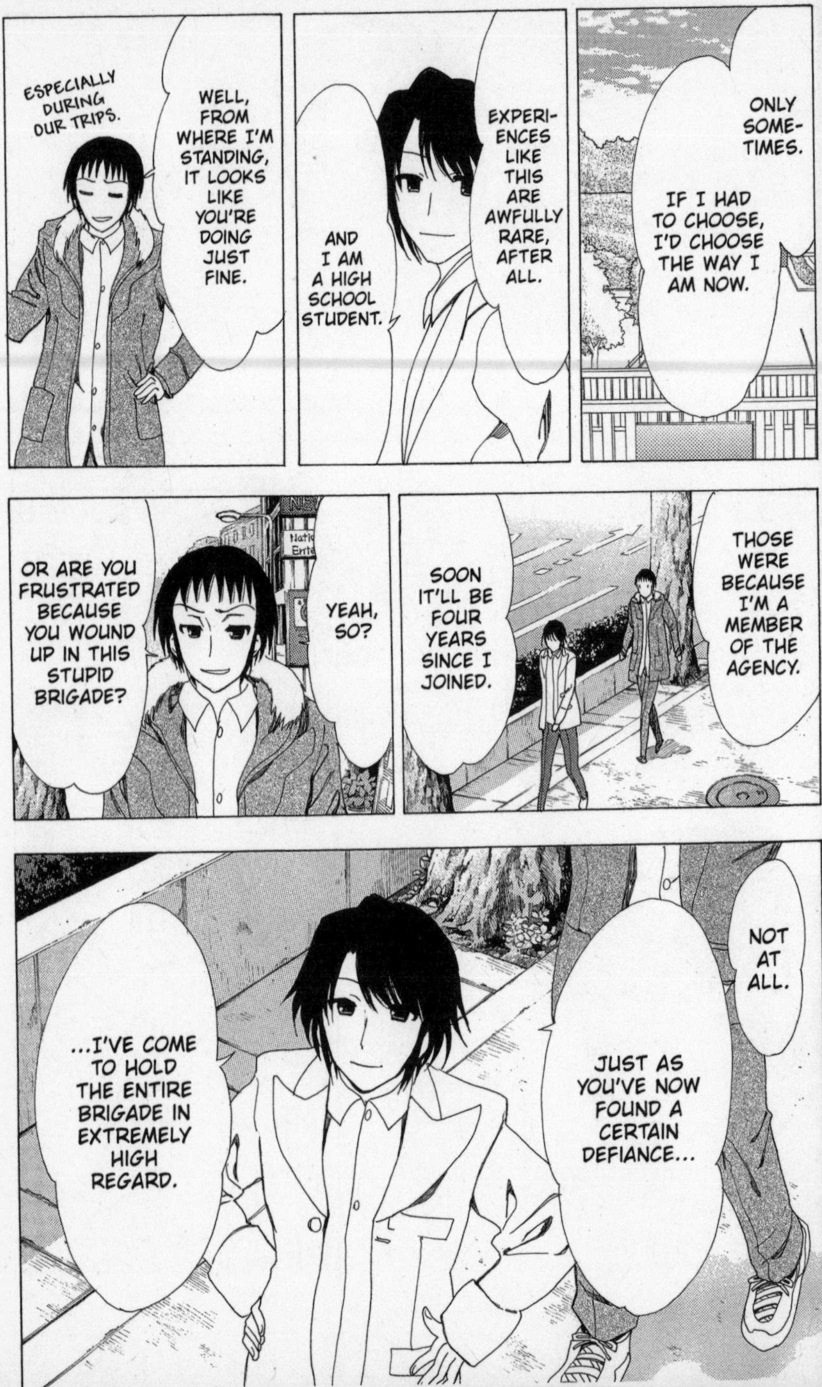
ONLY SOMETIMES.
IF I HAD TO CHOOSE, I'D CHOOSE THE WAY I AM NOW.
EXPERIENCES LIKE THIS ARE AWFULLY RARE, AFTER ALL.
AND I AM A HIGH SCHOOL STUDENT.
WELL, FROM WHERE I'M STANDING, IT LOOKS LIKE YOU'RE DOING JUST FINE.
ESPECIALLY DURING OUR TRIPS.
THOSE WERE BECAUSE I'M A MEMBER OF THE AGENCY.
SOON IT'LL BE FOUR YEARS SINCE I JOINED.
YEAH, SO?
OR ARE YOU FRUSTRATED BECAUSE YOU WOUND UP IN THIS STUPID BRIGADE?
NOT AT ALL.
JUST AS YOU'VE NOW FOUND A CERTAIN DEFIANCE...
...I'VE COME TO HOLD THE ENTIRE BRIGADE IN EXTREMELY HIGH REGARD.

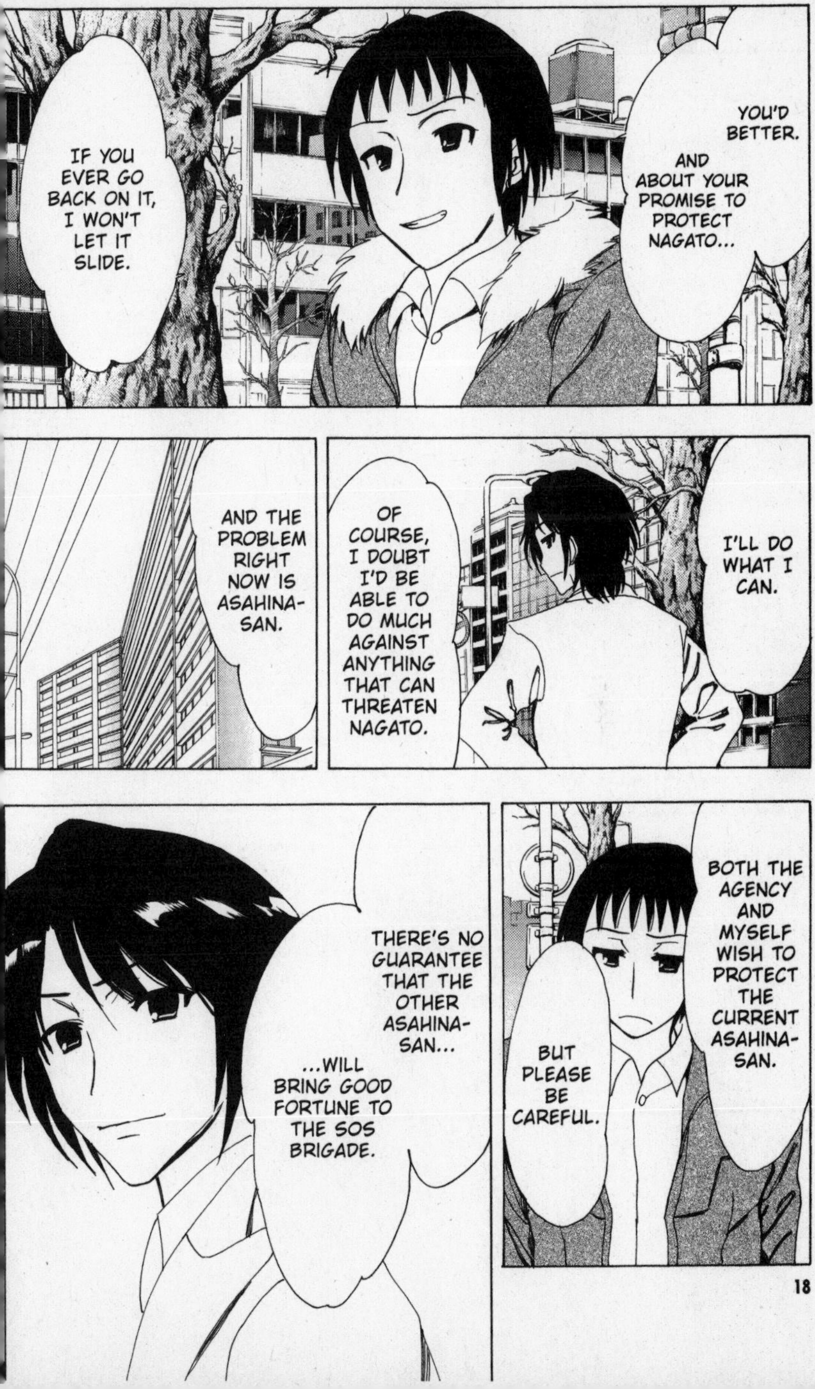
YOU'D BETTER.
AND ABOUT YOUR PROMISE TO PROTECT NAGATO...
IF YOU EVER GO BACK ON IT, I WON'T LET IT SLIDE.
I'LL DO WHAT I CAN.
OF COURSE, I DOUBT I'D BE ABLE TO DO MUCH AGAINST ANYTHING THAT CAN THREATEN NAGATO.
AND THE PROBLEM RIGHT NOW IS ASAHINA-SAN.
BOTH THE AGENCY AND MYSELF WISH TO PROTECT THE CURRENT ASAHINA-SAN.
BUT PLEASE BE CAREFUL.
THERE'S NO GUARANTEE THAT THE OTHER ASAHINA-SAN...
...WILL BRING GOOD FORTUNE TO THE SOS BRIGADE.

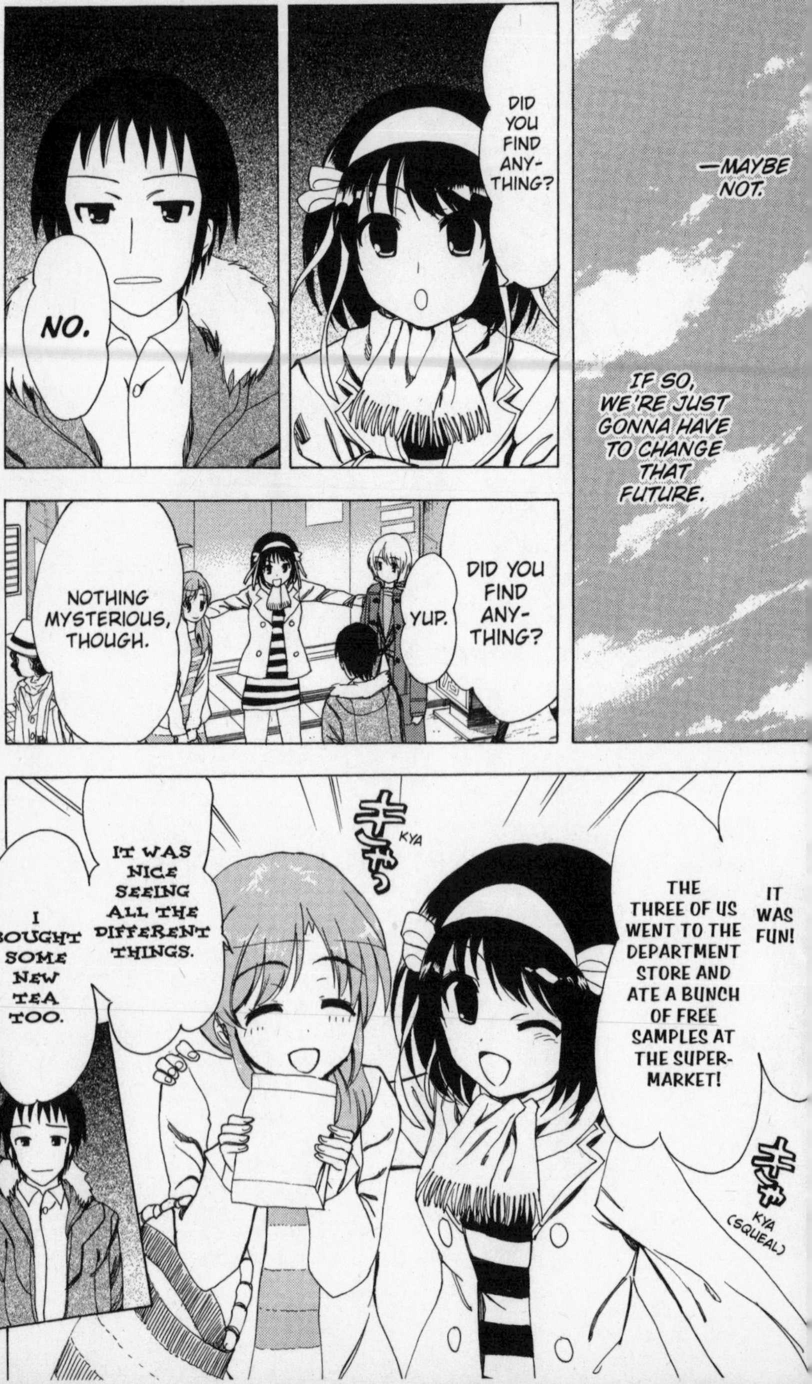
—MAYBE NOT.
IF SO, WE'RE JUST GONNA HAVE TO CHANGE THAT FUTURE.
DID YOU FIND ANYTHING?
NO.
DID YOU FIND ANYTHING?
YUP.
NOTHING MYSTERIOUS, THOUGH.
IT WAS FUN!
THE THREE OF US WENT TO THE DEPARTMENT STORE AND ATE A BUNCH OF FREE SAMPLES AT THE SUPERMARKET!
KYA (SQUEAL)
KYA
IT WAS NICE SEEING ALL THE DIFFERENT THINGS.
I BOUGHT SOME NEW TEA TOO.

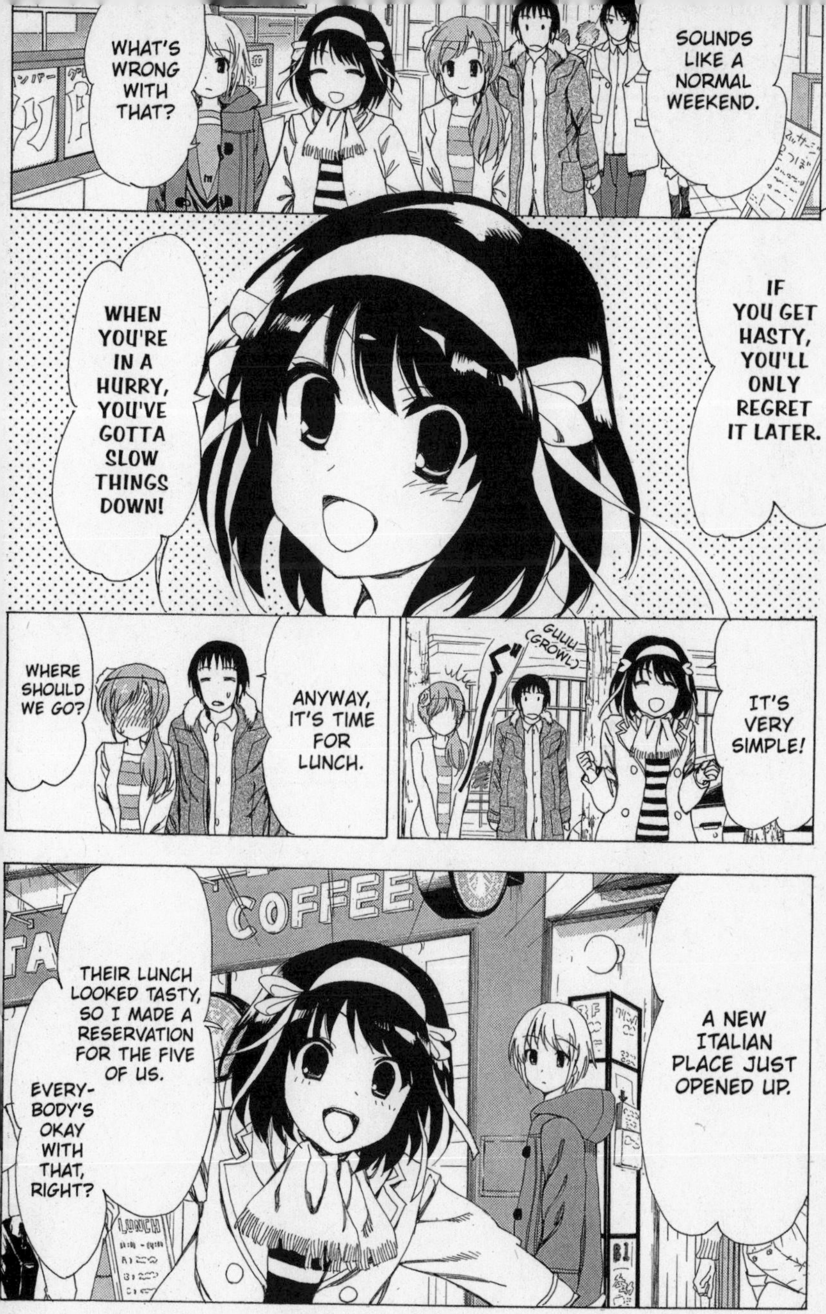
SOUNDS LIKE A NORMAL WEEKEND.
WHAT'S WRONG WITH THAT?
IF YOU GET HASTY, YOU'LL ONLY REGRET IT LATER.
WHEN YOU'RE IN A HURRY, YOU'VE GOTTA SLOW THINGS DOWN!
IT'S VERY SIMPLE!
GUUU (GROWL)
ANYWAY, IT'S TIME FOR LUNCH.
WHERE SHOULD WE GO?
A NEW ITALIAN PLACE JUST OPENED UP.
COFFEE
THEIR LUNCH LOOKED TASTY, SO I MADE A RESERVATION FOR THE FIVE OF US.
EVERYBODY'S OKAY WITH THAT, RIGHT?
LUNCH
B1

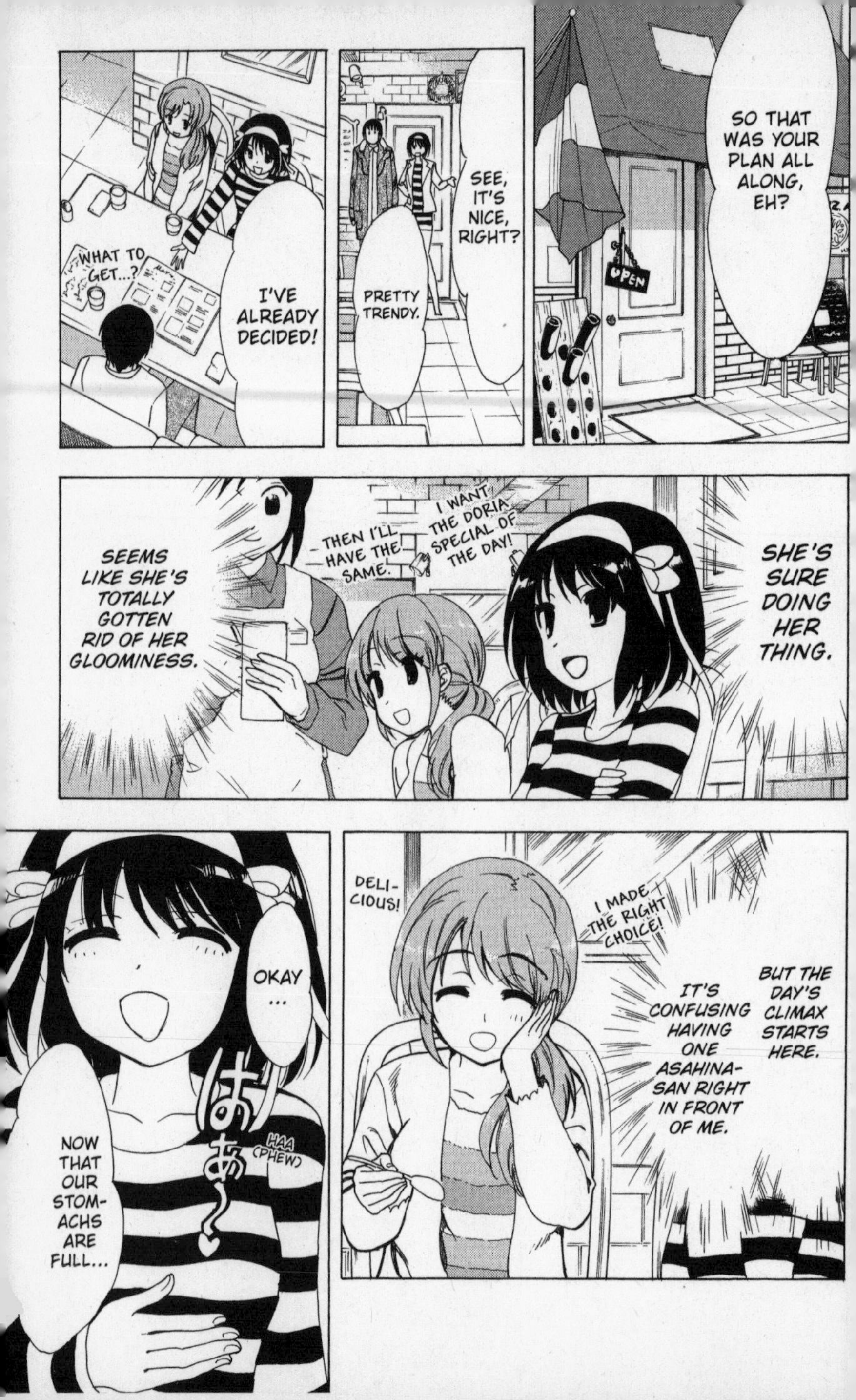
SO THAT WAS YOUR PLAN ALL ALONG, EH?
SEE, IT'S NICE, RIGHT?
PRETTY TRENDY.
I'VE ALREADY DECIDED!
WHAT TO GET...?
SHE'S SURE DOING HER THING.
I WANT THE DORIA SPECIAL OF THE DAY!
THEN I'LL HAVE THE SAME.
SEEMS LIKE SHE'S TOTALLY GOTTEN RID OF HER GLOOMINESS.
DELI-CIOUS!
I MADE THE RIGHT CHOICE!
IT'S CONFUSING HAVING ONE ASAHINA-SAN RIGHT IN FRONT OF ME.
BUT THE DAY'S CLIMAX STARTS HERE.
OKAY...
HAA (PHEW)
NOW THAT OUR STOM-ACHS ARE FULL...

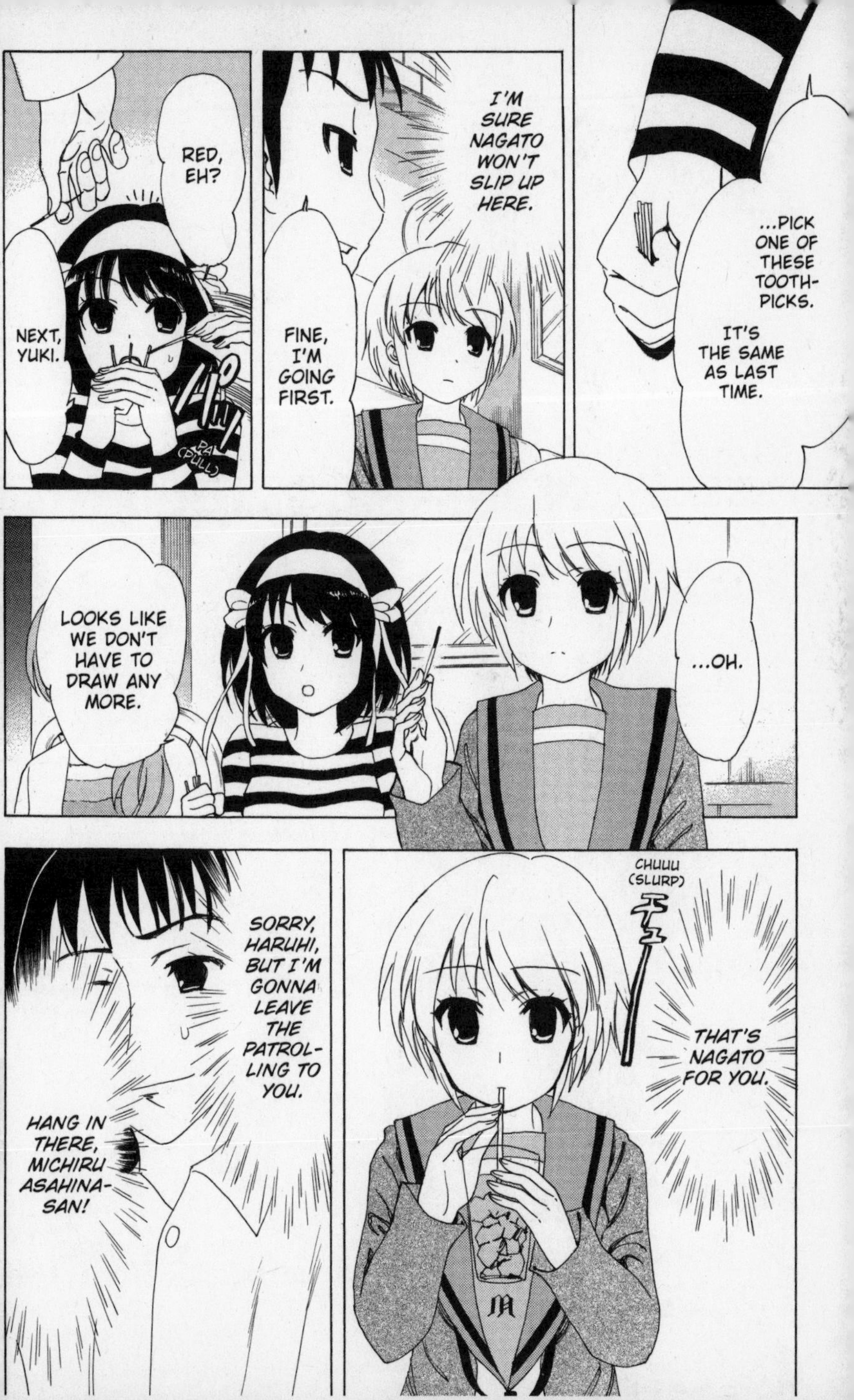
...PICK ONE OF THESE TOOTH-PICKS.
IT'S THE SAME AS LAST TIME.
I'M SURE NAGATO WON'T SLIP UP HERE.
FINE, I'M GOING FIRST.
RED, EH?
NEXT, YUKI.
PA (PULL)
...OH.
LOOKS LIKE WE DON'T HAVE TO DRAW ANY MORE.
CHUUU (SLURP)
THAT'S NAGATO FOR YOU.
SORRY, HARUHI, BUT I'M GONNA LEAVE THE PATROLLING TO YOU.
HANG IN THERE, MICHIRU ASAHINA-SAN!

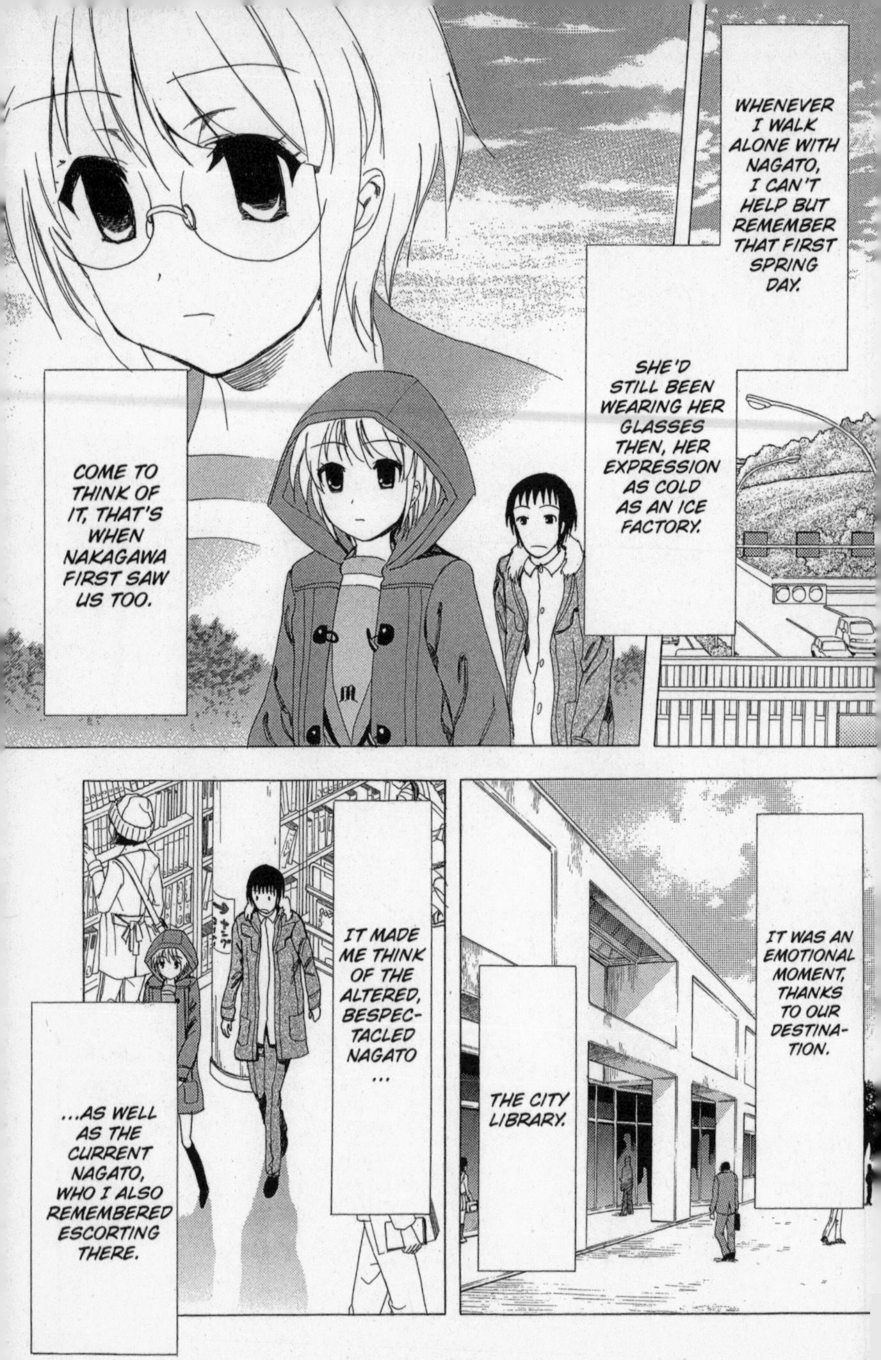
WHENEVER I WALK ALONE WITH NAGATO, I CAN'T HELP BUT REMEMBER THAT FIRST SPRING DAY.
SHE'D STILL BEEN WEARING HER GLASSES THEN, HER EXPRESSION AS COLD AS AN ICE FACTORY.
COME TO THINK OF IT, THAT'S WHEN NAKAGAWA FIRST SAW US TOO.
IT WAS AN EMOTIONAL MOMENT, THANKS TO OUR DESTINATION.
THE CITY LIBRARY.
IT MADE ME THINK OF THE ALTERED, BESPEC-TACLED NAGATO...
...AS WELL AS THE CURRENT NAGATO, WHO I ALSO REMEMBERED ESCORTING THERE.

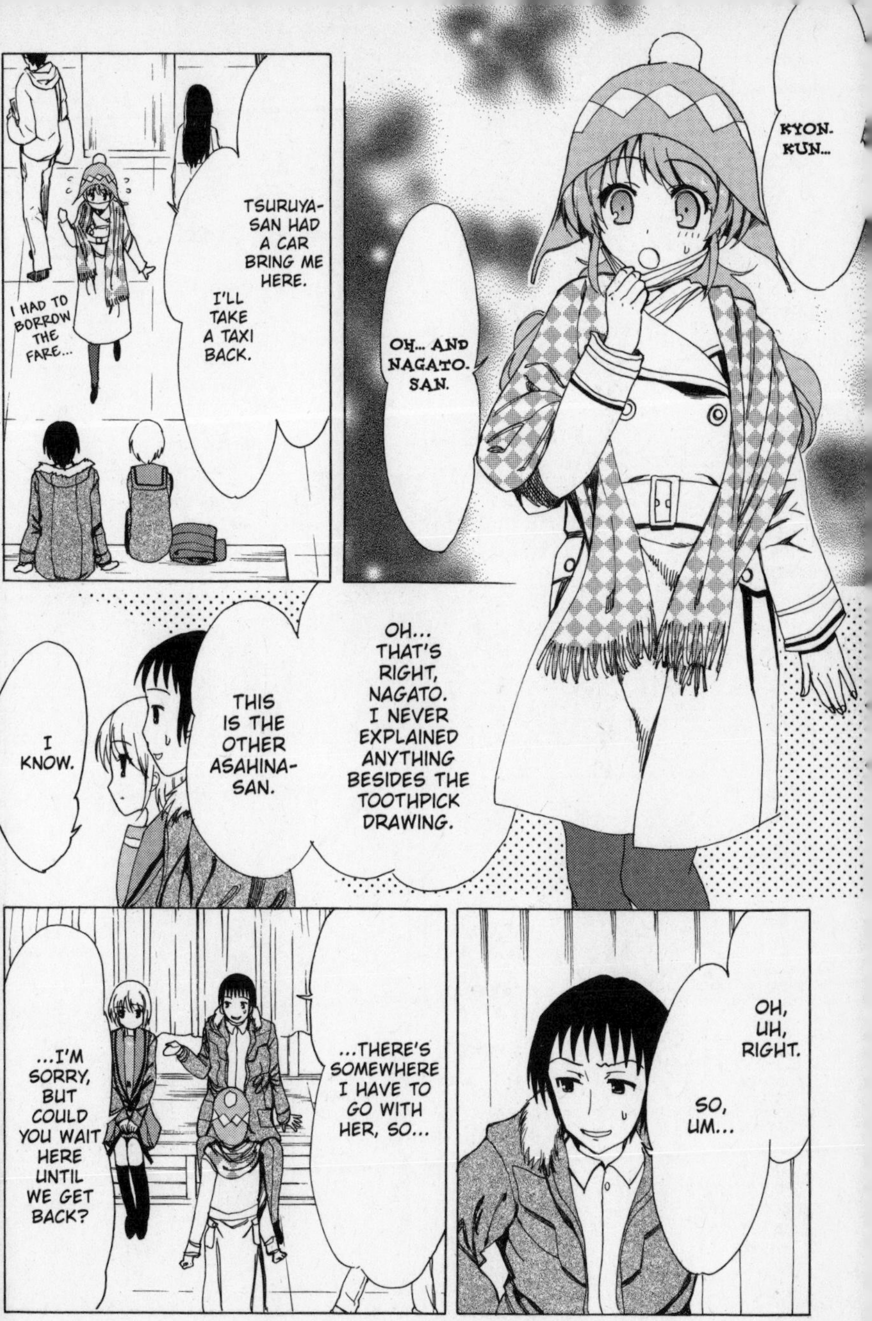
KYON-KUN...
OH... AND NAGATO-SAN.
TSURUYA-SAN HAD A CAR BRING ME HERE.
I'LL TAKE A TAXI BACK.
I HAD TO BORROW THE FARE...
OH... THAT'S RIGHT, NAGATO. I NEVER EXPLAINED ANYTHING BESIDES THE TOOTHPICK DRAWING.
THIS IS THE OTHER ASAHINA-SAN.
I KNOW.
OH, UH, RIGHT.
SO, UM...
...THERE'S SOMEWHERE I HAVE TO GO WITH HER, SO...
...I'M SORRY, BUT COULD YOU WAIT HERE UNTIL WE GET BACK?

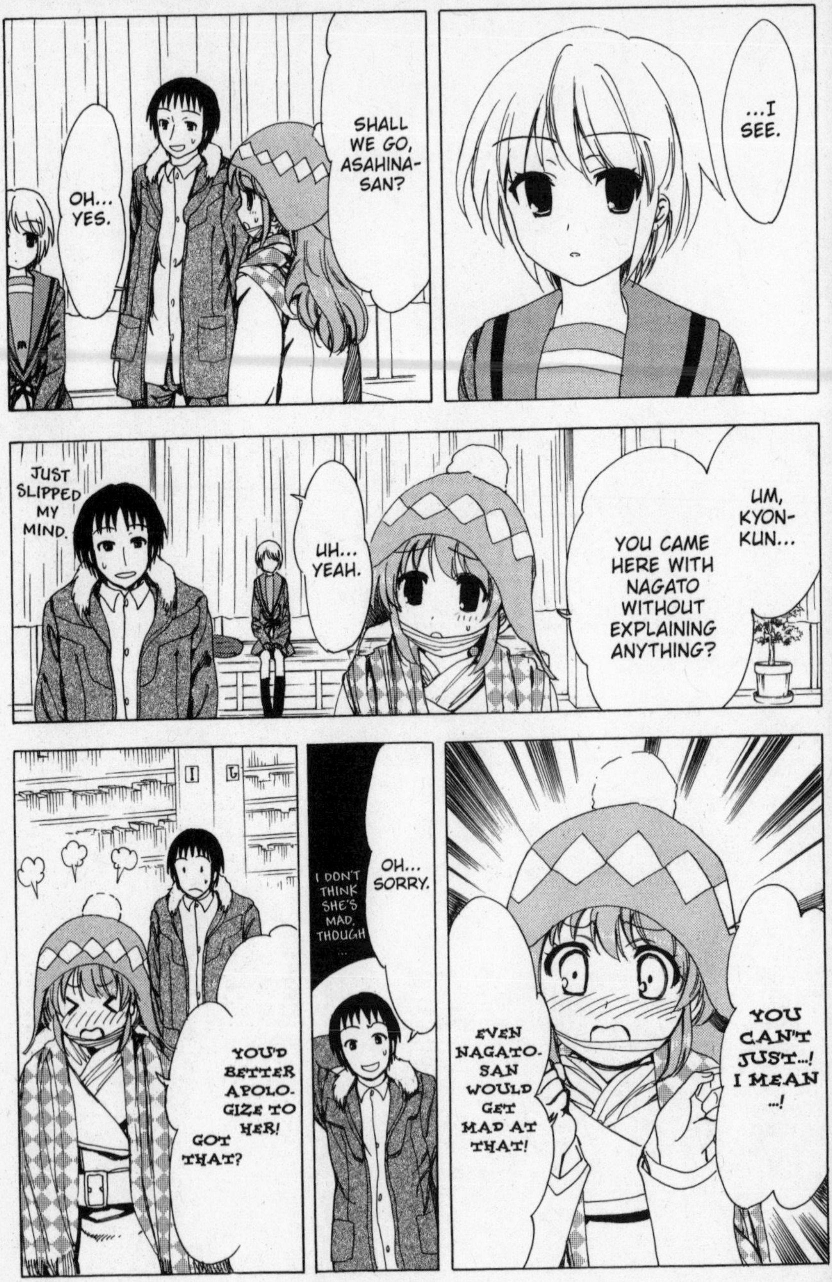
...I SEE.
SHALL WE GO, ASAHINA-SAN?
OH... YES.
UM, KYON-KUN...
YOU CAME HERE WITH NAGATO WITHOUT EXPLAINING ANYTHING?
UH... YEAH.
JUST SLIPPED MY MIND.
YOU CAN'T JUST...! I MEAN ...!
EVEN NAGATO-SAN WOULD GET MAD AT THAT!
OH... SORRY.
I DON'T THINK SHE'S MAD, THOUGH ...
YOU'D BETTER APOLOGIZE TO HER!
GOT THAT?

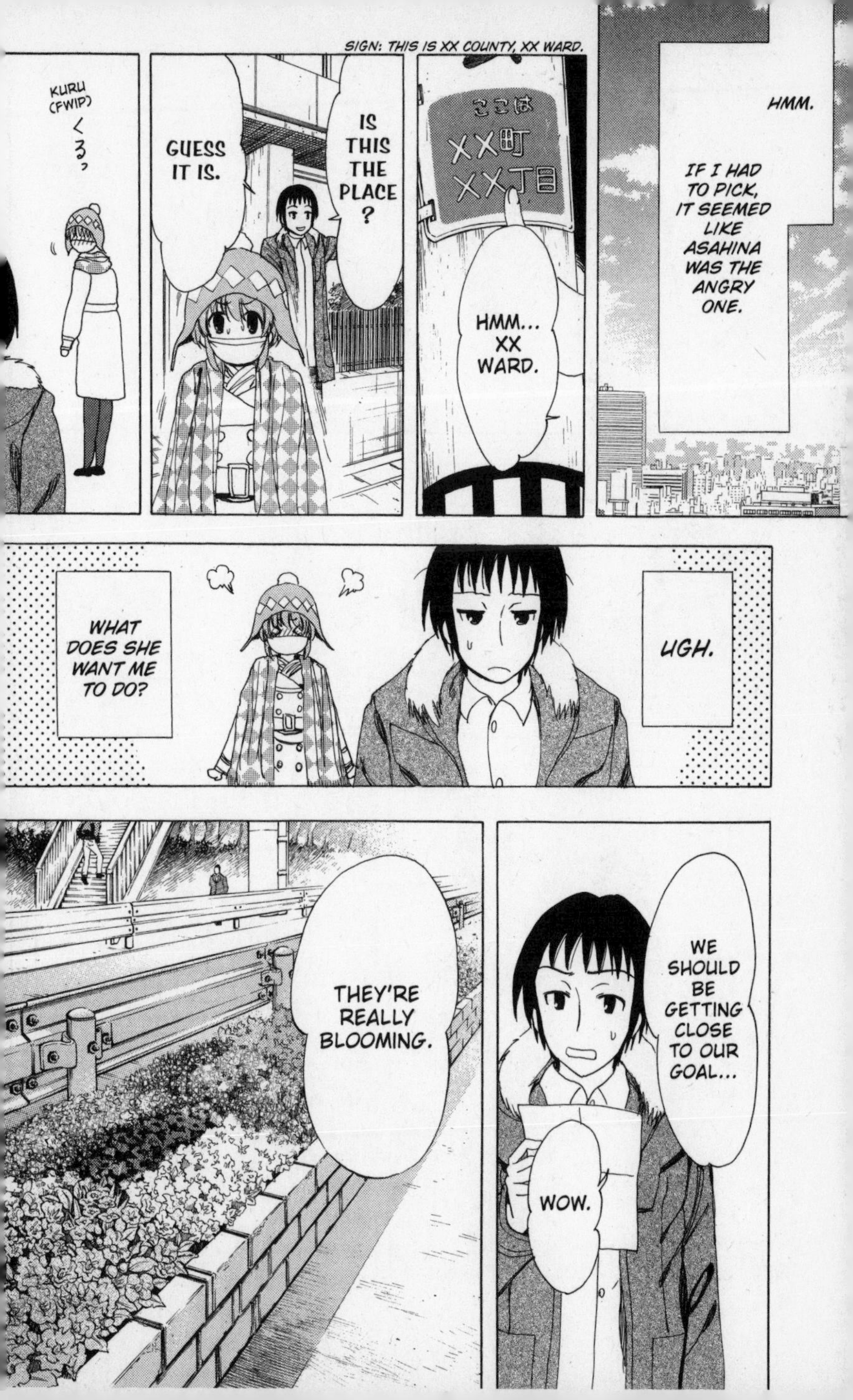
HMM.
IF I HAD TO PICK, IT SEEMED LIKE ASAHINA WAS THE ANGRY ONE.
SIGN: THIS IS XX COUNTY, XX WARD.
ここは XX町 XX丁目
HMM... XX WARD.
IS THIS THE PLACE?
GUESS IT IS.
KURU (FWIP)
くるっ
UGH.
WHAT DOES SHE WANT ME TO DO?
WE SHOULD BE GETTING CLOSE TO OUR GOAL...
WOW.
THEY'RE REALLY BLOOMING.

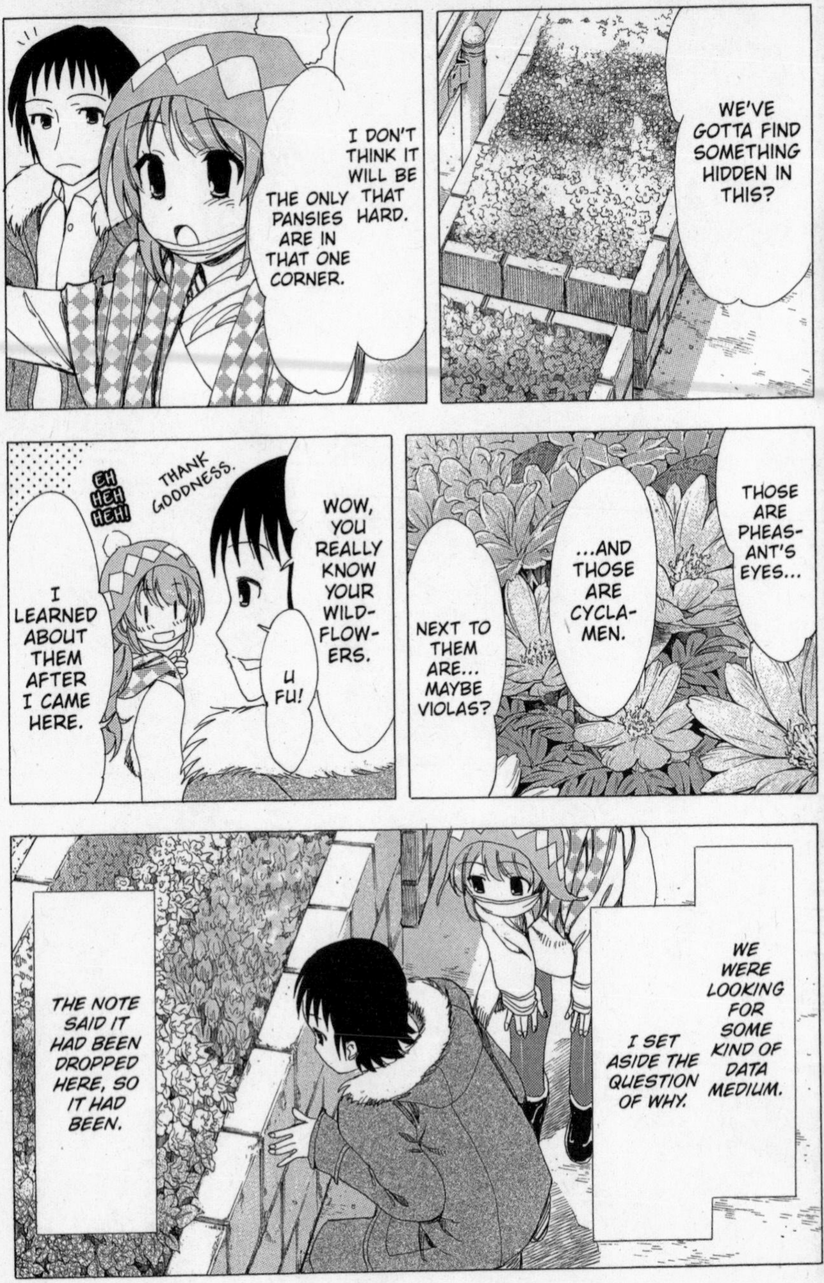
WE'VE GOTTA FIND SOMETHING HIDDEN IN THIS?
I DON'T THINK IT WILL BE THAT HARD.
THE ONLY PANSIES ARE IN THAT ONE CORNER.
THOSE ARE PHEASANT'S EYES...
...AND THOSE ARE CYCLAMEN.
NEXT TO THEM ARE... MAYBE VIOLAS?
WOW, YOU REALLY KNOW YOUR WILDFLOWERS.
U FU!
THANK GOODNESS.
EH HEH HEH!
I LEARNED ABOUT THEM AFTER I CAME HERE.
WE WERE LOOKING FOR SOME KIND OF DATA MEDIUM.
I SET ASIDE THE QUESTION OF WHY.
THE NOTE SAID IT HAD BEEN DROPPED HERE, SO IT HAD BEEN.

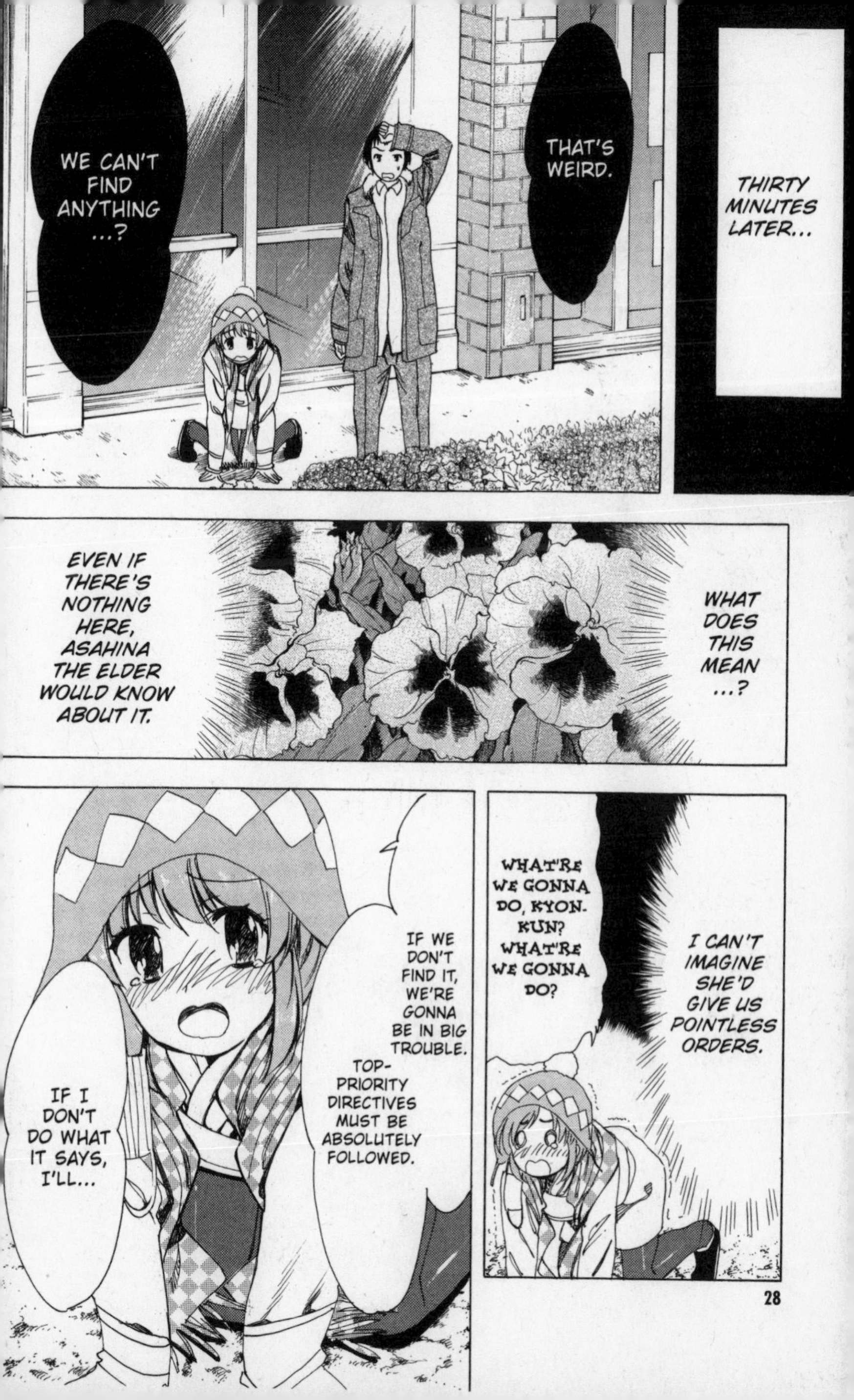
THIRTY MINUTES LATER...
THAT'S WEIRD.
WE CAN'T FIND ANYTHING ...?
WHAT DOES THIS MEAN ...?
EVEN IF THERE'S NOTHING HERE, ASAHINA THE ELDER WOULD KNOW ABOUT IT.
I CAN'T IMAGINE SHE'D GIVE US POINTLESS ORDERS.
WHAT'RE WE GONNA DO, KYON-KUN? WHAT'RE WE GONNA DO?
IF WE DON'T FIND IT, WE'RE GONNA BE IN BIG TROUBLE.
TOP-PRIORITY DIRECTIVES MUST BE ABSOLUTELY FOLLOWED.
IF I DON'T DO WHAT IT SAYS, I'LL...

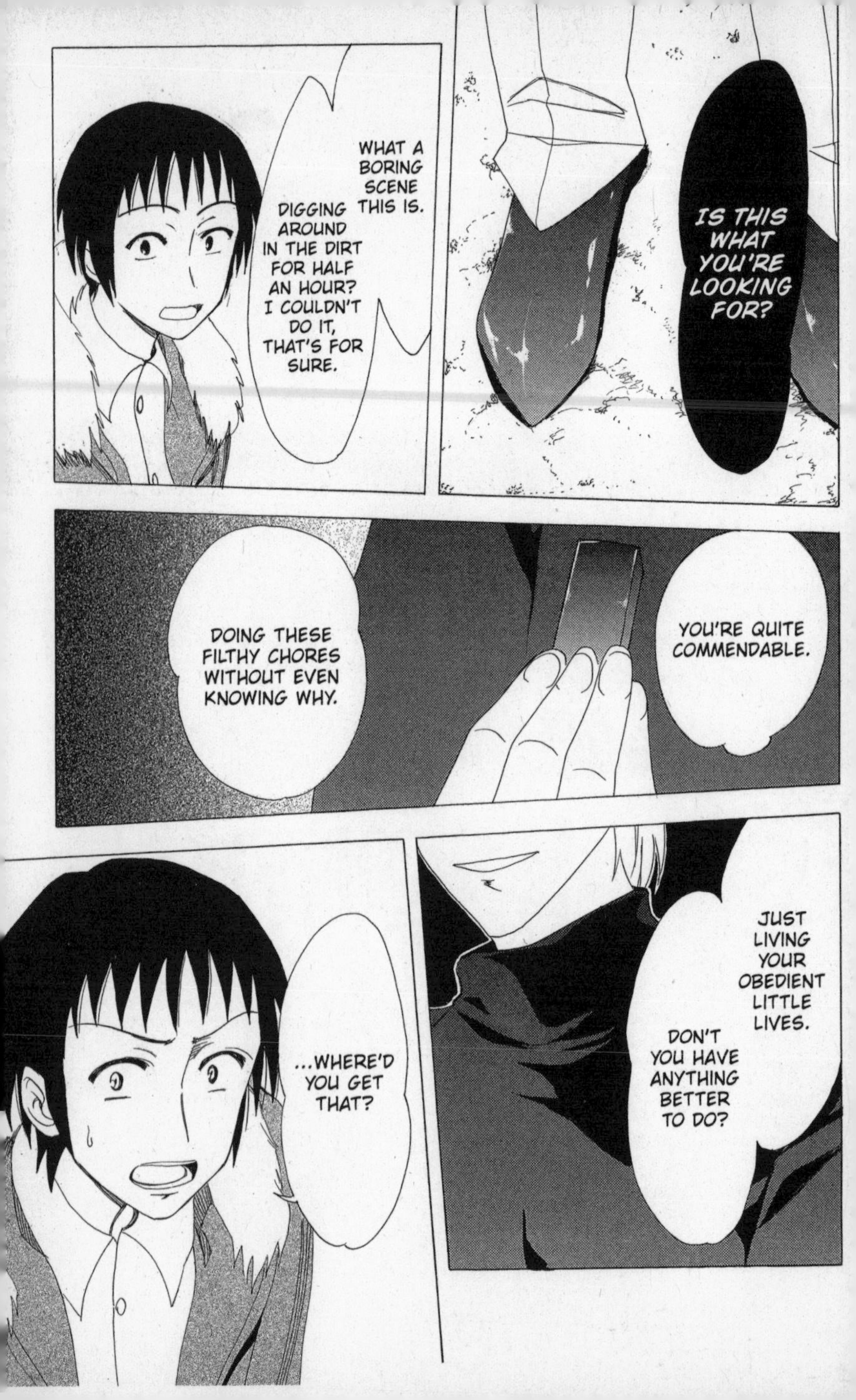
IS THIS WHAT YOU'RE LOOKING FOR?
WHAT A BORING SCENE THIS IS.
DIGGING AROUND IN THE DIRT FOR HALF AN HOUR? I COULDN'T DO IT, THAT'S FOR SURE.
YOU'RE QUITE COMMENDABLE.
DOING THESE FILTHY CHORES WITHOUT EVEN KNOWING WHY.
JUST LIVING YOUR OBEDIENT LITTLE LIVES.
DON'T YOU HAVE ANYTHING BETTER TO DO?
...WHERE'D YOU GET THAT?

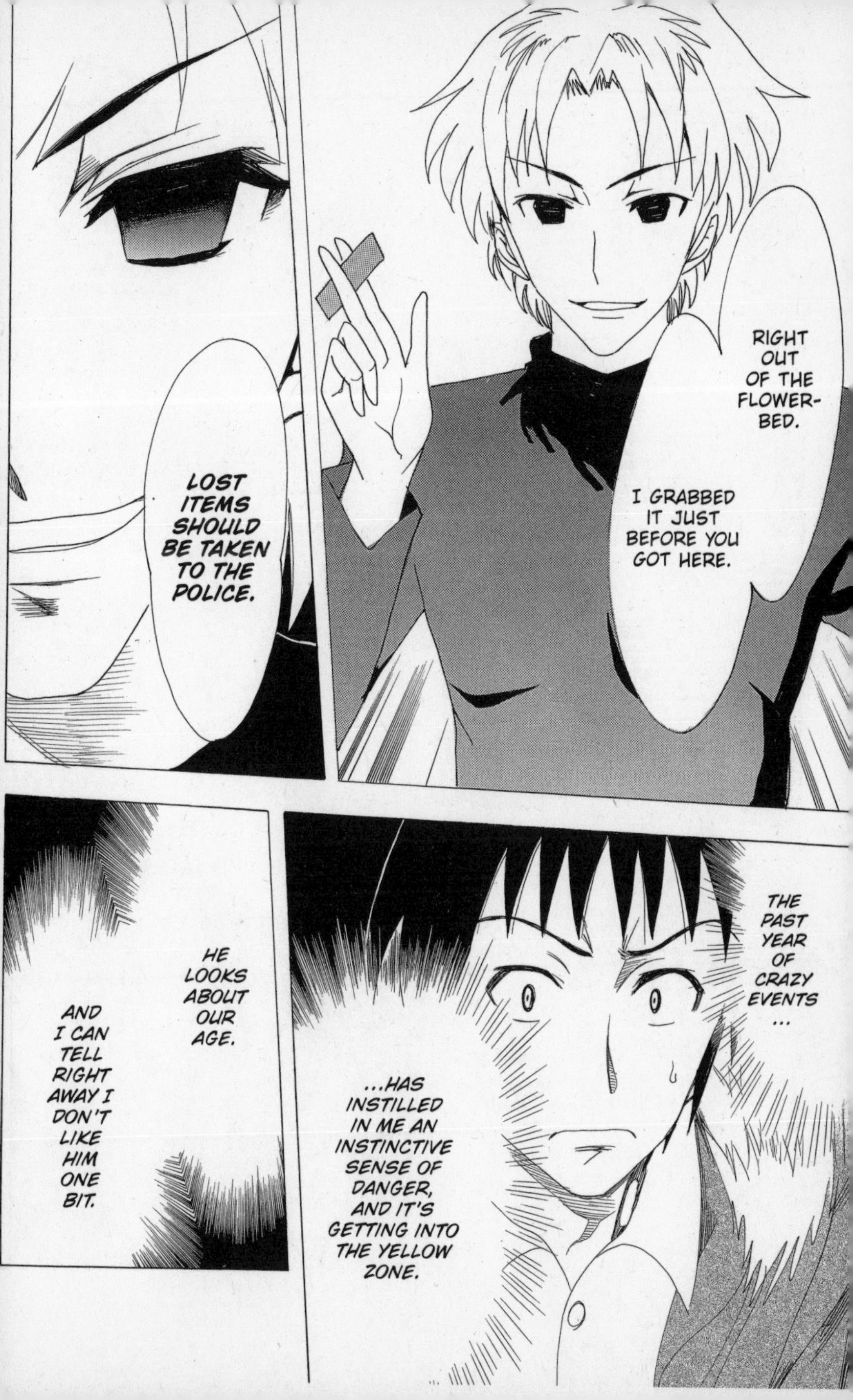
RIGHT OUT OF THE FLOWER-BED.
I GRABBED IT JUST BEFORE YOU GOT HERE.
LOST ITEMS SHOULD BE TAKEN TO THE POLICE.
THE PAST YEAR OF CRAZY EVENTS...
...HAS INSTILLED IN ME AN INSTINCTIVE SENSE OF DANGER, AND IT'S GETTING INTO THE YELLOW ZONE.
HE LOOKS ABOUT OUR AGE.
AND I CAN TELL RIGHT AWAY I DON'T LIKE HIM ONE BIT.

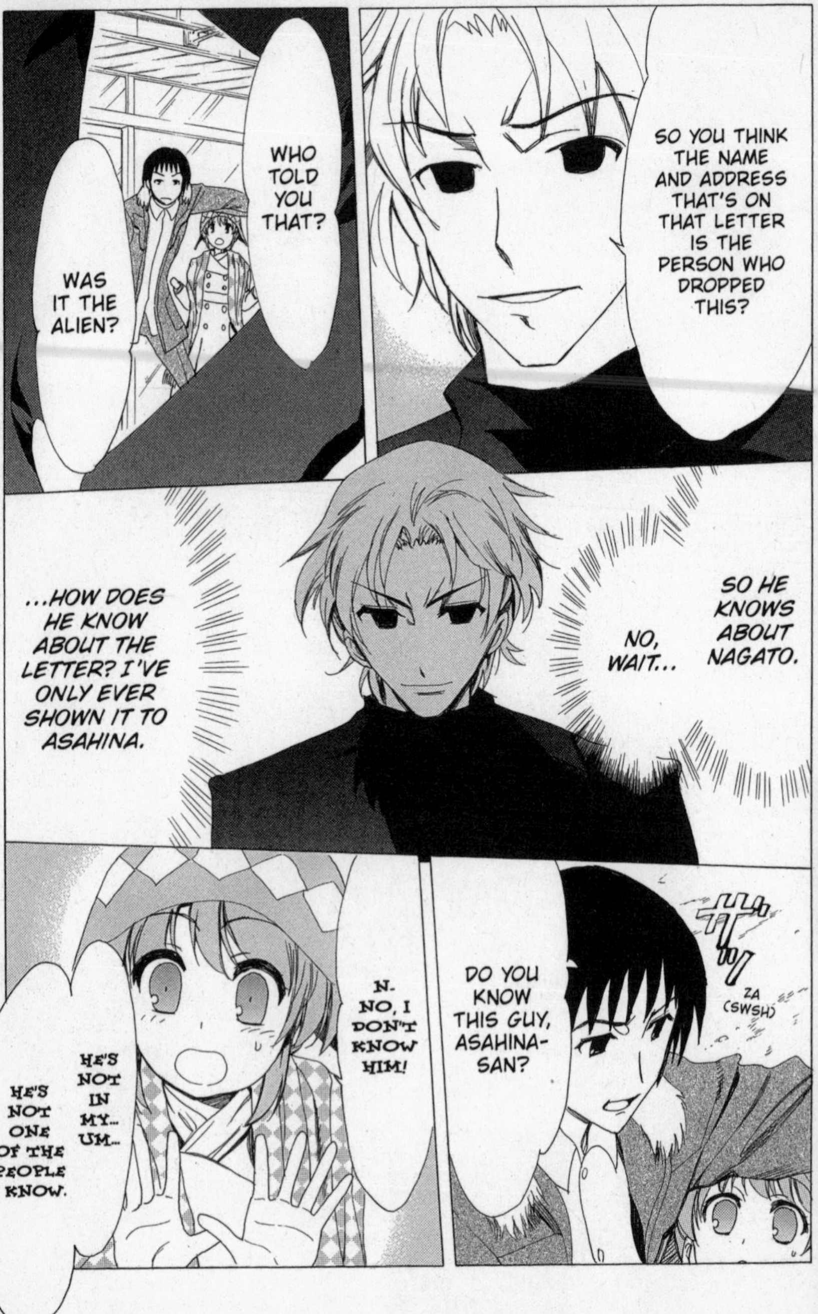
SO YOU THINK THE NAME AND ADDRESS THAT'S ON THAT LETTER IS THE PERSON WHO DROPPED THIS?
WHO TOLD YOU THAT?
WAS IT THE ALIEN?
SO HE KNOWS ABOUT NAGATO.
NO, WAIT...
...HOW DOES HE KNOW ABOUT THE LETTER? I'VE ONLY EVER SHOWN IT TO ASAHINA.
ZA (SWSH)
DO YOU KNOW THIS GUY, ASAHINA-SAN?
N-NO, I DON'T KNOW HIM!
HE'S NOT IN MY... UM...
HE'S NOT ONE OF THE PEOPLE I KNOW.

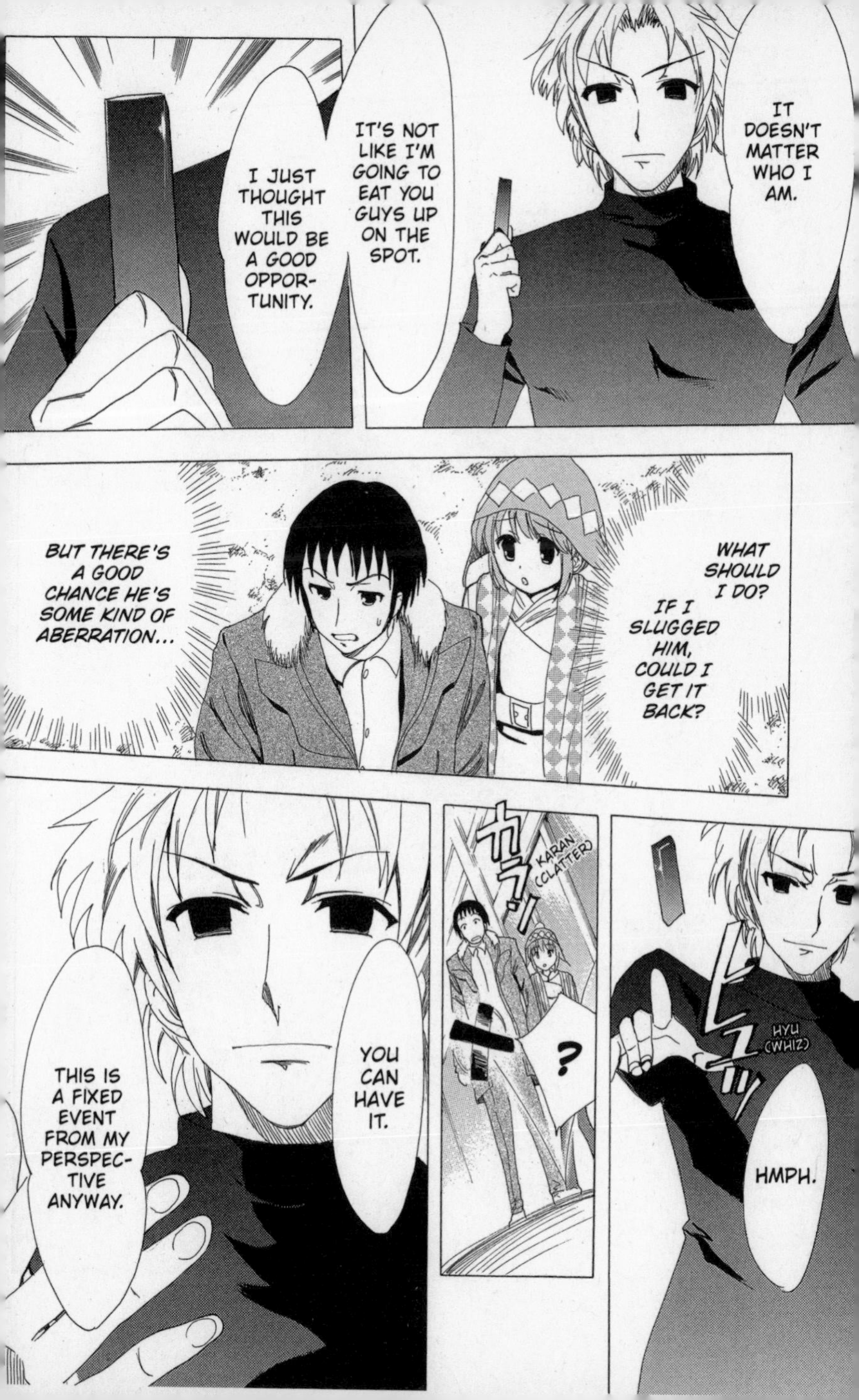
IT DOESN'T MATTER WHO I AM.
IT'S NOT LIKE I'M GOING TO EAT YOU GUYS UP ON THE SPOT.
I JUST THOUGHT THIS WOULD BE A GOOD OPPORTUNITY.
WHAT SHOULD I DO?
IF I SLUGGED HIM, COULD I GET IT BACK?
BUT THERE'S A GOOD CHANCE HE'S SOME KIND OF ABERRATION...
HYU (WHIZ)
HMPH.
KARAN (CLATTER)
?
YOU CAN HAVE IT.
THIS IS A FIXED EVENT FROM MY PERSPECTIVE ANYWAY.

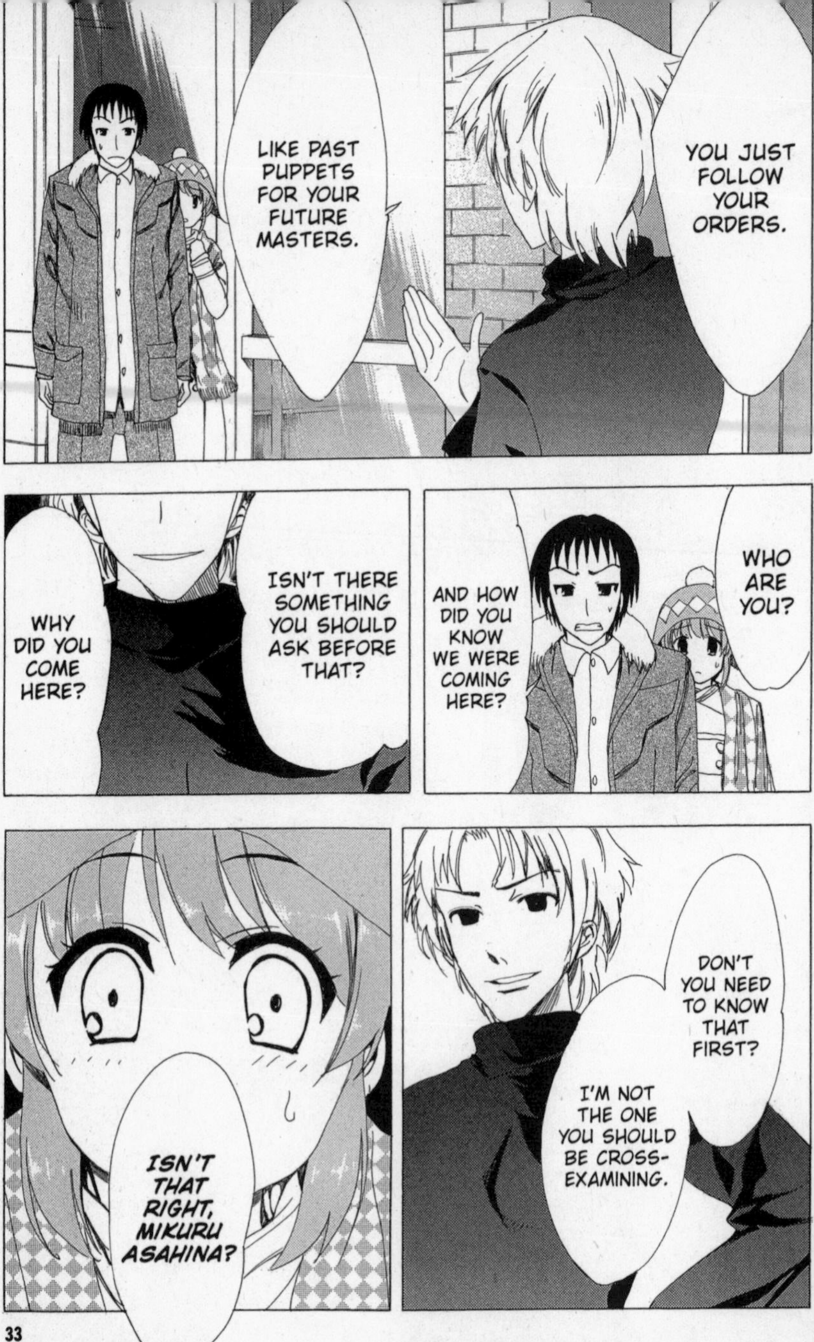
YOU JUST FOLLOW YOUR ORDERS.
LIKE PAST PUPPETS FOR YOUR FUTURE MASTERS.
WHO ARE YOU?
AND HOW DID YOU KNOW WE WERE COMING HERE?
ISN'T THERE SOMETHING YOU SHOULD ASK BEFORE THAT?
WHY DID YOU COME HERE?
DON'T YOU NEED TO KNOW THAT FIRST?
I'M NOT THE ONE YOU SHOULD BE CROSS-EXAMINING.
ISN'T THAT RIGHT, MIKURU ASAHINA?

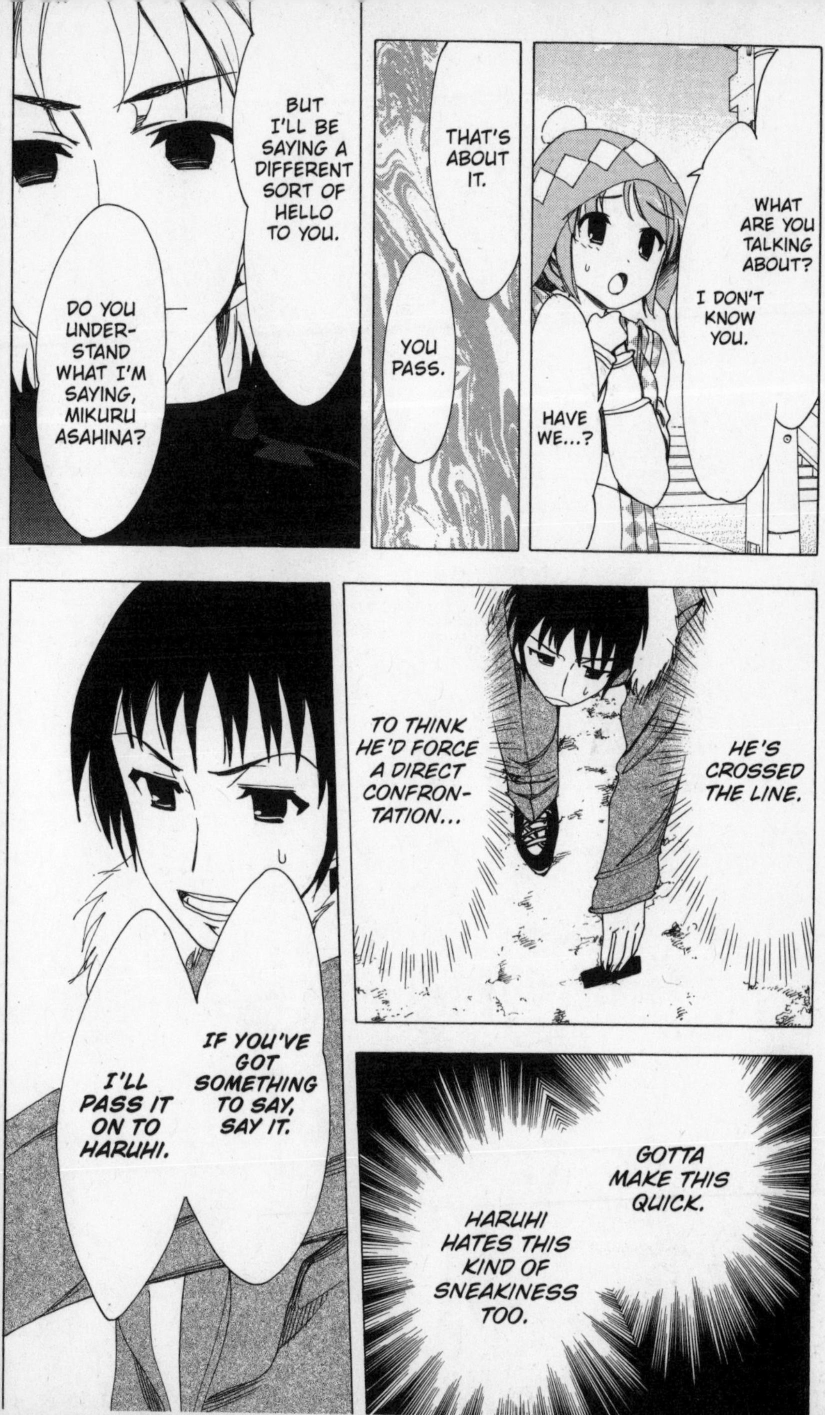
WHAT ARE YOU TALKING ABOUT? I DON'T KNOW YOU.
HAVE WE...?
THAT'S ABOUT IT.
YOU PASS.
BUT I'LL BE SAYING A DIFFERENT SORT OF HELLO TO YOU.
DO YOU UNDER-STAND WHAT I'M SAYING, MIKURU ASAHINA?
HE'S CROSSED THE LINE.
TO THINK HE'D FORCE A DIRECT CONFRON-TATION...
GOTTA MAKE THIS QUICK.
HARUHI HATES THIS KIND OF SNEAKINESS TOO.
IF YOU'VE GOT SOMETHING TO SAY, SAY IT.
I'LL PASS IT ON TO HARUHI.

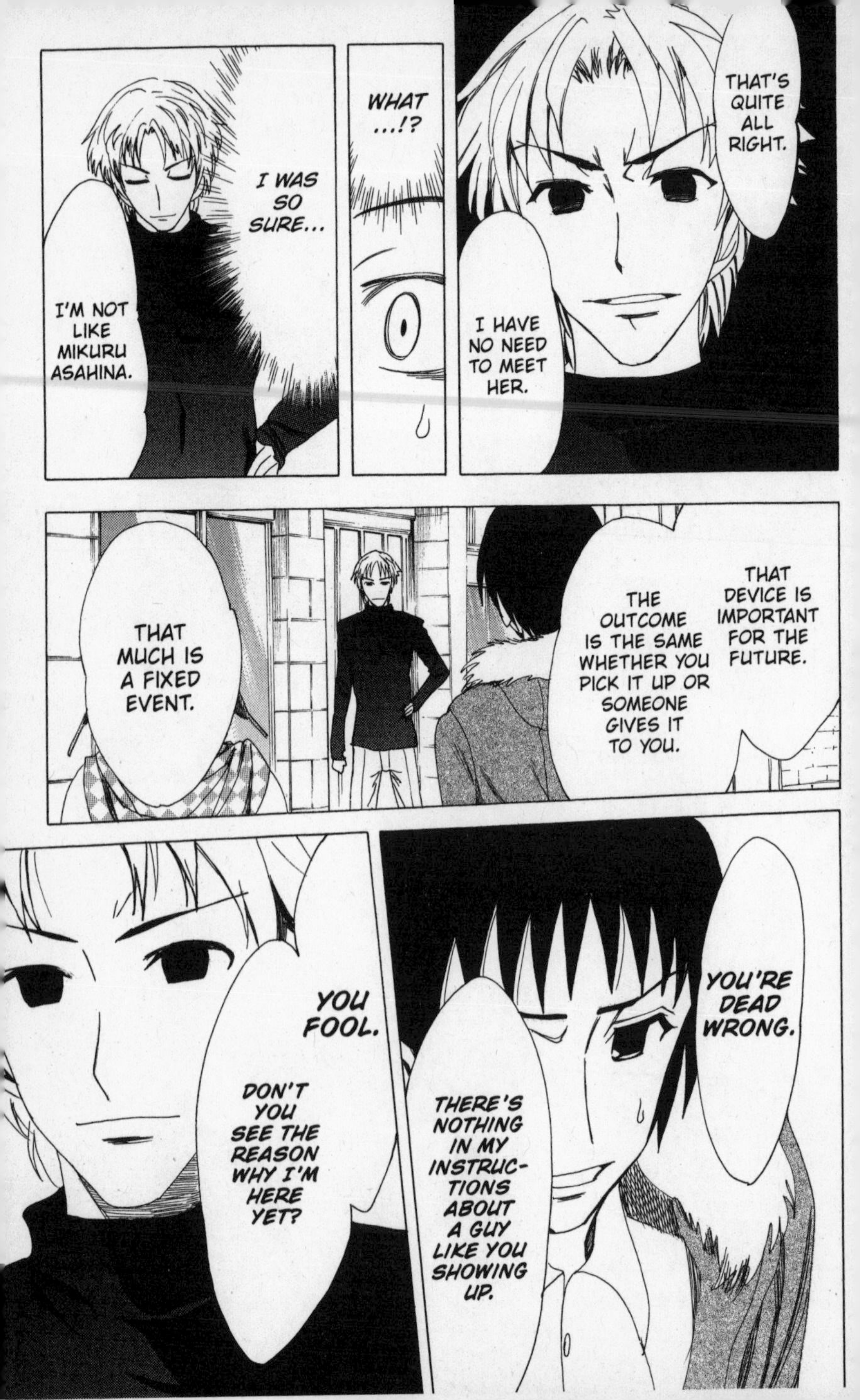
THAT'S QUITE ALL RIGHT.
I HAVE NO NEED TO MEET HER.
WHAT ...!?
I WAS SO SURE...
I'M NOT LIKE MIKURU ASAHINA.
THAT DEVICE IS IMPORTANT FOR THE FUTURE.
THE OUTCOME IS THE SAME WHETHER YOU PICK IT UP OR SOMEONE GIVES IT TO YOU.
THAT MUCH IS A FIXED EVENT.
YOU'RE DEAD WRONG.
THERE'S NOTHING IN MY INSTRUC-TIONS ABOUT A GUY LIKE YOU SHOWING UP.
YOU FOOL.
DON'T YOU SEE THE REASON WHY I'M HERE YET?

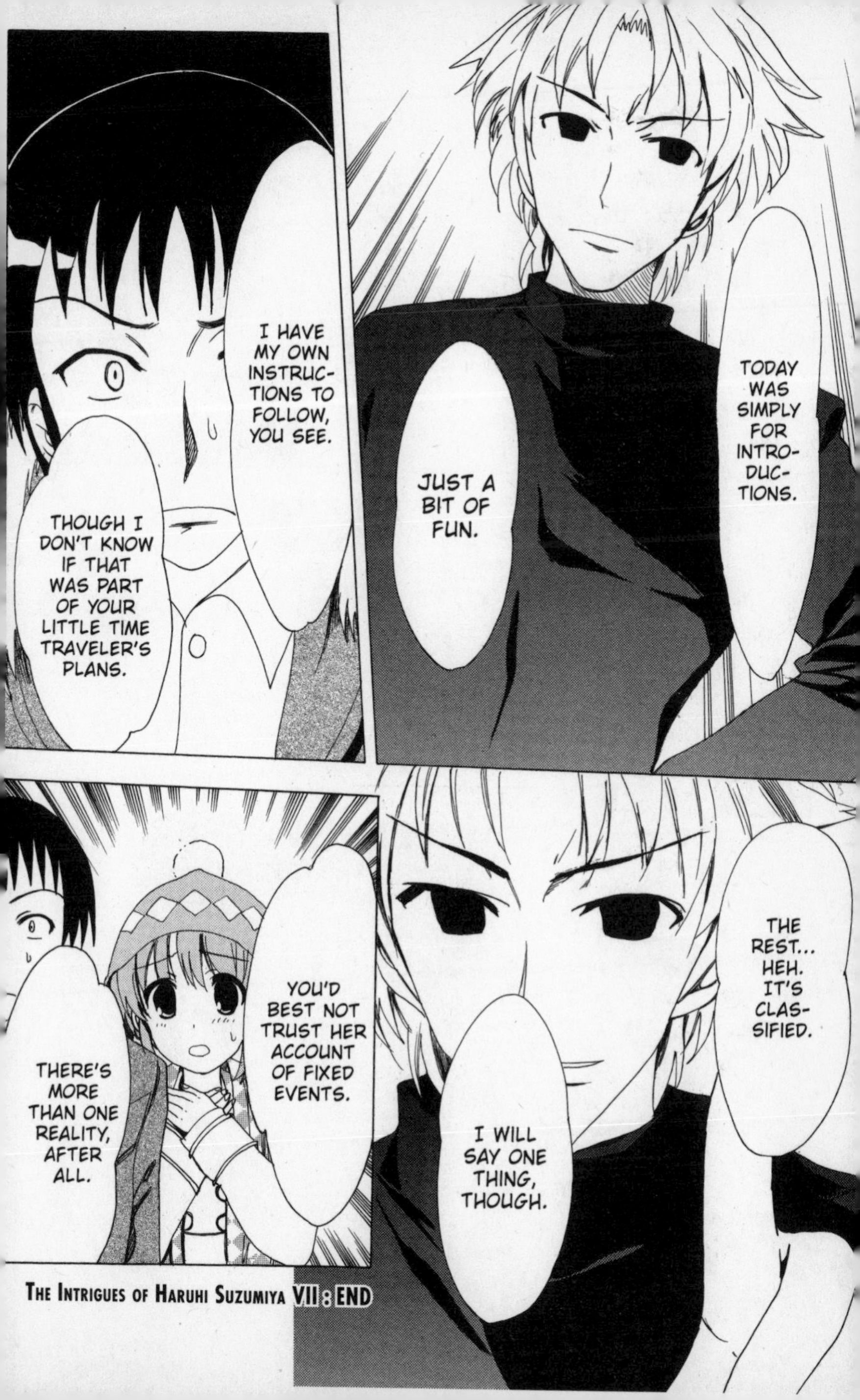
TODAY WAS SIMPLY FOR INTRO-DUC-TIONS.
JUST A BIT OF FUN.
I HAVE MY OWN INSTRUC-TIONS TO FOLLOW, YOU SEE.
THOUGH I DON'T KNOW IF THAT WAS PART OF YOUR LITTLE TIME TRAVELER'S PLANS.
THE REST... HEH. IT'S CLAS-SIFIED.
I WILL SAY ONE THING, THOUGH.
YOU'D BEST NOT TRUST HER ACCOUNT OF FIXED EVENTS.
THERE'S MORE THAN ONE REALITY, AFTER ALL.

THE INTRIGUES OF HARUHI SUZUMIYA VII : END

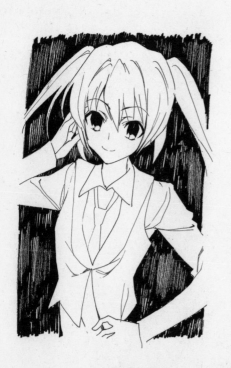

THE MELANCHOLY OF HARUHI SUZUMIYA

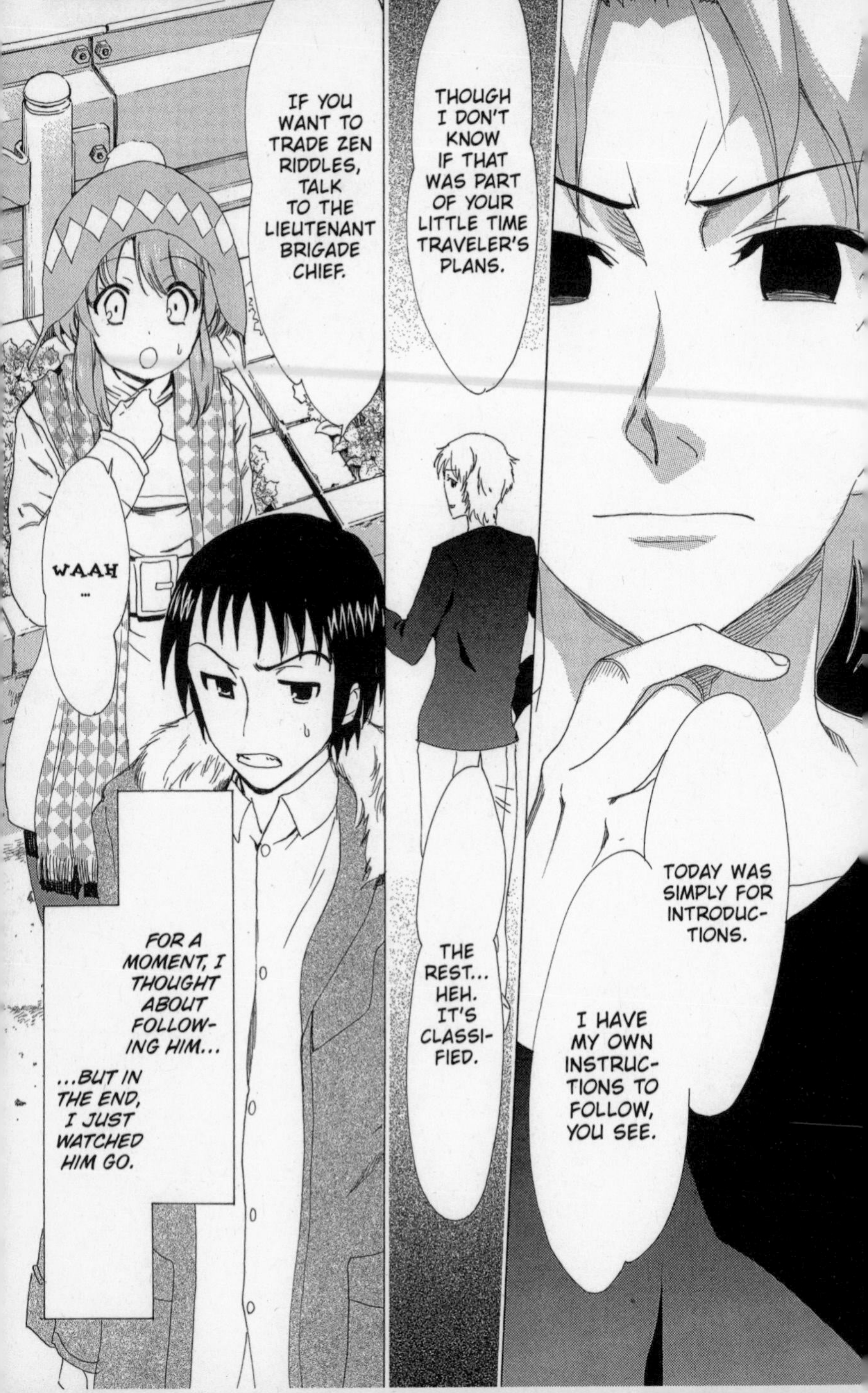
TODAY WAS SIMPLY FOR INTRODUC-TIONS.
I HAVE MY OWN INSTRUC-TIONS TO FOLLOW, YOU SEE.
THOUGH I DON'T KNOW IF THAT WAS PART OF YOUR LITTLE TIME TRAVELER'S PLANS.
THE REST... HEH. IT'S CLASSI-FIED.
IF YOU WANT TO TRADE ZEN RIDDLES, TALK TO THE LIEUTENANT BRIGADE CHIEF.
WAAH ...
FOR A MOMENT, I THOUGHT ABOUT FOLLOW-ING HIM...
...BUT IN THE END, I JUST WATCHED HIM GO.

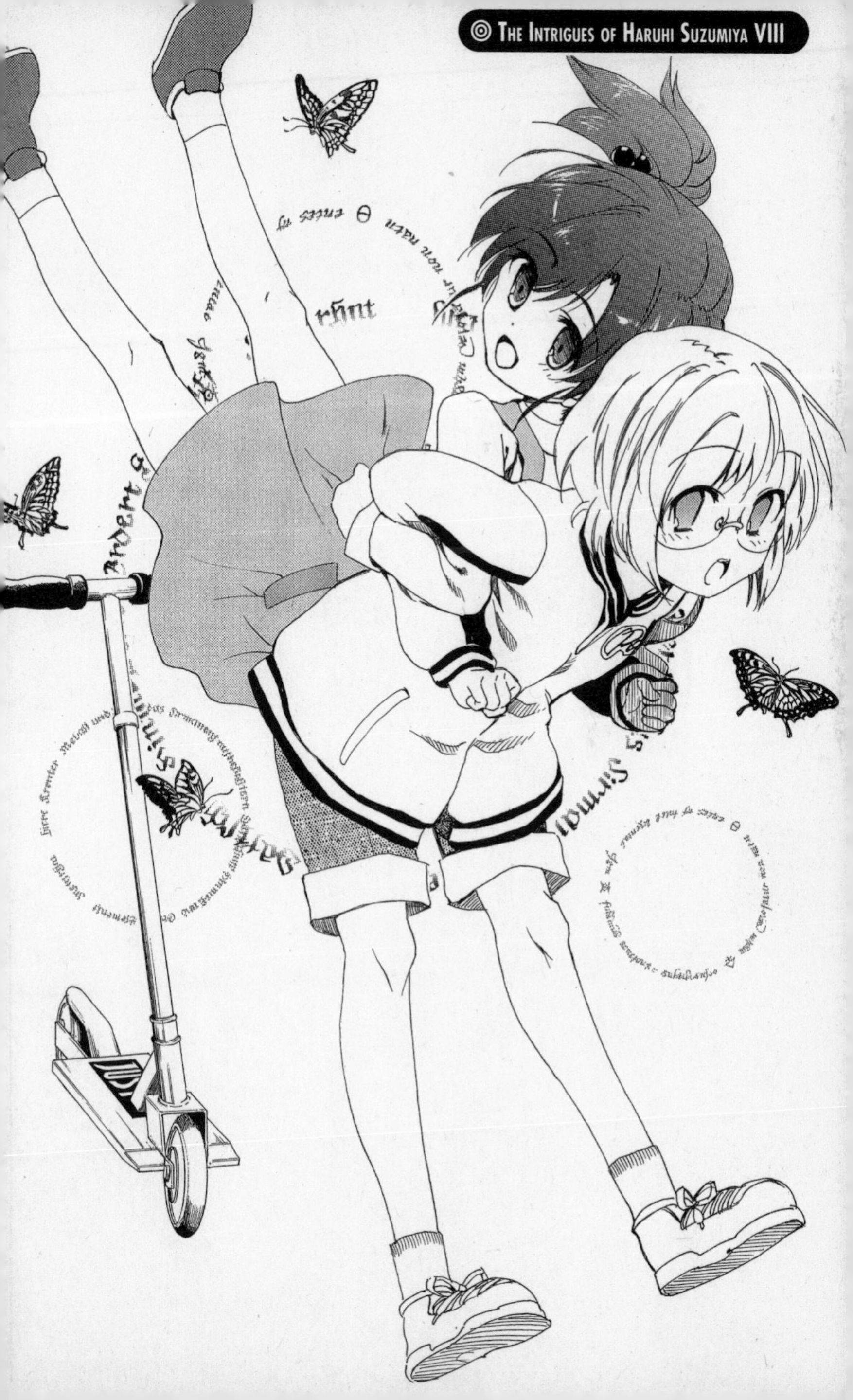

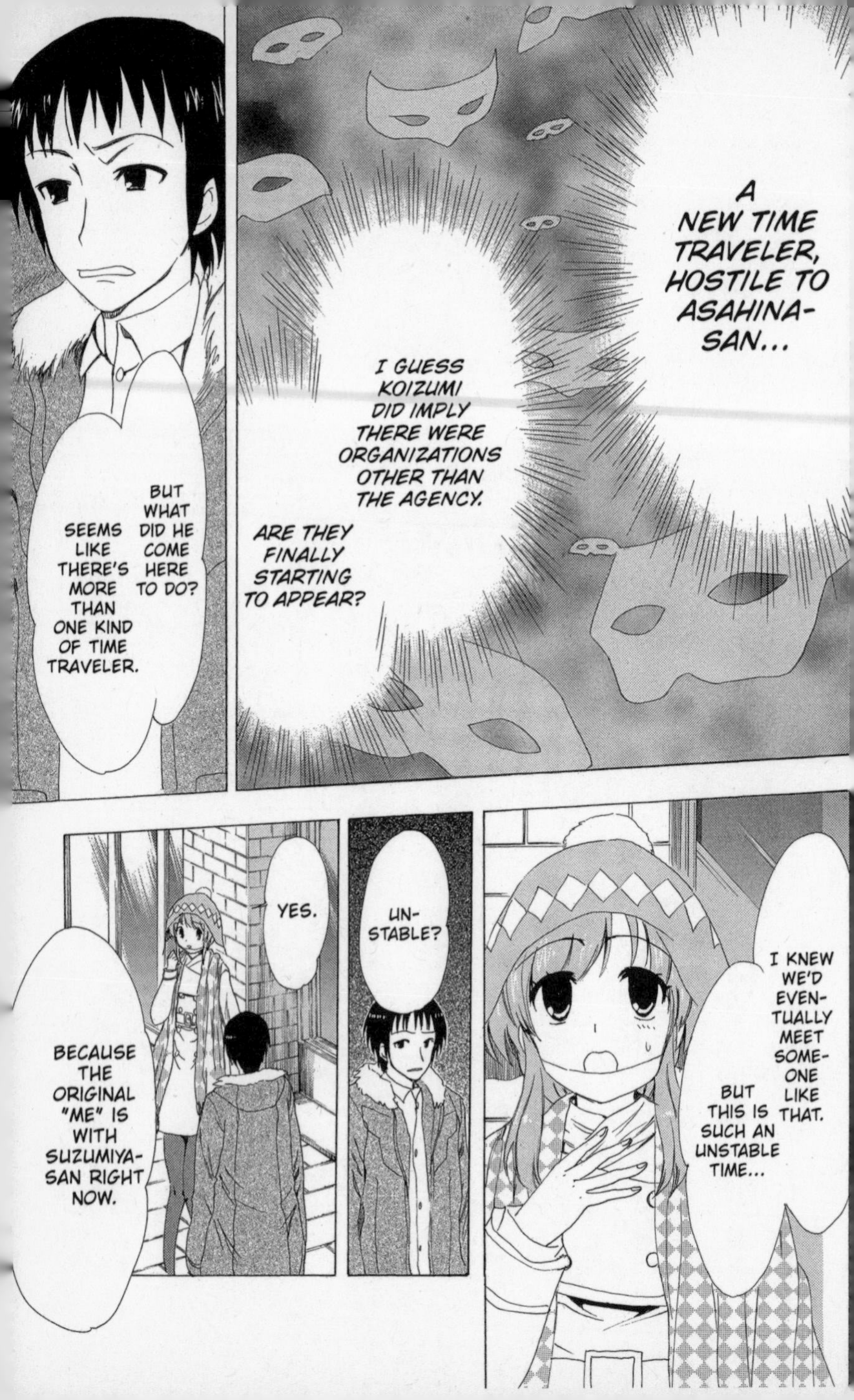
A NEW TIME TRAVELER, HOSTILE TO ASAHINA-SAN...
I GUESS KOIZUMI DID IMPLY THERE WERE ORGANIZATIONS OTHER THAN THE AGENCY.
ARE THEY FINALLY STARTING TO APPEAR?
BUT WHAT DID HE COME HERE TO DO?
SEEMS LIKE THERE'S MORE THAN ONE KIND OF TIME TRAVELER.
I KNEW WE'D EVENTUALLY MEET SOMEONE LIKE THAT.
BUT THIS IS SUCH AN UNSTABLE TIME...
UN-STABLE?
YES.
BECAUSE THE ORIGINAL "ME" IS WITH SUZUMIYA-SAN RIGHT NOW.

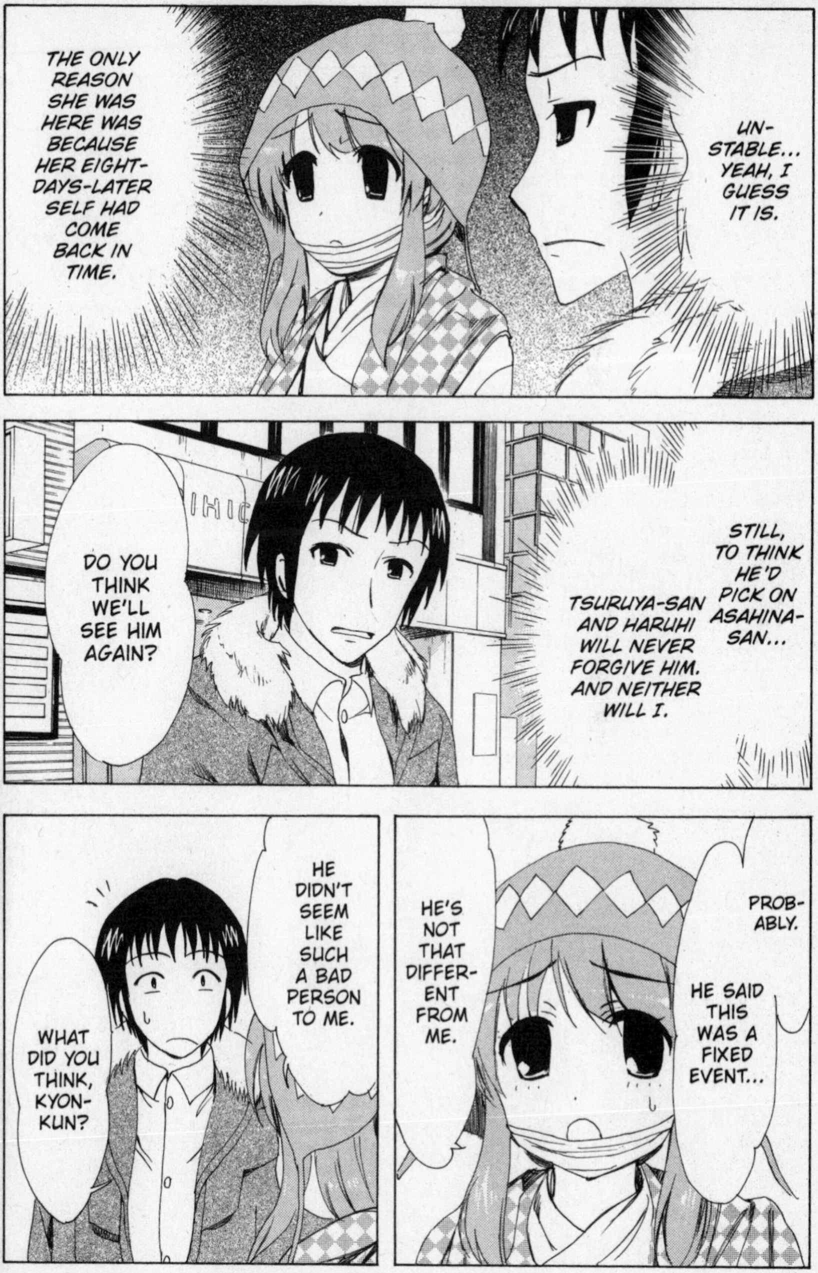
UN-STABLE... YEAH, I GUESS IT IS.
THE ONLY REASON SHE WAS HERE WAS BECAUSE HER EIGHT-DAYS-LATER SELF HAD COME BACK IN TIME.
STILL, TO THINK HE'D PICK ON ASAHINA-SAN...
TSURUYA-SAN AND HARUHI WILL NEVER FORGIVE HIM. AND NEITHER WILL I.
DO YOU THINK WE'LL SEE HIM AGAIN?
PROB-ABLY.
HE SAID THIS WAS A FIXED EVENT...
HE'S NOT THAT DIFFER-ENT FROM ME.
HE DIDN'T SEEM LIKE SUCH A BAD PERSON TO ME.
WHAT DID YOU THINK, KYON-KUN?

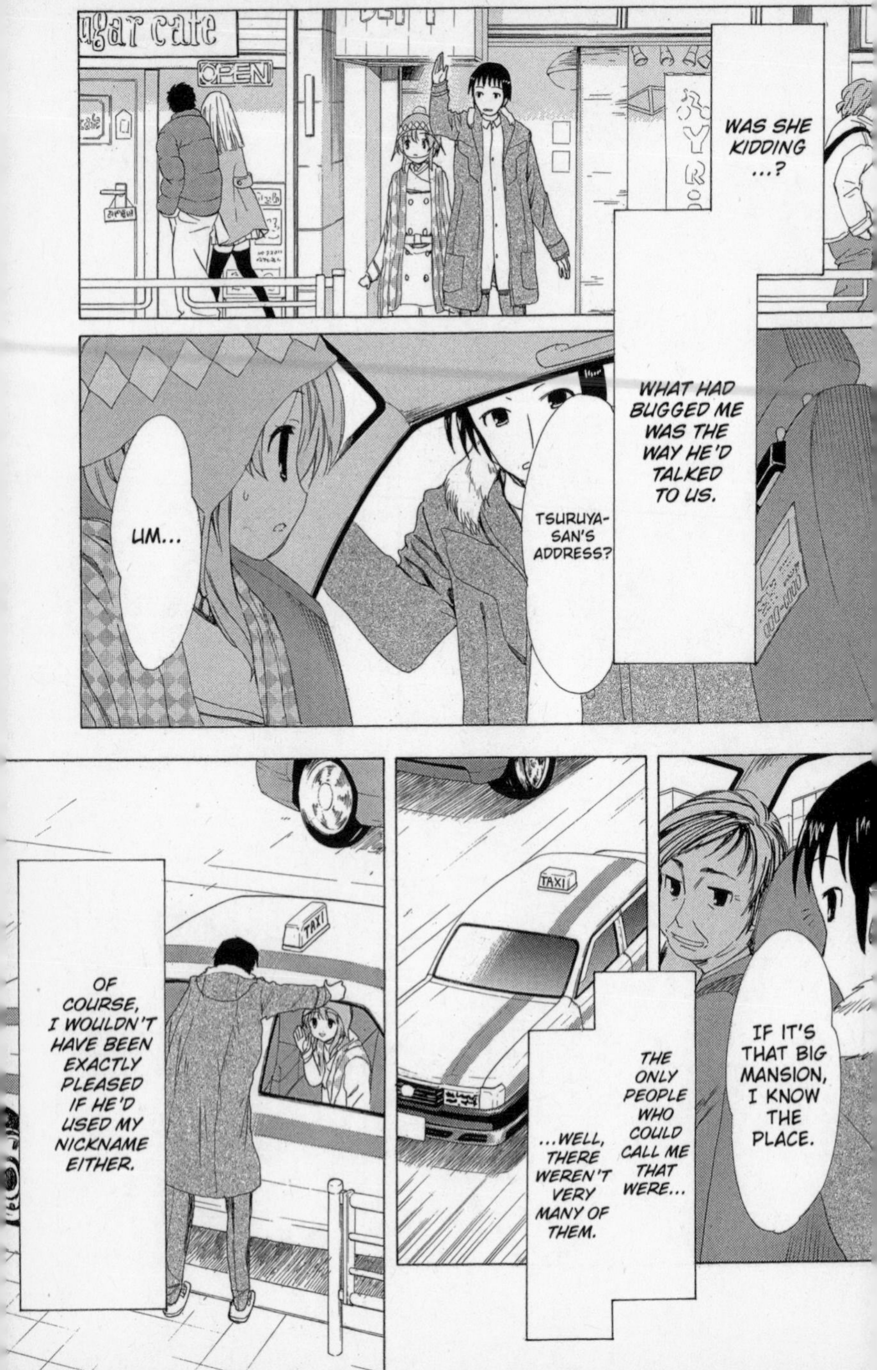
WAS SHE KIDDING ...?
OPEN
WHAT HAD BUGGED ME WAS THE WAY HE'D TALKED TO US.
TSURUYA-SAN'S ADDRESS?
UM...
IF IT'S THAT BIG MANSION, I KNOW THE PLACE.
THE ONLY PEOPLE WHO COULD CALL ME THAT WERE...
...WELL, THERE WEREN'T VERY MANY OF THEM.
TAXI
TAXI
OF COURSE, I WOULDN'T HAVE BEEN EXACTLY PLEASED IF HE'D USED MY NICKNAME EITHER.

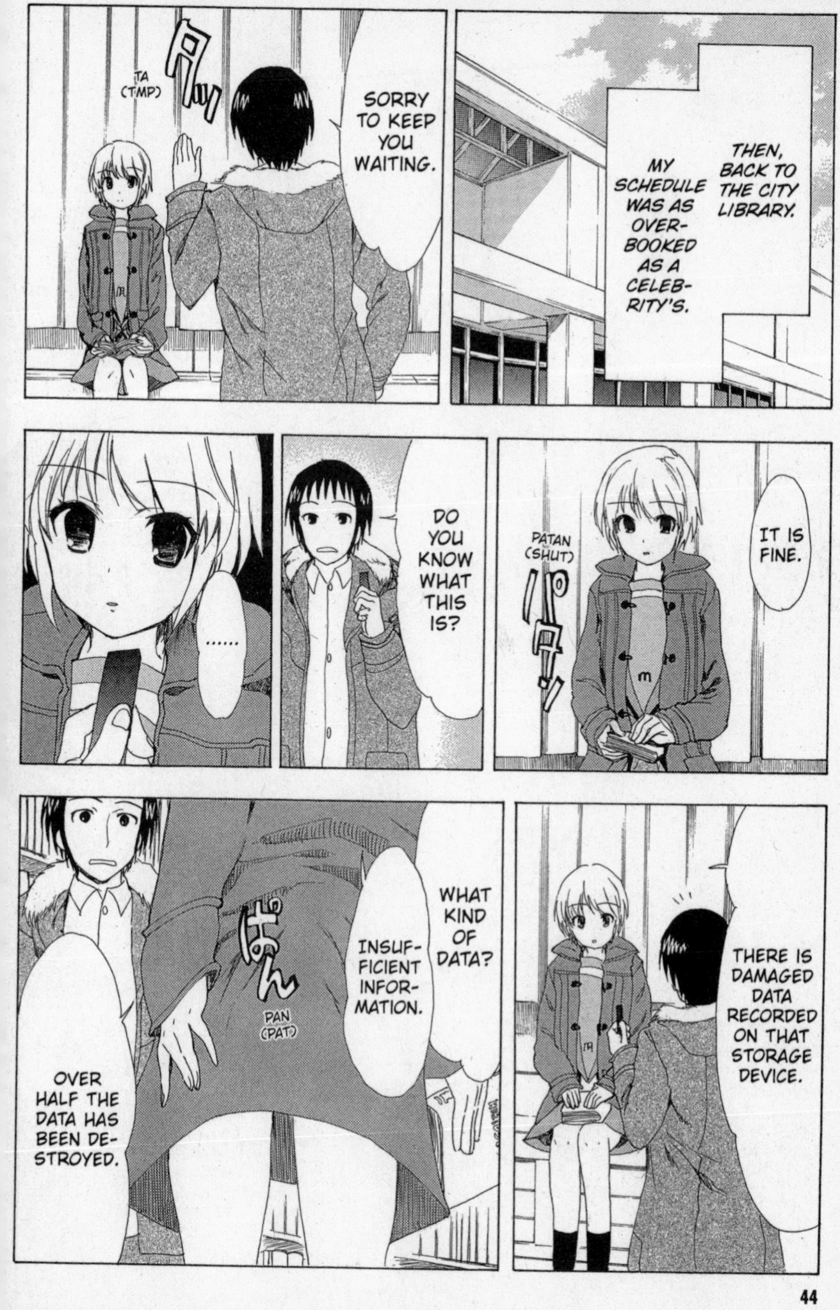
THEN, BACK TO THE CITY LIBRARY.
MY SCHEDULE WAS AS OVER-BOOKED AS A CELEBRITY'S.
SORRY TO KEEP YOU WAITING.
TA (TMP)
IT IS FINE.
PATAN (SHUT)
DO YOU KNOW WHAT THIS IS?
......
THERE IS DAMAGED DATA RECORDED ON THAT STORAGE DEVICE.
WHAT KIND OF DATA?
INSUFFICIENT INFORMATION.
PAN (PAT)
OVER HALF THE DATA HAS BEEN DESTROYED.

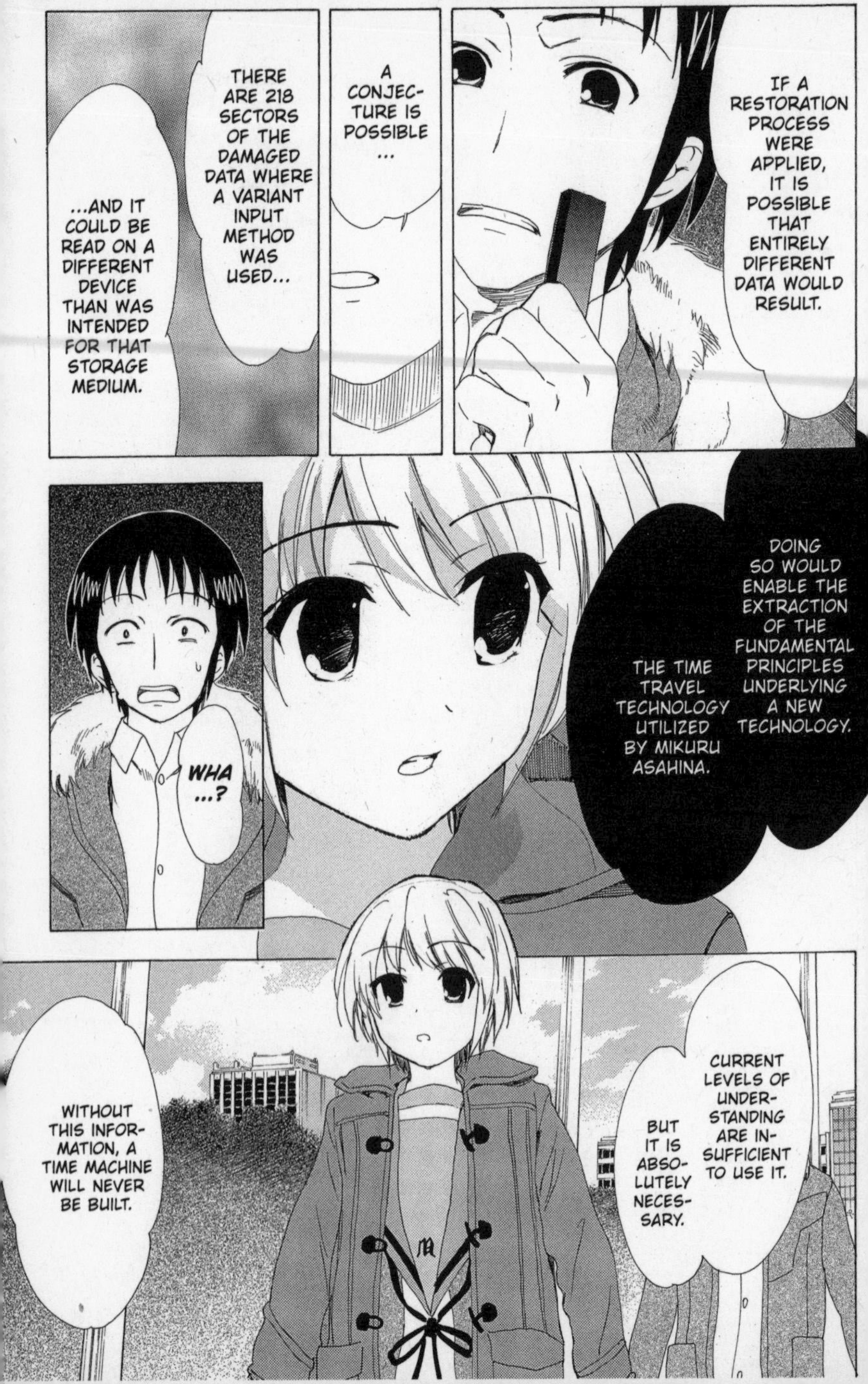
IF A RESTORATION PROCESS WERE APPLIED, IT IS POSSIBLE THAT ENTIRELY DIFFERENT DATA WOULD RESULT.
A CONJEC-TURE IS POSSIBLE ...
THERE ARE 218 SECTORS OF THE DAMAGED DATA WHERE A VARIANT INPUT METHOD WAS USED...
...AND IT COULD BE READ ON A DIFFERENT DEVICE THAN WAS INTENDED FOR THAT STORAGE MEDIUM.
DOING SO WOULD ENABLE THE EXTRACTION OF THE FUNDAMENTAL PRINCIPLES UNDERLYING A NEW TECHNOLOGY.
THE TIME TRAVEL TECHNOLOGY UTILIZED BY MIKURU ASAHINA.
WHA ...?
CURRENT LEVELS OF UNDER-STANDING ARE IN-SUFFICIENT TO USE IT.
BUT IT IS ABSO-LUTELY NECES-SARY.
WITHOUT THIS INFOR-MATION, A TIME MACHINE WILL NEVER BE BUILT.

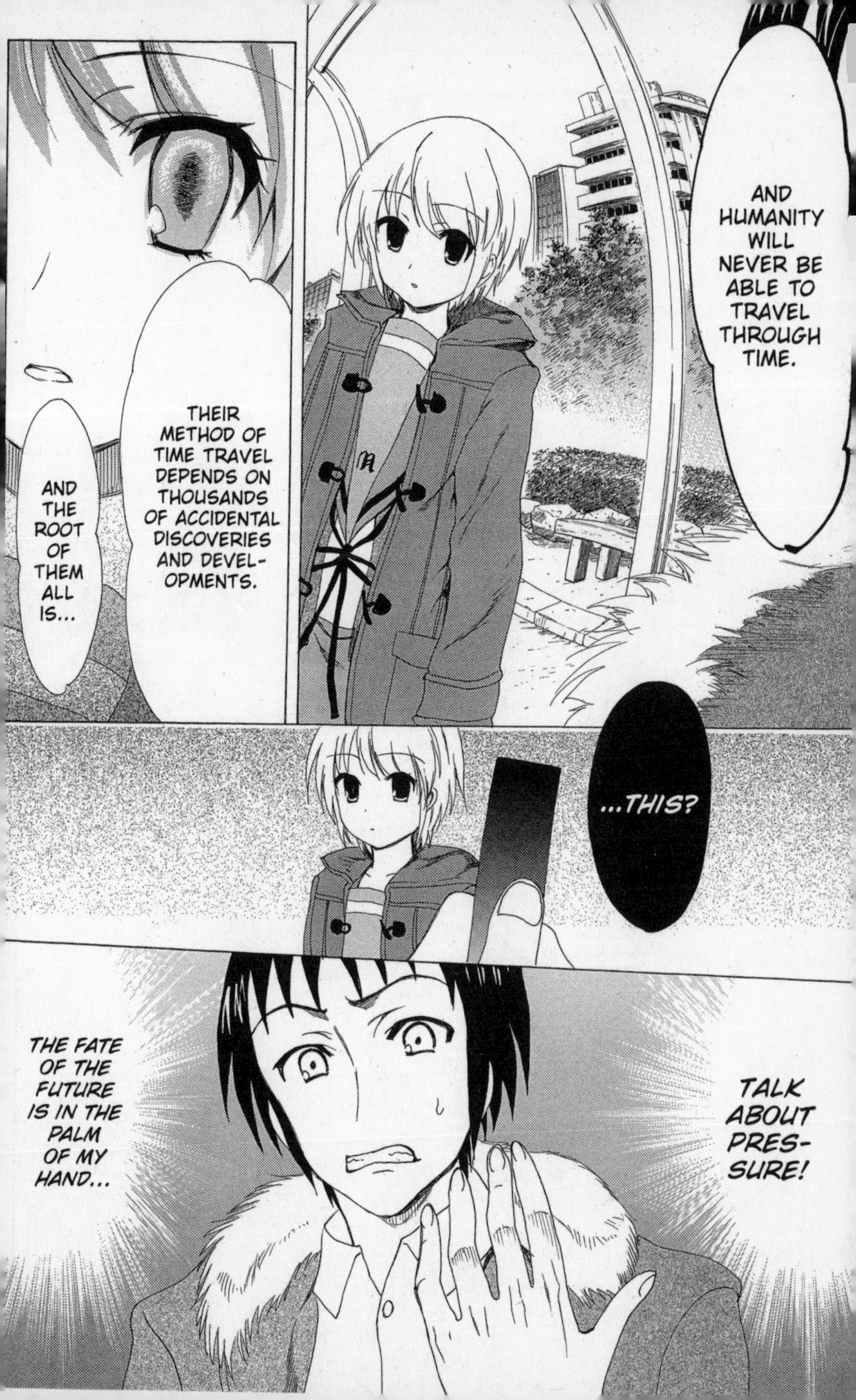
AND HUMANITY WILL NEVER BE ABLE TO TRAVEL THROUGH TIME.
THEIR METHOD OF TIME TRAVEL DEPENDS ON THOUSANDS OF ACCIDENTAL DISCOVERIES AND DEVEL-OPMENTS.
AND THE ROOT OF THEM ALL IS...
...THIS?
THE FATE OF THE FUTURE IS IN THE PALM OF MY HAND...
TALK ABOUT PRES-SURE!

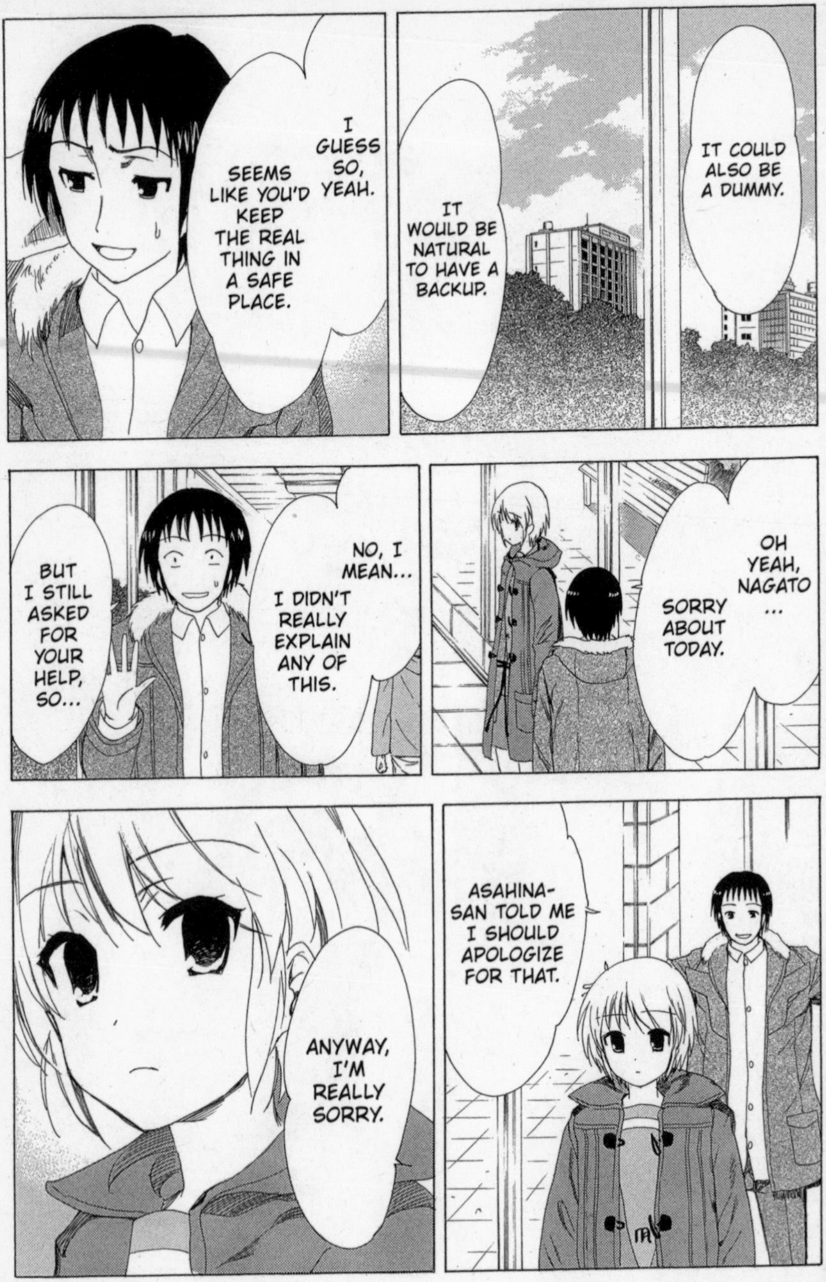
IT COULD ALSO BE A DUMMY.
IT WOULD BE NATURAL TO HAVE A BACKUP.
I GUESS SO, YEAH.
SEEMS LIKE YOU'D KEEP THE REAL THING IN A SAFE PLACE.
OH YEAH, NAGATO ...
SORRY ABOUT TODAY.
NO, I MEAN...
I DIDN'T REALLY EXPLAIN ANY OF THIS.
BUT I STILL ASKED FOR YOUR HELP, SO...
ASAHINA-SAN TOLD ME I SHOULD APOLOGIZE FOR THAT.
ANYWAY, I'M REALLY SORRY.

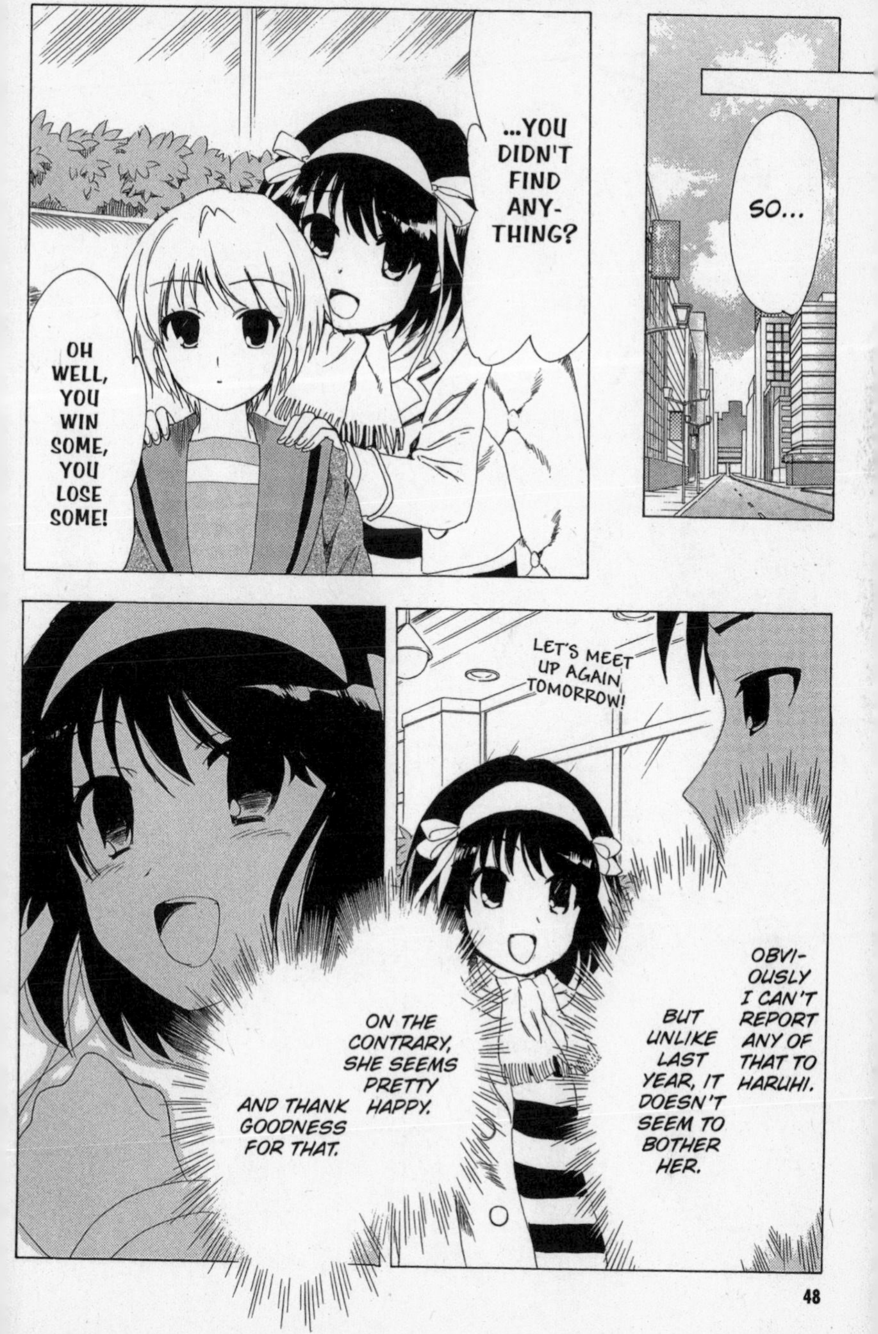
SO...
...YOU DIDN'T FIND ANYTHING?
OH WELL, YOU WIN SOME, YOU LOSE SOME!
LET'S MEET UP AGAIN TOMORROW!
OBVIOUSLY I CAN'T REPORT ANY OF THAT TO HARUHI.
BUT UNLIKE LAST YEAR, IT DOESN'T SEEM TO BOTHER HER.
ON THE CONTRARY, SHE SEEMS PRETTY HAPPY.
AND THANK GOODNESS FOR THAT.

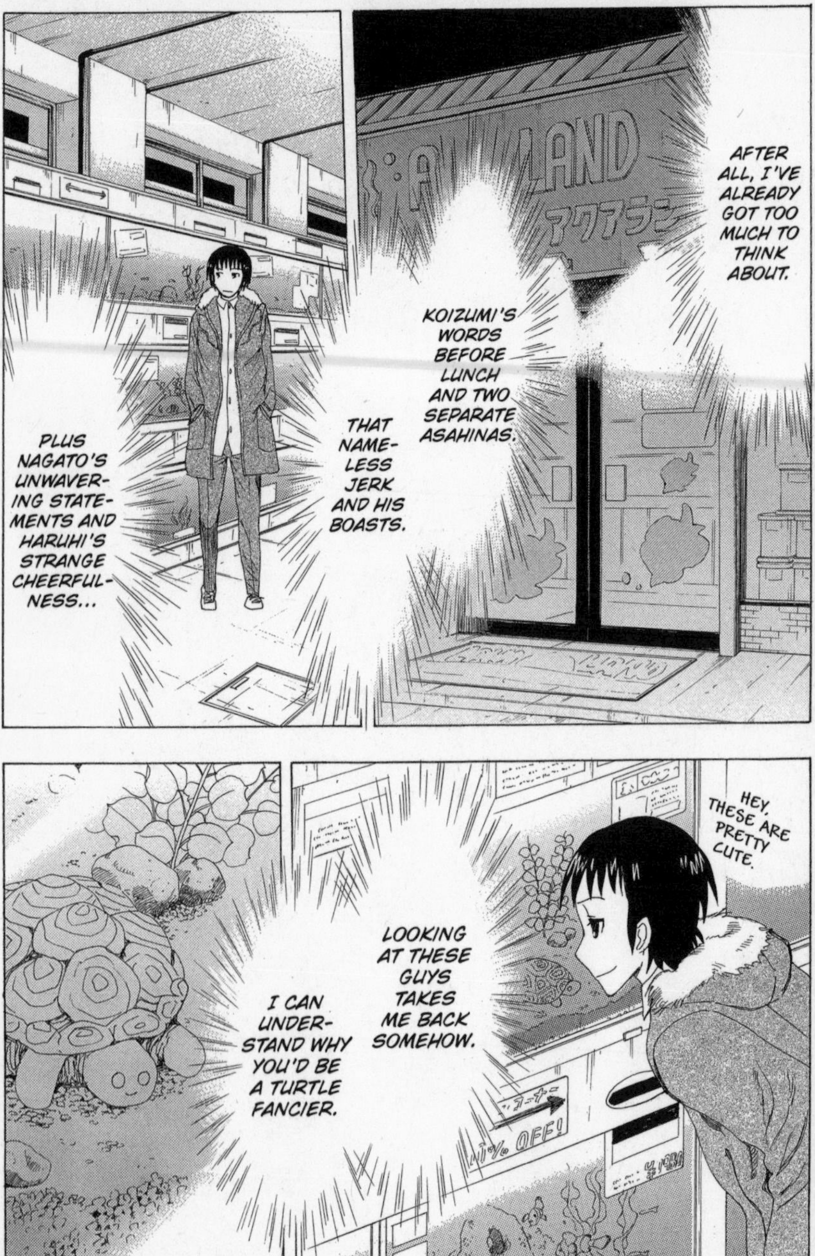
AFTER ALL, I'VE ALREADY GOT TOO MUCH TO THINK ABOUT.
KOIZUMI'S WORDS BEFORE LUNCH AND TWO SEPARATE ASAHINAS.
THAT NAMELESS JERK AND HIS BOASTS.
PLUS NAGATO'S UNWAVERING STATEMENTS AND HARUHI'S STRANGE CHEERFULNESS...
HEY, THESE ARE PRETTY CUTE.
LOOKING AT THESE GUYS TAKES ME BACK SOMEHOW.
I CAN UNDERSTAND WHY YOU'D BE A TURTLE FANCIER.

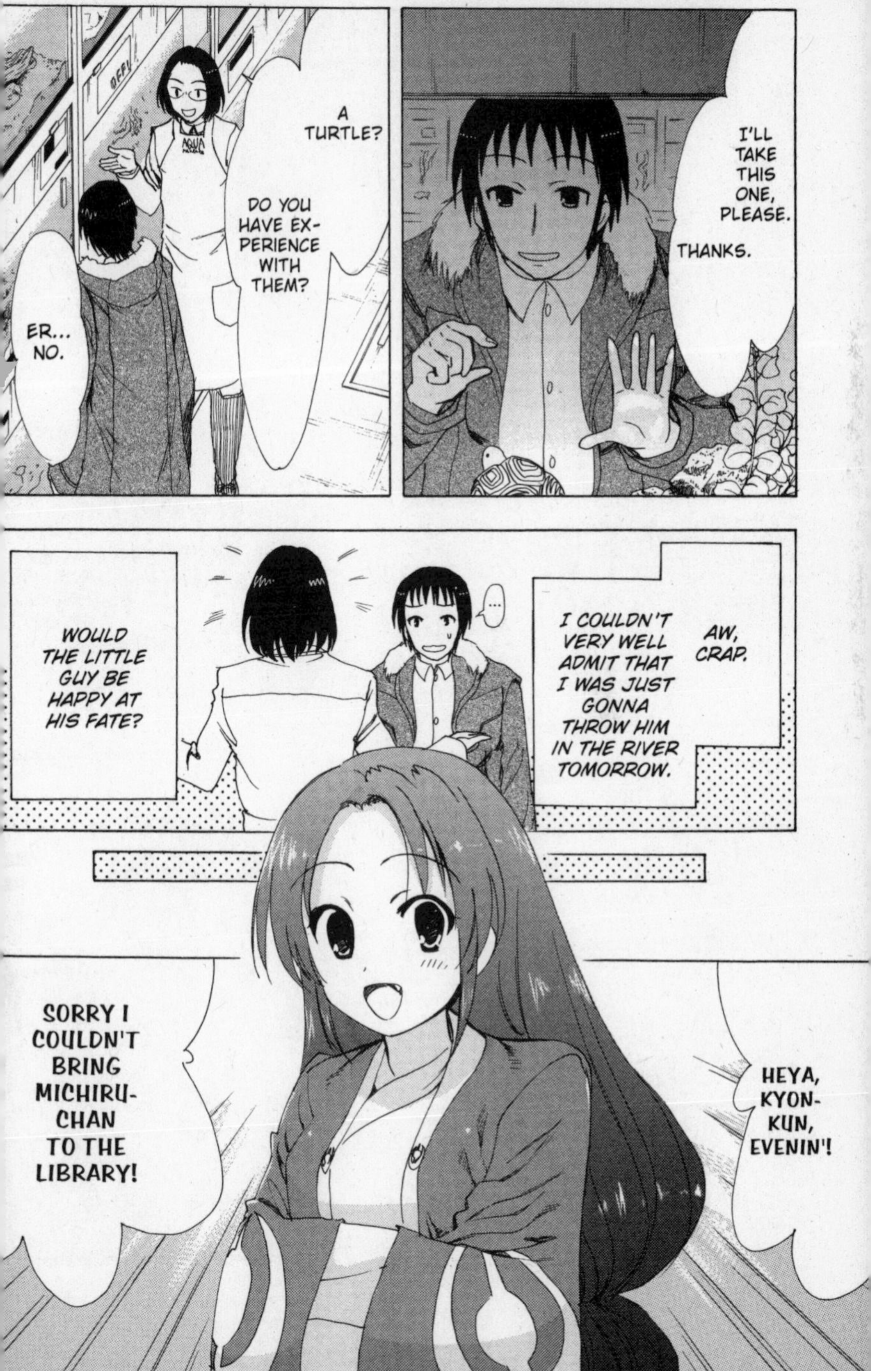
I'LL TAKE THIS ONE, PLEASE.
THANKS.
A TURTLE?
DO YOU HAVE EX-PERIENCE WITH THEM?
ER... NO.
AW, CRAP.
I COULDN'T VERY WELL ADMIT THAT I WAS JUST GONNA THROW HIM IN THE RIVER TOMORROW.
...
WOULD THE LITTLE GUY BE HAPPY AT HIS FATE?
HEYA, KYON-KUN, EVENIN'!
SORRY I COULDN'T BRING MICHIRU-CHAN TO THE LIBRARY!

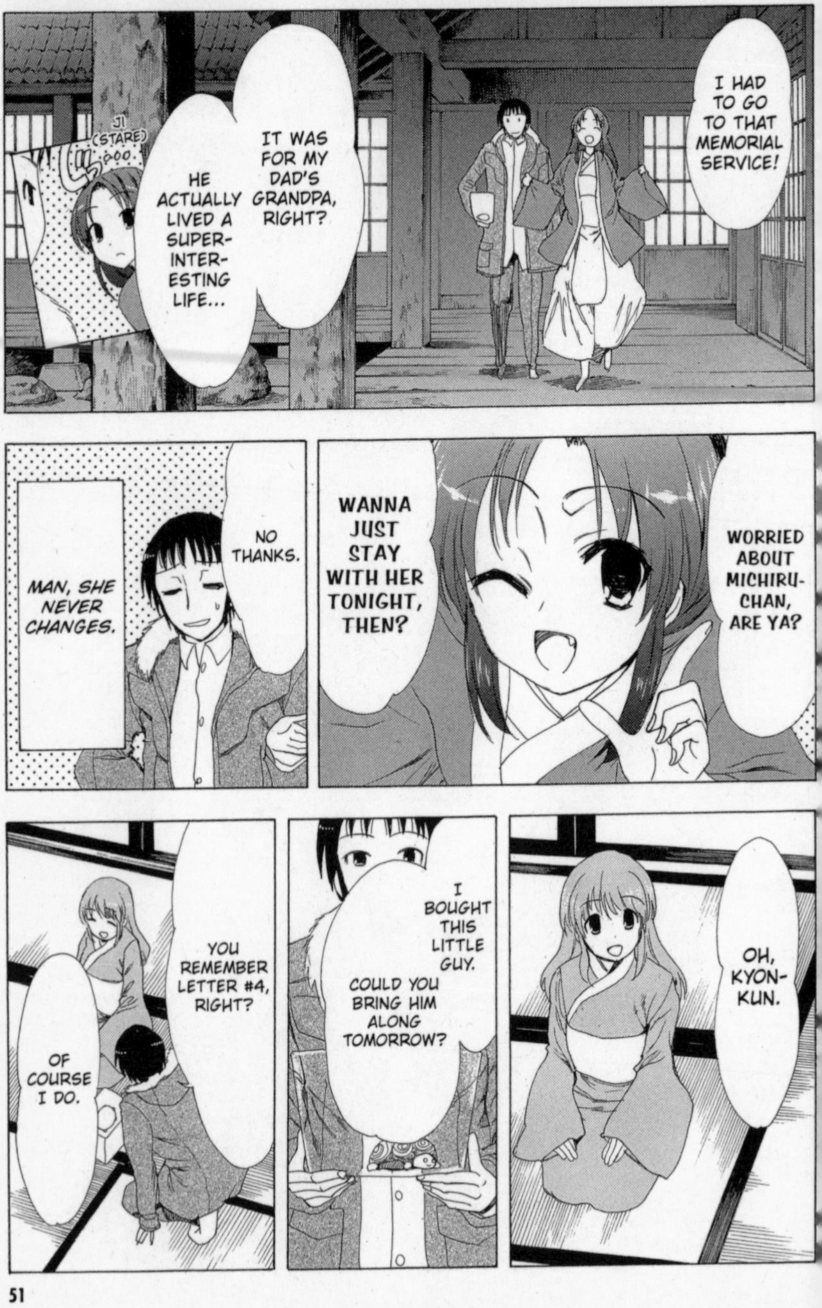
I HAD TO GO TO THAT MEMORIAL SERVICE!
IT WAS FOR MY DAD'S GRANDPA, RIGHT?
HE ACTUALLY LIVED A SUPER-INTERESTING LIFE...
JI (STARE)
WORRIED ABOUT MICHIRU-CHAN, ARE YA?
WANNA JUST STAY WITH HER TONIGHT, THEN?
NO THANKS.
MAN, SHE NEVER CHANGES.
OH, KYON-KUN.
I BOUGHT THIS LITTLE GUY.
COULD YOU BRING HIM ALONG TOMORROW?
YOU REMEMBER LETTER #4, RIGHT?
OF COURSE I DO.

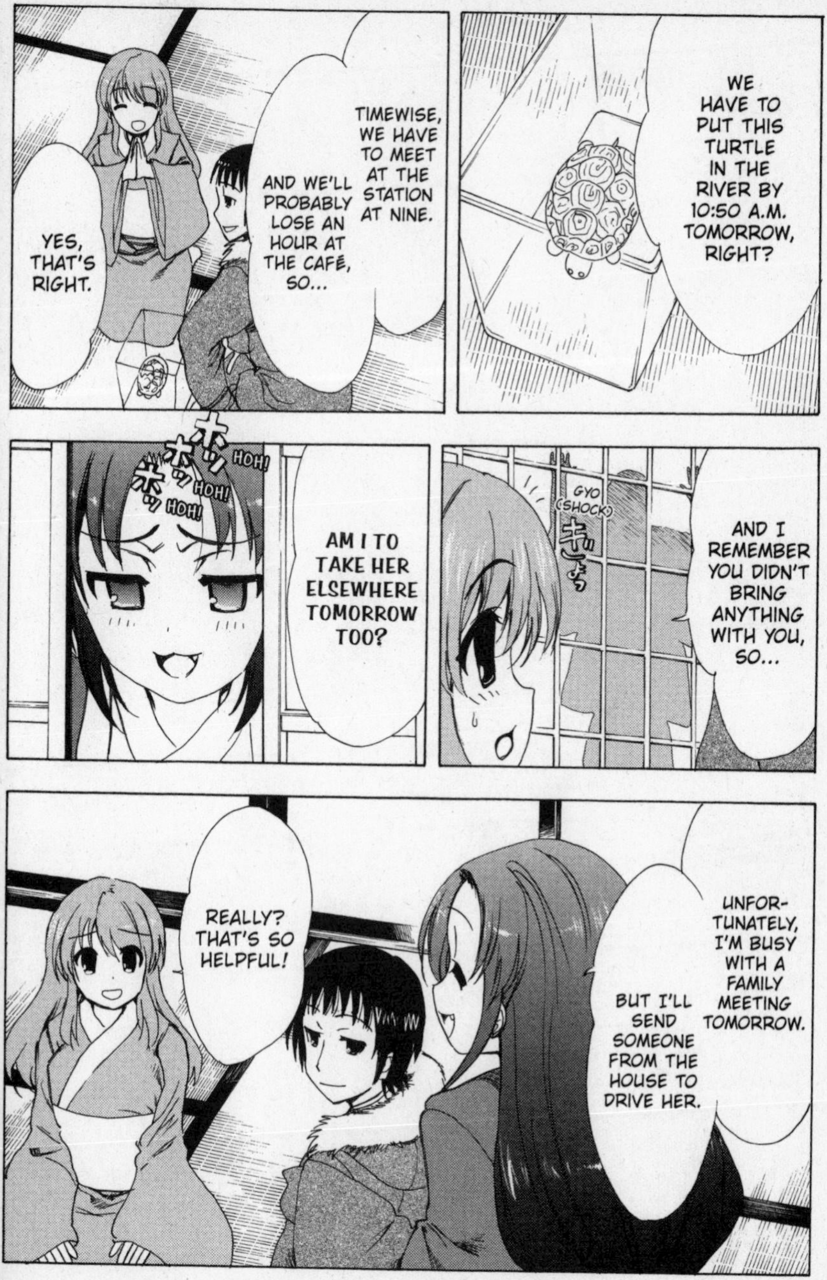
WE HAVE TO PUT THIS TURTLE IN THE RIVER BY 10:50 A.M. TOMORROW, RIGHT?
TIMEWISE, WE HAVE TO MEET AT THE STATION AT NINE.
AND WE'LL PROBABLY LOSE AN HOUR AT THE CAFÉ, SO...
YES, THAT'S RIGHT.
AND I REMEMBER YOU DIDN'T BRING ANYTHING WITH YOU, SO...
GYO (SHOCK)
ぎょっ
ホッ HOH!
ホッ HOH!
ホッ HOH!
AM I TO TAKE HER ELSEWHERE TOMORROW TOO?
UNFORTUNATELY, I'M BUSY WITH A FAMILY MEETING TOMORROW.
BUT I'LL SEND SOMEONE FROM THE HOUSE TO DRIVE HER.
REALLY? THAT'S SO HELPFUL!

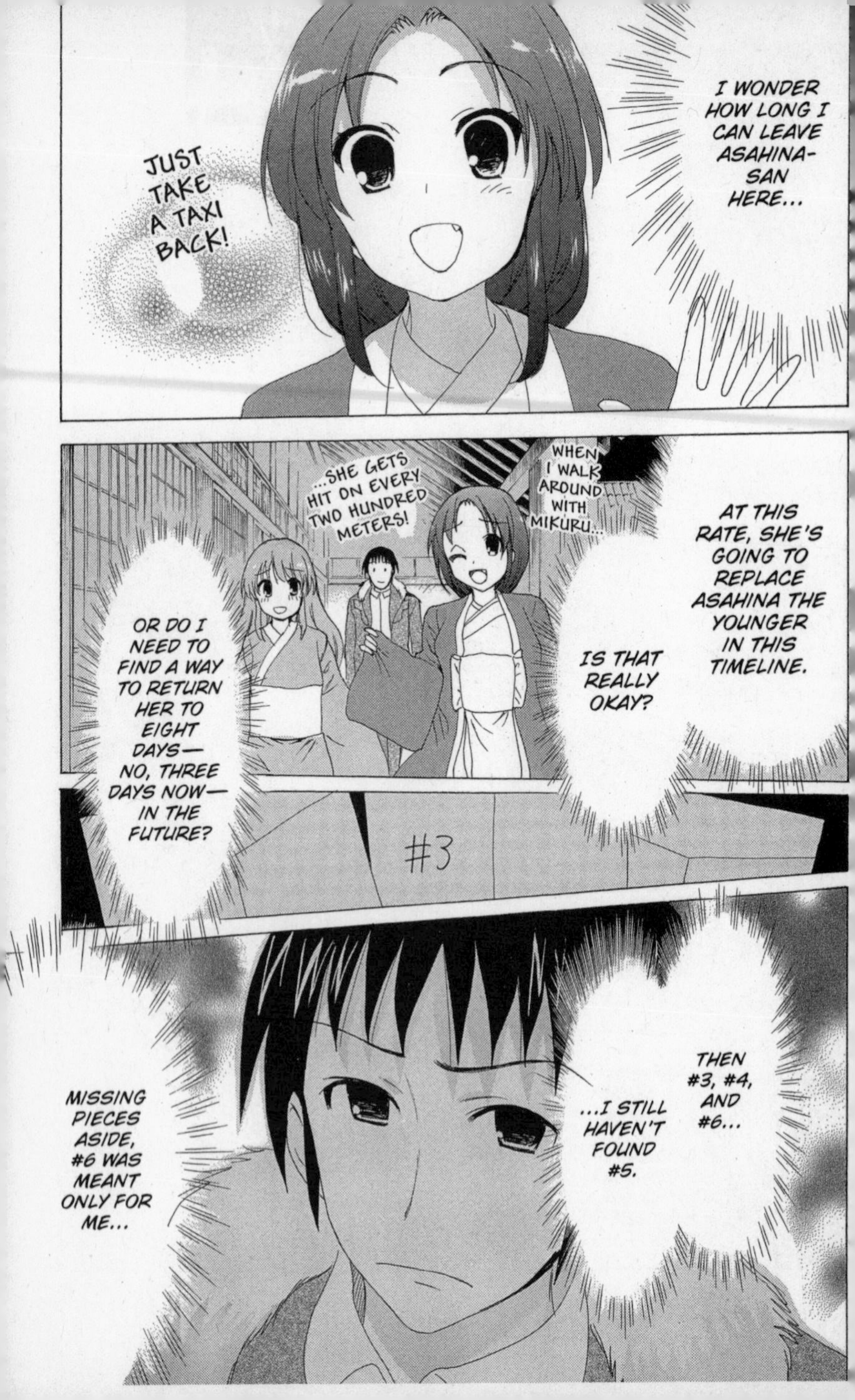
I WONDER HOW LONG I CAN LEAVE ASAHINA-SAN HERE...
JUST TAKE A TAXI BACK!
WHEN I WALK AROUND WITH MIKURU...
...SHE GETS HIT ON EVERY TWO HUNDRED METERS!
AT THIS RATE, SHE'S GOING TO REPLACE ASAHINA THE YOUNGER IN THIS TIMELINE.
IS THAT REALLY OKAY?
OR DO I NEED TO FIND A WAY TO RETURN HER TO EIGHT DAYS—NO, THREE DAYS NOW—IN THE FUTURE?
#3
THEN #3, #4, AND #6...
...I STILL HAVEN'T FOUND #5.
MISSING PIECES ASIDE, #6 WAS MEANT ONLY FOR ME...

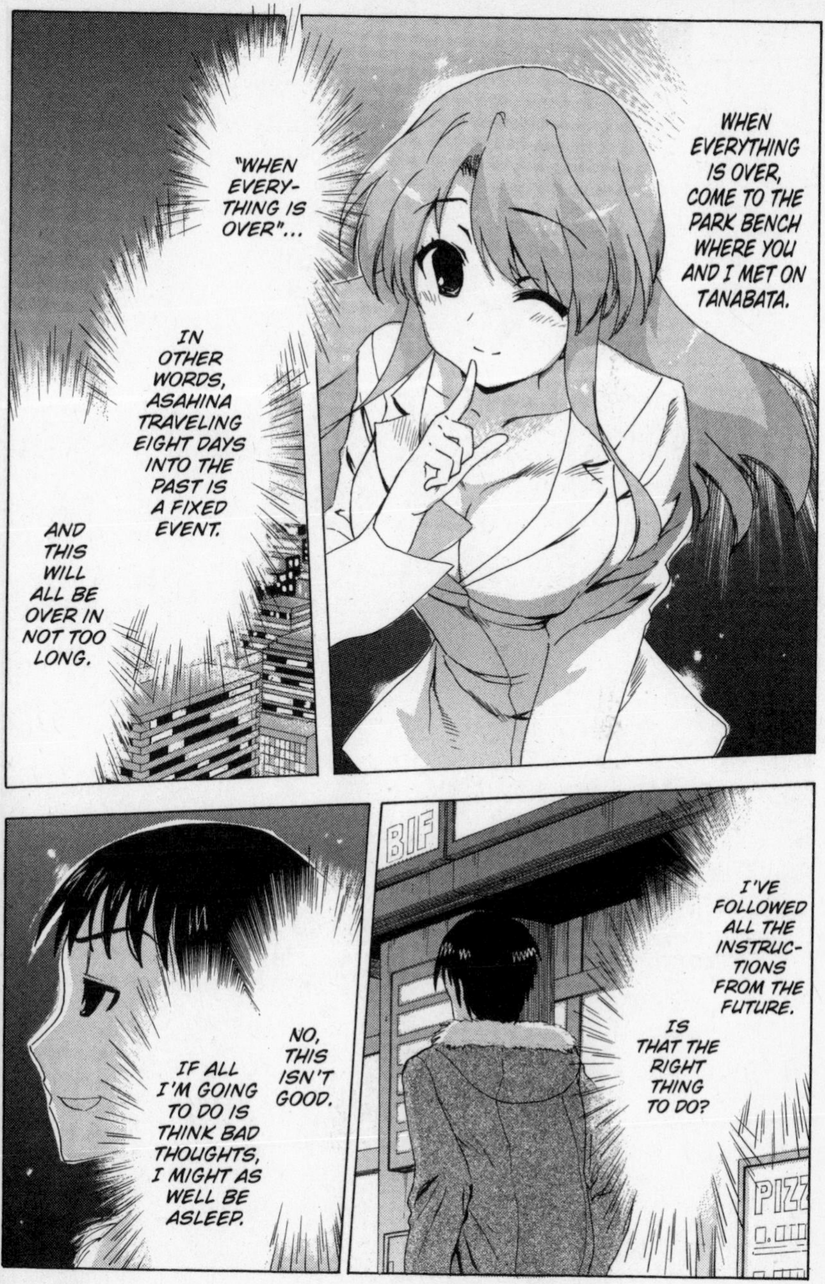
WHEN EVERYTHING IS OVER, COME TO THE PARK BENCH WHERE YOU AND I MET ON TANABATA.
"WHEN EVERY-THING IS OVER"...
IN OTHER WORDS, ASAHINA TRAVELING EIGHT DAYS INTO THE PAST IS A FIXED EVENT.
AND THIS WILL ALL BE OVER IN NOT TOO LONG.
I'VE FOLLOWED ALL THE INSTRUC-TIONS FROM THE FUTURE.
IS THAT THE RIGHT THING TO DO?
NO, THIS ISN'T GOOD.
IF ALL I'M GOING TO DO IS THINK BAD THOUGHTS, I MIGHT AS WELL BE ASLEEP.

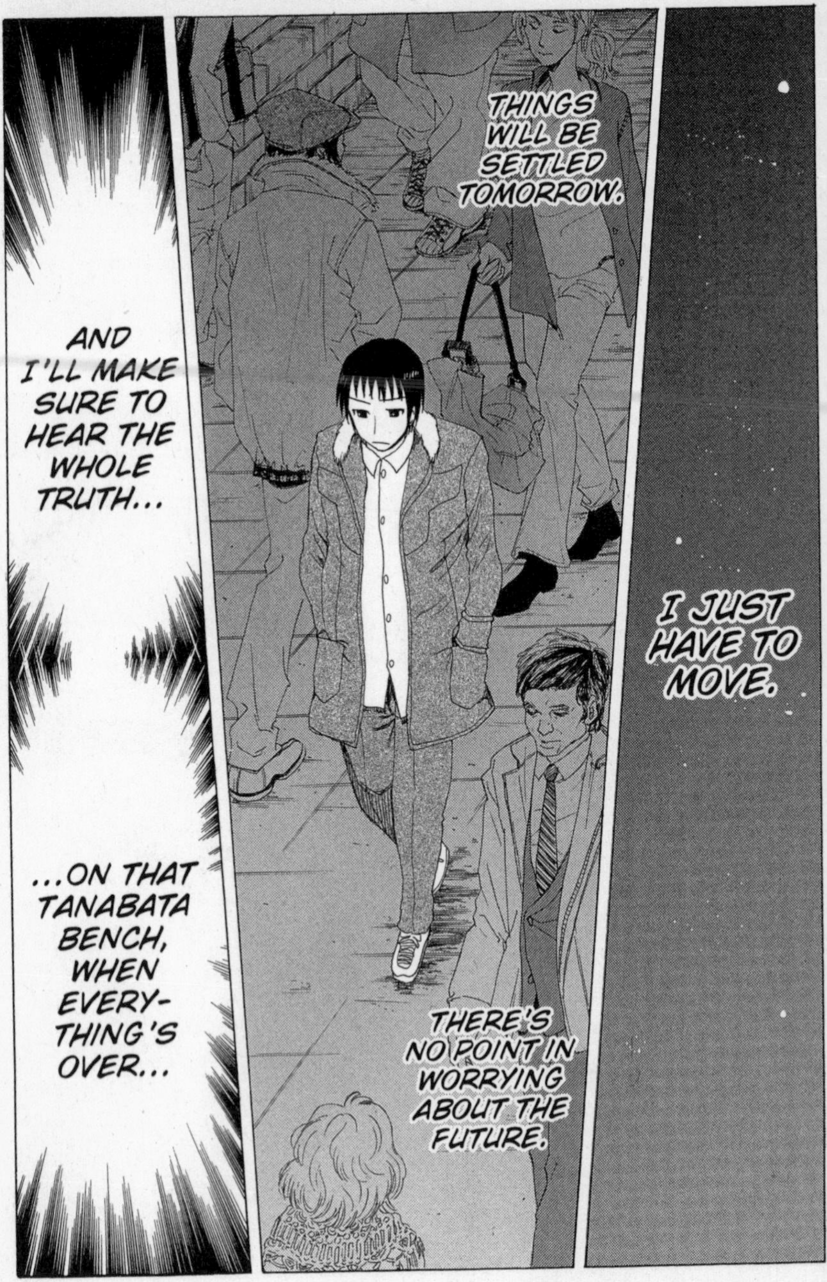
I JUST HAVE TO MOVE.
THINGS WILL BE SETTLED TOMORROW.
THERE'S NO POINT IN WORRYING ABOUT THE FUTURE.
AND I'LL MAKE SURE TO HEAR THE WHOLE TRUTH...
...ON THAT TANABATA BENCH, WHEN EVERY-THING'S OVER...

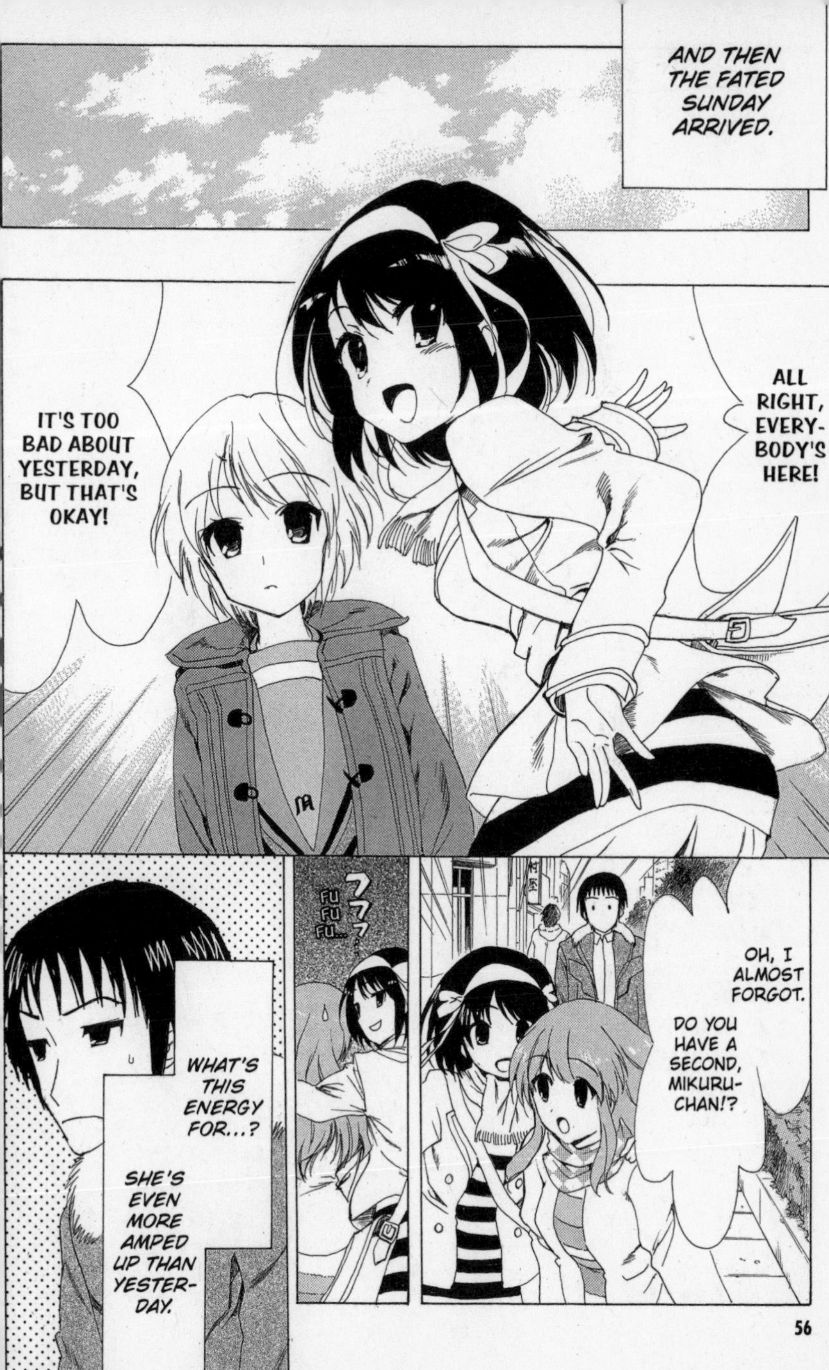
AND THEN THE FATED SUNDAY ARRIVED.
ALL RIGHT, EVERY-BODY'S HERE!
IT'S TOO BAD ABOUT YESTERDAY, BUT THAT'S OKAY!
OH, I ALMOST FORGOT.
DO YOU HAVE A SECOND, MIKURU-CHAN!?
FU FU FU...
WHAT'S THIS ENERGY FOR...?
SHE'S EVEN MORE AMPED UP THAN YESTER-DAY.

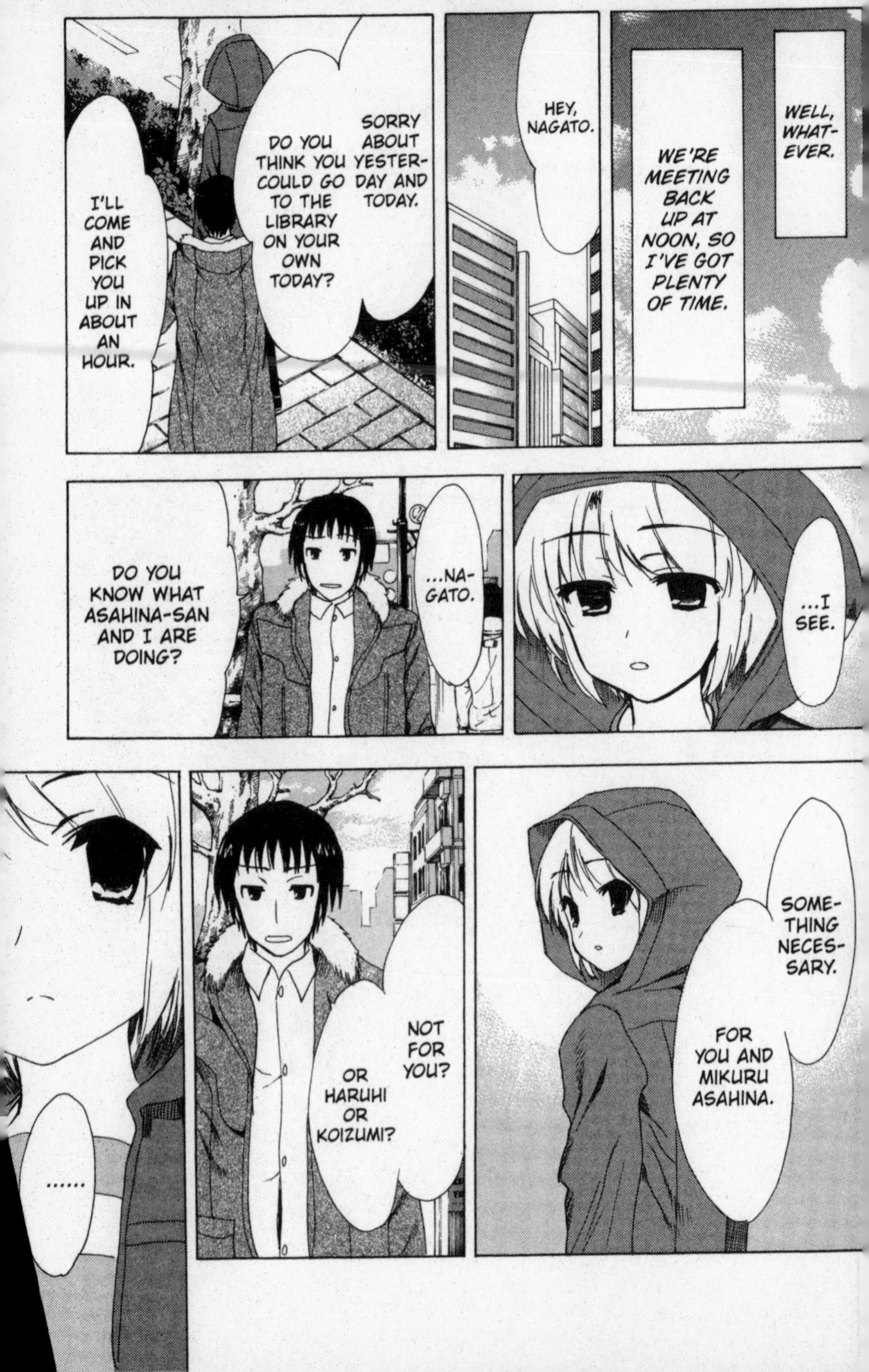
WELL, WHATEVER.
WE'RE MEETING BACK UP AT NOON, SO I'VE GOT PLENTY OF TIME.
HEY, NAGATO.
SORRY ABOUT YESTERDAY AND TODAY.
DO YOU THINK YOU COULD GO TO THE LIBRARY ON YOUR OWN TODAY?
I'LL COME AND PICK YOU UP IN ABOUT AN HOUR.
...I SEE.
...NAGATO.
DO YOU KNOW WHAT ASAHINA-SAN AND I ARE DOING?
SOMETHING NECESSARY.
FOR YOU AND MIKURU ASAHINA.
NOT FOR YOU?
OR HARUHI OR KOIZUMI?
......

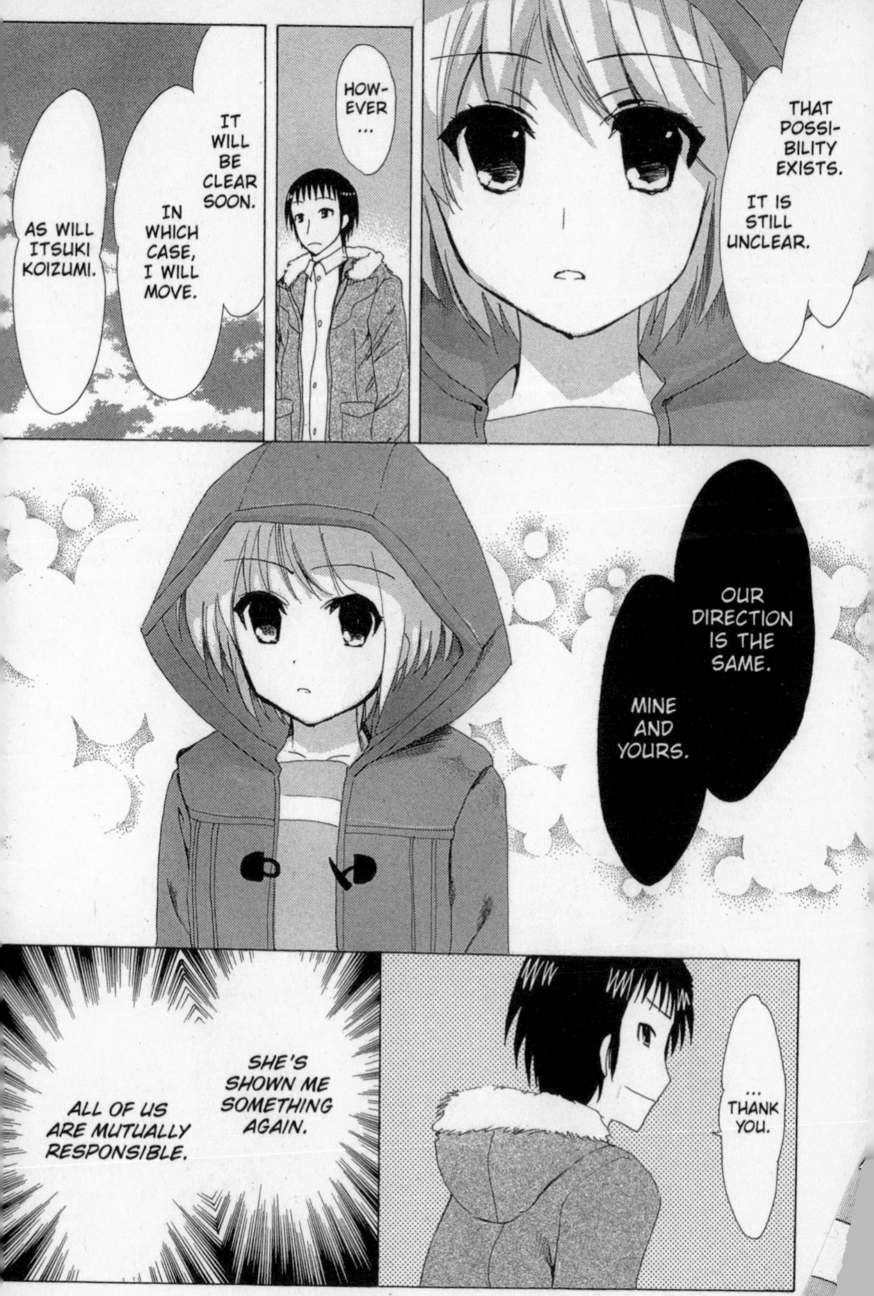
THAT POSSIBILITY EXISTS.
IT IS STILL UNCLEAR.
HOWEVER...
IT WILL BE CLEAR SOON.
IN WHICH CASE, I WILL MOVE.
AS WILL ITSUKI KOIZUMI.
OUR DIRECTION IS THE SAME.
MINE AND YOURS.
...THANK YOU.
SHE'S SHOWN ME SOMETHING AGAIN.
ALL OF US ARE MUTUALLY RESPONSIBLE.

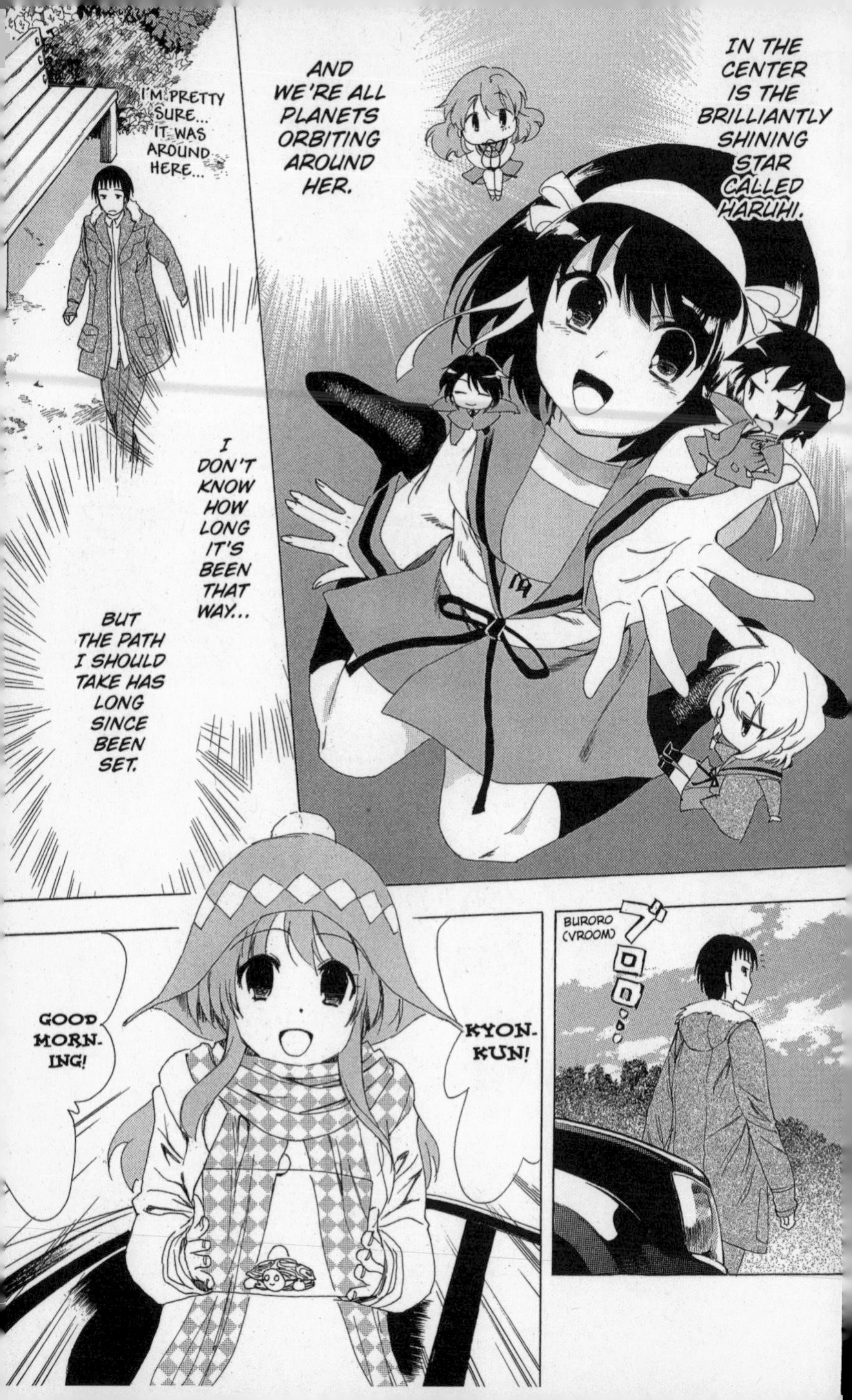
IN THE CENTER IS THE BRILLIANTLY SHINING STAR CALLED HARUHI.
AND WE'RE ALL PLANETS ORBITING AROUND HER.
I'M PRETTY SURE... IT WAS AROUND HERE...
I DON'T KNOW HOW LONG IT'S BEEN THAT WAY...
BUT THE PATH I SHOULD TAKE HAS LONG SINCE BEEN SET.
BURORO (VROOM)
KYON-KUN!
GOOD MORN-ING!

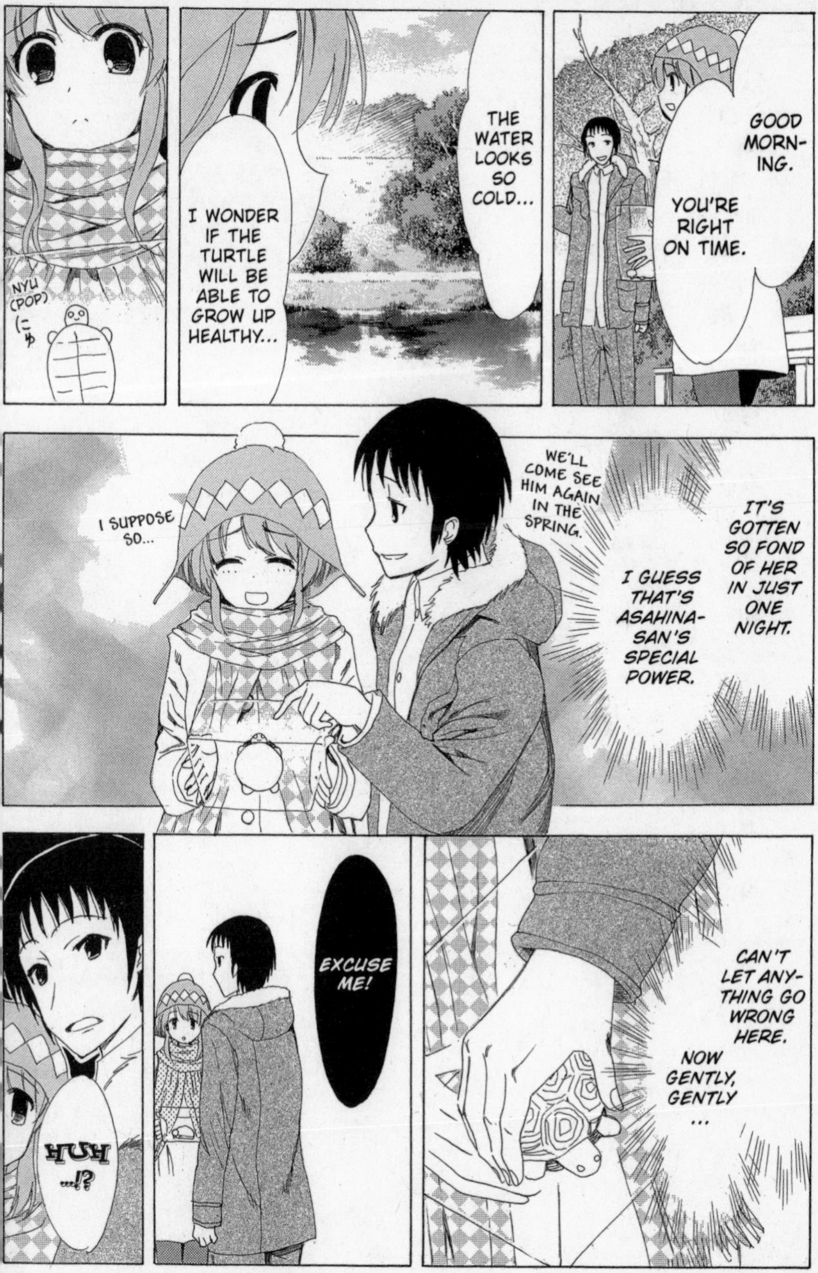
GOOD MORNING.
YOU'RE RIGHT ON TIME.
THE WATER LOOKS SO COLD...
I WONDER IF THE TURTLE WILL BE ABLE TO GROW UP HEALTHY...
NYU (POP)
にゅ
WE'LL COME SEE HIM AGAIN IN THE SPRING.
I SUPPOSE SO...
IT'S GOTTEN SO FOND OF HER IN JUST ONE NIGHT.
I GUESS THAT'S ASAHINA-SAN'S SPECIAL POWER.
CAN'T LET ANYTHING GO WRONG HERE.
NOW GENTLY, GENTLY...
EXCUSE ME!
HUH ...!?

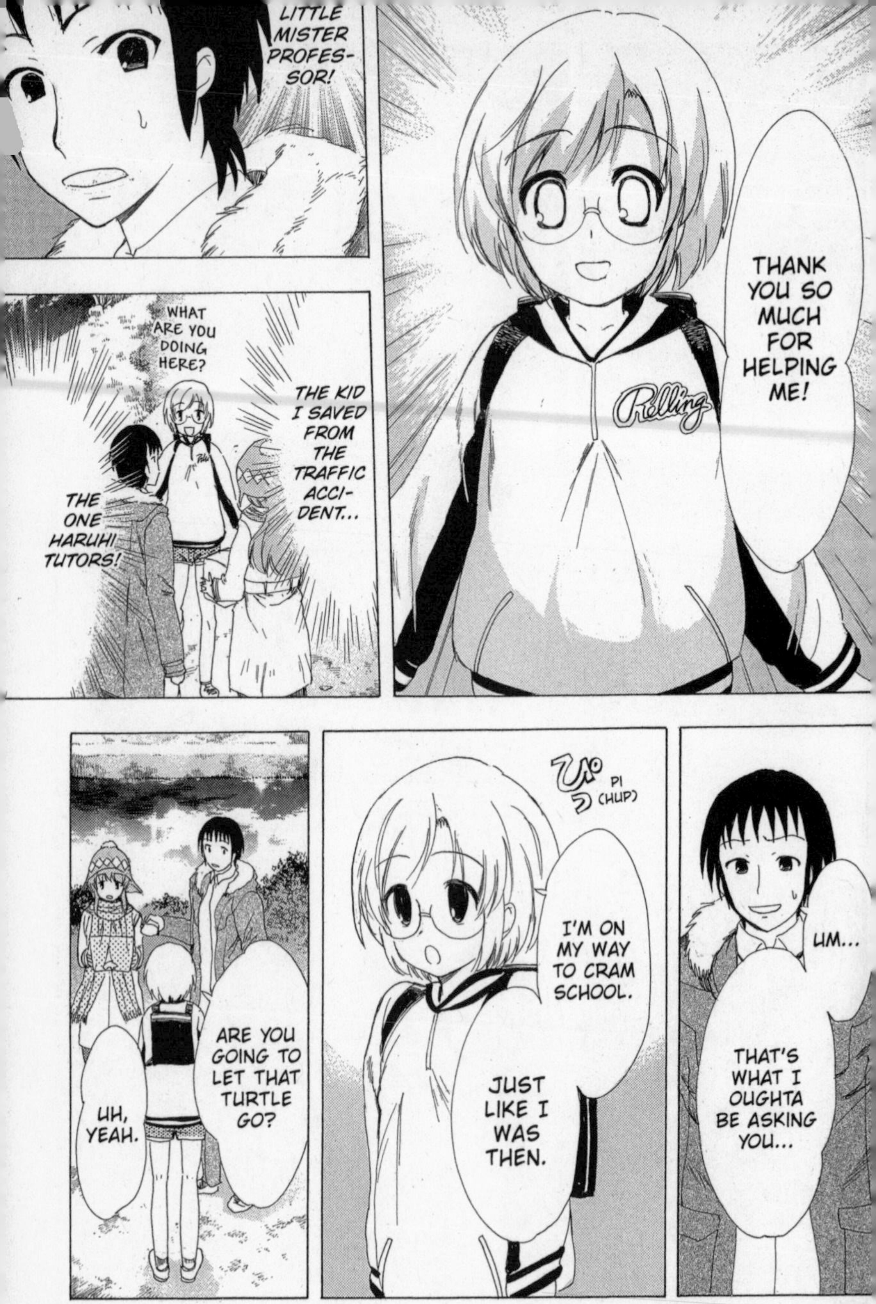
THANK YOU SO MUCH FOR HELPING ME!
LITTLE MISTER PROFES-SOR!
THE KID I SAVED FROM THE TRAFFIC ACCI-DENT...
WHAT ARE YOU DOING HERE?
THE ONE HARUHI TUTORS!
UM...
THAT'S WHAT I OUGHTA BE ASKING YOU...
ぴっ
PI (HUP)
I'M ON MY WAY TO CRAM SCHOOL.
JUST LIKE I WAS THEN.
ARE YOU GOING TO LET THAT TURTLE GO?
UH, YEAH.

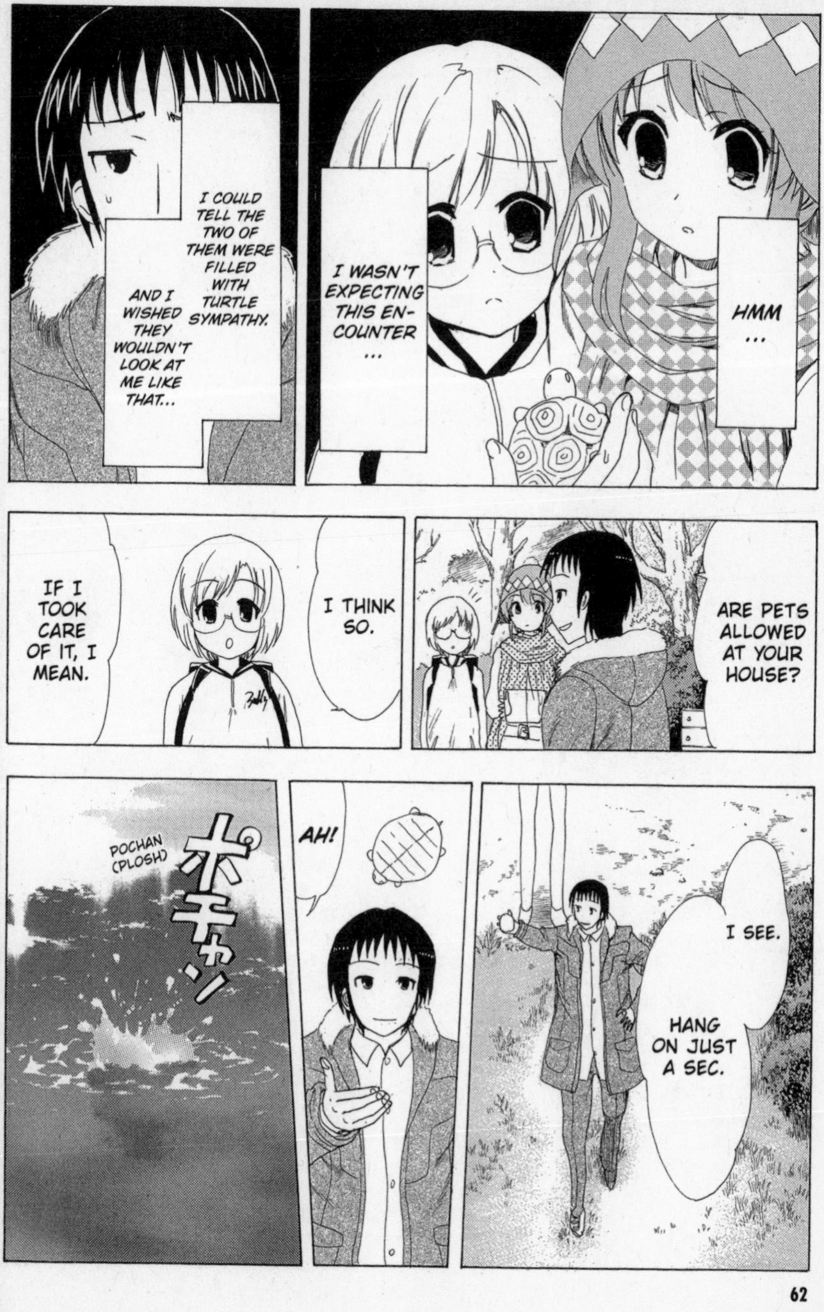
HMM ...
I WASN'T EXPECTING THIS EN-COUNTER ...
I COULD TELL THE TWO OF THEM WERE FILLED WITH TURTLE SYMPATHY.
AND I WISHED THEY WOULDN'T LOOK AT ME LIKE THAT...
ARE PETS ALLOWED AT YOUR HOUSE?
I THINK SO.
IF I TOOK CARE OF IT, I MEAN.
I SEE.
HANG ON JUST A SEC.
AH!
ポチャン
POCHAN (PLOSH)

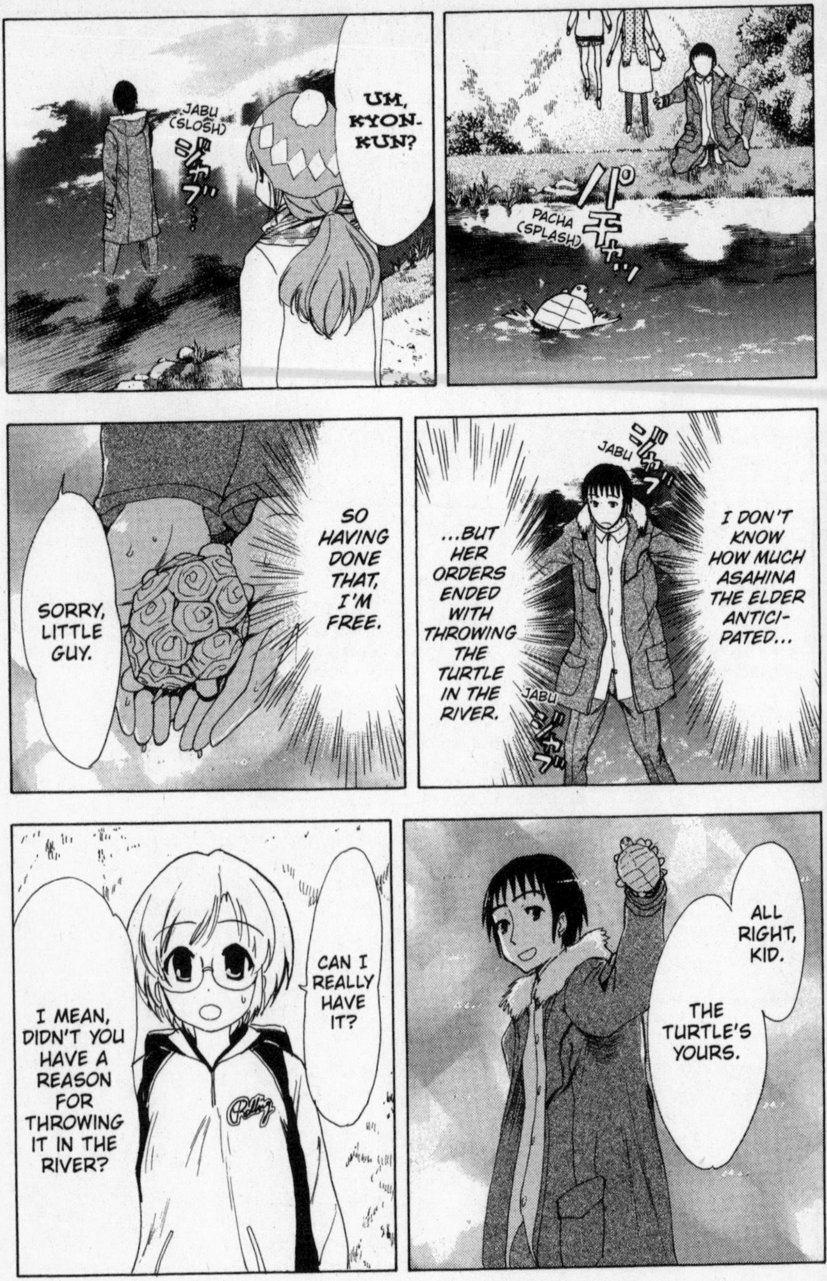
PACHA (SPLASH)
パチャッ
JABU (SLOSH)
ジャブ…
UM, KYON-KUN?
JABU
ジャブ
I DON'T KNOW HOW MUCH ASAHINA THE ELDER ANTICIPATED...
...BUT HER ORDERS ENDED WITH THROWING THE TURTLE IN THE RIVER.
JABU
ジャブ
SO HAVING DONE THAT, I'M FREE.
SORRY, LITTLE GUY.
ALL RIGHT, KID.
THE TURTLE'S YOURS.
CAN I REALLY HAVE IT?
I MEAN, DIDN'T YOU HAVE A REASON FOR THROWING IT IN THE RIVER?

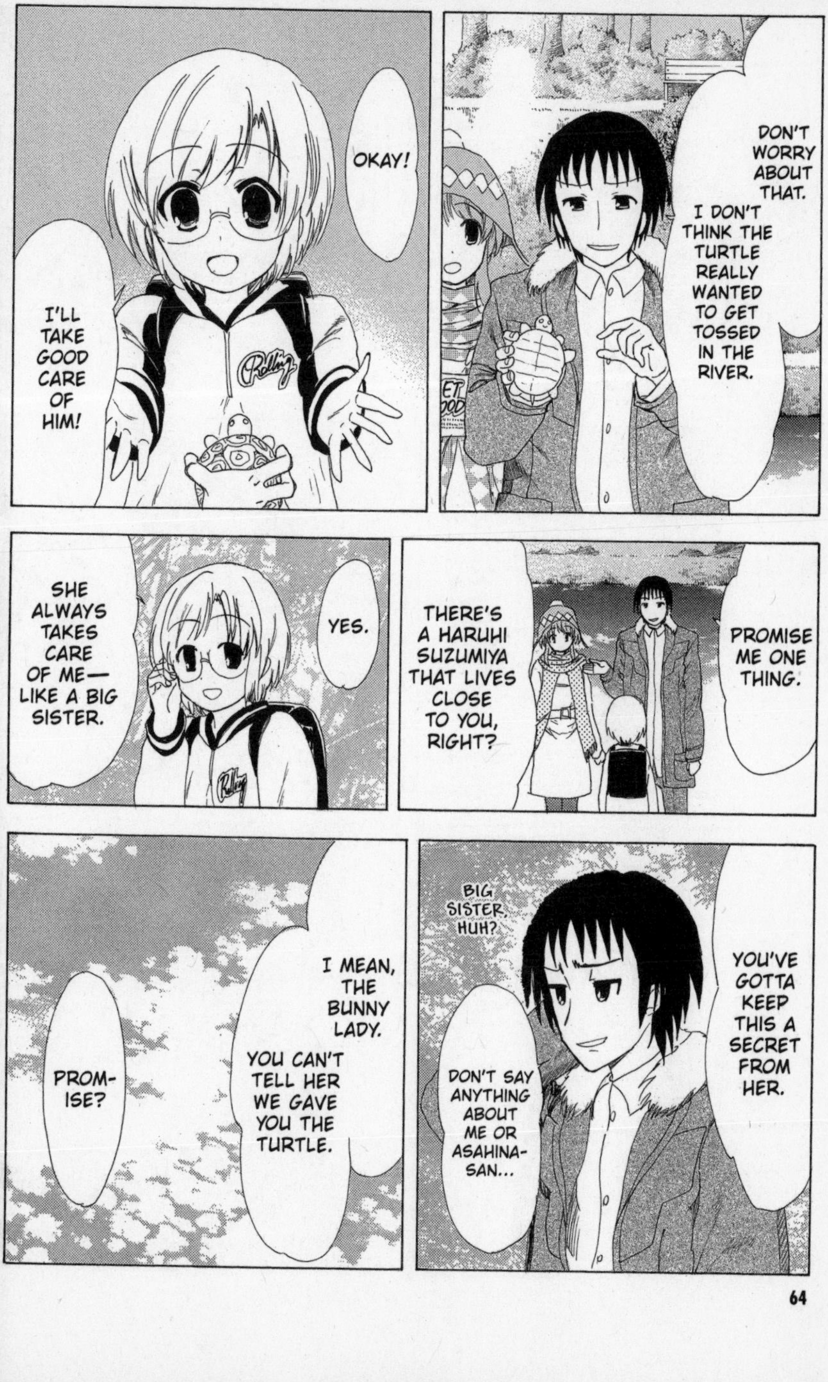
DON'T WORRY ABOUT THAT.
I DON'T THINK THE TURTLE REALLY WANTED TO GET TOSSED IN THE RIVER.
OKAY!
I'LL TAKE GOOD CARE OF HIM!
PROMISE ME ONE THING.
THERE'S A HARUHI SUZUMIYA THAT LIVES CLOSE TO YOU, RIGHT?
YES.
SHE ALWAYS TAKES CARE OF ME—LIKE A BIG SISTER.
BIG SISTER, HUH?
YOU'VE GOTTA KEEP THIS A SECRET FROM HER.
DON'T SAY ANYTHING ABOUT ME OR ASAHINA-SAN...
I MEAN, THE BUNNY LADY.
YOU CAN'T TELL HER WE GAVE YOU THE TURTLE.
PROM-ISE?

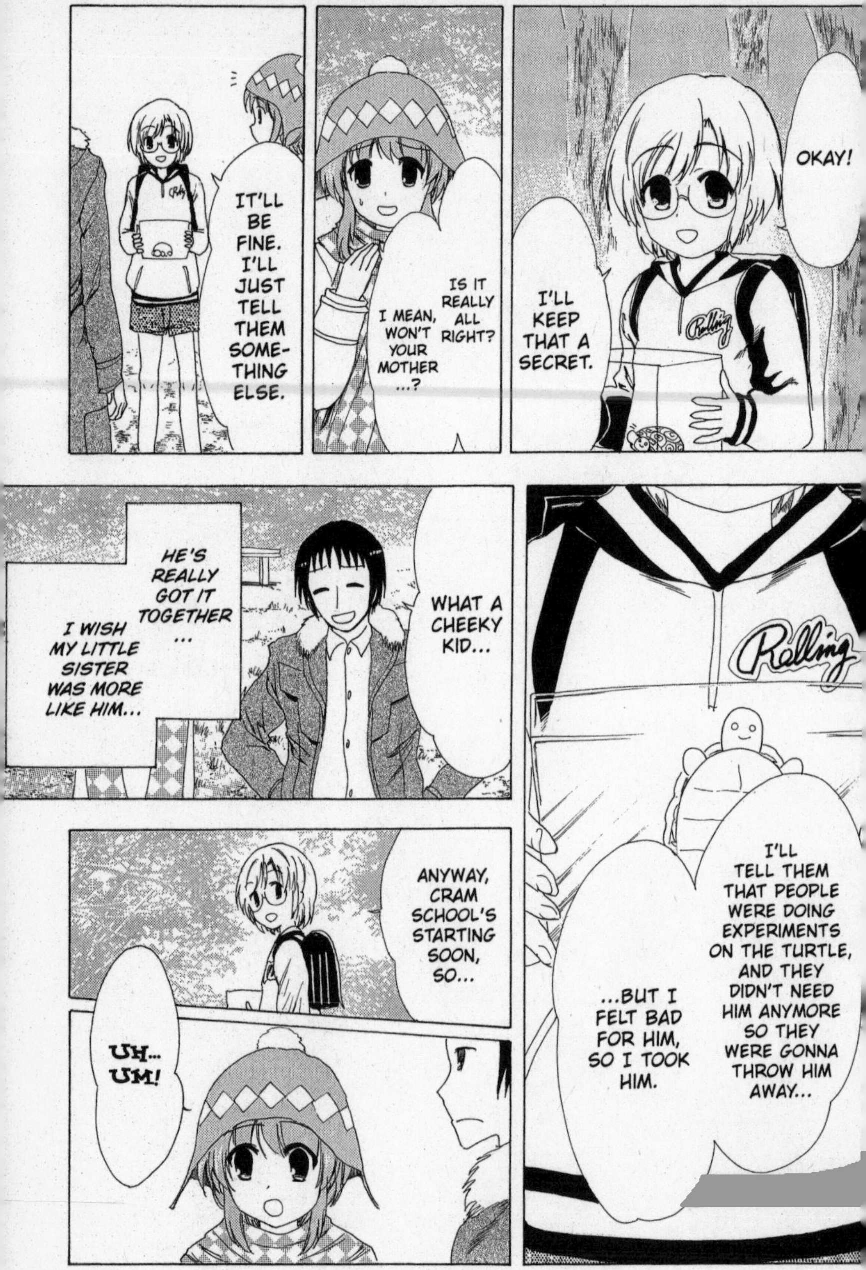
OKAY!
I'LL KEEP THAT A SECRET.
IS IT REALLY ALL RIGHT?
I MEAN, WON'T YOUR MOTHER ...?
IT'LL BE FINE. I'LL JUST TELL THEM SOMETHING ELSE.
I'LL TELL THEM THAT PEOPLE WERE DOING EXPERIMENTS ON THE TURTLE, AND THEY DIDN'T NEED HIM ANYMORE SO THEY WERE GONNA THROW HIM AWAY...
...BUT I FELT BAD FOR HIM, SO I TOOK HIM.
WHAT A CHEEKY KID...
HE'S REALLY GOT IT TOGETHER...
I WISH MY LITTLE SISTER WAS MORE LIKE HIM...
ANYWAY, CRAM SCHOOL'S STARTING SOON, SO...
UH... UM!

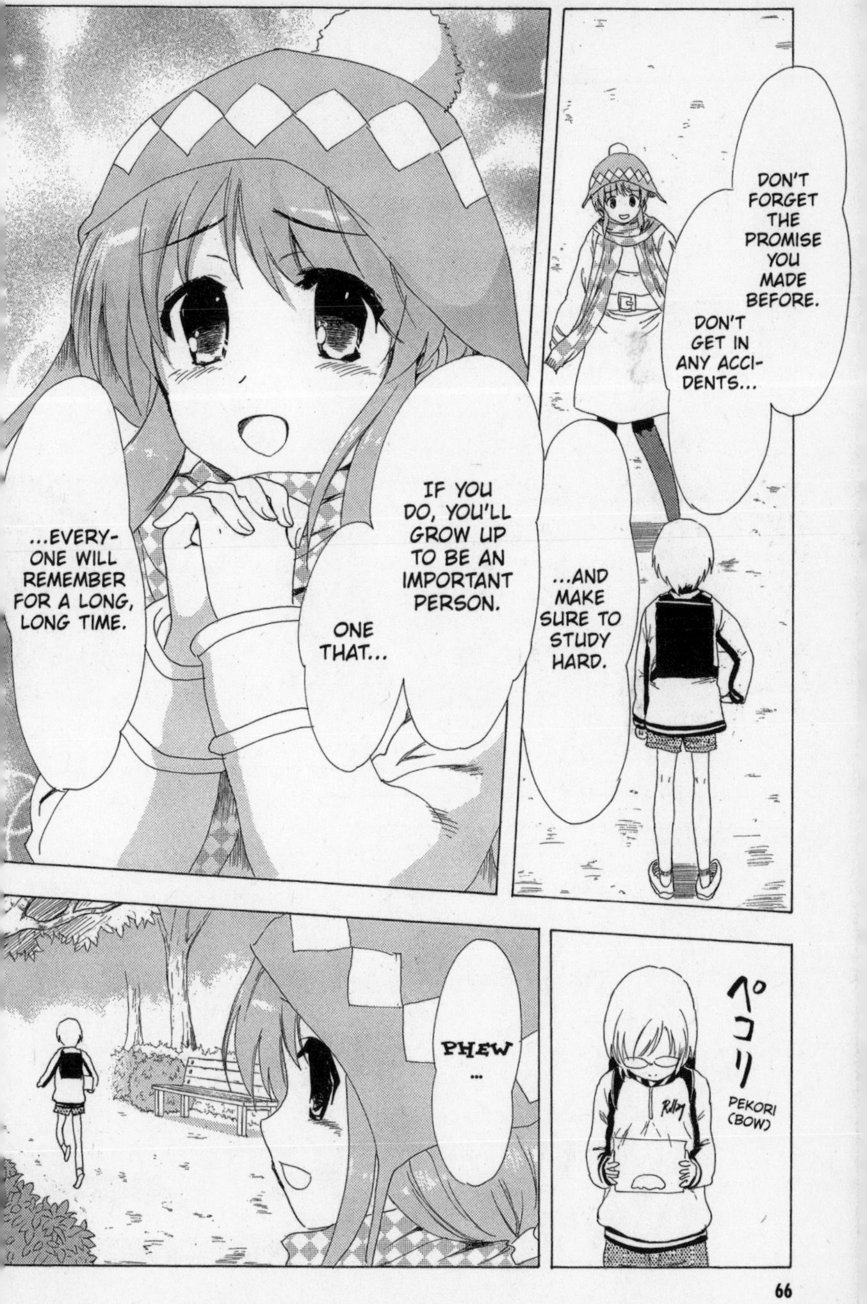
DON'T FORGET THE PROMISE YOU MADE BEFORE.
DON'T GET IN ANY ACCI-DENTS...
...AND MAKE SURE TO STUDY HARD.
IF YOU DO, YOU'LL GROW UP TO BE AN IMPORTANT PERSON.
ONE THAT...
...EVERY-ONE WILL REMEMBER FOR A LONG, LONG TIME.
ペコリ
PEKORI (BOW)
PHEW ...

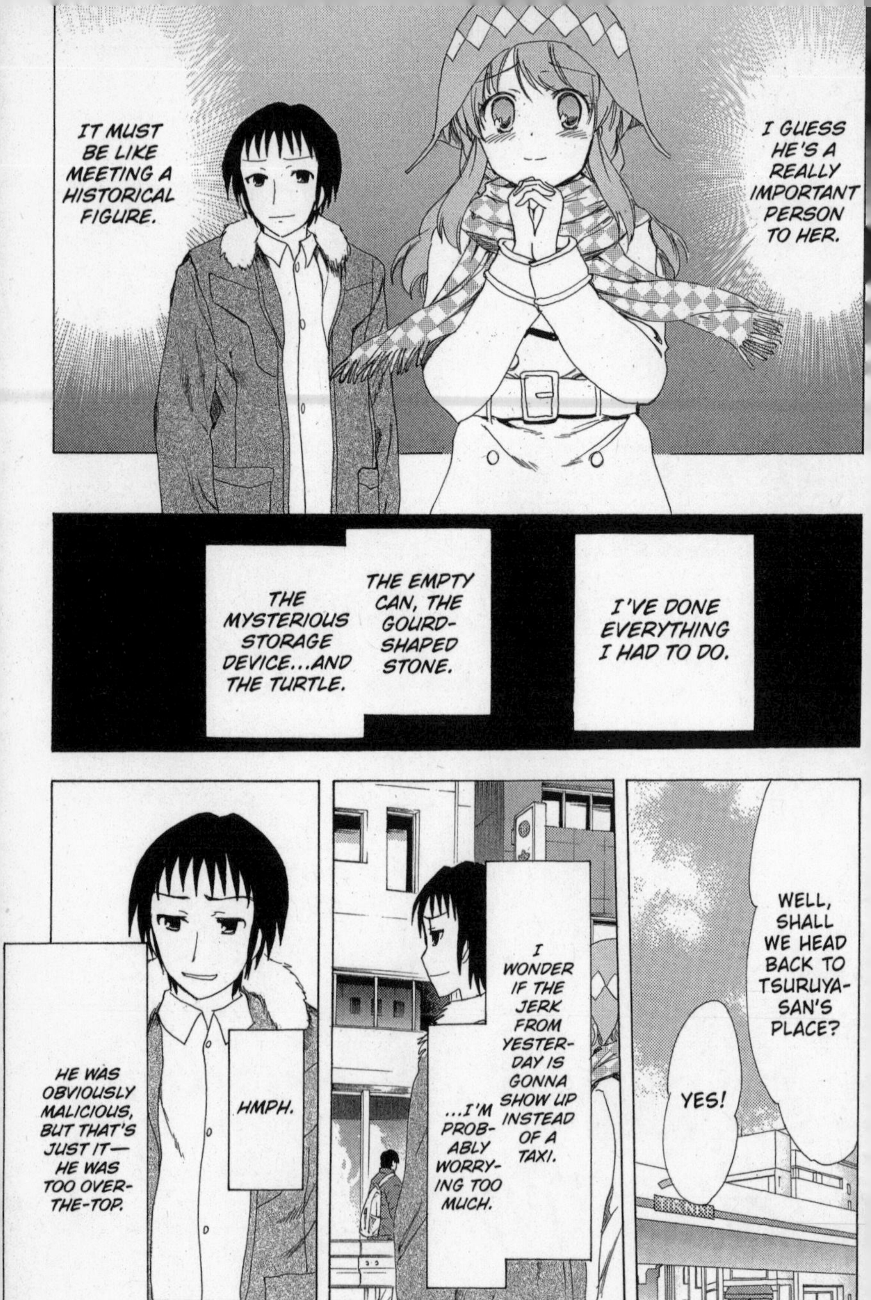
I GUESS HE'S A REALLY IMPORTANT PERSON TO HER.
IT MUST BE LIKE MEETING A HISTORICAL FIGURE.
I'VE DONE EVERYTHING I HAD TO DO.
THE EMPTY CAN, THE GOURD-SHAPED STONE.
THE MYSTERIOUS STORAGE DEVICE...AND THE TURTLE.
WELL, SHALL WE HEAD BACK TO TSURUYA-SAN'S PLACE?
YES!
I WONDER IF THE JERK FROM YESTERDAY IS GONNA SHOW UP INSTEAD OF A TAXI.
...I'M PROBABLY WORRYING TOO MUCH.
HMPH.
HE WAS OBVIOUSLY MALICIOUS, BUT THAT'S JUST IT—HE WAS TOO OVER-THE-TOP.

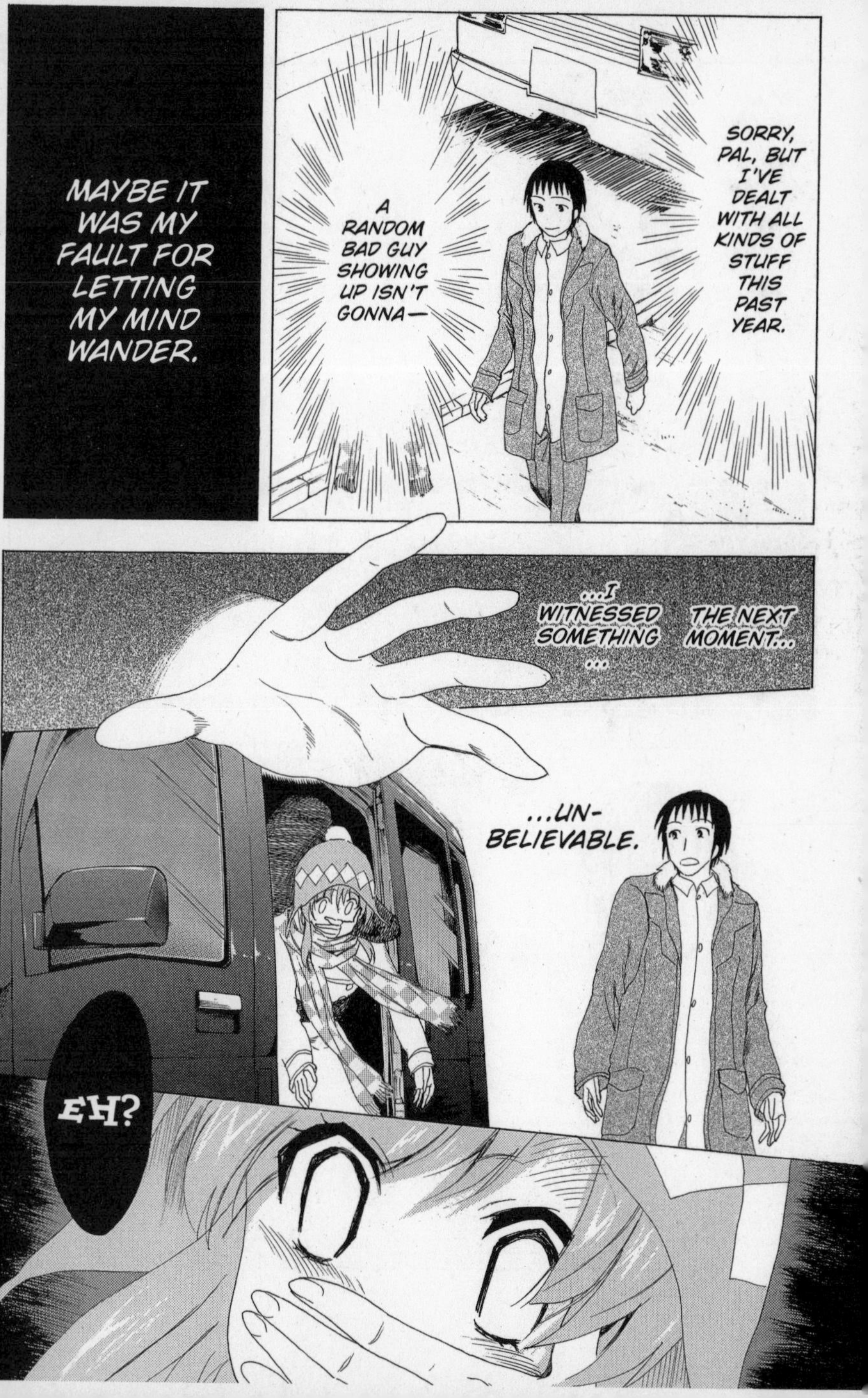
SORRY, PAL, BUT I'VE DEALT WITH ALL KINDS OF STUFF THIS PAST YEAR.
A RANDOM BAD GUY SHOWING UP ISN'T GONNA—
MAYBE IT WAS MY FAULT FOR LETTING MY MIND WANDER.
THE NEXT MOMENT...
...I WITNESSED SOMETHING ...
...UN-BELIEVABLE.
EH?

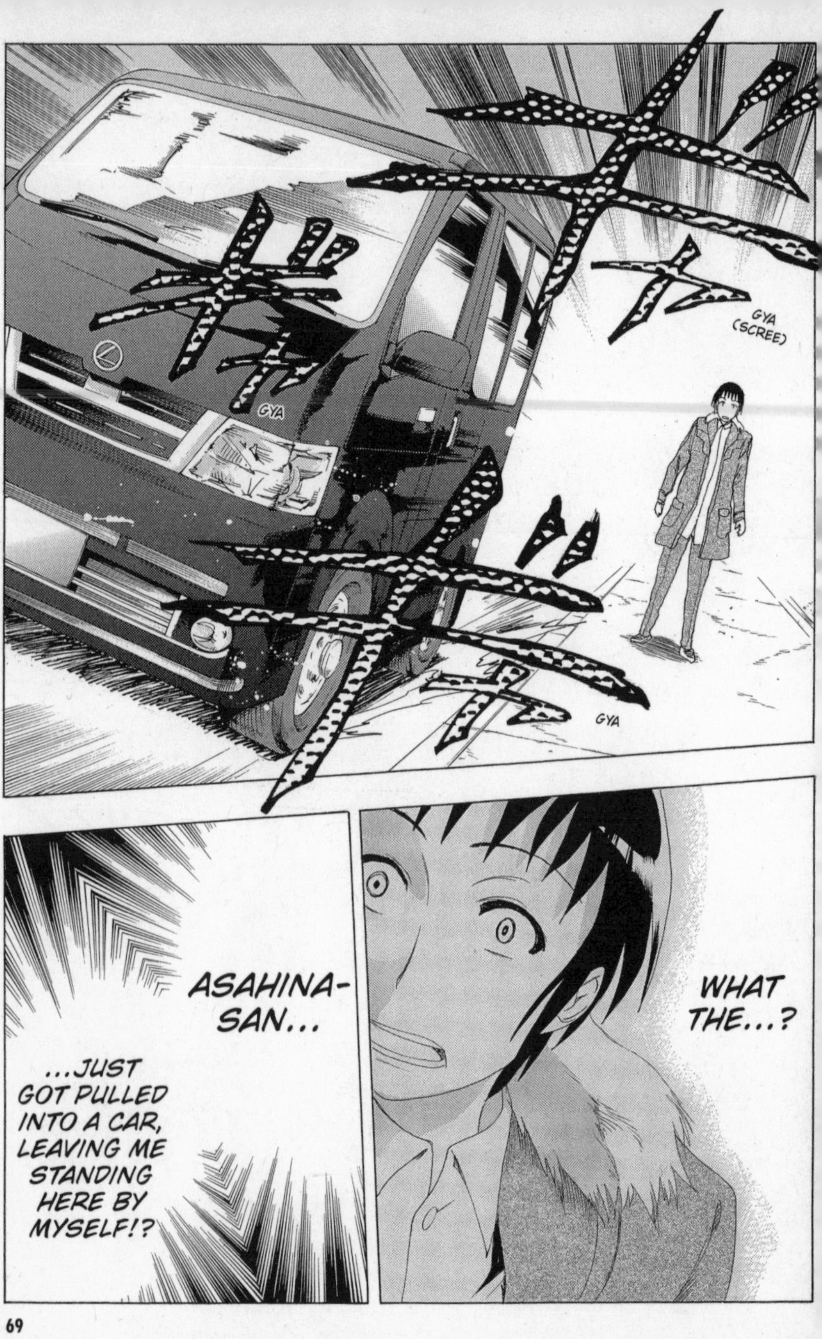

GYA (SCREE)
GYA
GYA
WHAT THE...?
ASAHINA-SAN...
...JUST GOT PULLED INTO A CAR, LEAVING ME STANDING HERE BY MYSELF!?

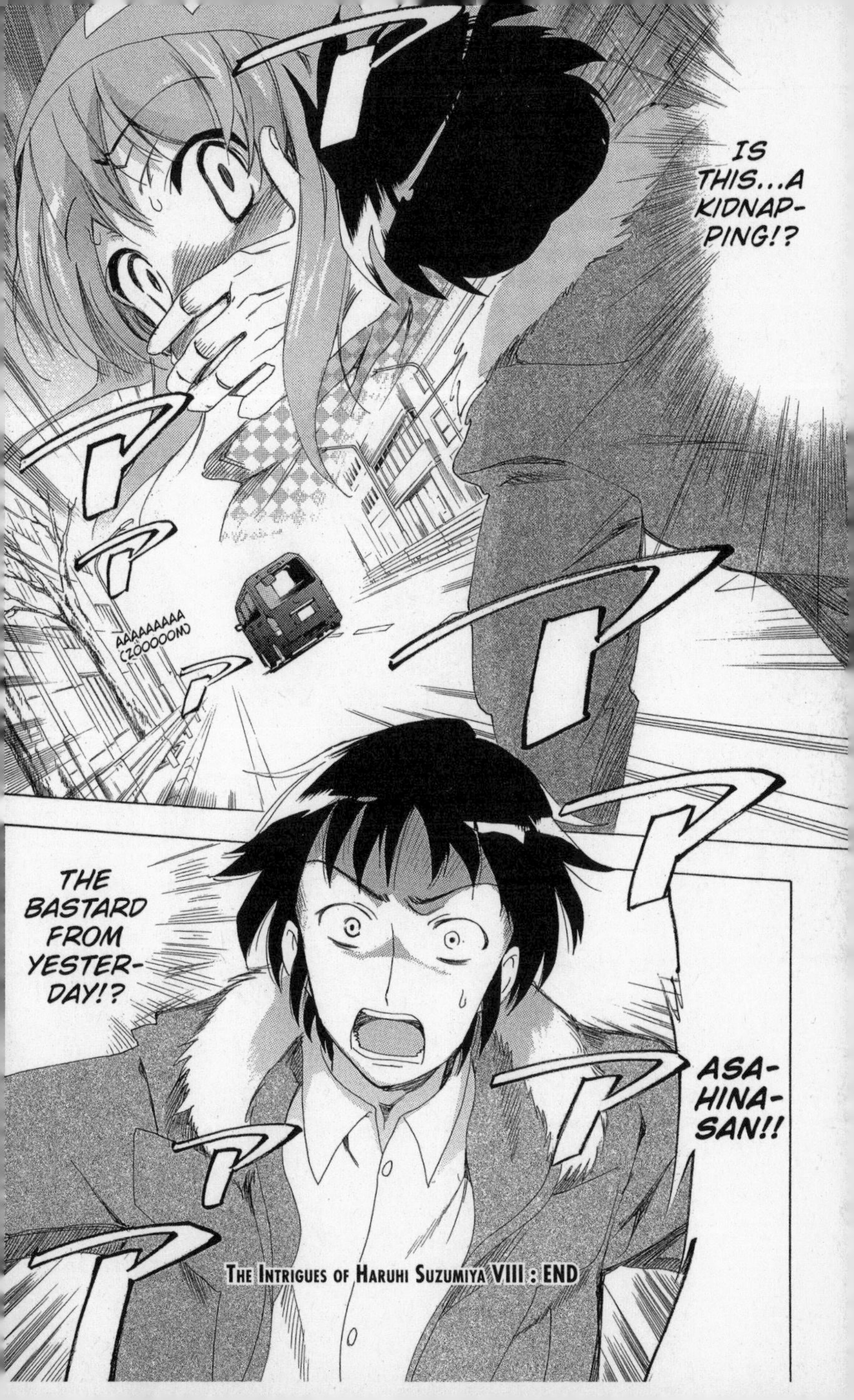
IS THIS...A KIDNAPPING!?
AAAAAAAAA (ZOOOOOM)
THE BASTARD FROM YESTERDAY!?
ASAHINA-SAN!!
THE INTRIGUES OF HARUHI SUZUMIYA VIII : END

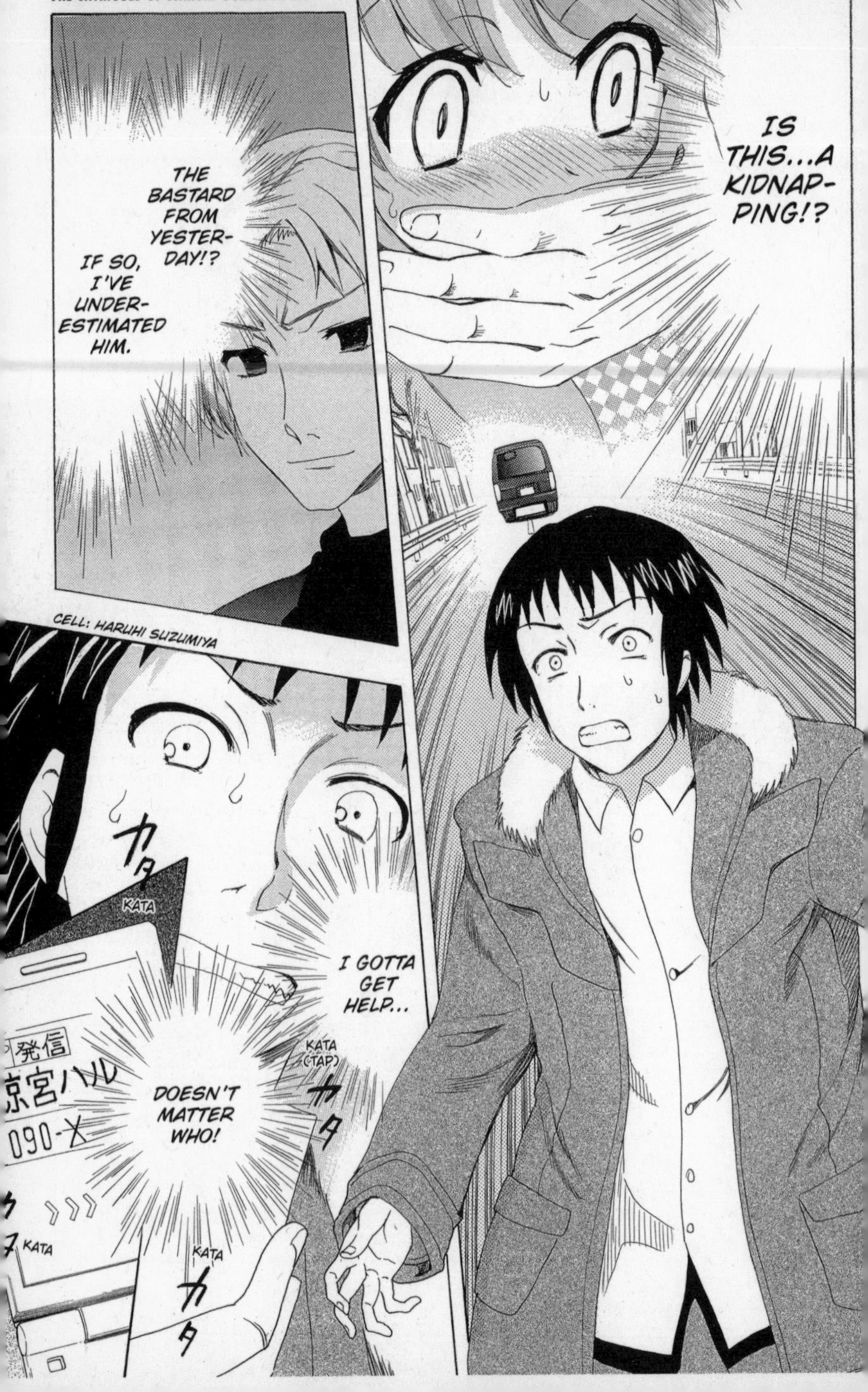
IS THIS...A KIDNAPPING!?
THE BASTARD FROM YESTERDAY!?
IF SO, I'VE UNDERESTIMATED HIM.
CELL: HARUHI SUZUMIYA
I GOTTA GET HELP...
KATA (TAP)
KATA
DOESN'T MATTER WHO!
KATA
KATA
発信
涼宮ハル
090-X

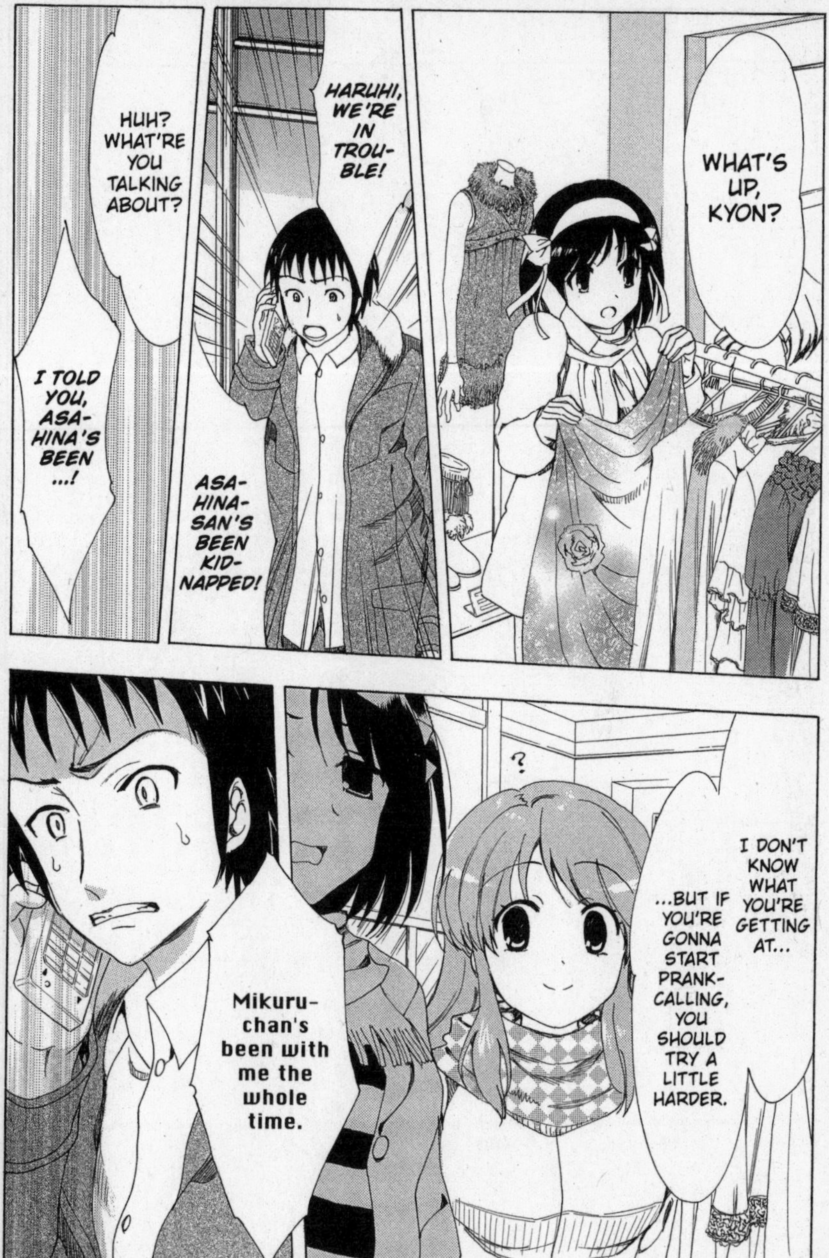
WHAT'S UP, KYON?
HARUHI, WE'RE IN TROU-BLE!
ASA-HINA-SAN'S BEEN KID-NAPPED!
HUH? WHAT'RE YOU TALKING ABOUT?
I TOLD YOU, ASA-HINA'S BEEN ...!
?
I DON'T KNOW WHAT YOU'RE GETTING AT...
...BUT IF YOU'RE GONNA START PRANK-CALLING, YOU SHOULD TRY A LITTLE HARDER.
Mikuru-chan's been with me the whole time.

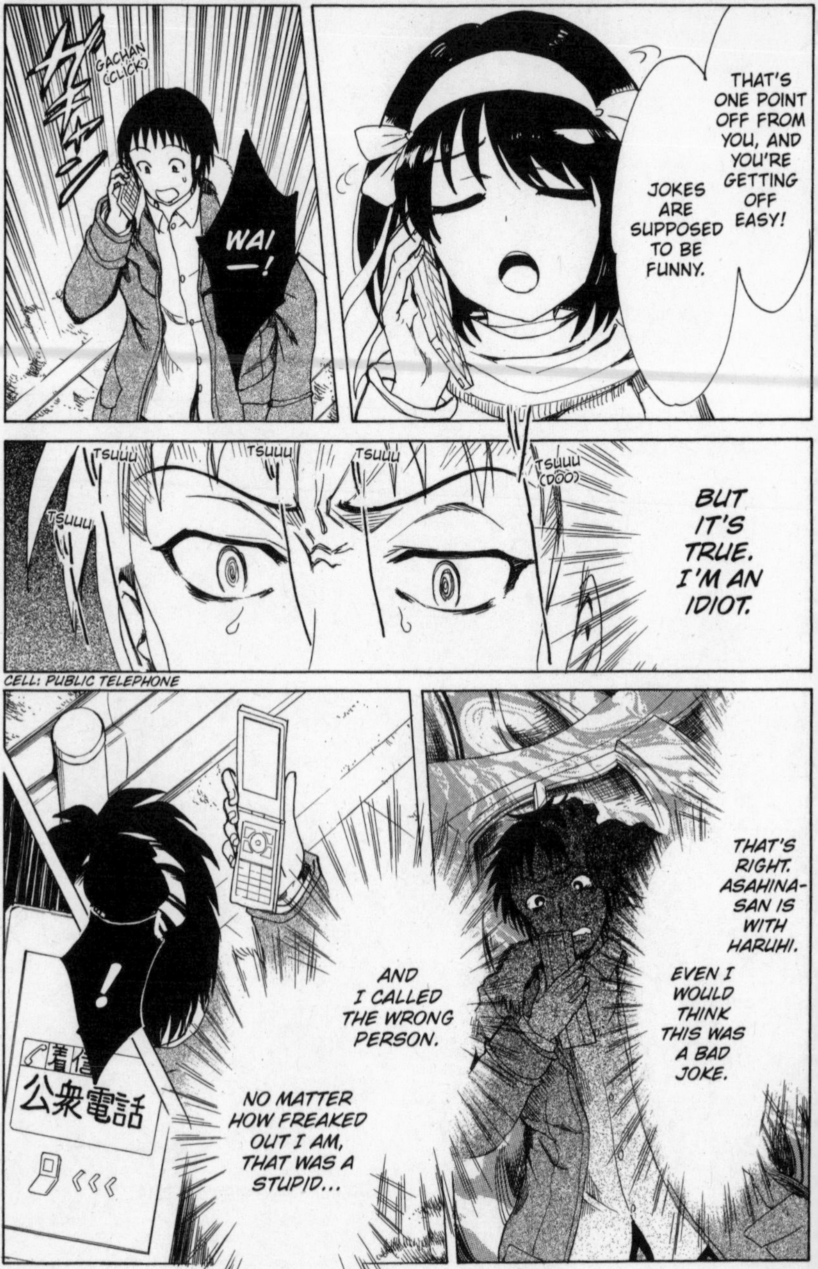
THAT'S ONE POINT OFF FROM YOU, AND YOU'RE GETTING OFF EASY!
JOKES ARE SUPPOSED TO BE FUNNY.
GACHAN (CLICK)
WAI—!
TSUUU
TSUUU
TSUUU
TSUUU (DOO)
TSUUU
BUT IT'S TRUE. I'M AN IDIOT.
THAT'S RIGHT. ASAHINA-SAN IS WITH HARUHI.
EVEN I WOULD THINK THIS WAS A BAD JOKE.
AND I CALLED THE WRONG PERSON.
CELL: PUBLIC TELEPHONE
着信
公衆電話
!
NO MATTER HOW FREAKED OUT I AM, THAT WAS A STUPID...

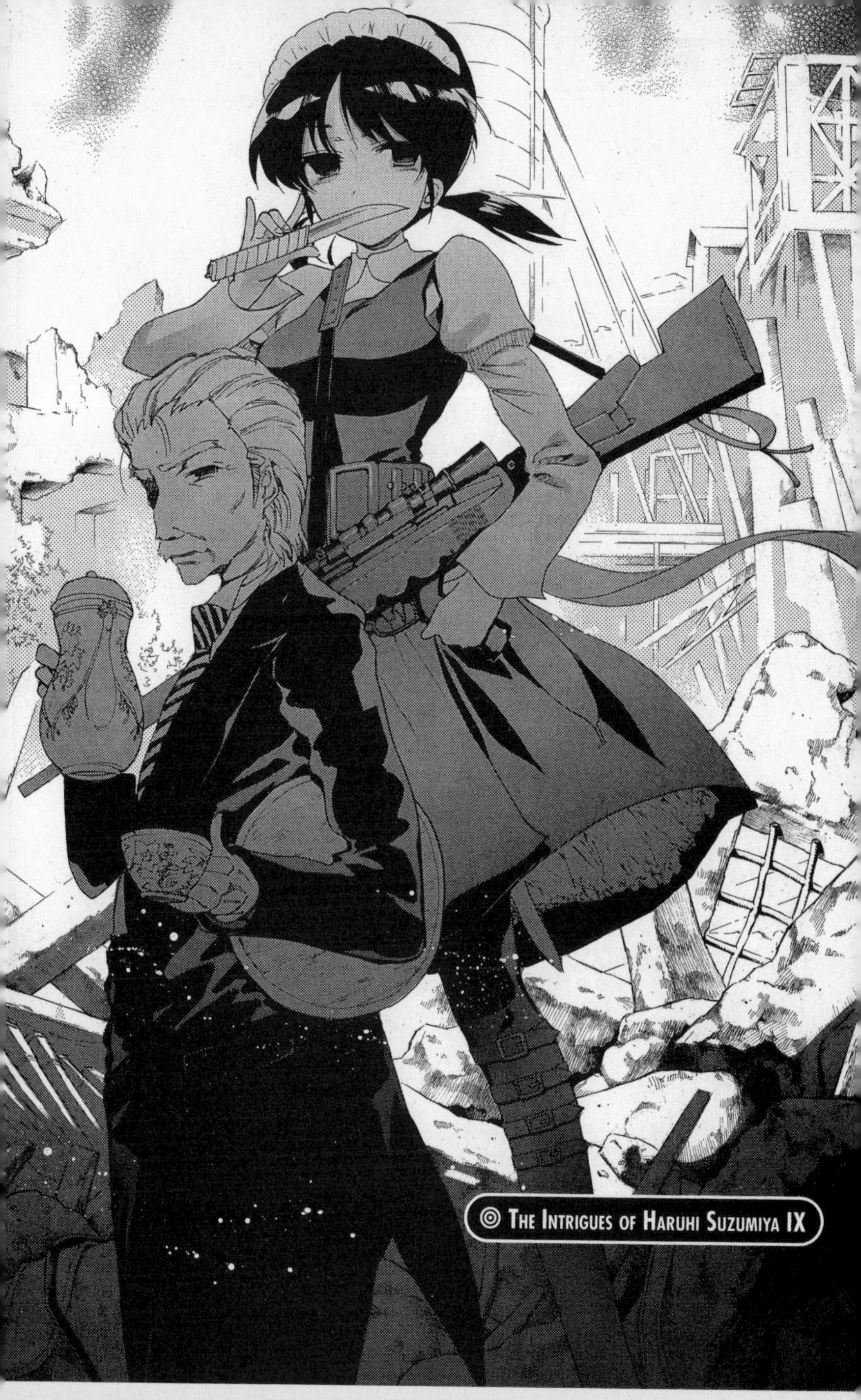
◎ The Intrigues of Haruhi Suzumiya IX

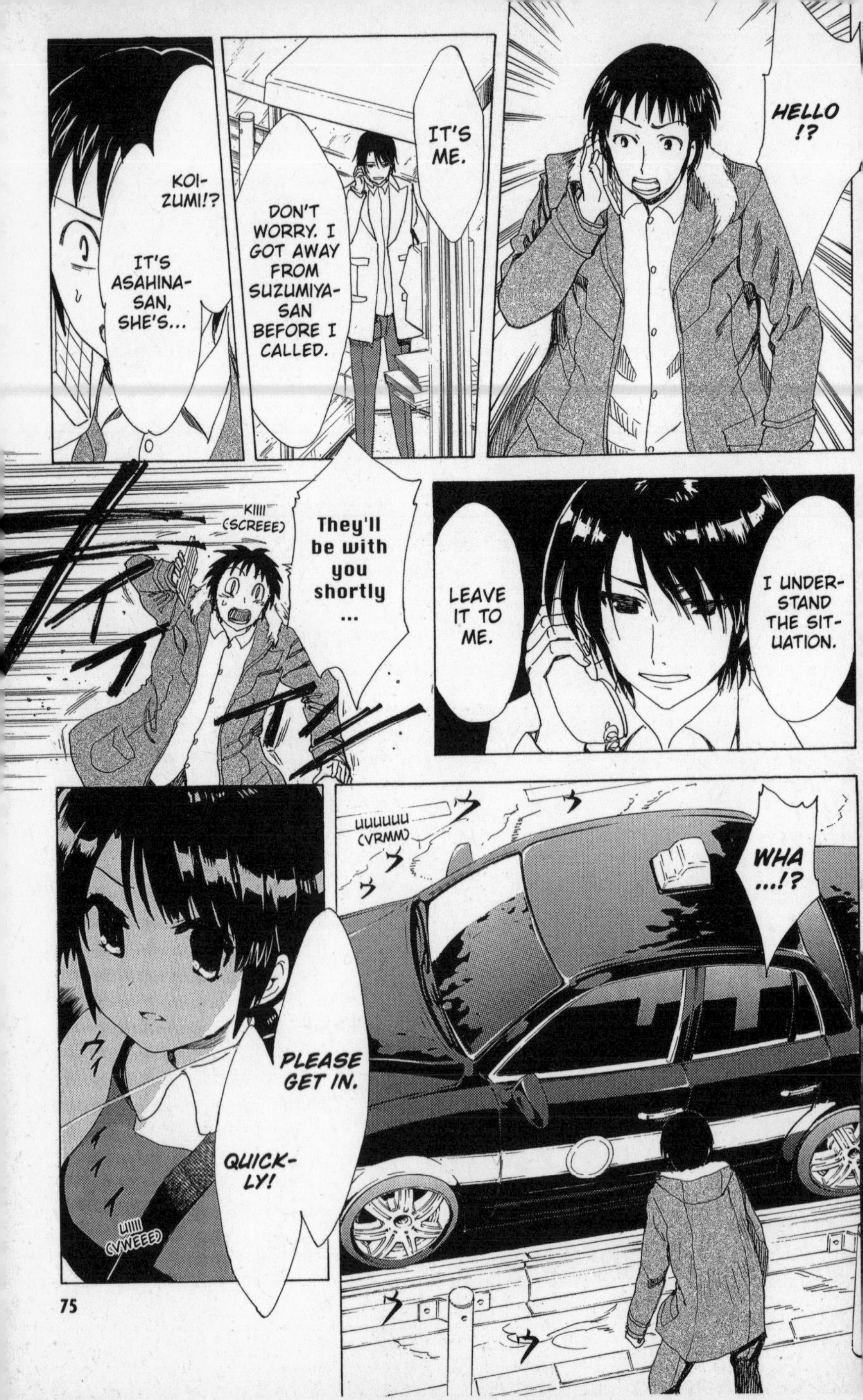
HELLO !?
IT'S ME.
DON'T WORRY. I GOT AWAY FROM SUZUMIYA-SAN BEFORE I CALLED.
KOI-ZUMI!?
IT'S ASAHINA-SAN, SHE'S...
I UNDER-STAND THE SIT-UATION.
LEAVE IT TO ME.
They'll be with you shortly ...
KIIII (SCREEE)
WHA ...!?
UUUUUU (VRMM)
PLEASE GET IN.
QUICK-LY!
UIIII (VWEEE)

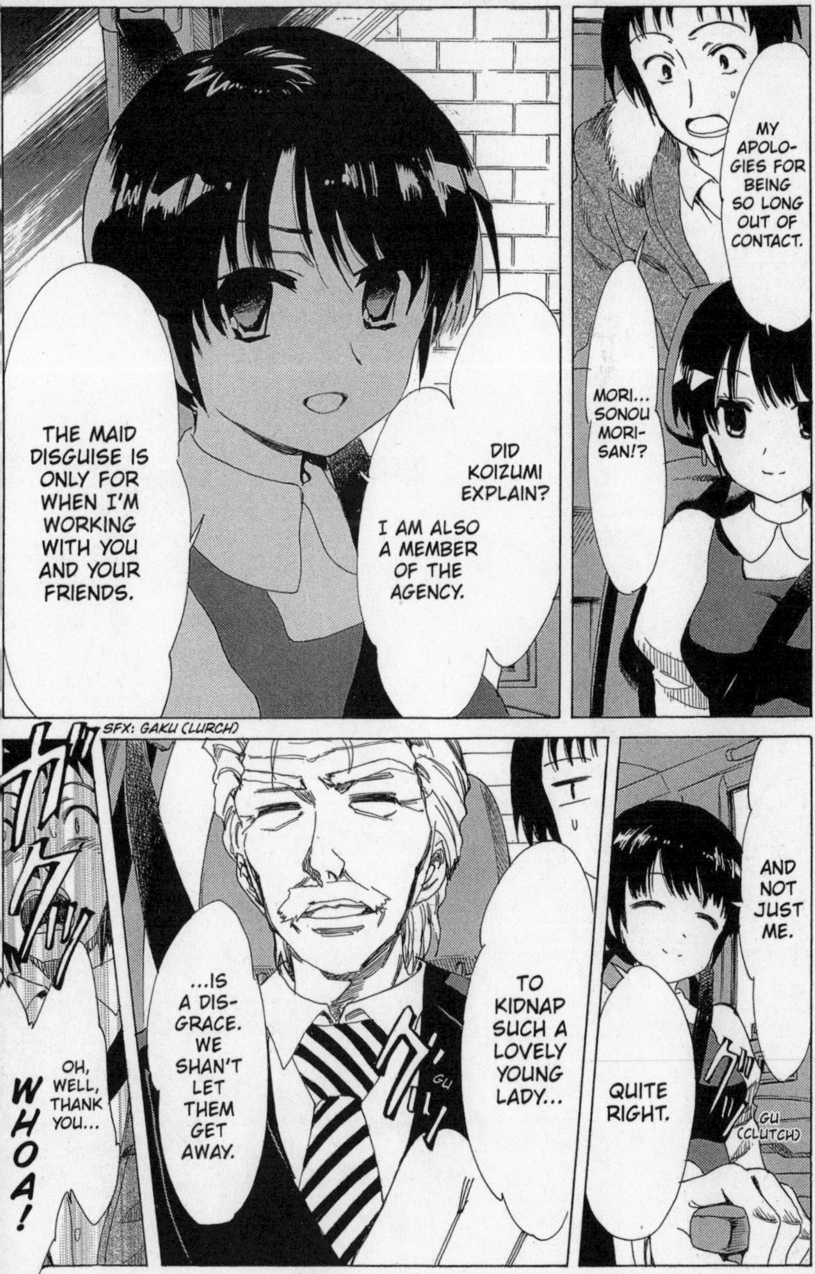
MY APOLOGIES FOR BEING SO LONG OUT OF CONTACT.
MORI... SONOU MORI-SAN!?
DID KOIZUMI EXPLAIN?
I AM ALSO A MEMBER OF THE AGENCY.
THE MAID DISGUISE IS ONLY FOR WHEN I'M WORKING WITH YOU AND YOUR FRIENDS.
SFX: GAKU (LURCH)
AND NOT JUST ME.
QUITE RIGHT.
GU (CLUTCH)
TO KIDNAP SUCH A LOVELY YOUNG LADY...
...IS A DISGRACE. WE SHAN'T LET THEM GET AWAY.
GU
OH, WELL, THANK YOU...
WHOA!

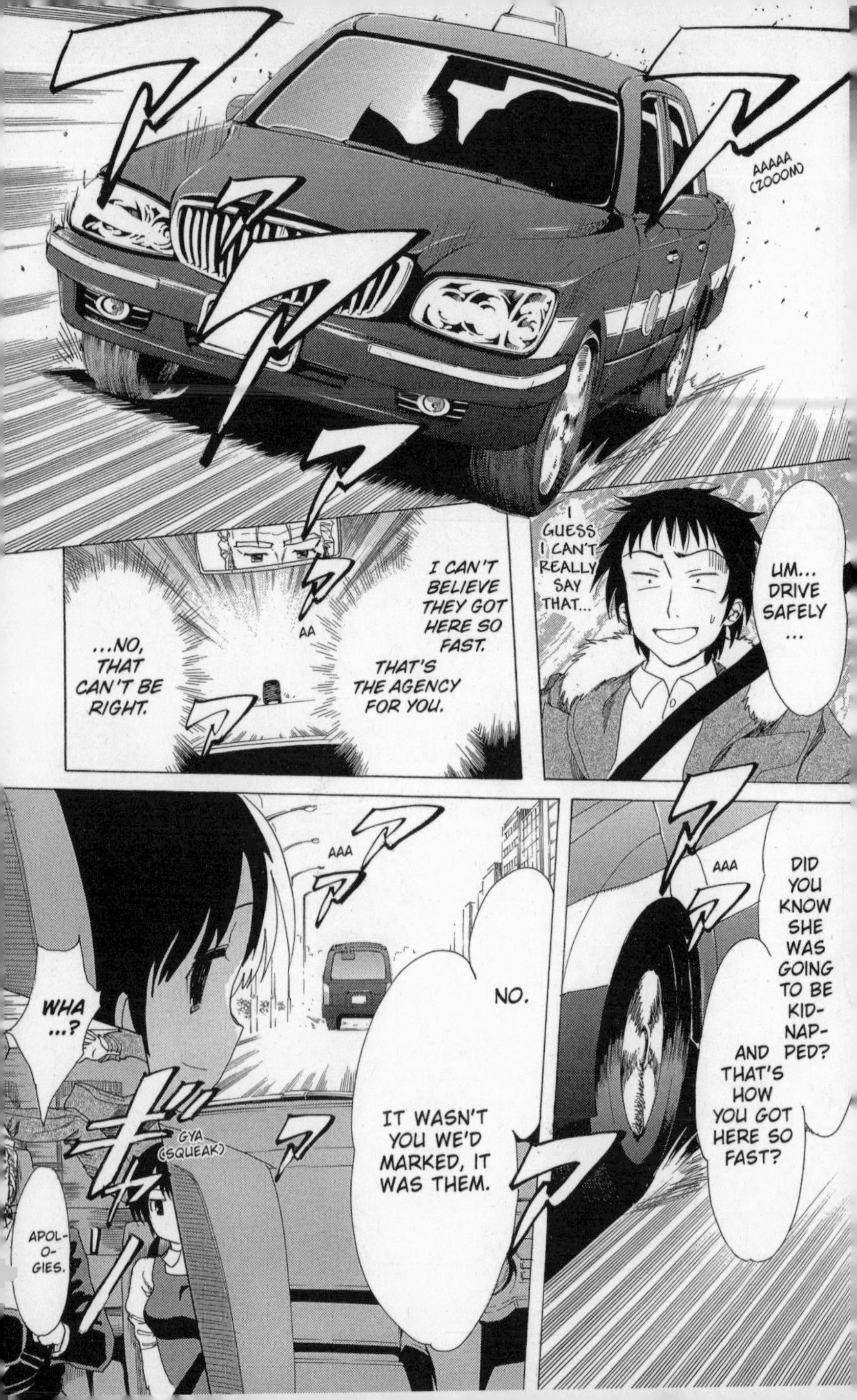
AAAAA (ZOOOM)
UM... DRIVE SAFELY...
I GUESS I CAN'T REALLY SAY THAT...
I CAN'T BELIEVE THEY GOT HERE SO FAST.
AA
THAT'S THE AGENCY FOR YOU.
...NO, THAT CAN'T BE RIGHT.
AAA
DID YOU KNOW SHE WAS GOING TO BE KIDNAPPED?
AND THAT'S HOW YOU GOT HERE SO FAST?
NO.
IT WASN'T YOU WE'D MARKED, IT WAS THEM.
AAA
WHA...?
GYA (SQUEAK)
APOLOGIES.

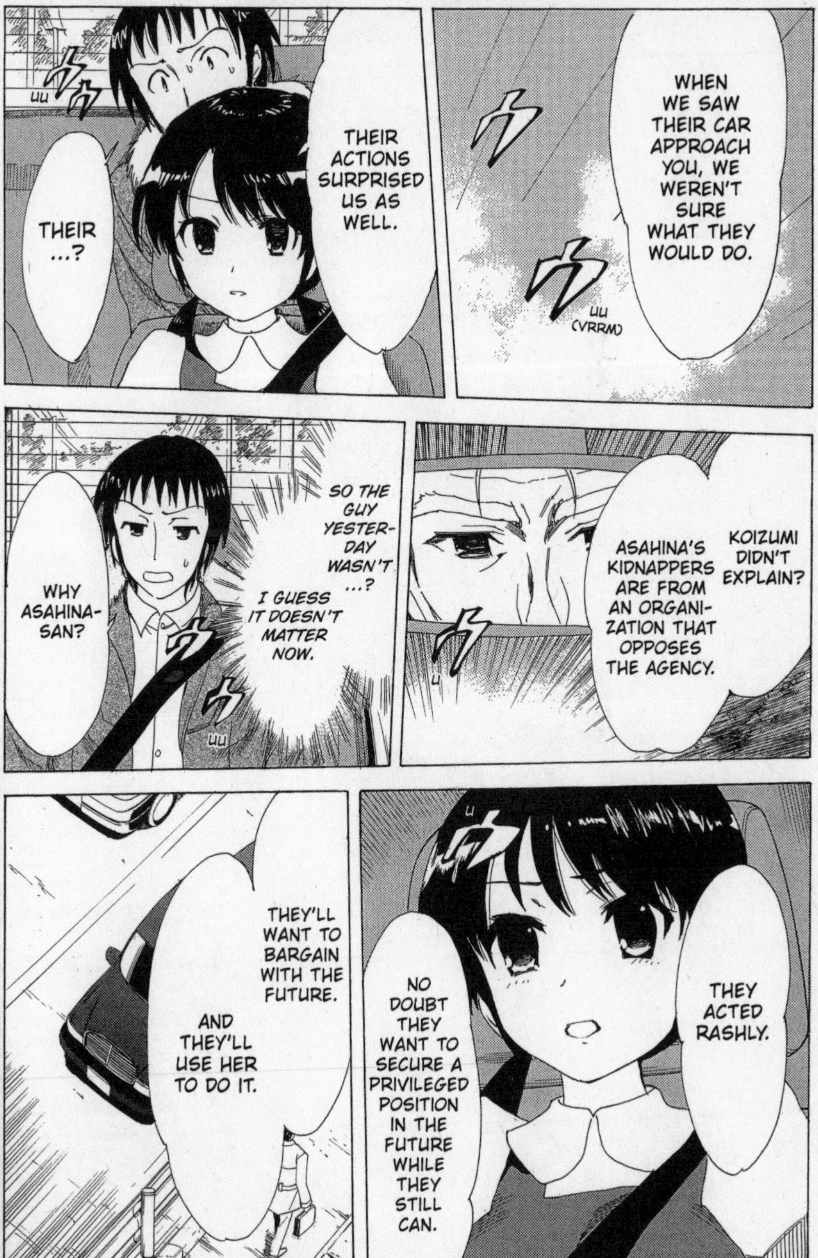
WHEN WE SAW THEIR CAR APPROACH YOU, WE WEREN'T SURE WHAT THEY WOULD DO.
UU (VRRM)
THEIR ACTIONS SURPRISED US AS WELL.
UU
THEIR ...?
KOIZUMI DIDN'T EXPLAIN?
ASAHINA'S KIDNAPPERS ARE FROM AN ORGANIZATION THAT OPPOSES THE AGENCY.
U
SO THE GUY YESTERDAY WASN'T ...?
I GUESS IT DOESN'T MATTER NOW.
WHY ASAHINA-SAN?
UU
U
THEY ACTED RASHLY.
NO DOUBT THEY WANT TO SECURE A PRIVILEGED POSITION IN THE FUTURE WHILE THEY STILL CAN.
THEY'LL WANT TO BARGAIN WITH THE FUTURE.
AND THEY'LL USE HER TO DO IT.

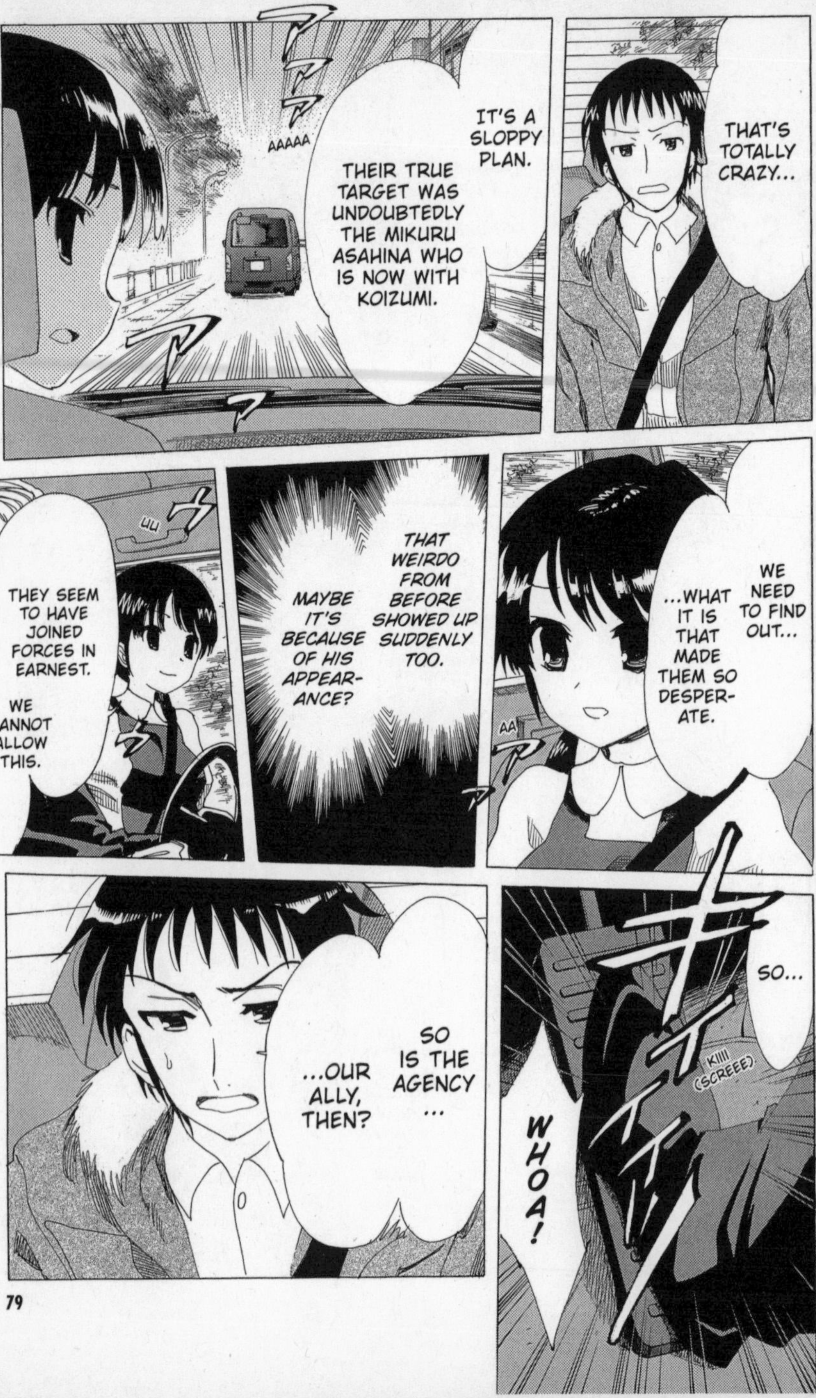
THAT'S TOTALLY CRAZY...
IT'S A SLOPPY PLAN.
THEIR TRUE TARGET WAS UNDOUBTEDLY THE MIKURU ASAHINA WHO IS NOW WITH KOIZUMI.
AAAAA
WE NEED TO FIND OUT...
...WHAT IT IS THAT MADE THEM SO DESPERATE.
AA
THAT WEIRDO FROM BEFORE SHOWED UP SUDDENLY TOO.
MAYBE IT'S BECAUSE OF HIS APPEARANCE?
UU
THEY SEEM TO HAVE JOINED FORCES IN EARNEST.
WE CANNOT ALLOW THIS.
SO...
KIIII (SCREEE)
WHOA!
SO IS THE AGENCY...
...OUR ALLY, THEN?

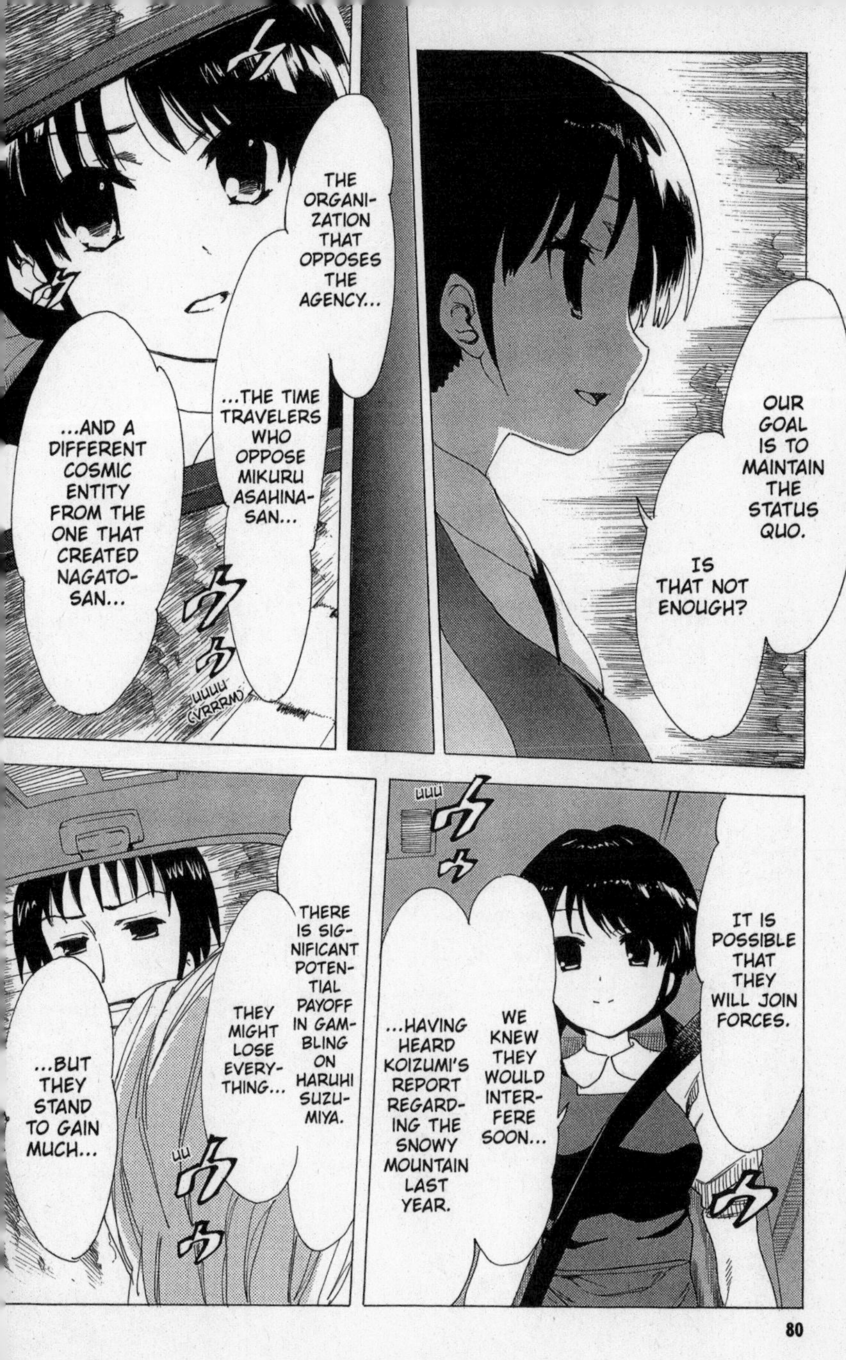
OUR GOAL IS TO MAINTAIN THE STATUS QUO.
IS THAT NOT ENOUGH?
THE ORGANIZATION THAT OPPOSES THE AGENCY...
...THE TIME TRAVELERS WHO OPPOSE MIKURU ASAHINA-SAN...
...AND A DIFFERENT COSMIC ENTITY FROM THE ONE THAT CREATED NAGATO-SAN...
UUUU (VRRRM)
UUU
IT IS POSSIBLE THAT THEY WILL JOIN FORCES.
WE KNEW THEY WOULD INTERFERE SOON...
...HAVING HEARD KOIZUMI'S REPORT REGARDING THE SNOWY MOUNTAIN LAST YEAR.
THERE IS SIGNIFICANT POTENTIAL PAYOFF IN GAMBLING ON HARUHI SUZUMIYA.
THEY MIGHT LOSE EVERYTHING...
...BUT THEY STAND TO GAIN MUCH...
UU

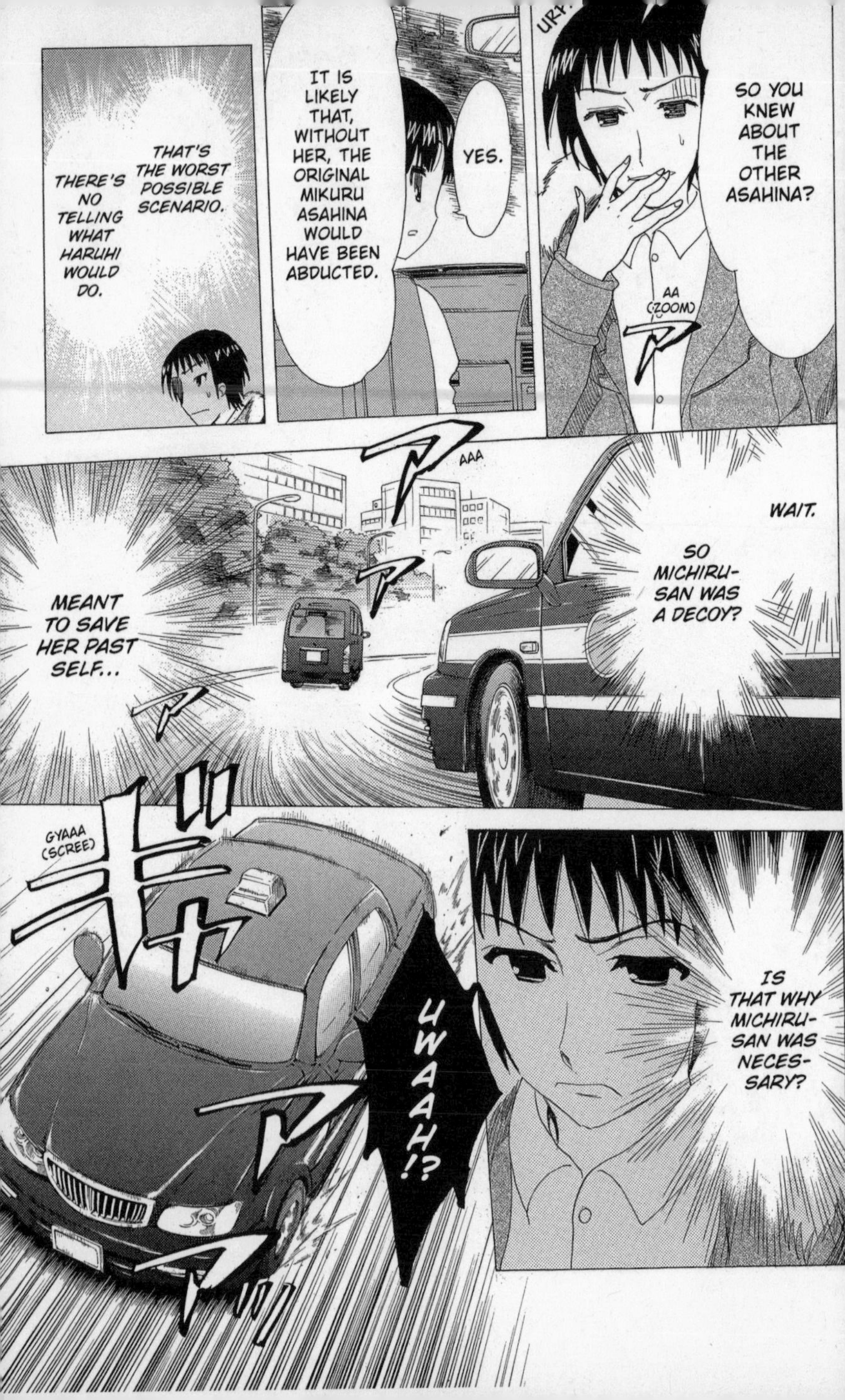
SO YOU KNEW ABOUT THE OTHER ASAHINA?
URY...
AA (ZOOM)
YES.
IT IS LIKELY THAT, WITHOUT HER, THE ORIGINAL MIKURU ASAHINA WOULD HAVE BEEN ABDUCTED.
THAT'S THE WORST POSSIBLE SCENARIO.
THERE'S NO TELLING WHAT HARUHI WOULD DO.
WAIT.
SO MICHIRU-SAN WAS A DECOY?
AAA
MEANT TO SAVE HER PAST SELF...
IS THAT WHY MICHIRU-SAN WAS NECES-SARY?
UWAAAH!?
GYAAA (SCREE)

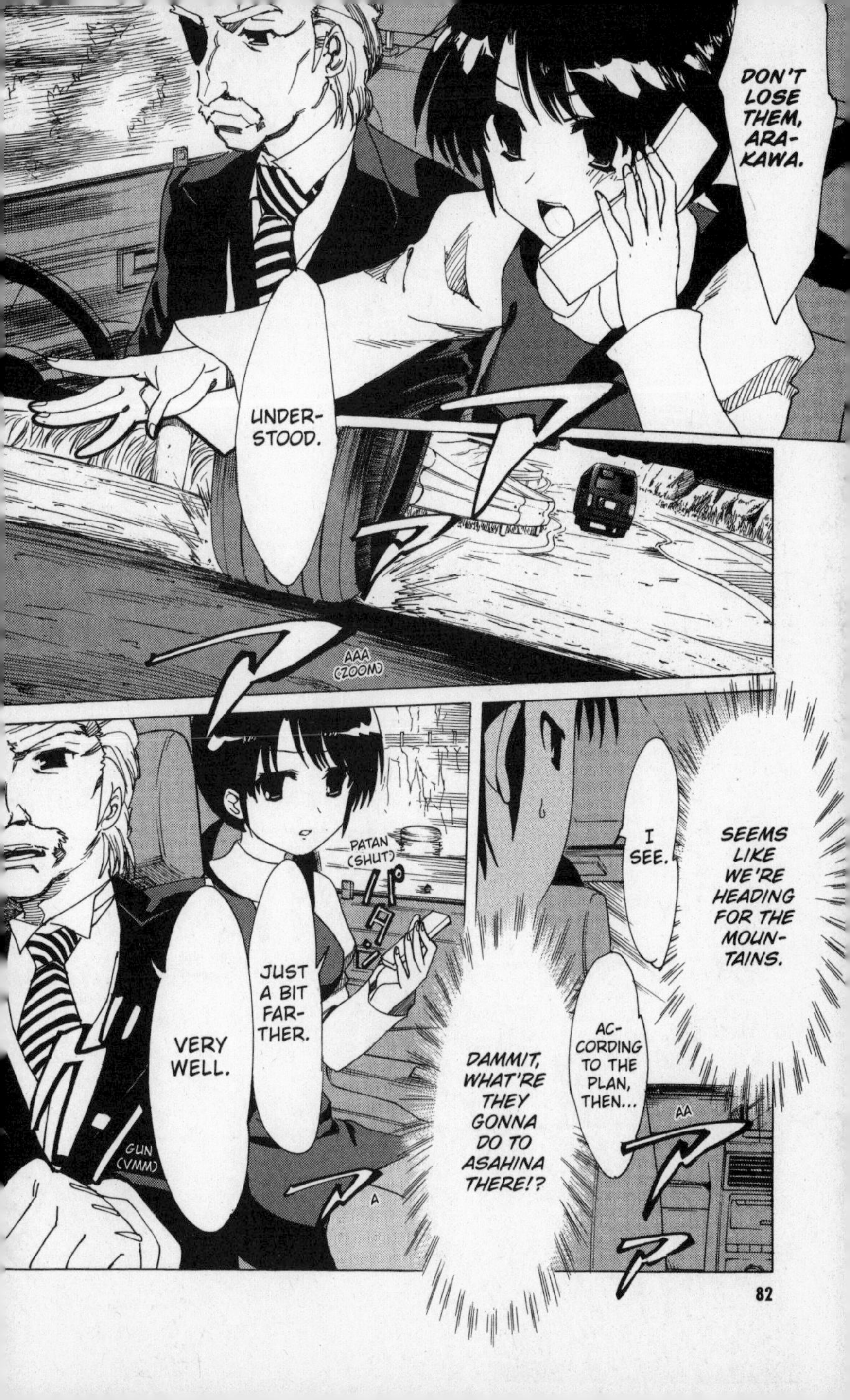
DON'T LOSE THEM, ARA-KAWA.
UNDER-STOOD.
AAA (ZOOM)
SEEMS LIKE WE'RE HEADING FOR THE MOUN-TAINS.
I SEE.
AC-CORDING TO THE PLAN, THEN...
DAMMIT, WHAT'RE THEY GONNA DO TO ASAHINA THERE!?
AA
PATAN (SHUT)
JUST A BIT FAR-THER.
VERY WELL.
GUN (VMM)
A

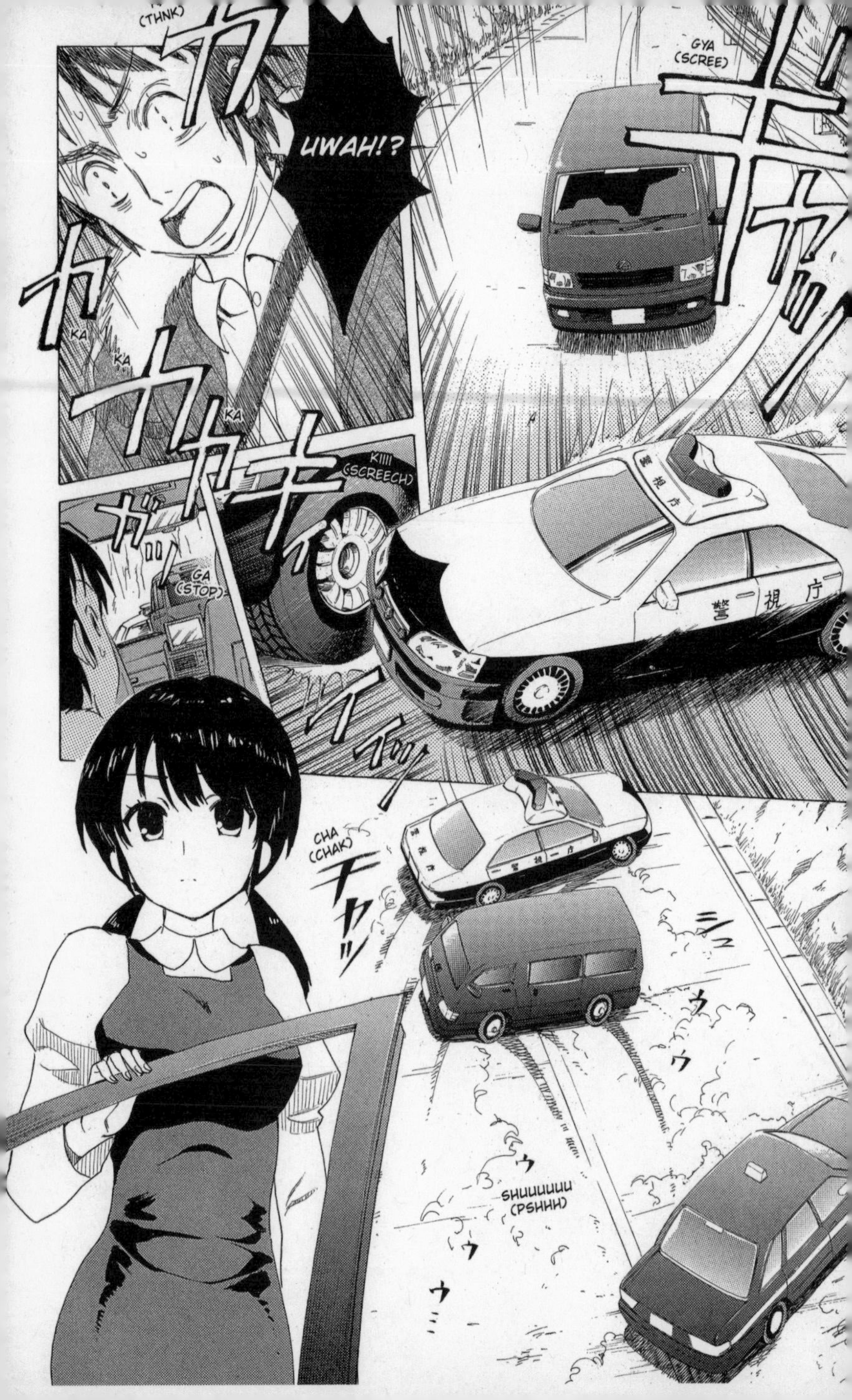
GYA
(SCREE)
(THNK)
UWAH!?
KA
KA
KA
KIIII
(SCREECH)
GA
(STOP)
CHA
(CHAK)
SHUUUUUU
(PSHHH)

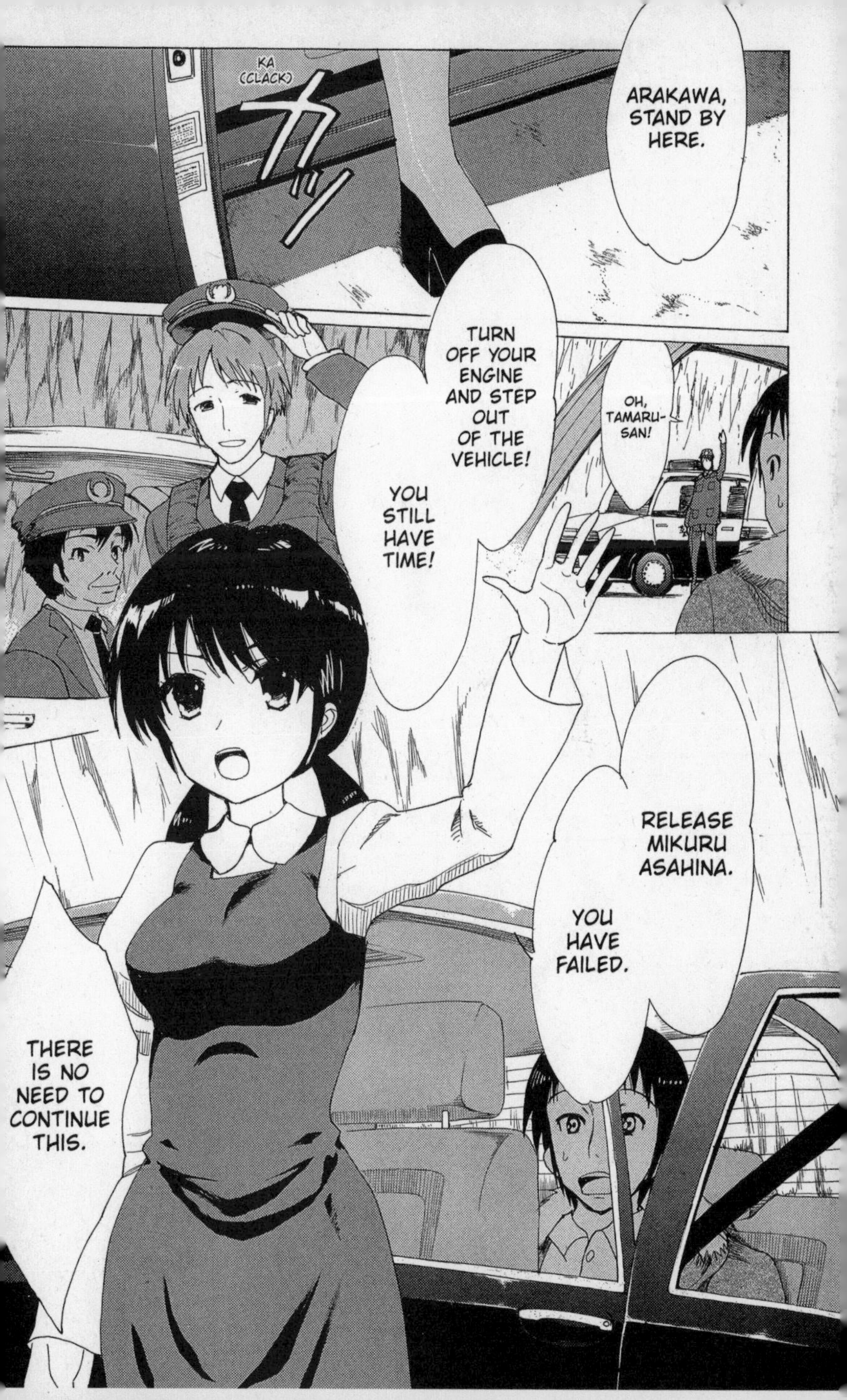
ARAKAWA, STAND BY HERE.
KA (CLACK)
カッ
OH, TAMARU-SAN!
TURN OFF YOUR ENGINE AND STEP OUT OF THE VEHICLE!
YOU STILL HAVE TIME!
RELEASE MIKURU ASAHINA.
YOU HAVE FAILED.
THERE IS NO NEED TO CONTINUE THIS.

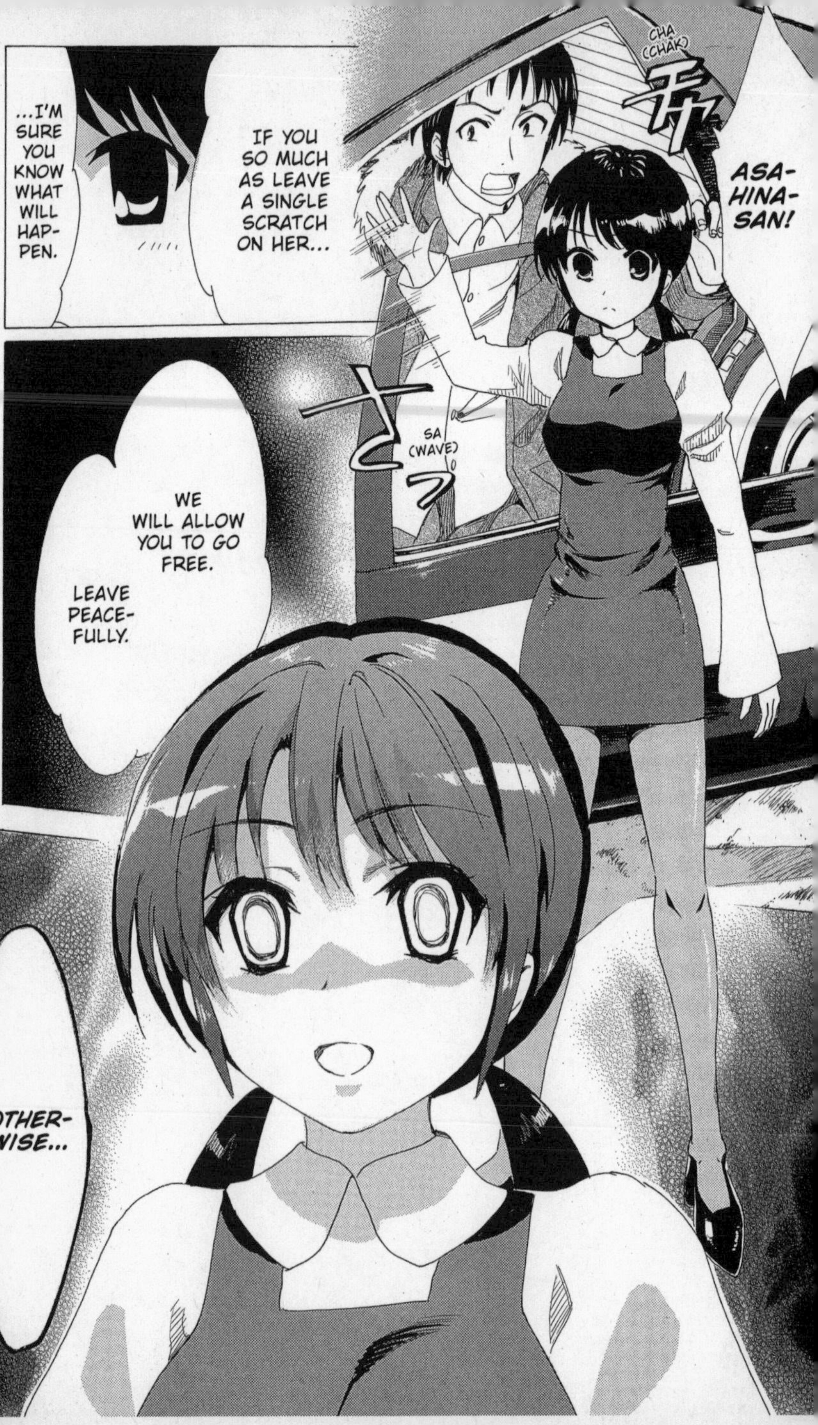
チャ
CHA (CHAK)
ASA-HINA-SAN!
IF YOU SO MUCH AS LEAVE A SINGLE SCRATCH ON HER...
...I'M SURE YOU KNOW WHAT WILL HAP-PEN.
さっ
SA (WAVE)
WE WILL ALLOW YOU TO GO FREE.
LEAVE PEACE-FULLY.
OTHER-WISE...

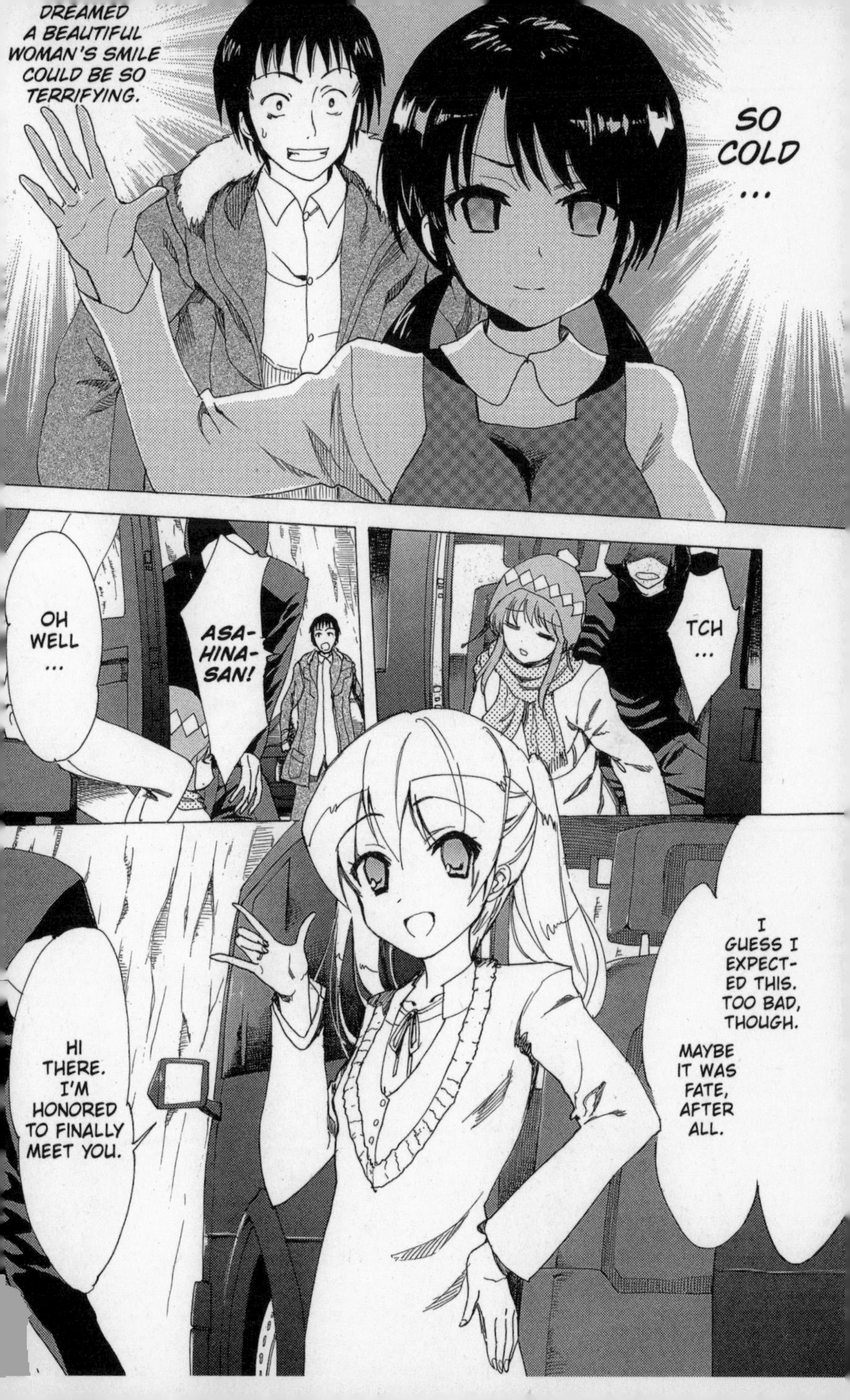
SO COLD ...
DREAMED A BEAUTIFUL WOMAN'S SMILE COULD BE SO TERRIFYING.
TCH ...
ASA-HINA-SAN!
OH WELL ...
I GUESS I EXPECT-ED THIS. TOO BAD, THOUGH.
MAYBE IT WAS FATE, AFTER ALL.
HI THERE. I'M HONORED TO FINALLY MEET YOU.

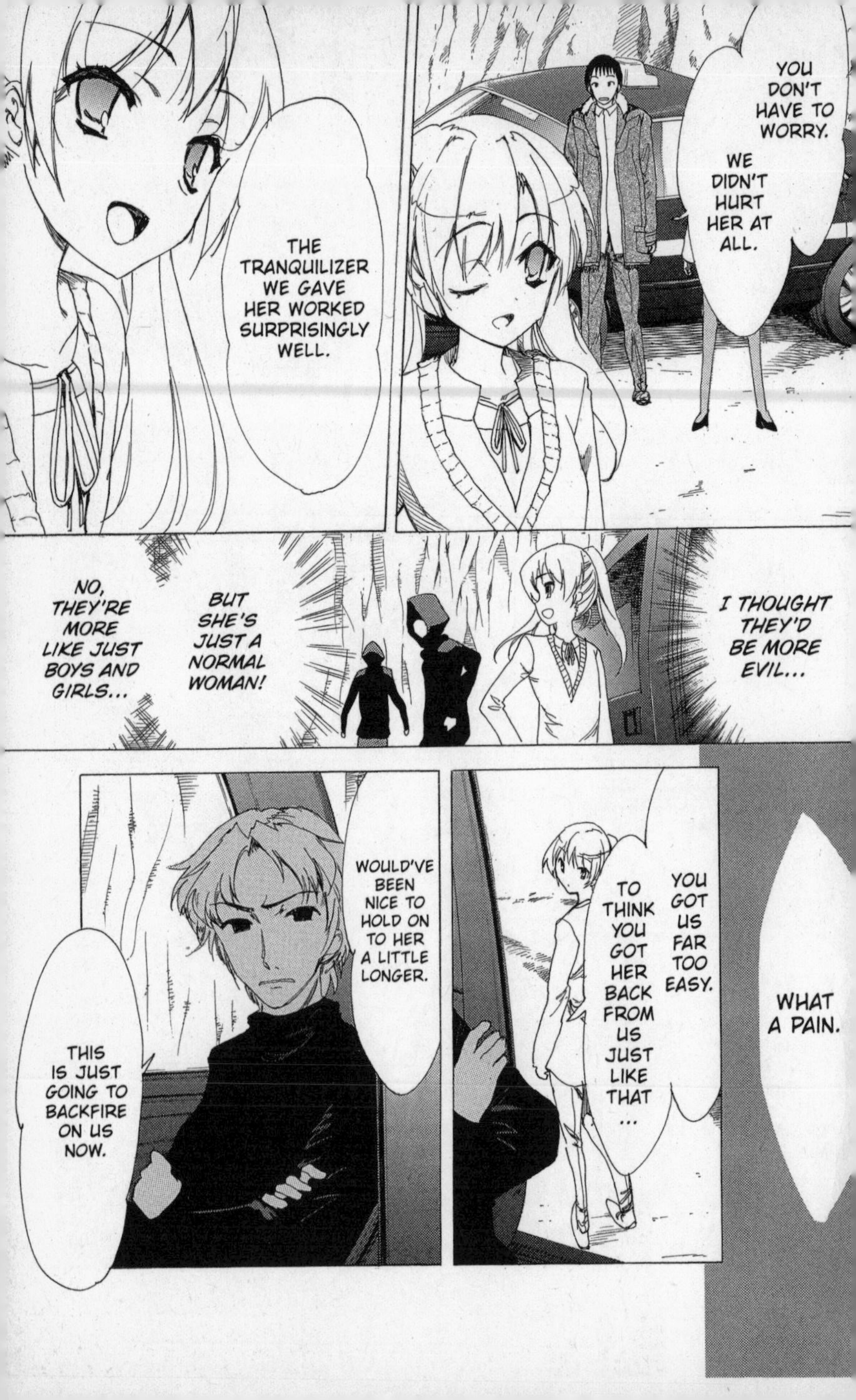
YOU DON'T HAVE TO WORRY.
WE DIDN'T HURT HER AT ALL.
THE TRANQUILIZER WE GAVE HER WORKED SURPRISINGLY WELL.
I THOUGHT THEY'D BE MORE EVIL...
BUT SHE'S JUST A NORMAL WOMAN!
NO, THEY'RE MORE LIKE JUST BOYS AND GIRLS...
WHAT A PAIN.
YOU GOT US FAR TOO EASY.
TO THINK YOU GOT HER BACK FROM US JUST LIKE THAT...
WOULD'VE BEEN NICE TO HOLD ON TO HER A LITTLE LONGER.
THIS IS JUST GOING TO BACKFIRE ON US NOW.

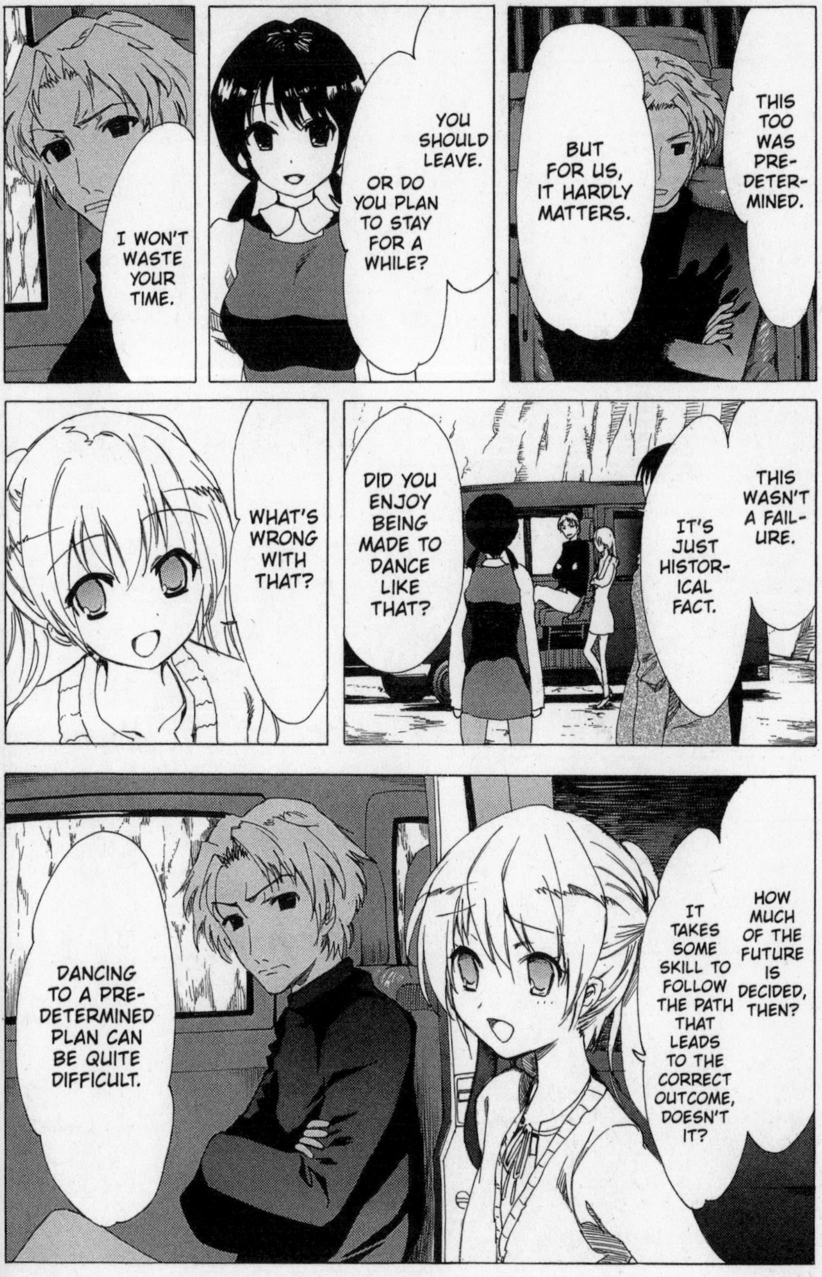
THIS TOO WAS PRE-DETERMINED.
BUT FOR US, IT HARDLY MATTERS.
YOU SHOULD LEAVE.
OR DO YOU PLAN TO STAY FOR A WHILE?
I WON'T WASTE YOUR TIME.
THIS WASN'T A FAILURE.
IT'S JUST HISTORICAL FACT.
DID YOU ENJOY BEING MADE TO DANCE LIKE THAT?
WHAT'S WRONG WITH THAT?
HOW MUCH OF THE FUTURE IS DECIDED, THEN?
IT TAKES SOME SKILL TO FOLLOW THE PATH THAT LEADS TO THE CORRECT OUTCOME, DOESN'T IT?
DANCING TO A PRE-DETERMINED PLAN CAN BE QUITE DIFFICULT.

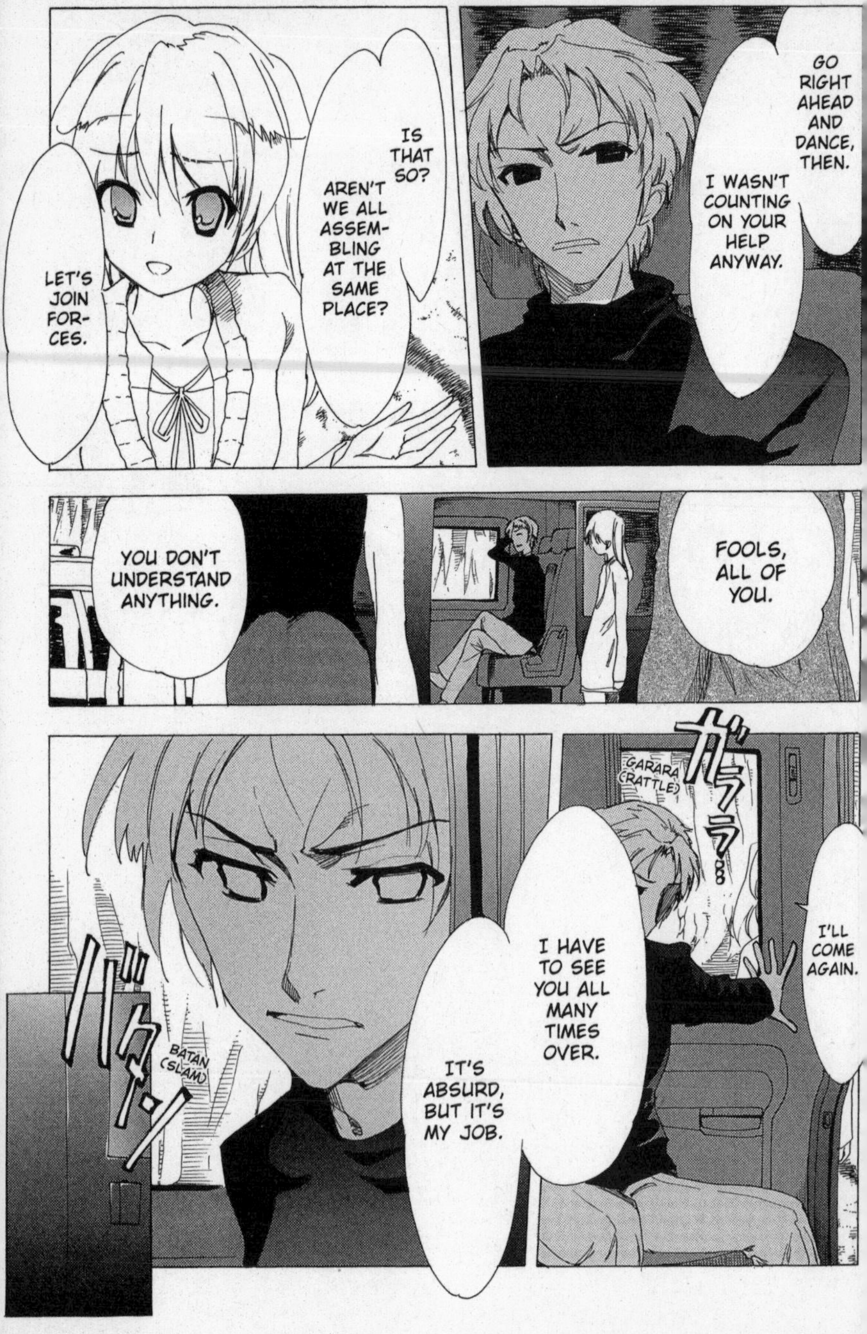
GO RIGHT AHEAD AND DANCE, THEN.
I WASN'T COUNTING ON YOUR HELP ANYWAY.
IS THAT SO?
AREN'T WE ALL ASSEM-BLING AT THE SAME PLACE?
LET'S JOIN FOR-CES.
FOOLS, ALL OF YOU.
YOU DON'T UNDERSTAND ANYTHING.
GARARA (RATTLE)
I'LL COME AGAIN.
I HAVE TO SEE YOU ALL MANY TIMES OVER.
IT'S ABSURD, BUT IT'S MY JOB.
BATAN (SLAM)

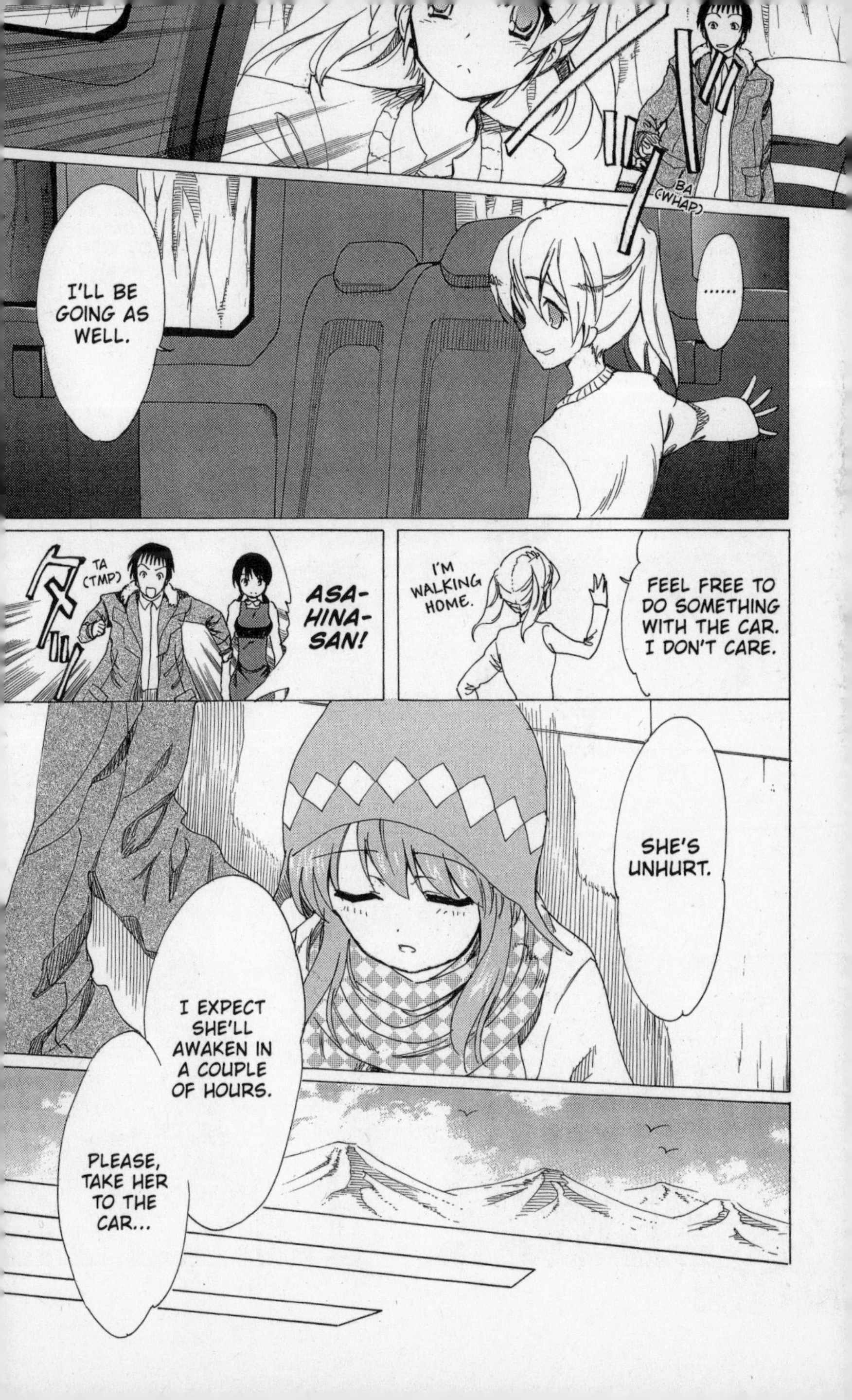
BA (WHAP)
......
I'LL BE GOING AS WELL.
FEEL FREE TO DO SOMETHING WITH THE CAR. I DON'T CARE.
I'M WALKING HOME.
ASA-HINA-SAN!
TA (TMP)
SHE'S UNHURT.
I EXPECT SHE'LL AWAKEN IN A COUPLE OF HOURS.
PLEASE, TAKE HER TO THE CAR...

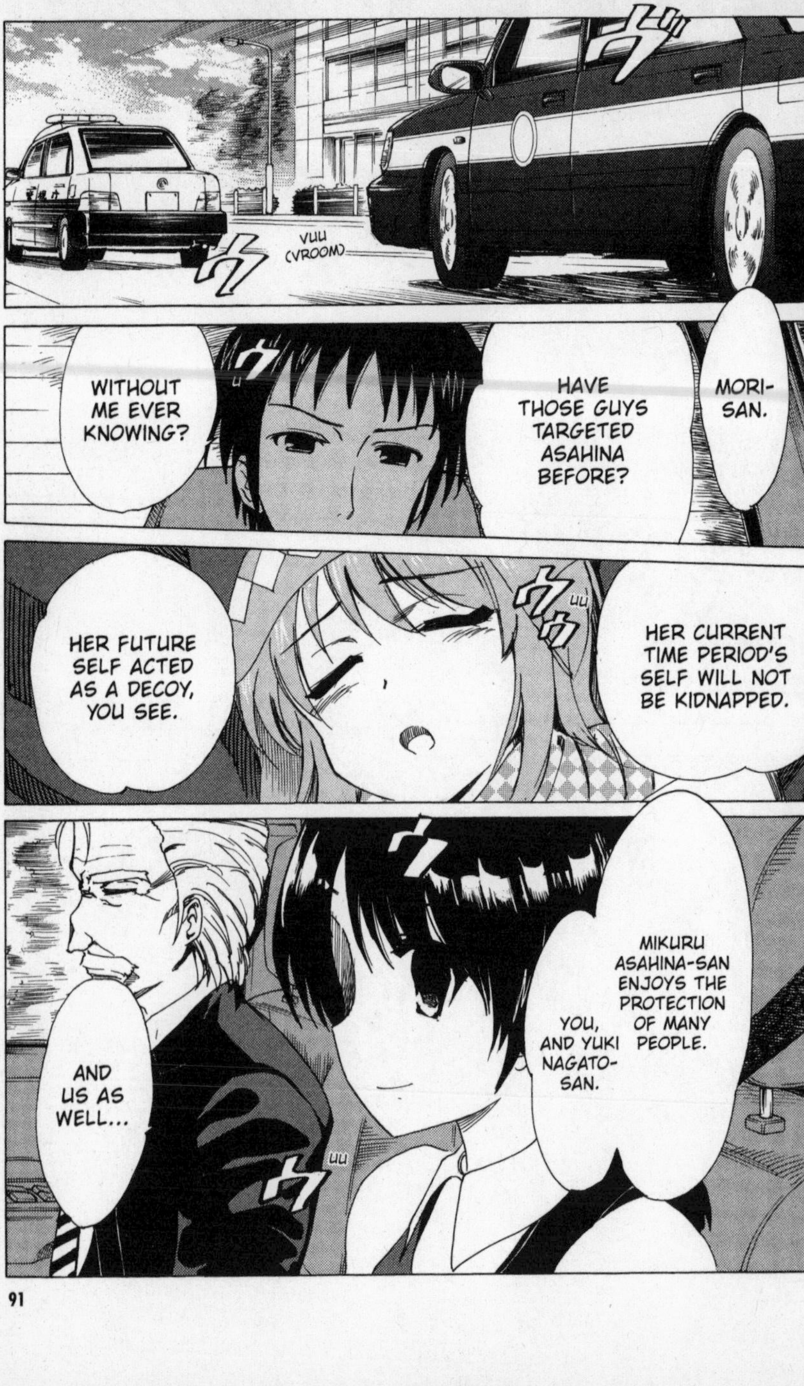
VUU (VROOM)
MORI-SAN.
HAVE THOSE GUYS TARGETED ASAHINA BEFORE?
WITHOUT ME EVER KNOWING?
UU
HER CURRENT TIME PERIOD'S SELF WILL NOT BE KIDNAPPED.
HER FUTURE SELF ACTED AS A DECOY, YOU SEE.
MIKURU ASAHINA-SAN ENJOYS THE PROTECTION OF MANY PEOPLE.
YOU, AND YUKI NAGATO-SAN.
UU
AND US AS WELL...

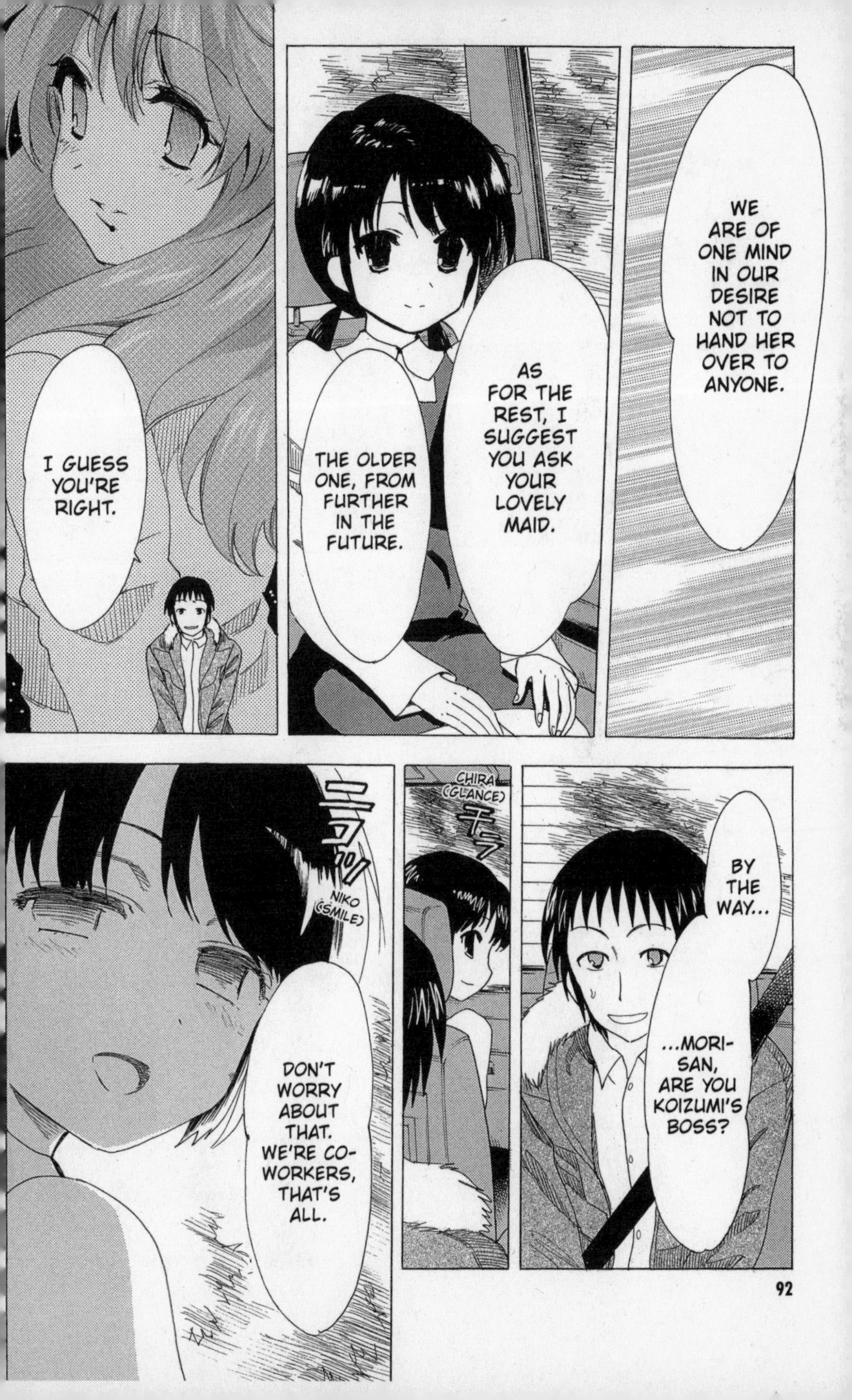
WE ARE OF ONE MIND IN OUR DESIRE NOT TO HAND HER OVER TO ANYONE.
AS FOR THE REST, I SUGGEST YOU ASK YOUR LOVELY MAID.
THE OLDER ONE, FROM FURTHER IN THE FUTURE.
I GUESS YOU'RE RIGHT.
BY THE WAY...
...MORI-SAN, ARE YOU KOIZUMI'S BOSS?
CHIRA (GLANCE)
NIKO (SMILE)
DON'T WORRY ABOUT THAT. WE'RE CO-WORKERS, THAT'S ALL.

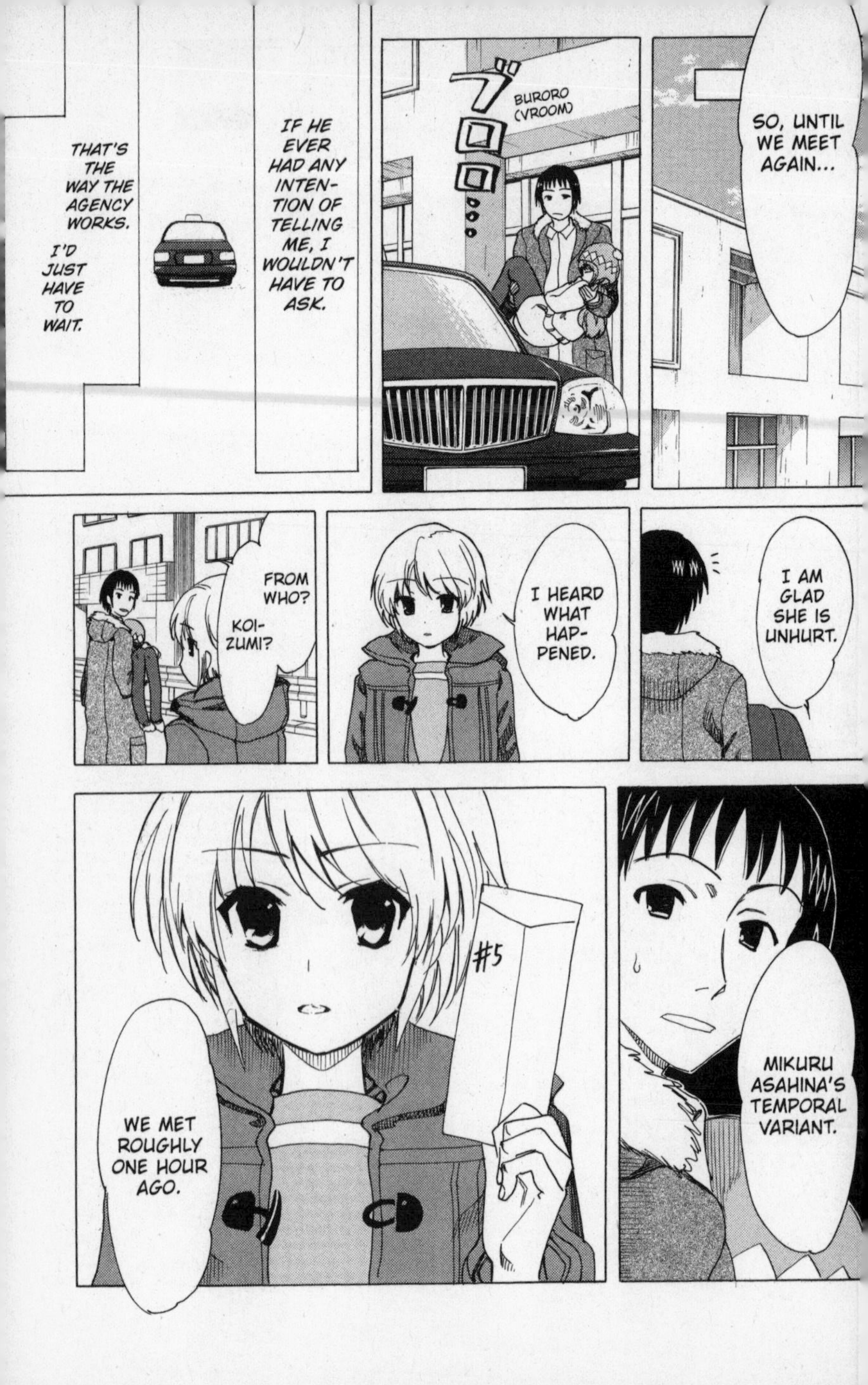
SO, UNTIL WE MEET AGAIN...
BURORO (VROOM)
IF HE EVER HAD ANY INTENTION OF TELLING ME, I WOULDN'T HAVE TO ASK.
THAT'S THE WAY THE AGENCY WORKS.
I'D JUST HAVE TO WAIT.
I AM GLAD SHE IS UNHURT.
I HEARD WHAT HAPPENED.
FROM WHO?
KOI-ZUMI?
MIKURU ASAHINA'S TEMPORAL VARIANT.
#5
WE MET ROUGHLY ONE HOUR AGO.

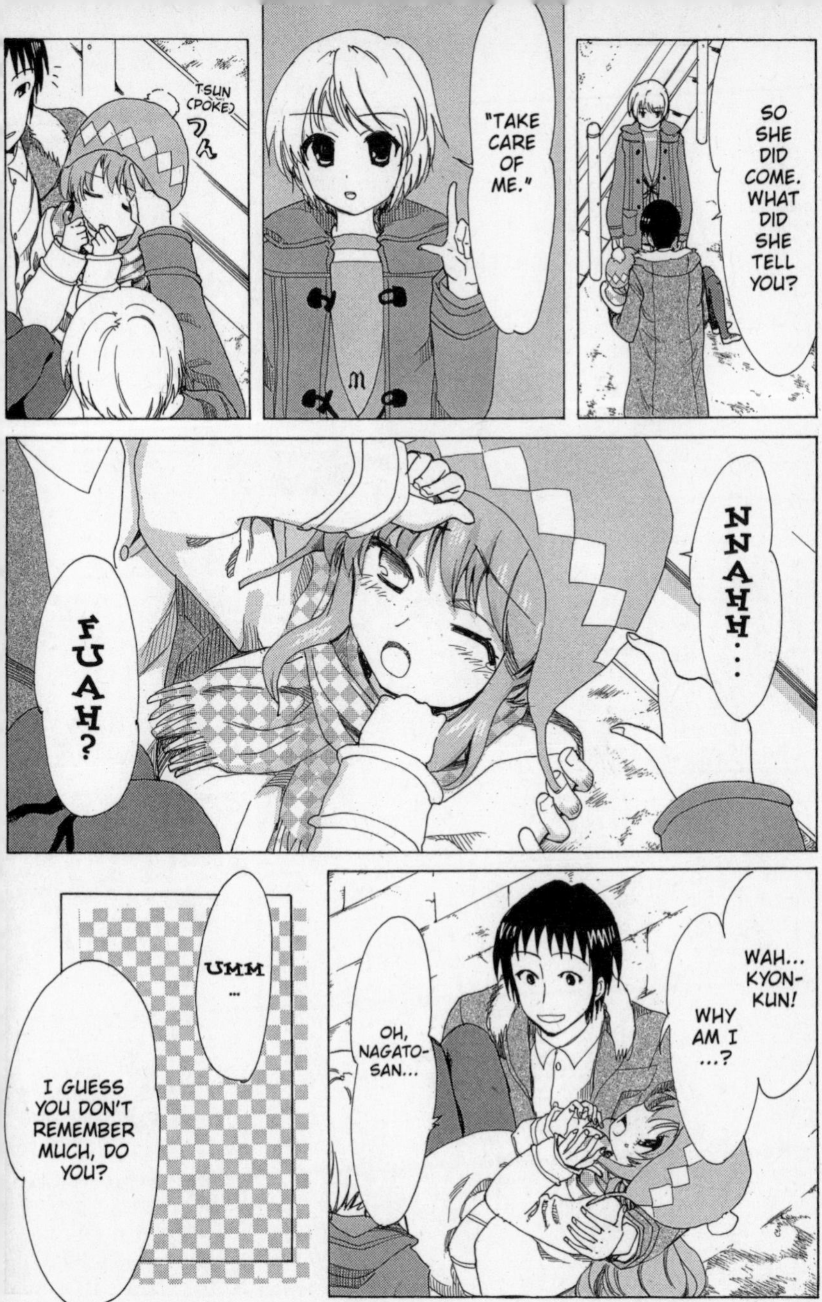
SO SHE DID COME. WHAT DID SHE TELL YOU?
"TAKE CARE OF ME."
TSUN (POKE)
つん
NNAHH...
FUAH?
WAH... KYON-KUN!
WHY AM I ...?
OH, NAGATO-SAN...
UMM ...
I GUESS YOU DON'T REMEMBER MUCH, DO YOU?

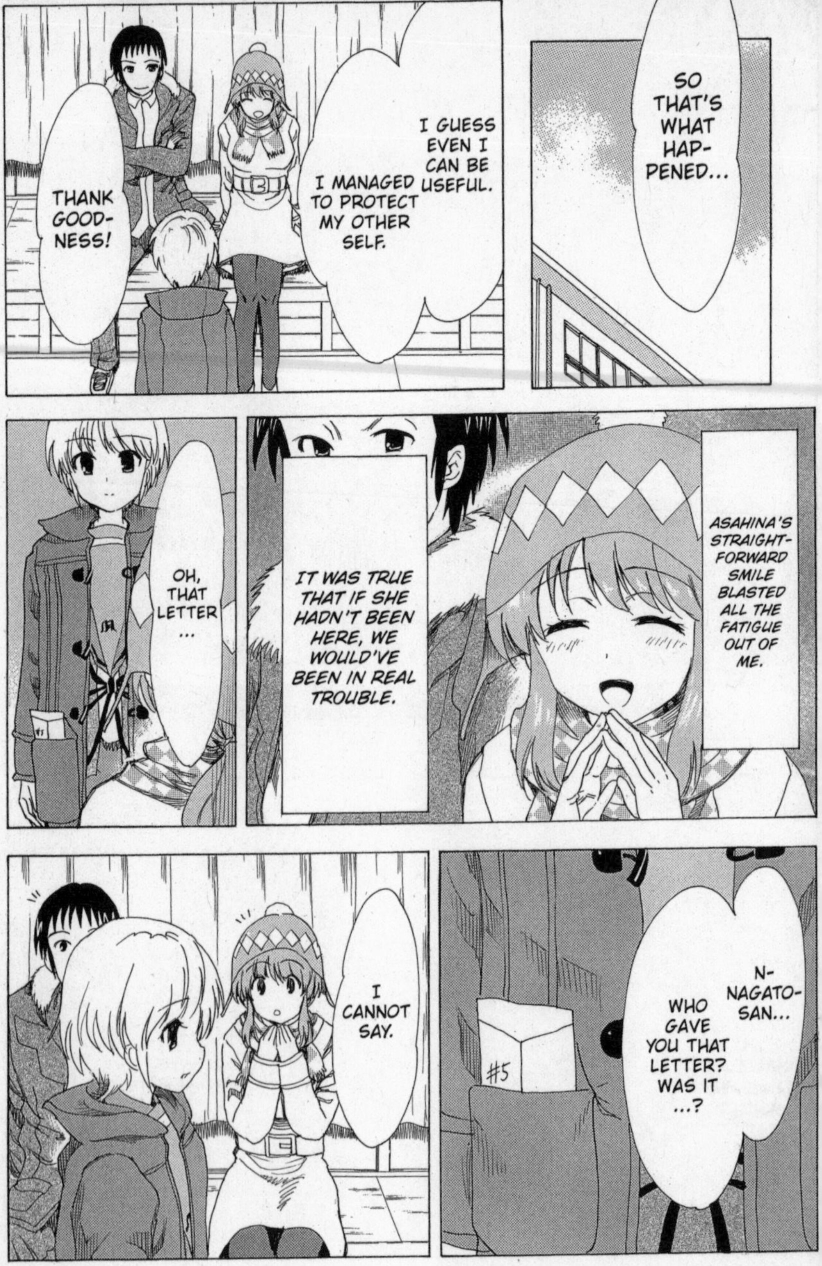
SO THAT'S WHAT HAP-PENED...
I GUESS EVEN I CAN BE USEFUL.
I MANAGED TO PROTECT MY OTHER SELF.
THANK GOOD-NESS!
ASAHINA'S STRAIGHT-FORWARD SMILE BLASTED ALL THE FATIGUE OUT OF ME.
IT WAS TRUE THAT IF SHE HADN'T BEEN HERE, WE WOULD'VE BEEN IN REAL TROUBLE.
OH, THAT LETTER ...
N-NAGATO-SAN...
WHO GAVE YOU THAT LETTER? WAS IT ...?
#5
I CANNOT SAY.

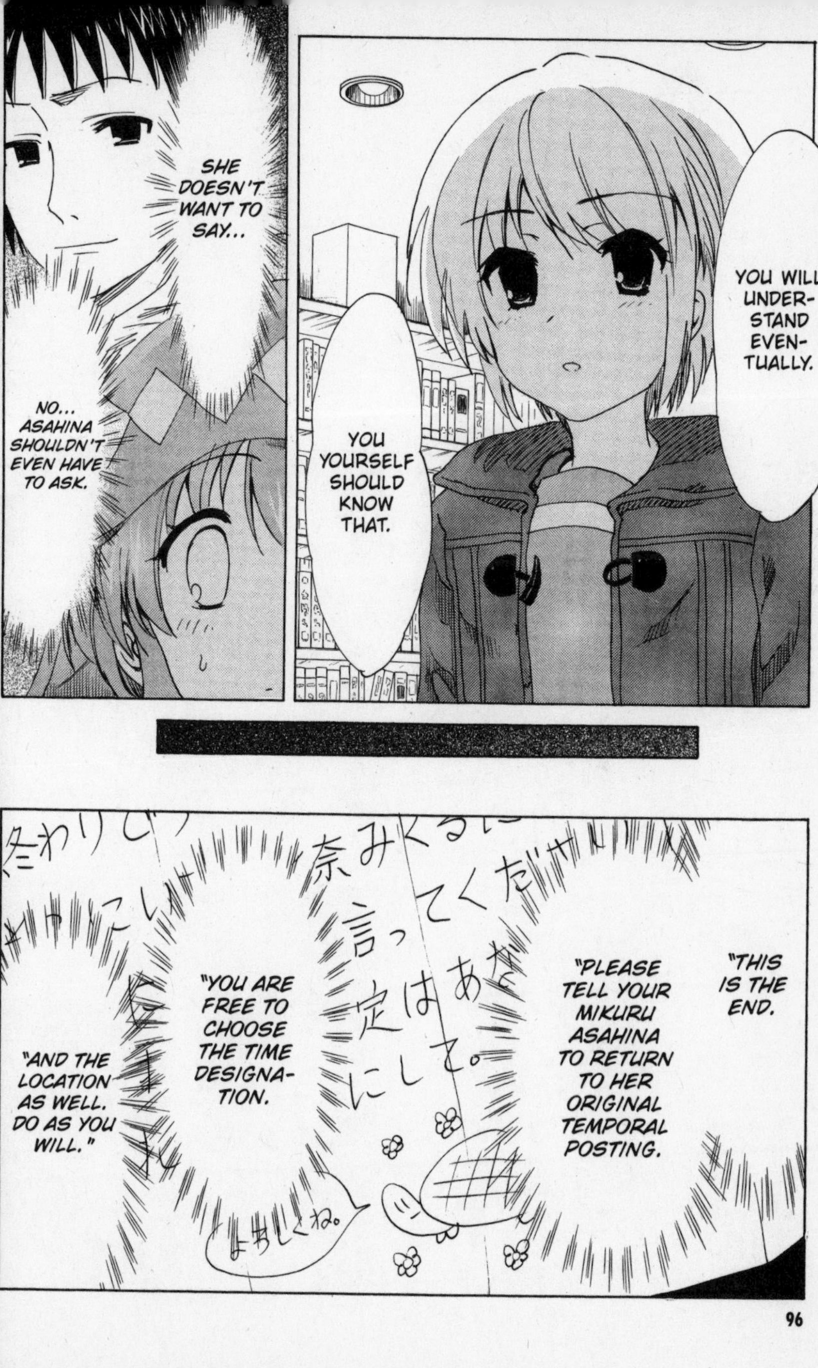
YOU WILL UNDER-STAND EVEN-TUALLY.
YOU YOURSELF SHOULD KNOW THAT.
SHE DOESN'T WANT TO SAY...
NO... ASAHINA SHOULDN'T EVEN HAVE TO ASK.
"THIS IS THE END.
"PLEASE TELL YOUR MIKURU ASAHINA TO RETURN TO HER ORIGINAL TEMPORAL POSTING.
"YOU ARE FREE TO CHOOSE THE TIME DESIGNA-TION.
"AND THE LOCATION AS WELL. DO AS YOU WILL."
よろしくね。

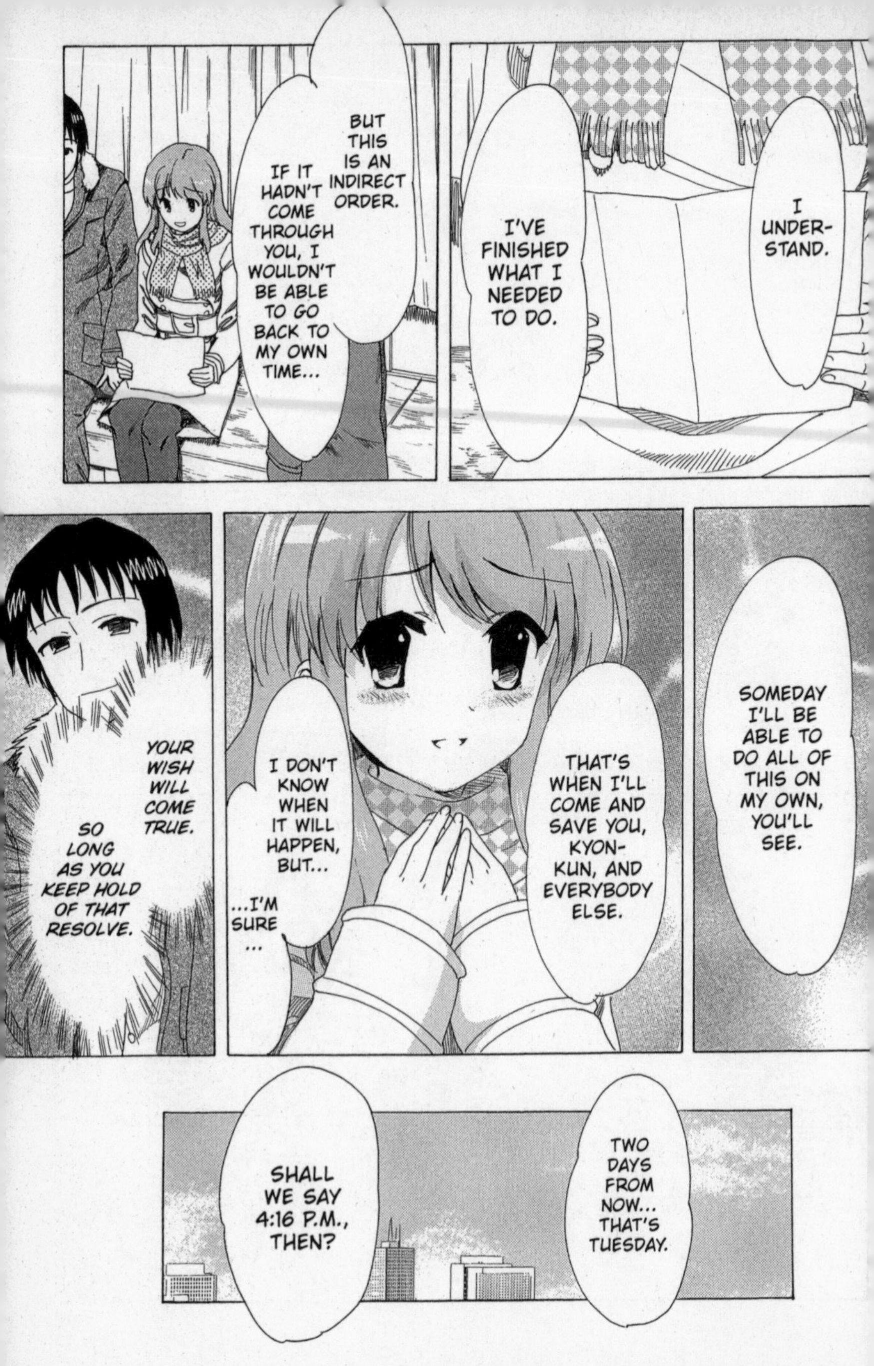
I UNDER-STAND.
I'VE FINISHED WHAT I NEEDED TO DO.
BUT THIS IS AN INDIRECT ORDER.
IF IT HADN'T COME THROUGH YOU, I WOULDN'T BE ABLE TO GO BACK TO MY OWN TIME...
SOMEDAY I'LL BE ABLE TO DO ALL OF THIS ON MY OWN, YOU'LL SEE.
THAT'S WHEN I'LL COME AND SAVE YOU, KYON-KUN, AND EVERYBODY ELSE.
I DON'T KNOW WHEN IT WILL HAPPEN, BUT...
...I'M SURE...
YOUR WISH WILL COME TRUE.
SO LONG AS YOU KEEP HOLD OF THAT RESOLVE.
TWO DAYS FROM NOW... THAT'S TUESDAY.
SHALL WE SAY 4:16 P.M., THEN?

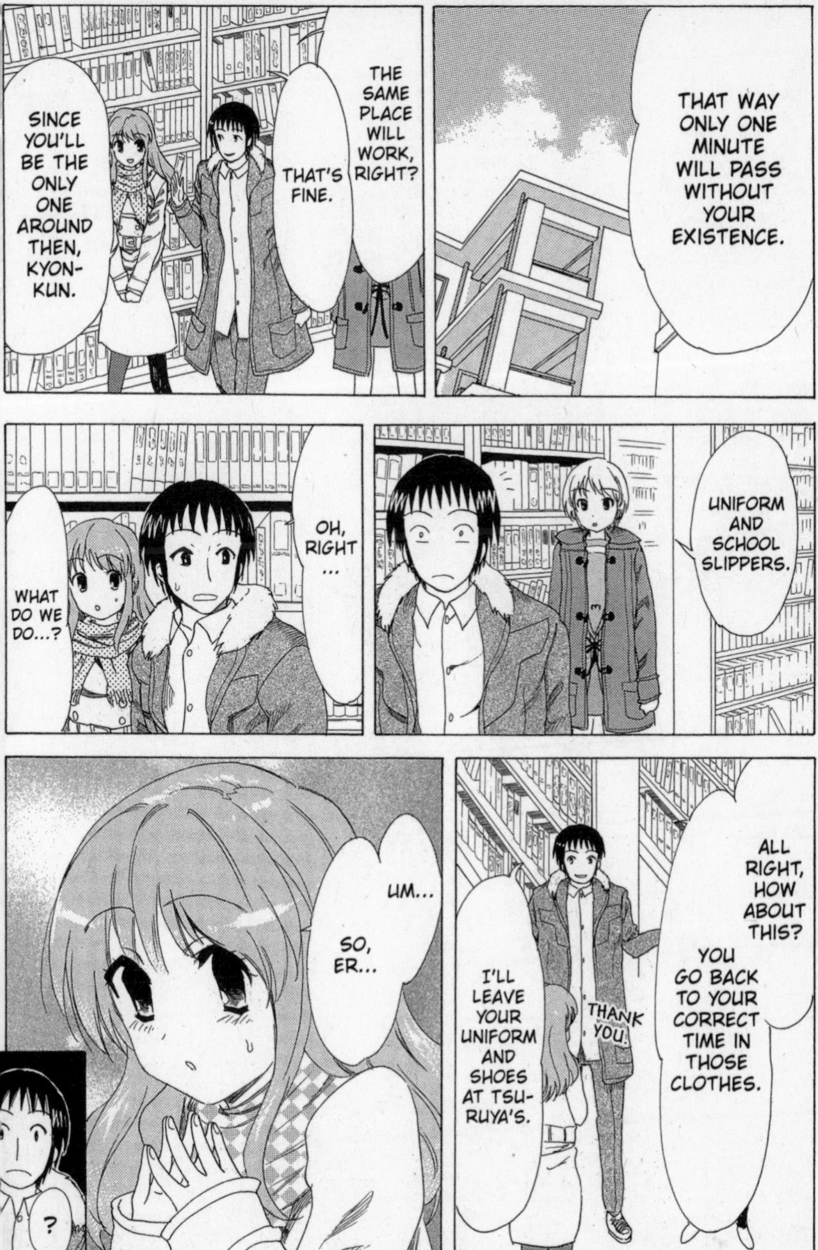
THAT WAY ONLY ONE MINUTE WILL PASS WITHOUT YOUR EXISTENCE.
THE SAME PLACE WILL WORK, RIGHT?
THAT'S FINE.
SINCE YOU'LL BE THE ONLY ONE AROUND THEN, KYON-KUN.
UNIFORM AND SCHOOL SLIPPERS.
OH, RIGHT ...
WHAT DO WE DO...?
ALL RIGHT, HOW ABOUT THIS?
YOU GO BACK TO YOUR CORRECT TIME IN THOSE CLOTHES.
THANK YOU.
I'LL LEAVE YOUR UNIFORM AND SHOES AT TSU-RUYA'S.
UM...
SO, ER...
?

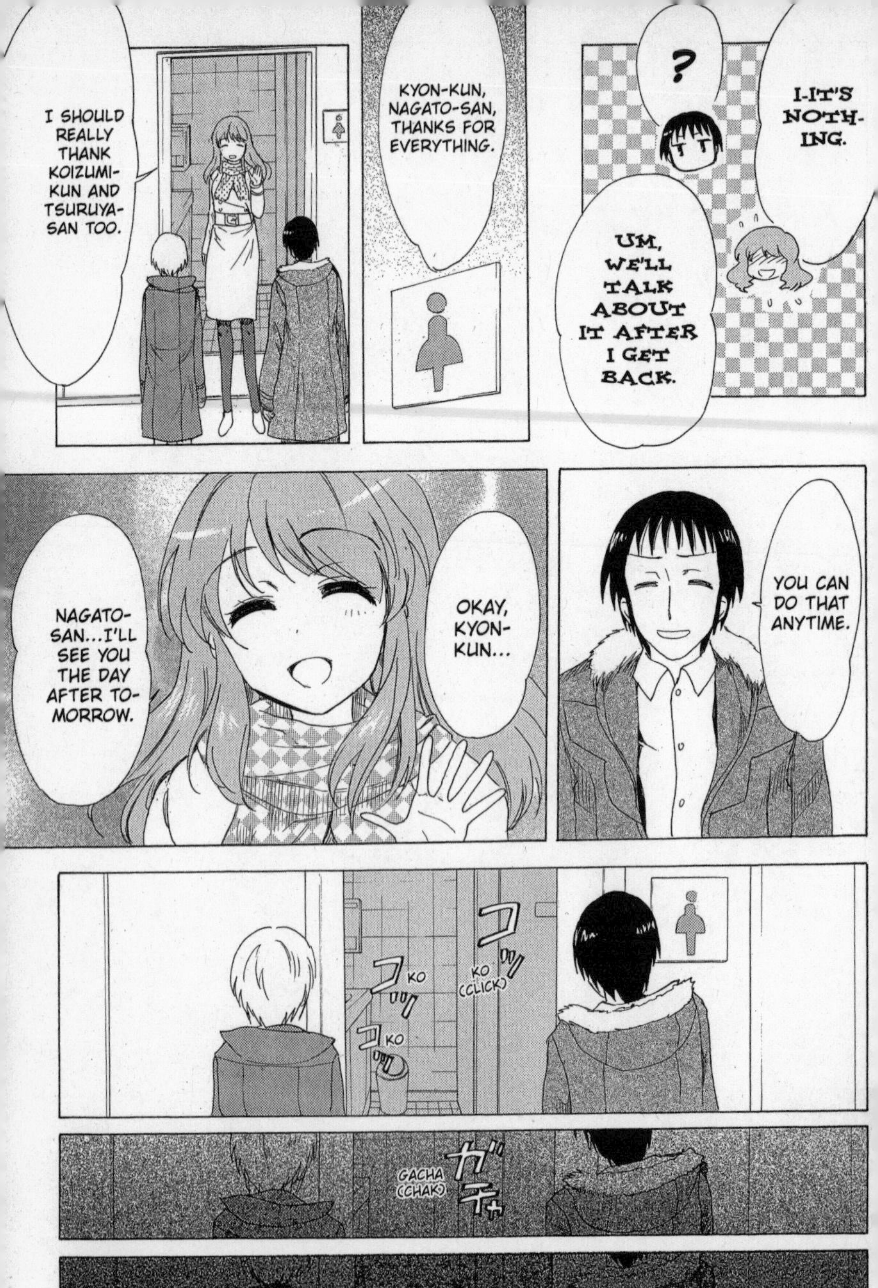
?
I-IT'S NOTH-ING.
UM, WE'LL TALK ABOUT IT AFTER I GET BACK.
KYON-KUN, NAGATO-SAN, THANKS FOR EVERYTHING.
I SHOULD REALLY THANK KOIZUMI-KUN AND TSURUYA-SAN TOO.
YOU CAN DO THAT ANYTIME.
OKAY, KYON-KUN...
NAGATO-SAN...I'LL SEE YOU THE DAY AFTER TO-MORROW.
KO (CLICK)
KO
KO
GACHA (CHAK)

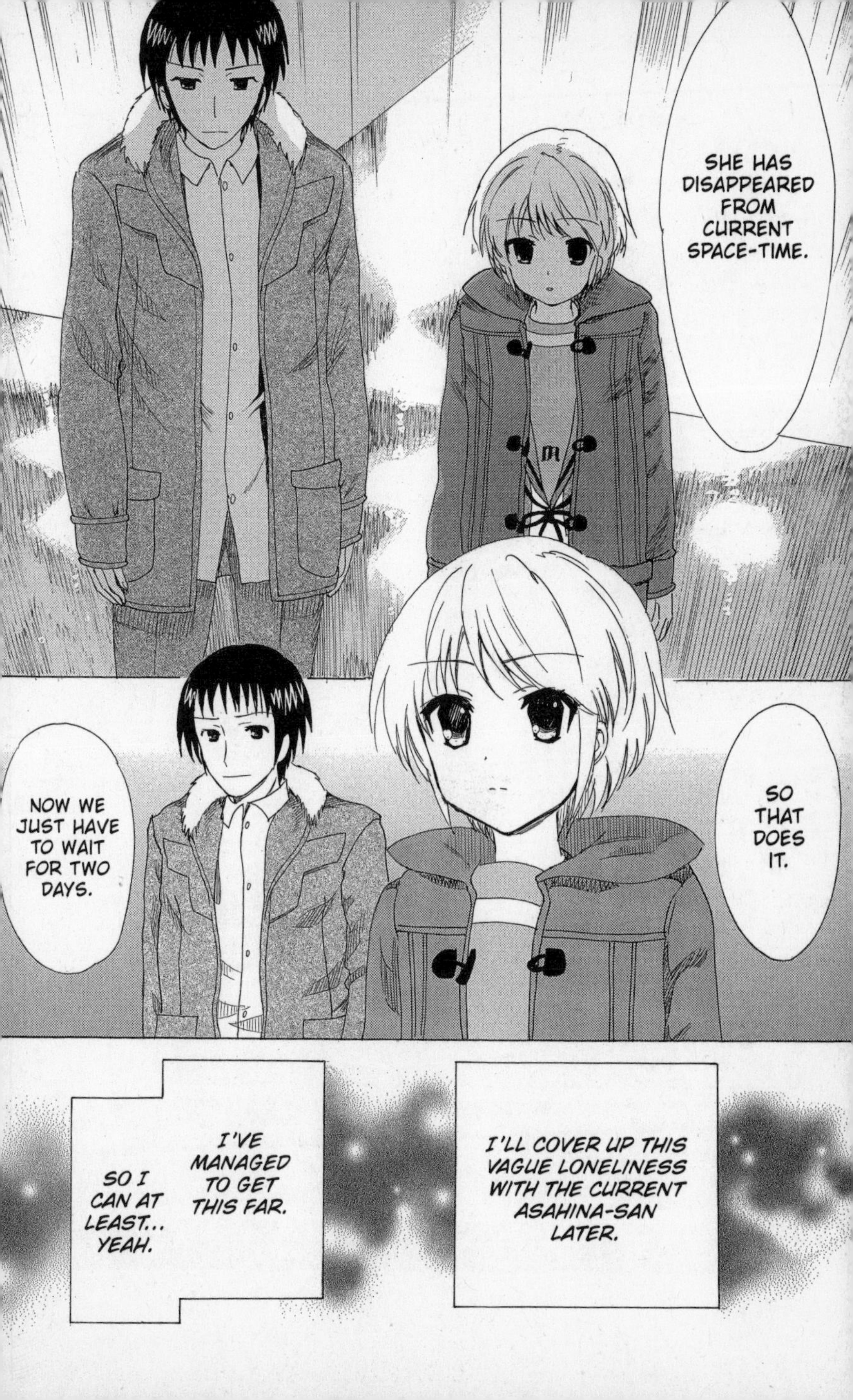
SHE HAS DISAPPEARED FROM CURRENT SPACE-TIME.
SO THAT DOES IT.
NOW WE JUST HAVE TO WAIT FOR TWO DAYS.
I'LL COVER UP THIS VAGUE LONELINESS WITH THE CURRENT ASAHINA-SAN LATER.
I'VE MANAGED TO GET THIS FAR.
SO I CAN AT LEAST... YEAH.

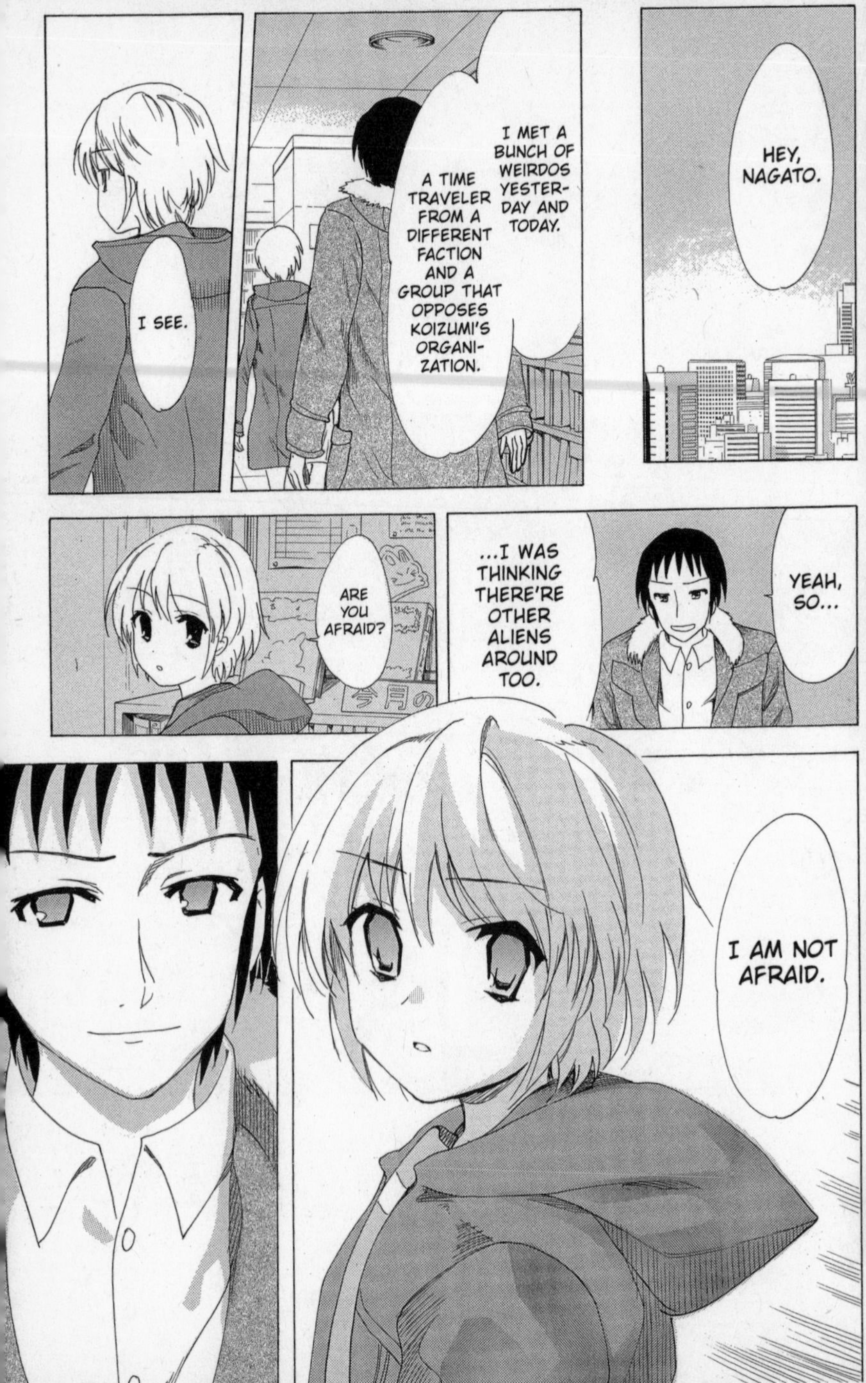
HEY, NAGATO.
I MET A BUNCH OF WEIRDOS YESTER-DAY AND TODAY.
A TIME TRAVELER FROM A DIFFERENT FACTION AND A GROUP THAT OPPOSES KOIZUMI'S ORGANI-ZATION.
I SEE.
YEAH, SO...
...I WAS THINKING THERE'RE OTHER ALIENS AROUND TOO.
ARE YOU AFRAID?
今月の
I AM NOT AFRAID.

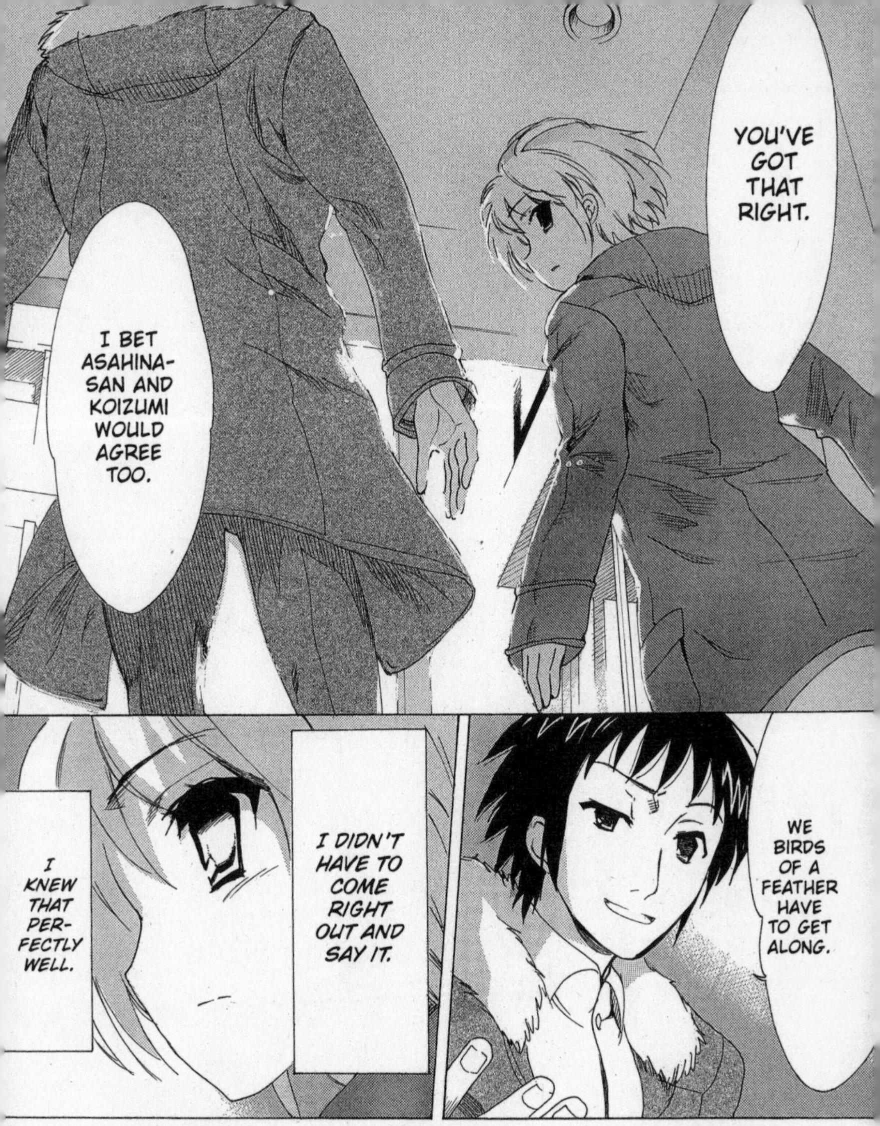
I BET ASAHINA-SAN AND KOIZUMI WOULD AGREE TOO.
YOU'VE GOT THAT RIGHT.
WE BIRDS OF A FEATHER HAVE TO GET ALONG.
I DIDN'T HAVE TO COME RIGHT OUT AND SAY IT.
I KNEW THAT PERFECTLY WELL.

THE SOS BRIGADE WASN'T A GROUP OF FIVE PEOPLE.

IT WAS A SINGLE UNIT.

THERE WAS NO NEED TO EXPLAIN THAT TO THE PERSON WHO'D LONG UNDERSTOOD IT MUCH BETTER THAN I EVER HAD.

THE INTRIGUES OF HARUHI SUZUMIYA IX : END

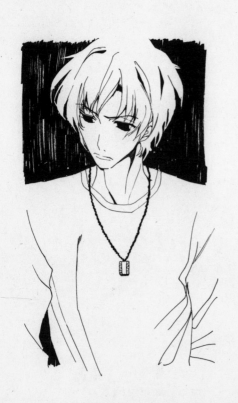

THE MELANCHOLY OF HARUHI SUZUMIYA

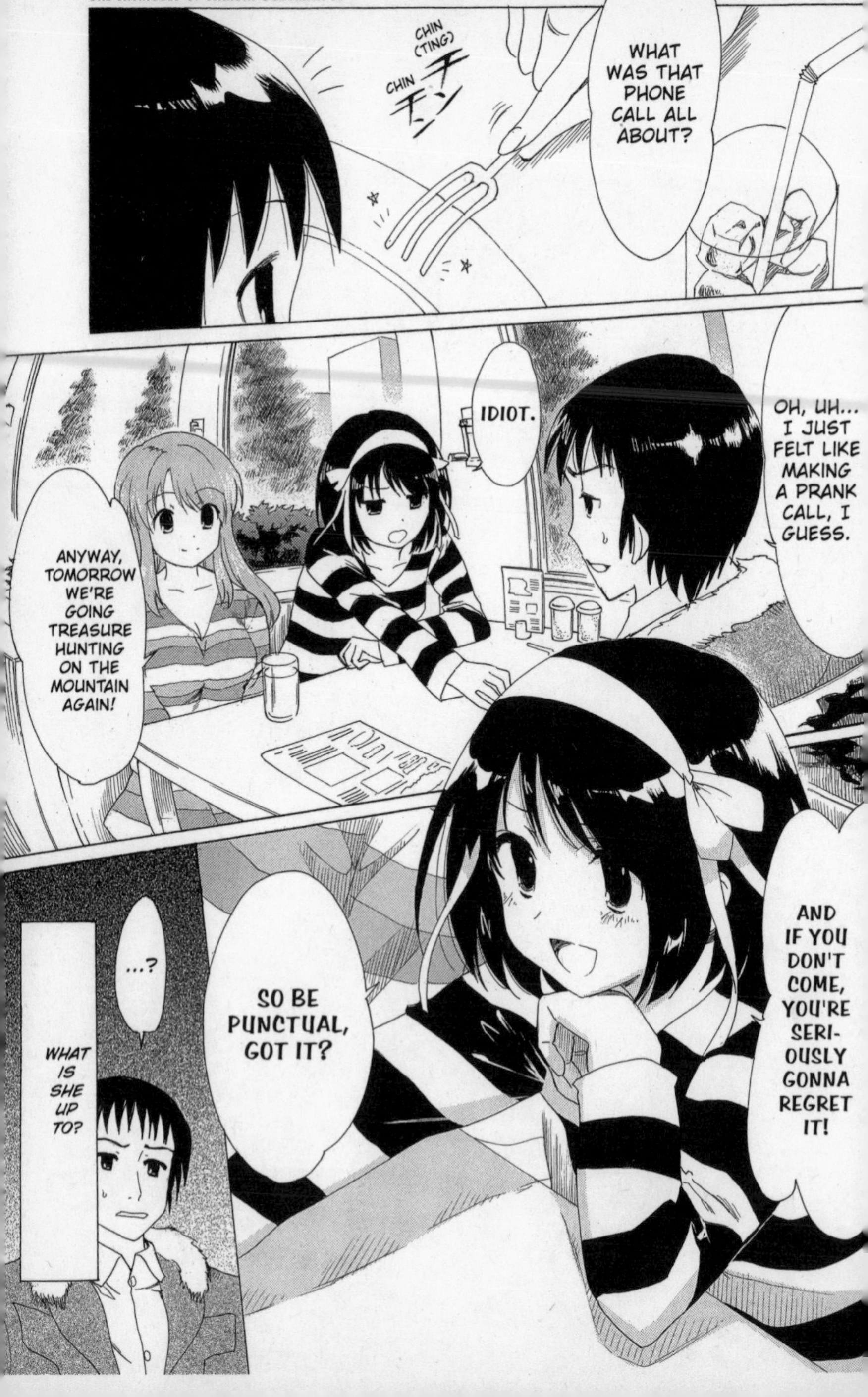
WHAT WAS THAT PHONE CALL ALL ABOUT?
CHIN (TING)
CHIN
OH, UH... I JUST FELT LIKE MAKING A PRANK CALL, I GUESS.
IDIOT.
ANYWAY, TOMORROW WE'RE GOING TREASURE HUNTING ON THE MOUNTAIN AGAIN!
AND IF YOU DON'T COME, YOU'RE SERI-OUSLY GONNA REGRET IT!
SO BE PUNCTUAL, GOT IT?
...?
WHAT IS SHE UP TO?

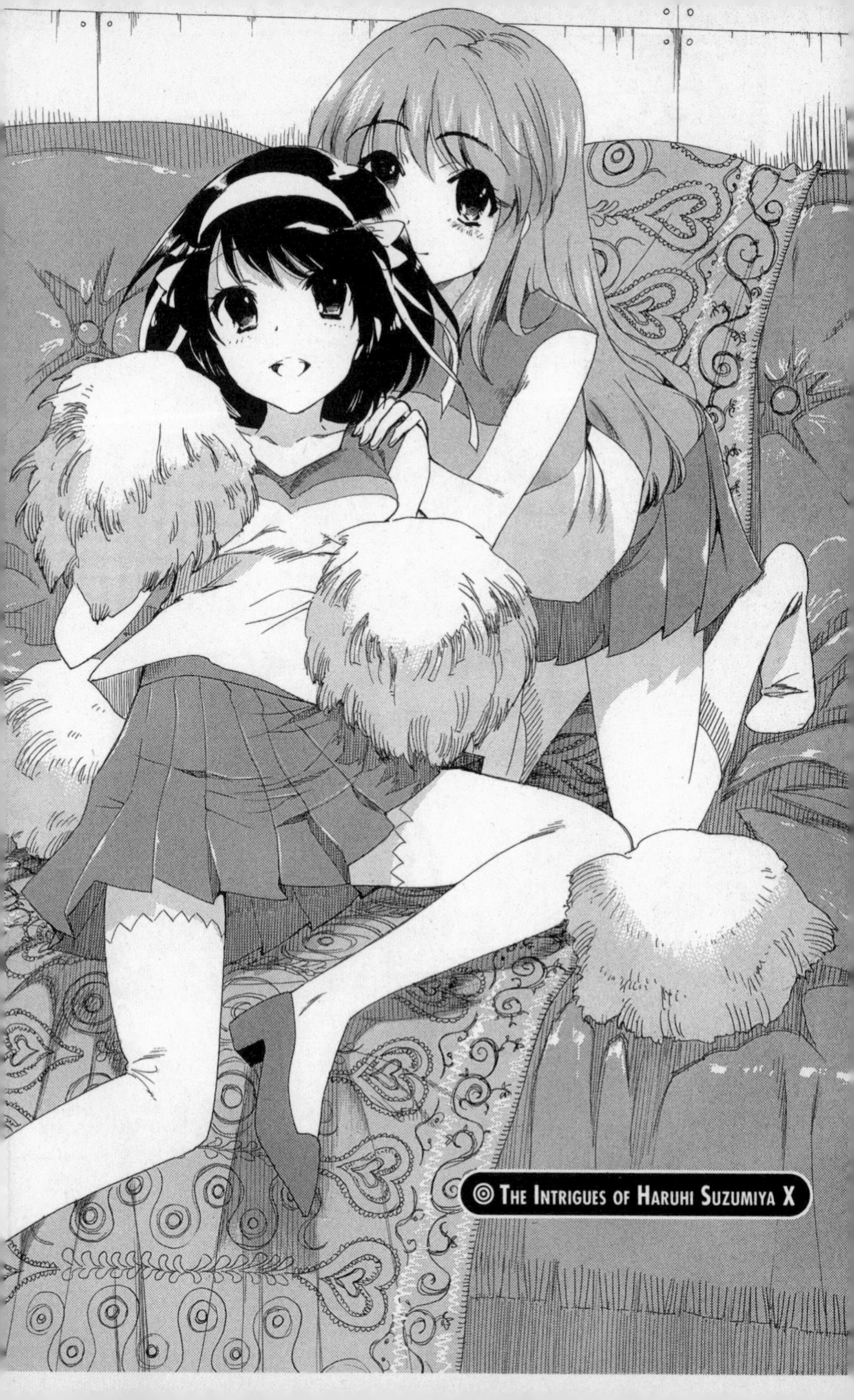
◎ The Intrigues of Haruhi Suzumiya X

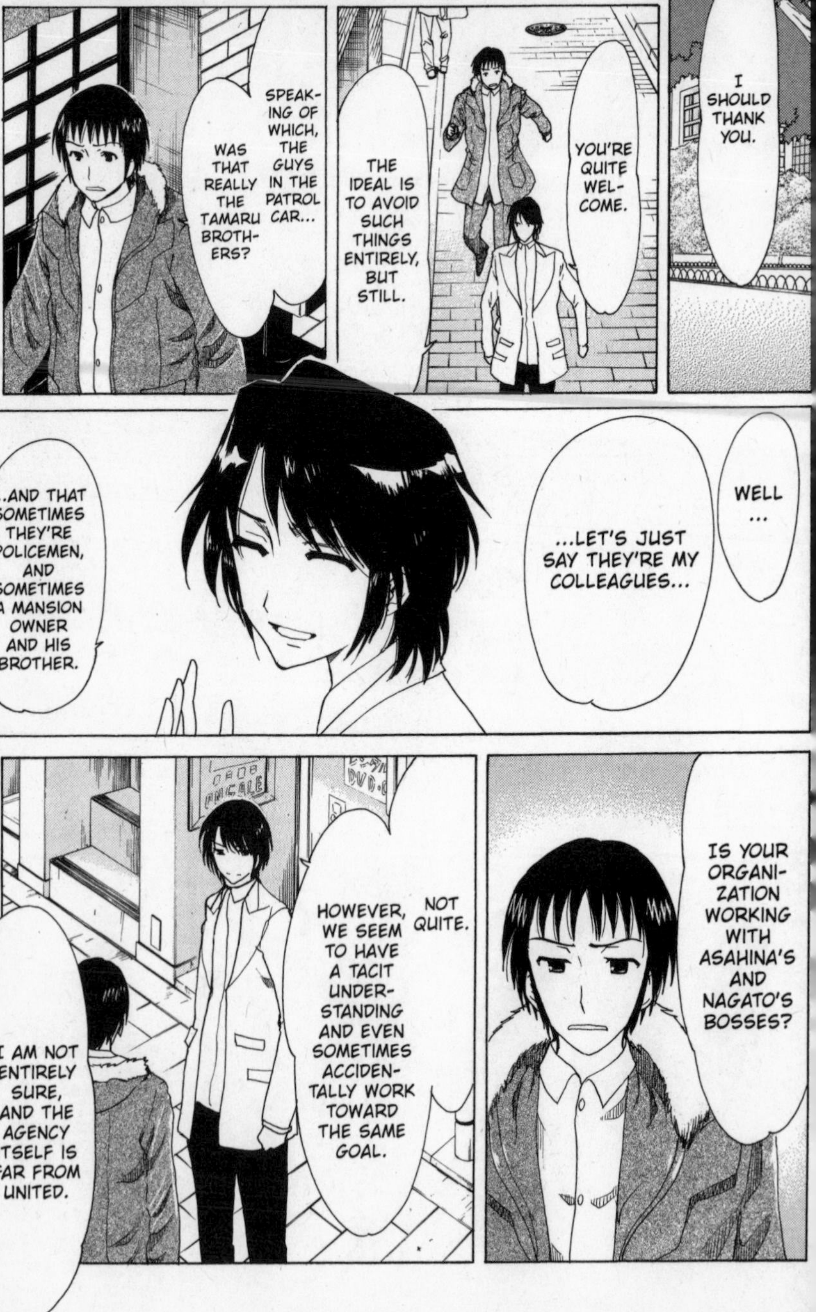
I SHOULD THANK YOU.
YOU'RE QUITE WEL-COME.
THE IDEAL IS TO AVOID SUCH THINGS ENTIRELY, BUT STILL.
SPEAK-ING OF WHICH, THE GUYS IN THE PATROL CAR...
WAS THAT REALLY THE TAMARU BROTH-ERS?
WELL...
...LET'S JUST SAY THEY'RE MY COLLEAGUES...
...AND THAT SOMETIMES THEY'RE POLICEMEN, AND SOMETIMES A MANSION OWNER AND HIS BROTHER.
IS YOUR ORGANI-ZATION WORKING WITH ASAHINA'S AND NAGATO'S BOSSES?
NOT QUITE.
HOWEVER, WE SEEM TO HAVE A TACIT UNDER-STANDING AND EVEN SOMETIMES ACCIDEN-TALLY WORK TOWARD THE SAME GOAL.
I AM NOT ENTIRELY SURE, AND THE AGENCY ITSELF IS FAR FROM UNITED.

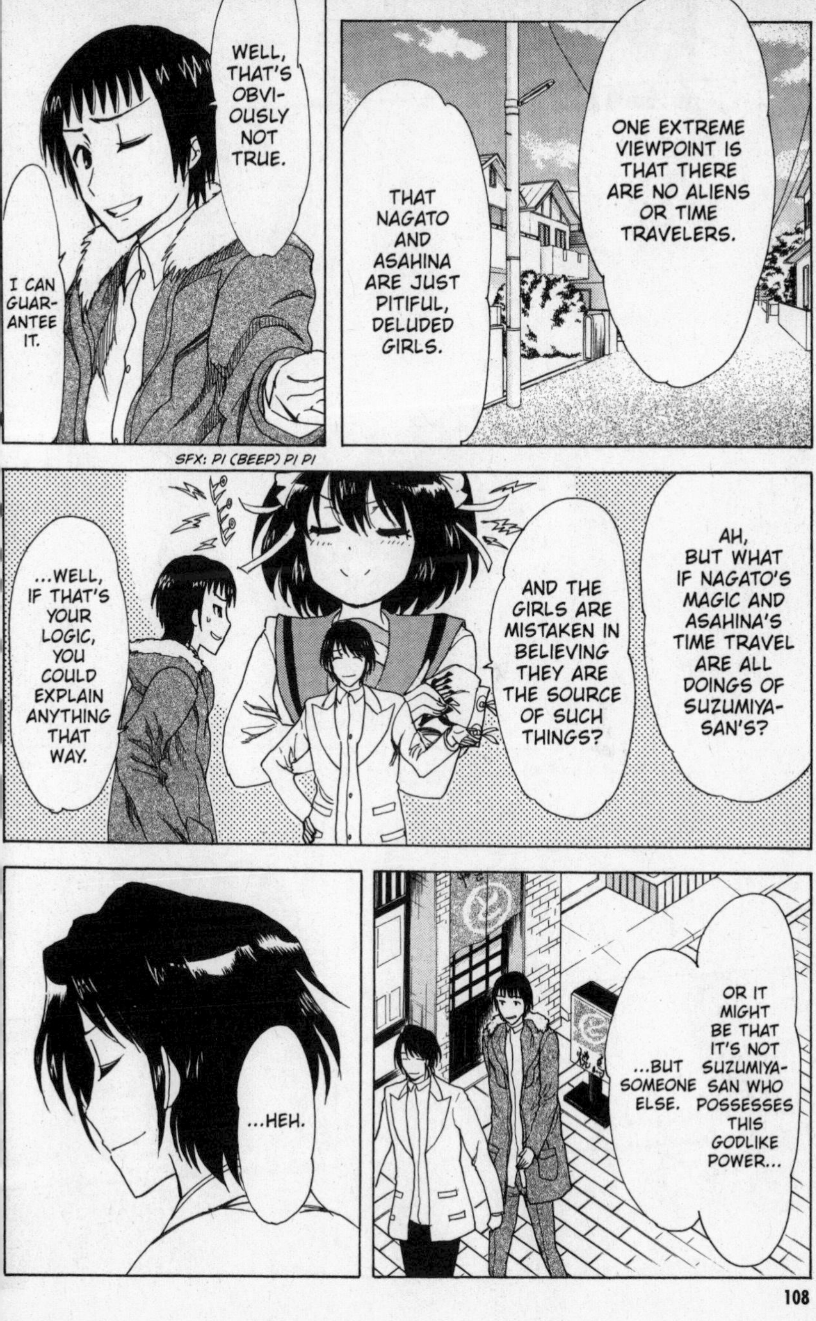
ONE EXTREME VIEWPOINT IS THAT THERE ARE NO ALIENS OR TIME TRAVELERS.
THAT NAGATO AND ASAHINA ARE JUST PITIFUL, DELUDED GIRLS.
WELL, THAT'S OBVIOUSLY NOT TRUE.
I CAN GUARANTEE IT.
SFX: PI (BEEP) PI PI
AH, BUT WHAT IF NAGATO'S MAGIC AND ASAHINA'S TIME TRAVEL ARE ALL DOINGS OF SUZUMIYA-SAN'S?
AND THE GIRLS ARE MISTAKEN IN BELIEVING THEY ARE THE SOURCE OF SUCH THINGS?
...WELL, IF THAT'S YOUR LOGIC, YOU COULD EXPLAIN ANYTHING THAT WAY.
OR IT MIGHT BE THAT IT'S NOT SUZUMIYA-SAN WHO POSSESSES THIS GODLIKE POWER...
...BUT SOMEONE ELSE.
...HEH.

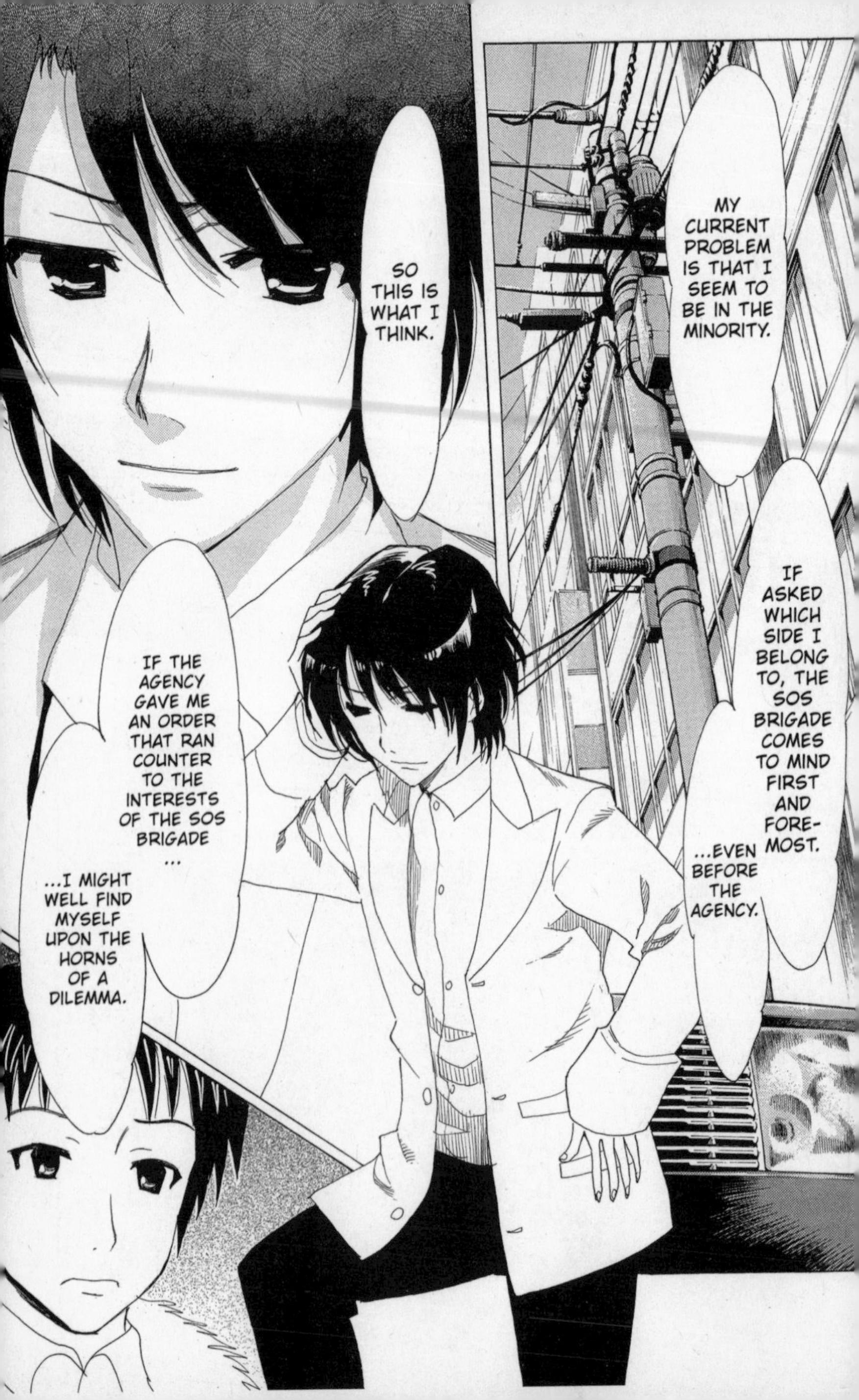
MY CURRENT PROBLEM IS THAT I SEEM TO BE IN THE MINORITY.
IF ASKED WHICH SIDE I BELONG TO, THE SOS BRIGADE COMES TO MIND FIRST AND FORE-MOST.
...EVEN BEFORE THE AGENCY.
SO THIS IS WHAT I THINK.
IF THE AGENCY GAVE ME AN ORDER THAT RAN COUNTER TO THE INTERESTS OF THE SOS BRIGADE ...
...I MIGHT WELL FIND MYSELF UPON THE HORNS OF A DILEMMA.

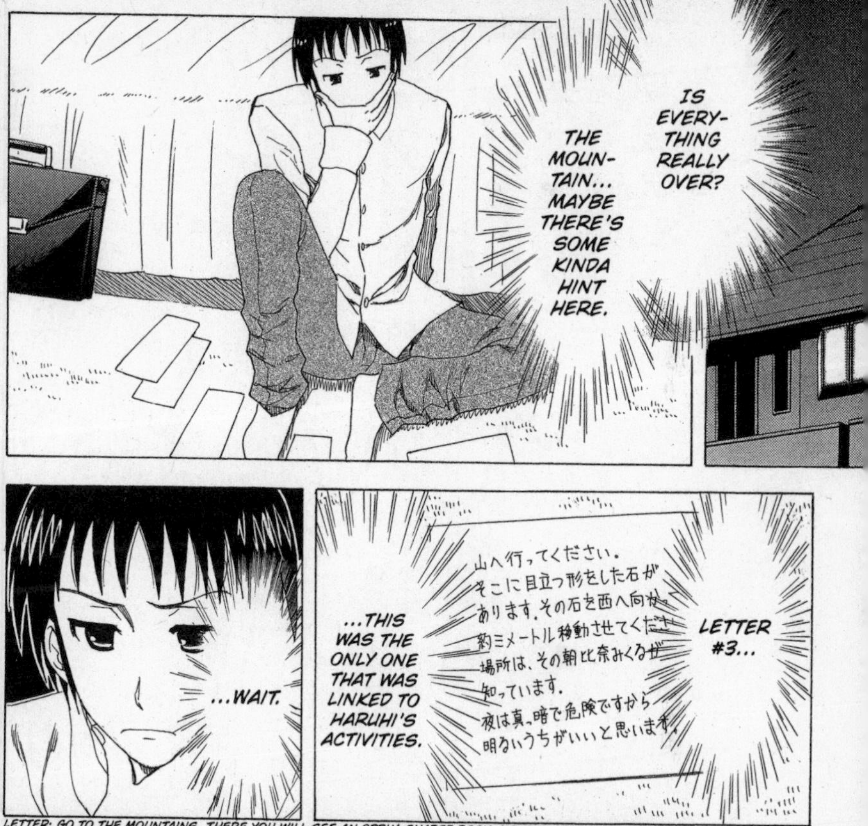
IS EVERY-THING REALLY OVER?
THE MOUN-TAIN... MAYBE THERE'S SOME KINDA HINT HERE.
LETTER #3...
山へ行ってください。
そこに目立つ形をした石が
あります。その石を西へ向かって
約三メートル移動させてください。
場所は、その朝比奈みくるが
知っています。
夜は真っ暗で危険ですから
明るいうちがいいと思います。
...THIS WAS THE ONLY ONE THAT WAS LINKED TO HARUHI'S ACTIVITIES.
...WAIT.

LETTER: GO TO THE MOUNTAINS. THERE YOU WILL SEE AN ODDLY-SHAPED ROCK. MOVE IT APPROXIMATELY THREE METERS WEST. YOUR MIKURU ASAHINA WILL KNOW THE PLACE. IT WILL BE VERY DARK AFTER NIGHTFALL, SO TRY TO FINISH DURING THE DAYLIGHT.

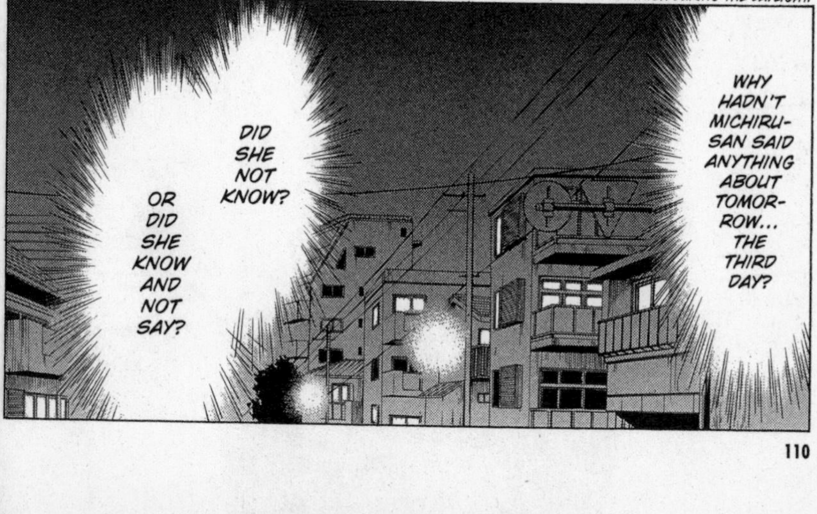
WHY HADN'T MICHIRU-SAN SAID ANYTHING ABOUT TOMOR-ROW... THE THIRD DAY?
DID SHE NOT KNOW?
OR DID SHE KNOW AND NOT SAY?

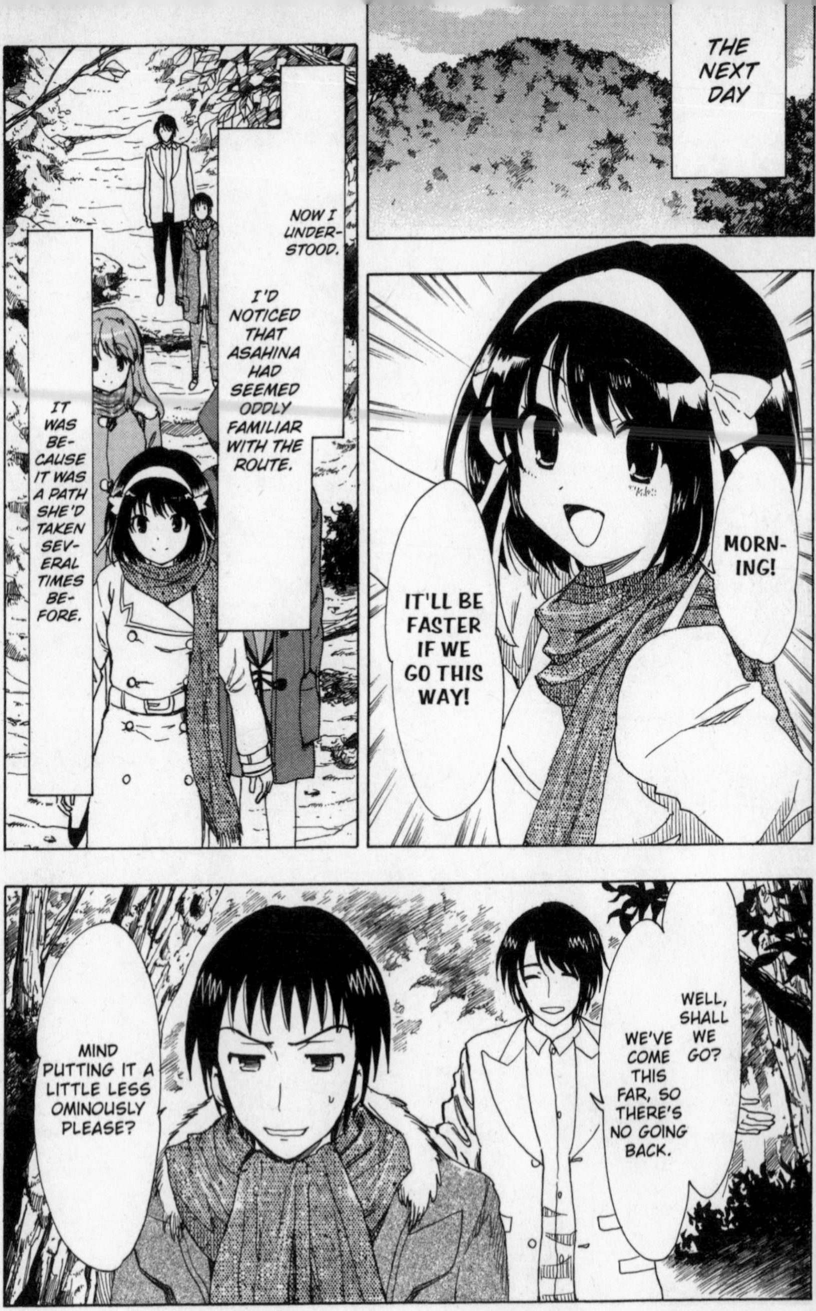
THE NEXT DAY
MORNING!
IT'LL BE FASTER IF WE GO THIS WAY!
NOW I UNDERSTOOD.
I'D NOTICED THAT ASAHINA HAD SEEMED ODDLY FAMILIAR WITH THE ROUTE.
IT WAS BECAUSE IT WAS A PATH SHE'D TAKEN SEVERAL TIMES BEFORE.
WELL, SHALL WE GO?
WE'VE COME THIS FAR, SO THERE'S NO GOING BACK.
MIND PUTTING IT A LITTLE LESS OMINOUSLY PLEASE?

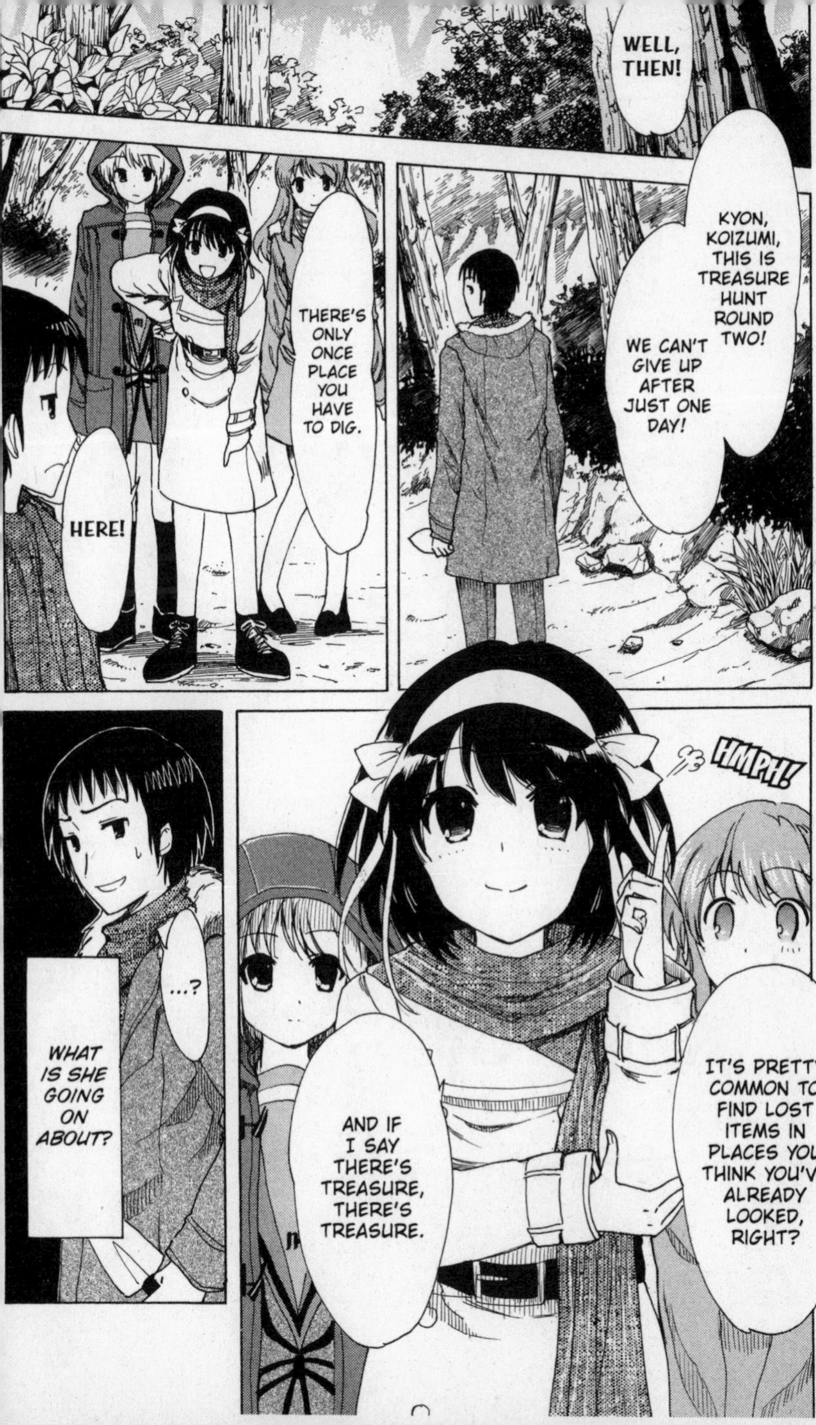
WELL, THEN!
KYON, KOIZUMI, THIS IS TREASURE HUNT ROUND TWO!
WE CAN'T GIVE UP AFTER JUST ONE DAY!
THERE'S ONLY ONCE PLACE YOU HAVE TO DIG.
HERE!
HMPH!
IT'S PRETTY COMMON TO FIND LOST ITEMS IN PLACES YOU THINK YOU'VE ALREADY LOOKED, RIGHT?
AND IF I SAY THERE'S TREASURE, THERE'S TREASURE.
...?
WHAT IS SHE GOING ON ABOUT?

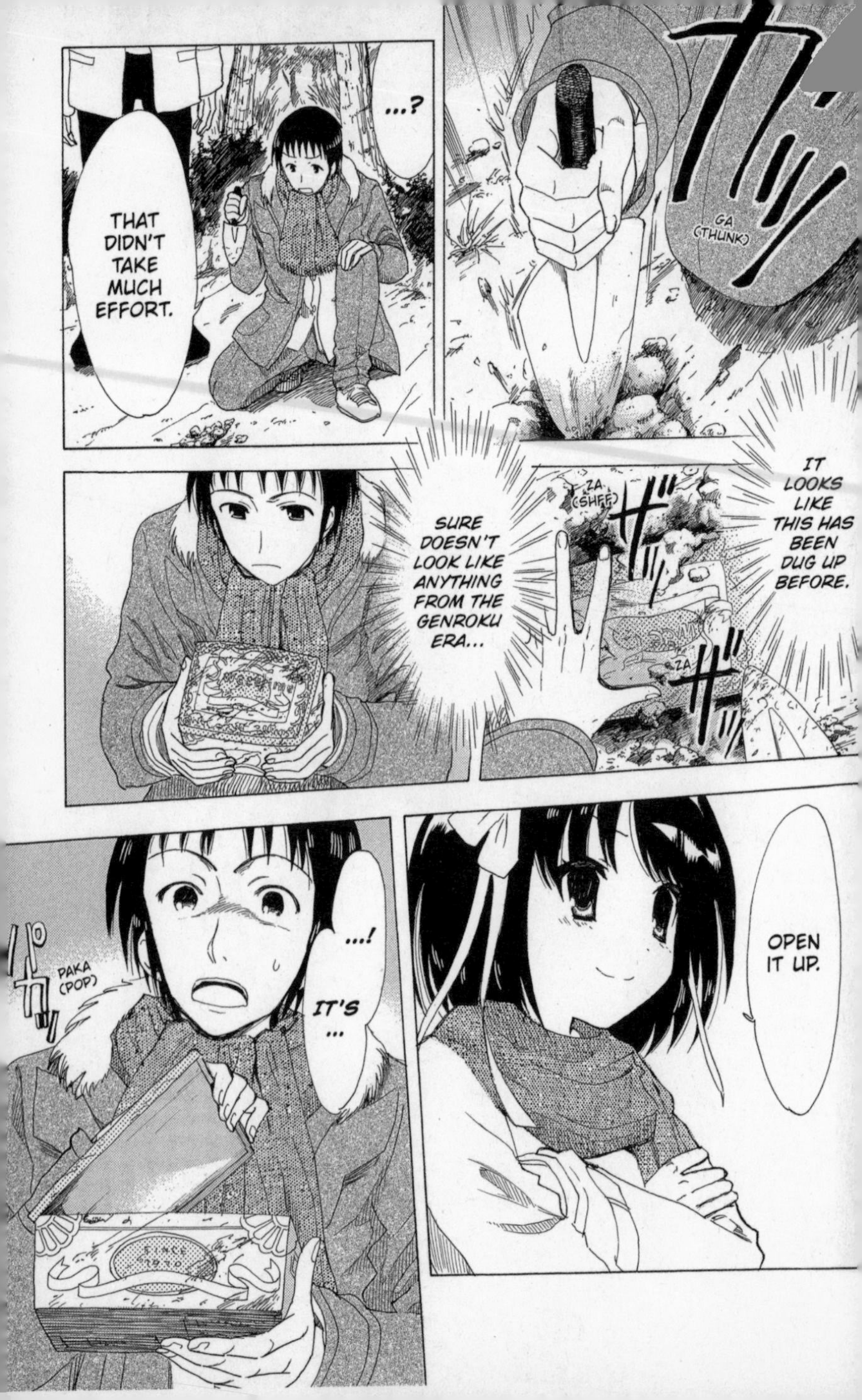
GA (THUNK)
...?
THAT DIDN'T TAKE MUCH EFFORT.
ZA (SHFF)
IT LOOKS LIKE THIS HAS BEEN DUG UP BEFORE.
ZA
SURE DOESN'T LOOK LIKE ANYTHING FROM THE GENROKU ERA...
OPEN IT UP.
...!
IT'S ...
PAKA (POP)

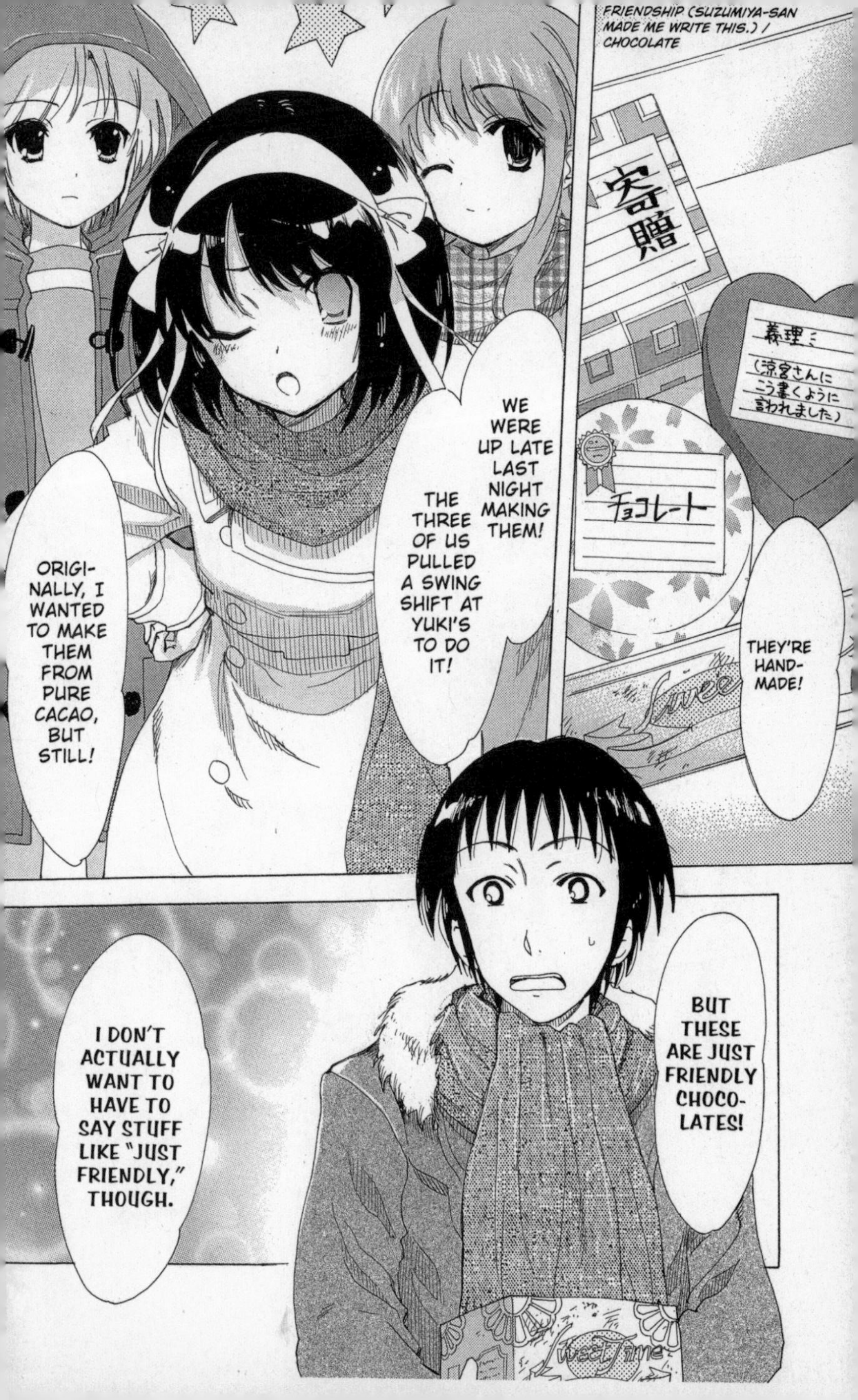
FRIENDSHIP (SUZUMIYA-SAN MADE ME WRITE THIS.) / CHOCOLATE
寄贈
義理
(涼宮さんにこう書くように言われました)
チョコレート
THEY'RE HAND-MADE!
WE WERE UP LATE LAST NIGHT MAKING THEM!
THE THREE OF US PULLED A SWING SHIFT AT YUKI'S TO DO IT!
ORIGI-NALLY, I WANTED TO MAKE THEM FROM PURE CACAO, BUT STILL!
BUT THESE ARE JUST FRIENDLY CHOCO-LATES!
I DON'T ACTUALLY WANT TO HAVE TO SAY STUFF LIKE "JUST FRIENDLY," THOUGH.

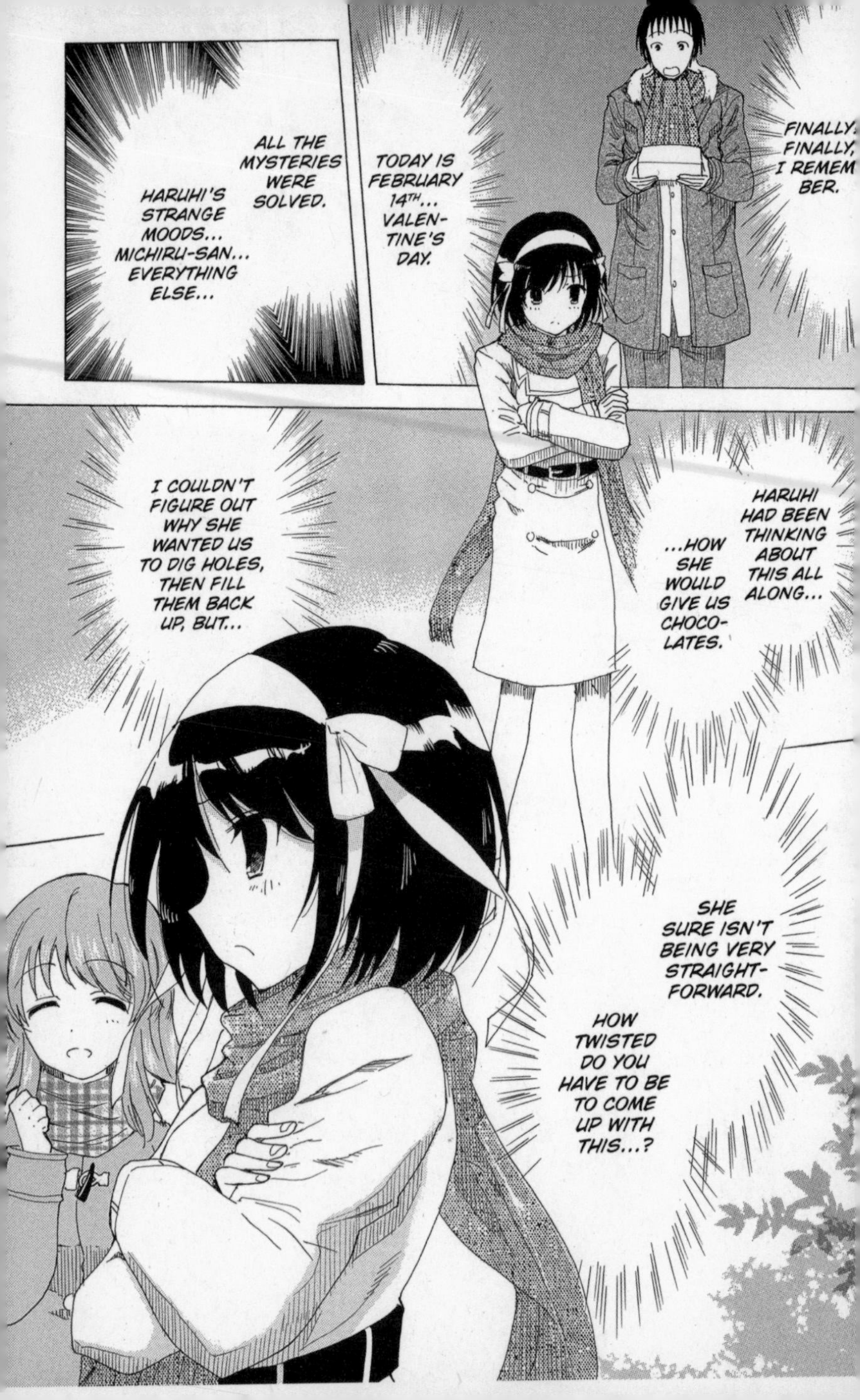
FINALLY. FINALLY, I REMEMBER.
TODAY IS FEBRUARY 14TH... VALENTINE'S DAY.
ALL THE MYSTERIES WERE SOLVED.
HARUHI'S STRANGE MOODS... MICHIRU-SAN... EVERYTHING ELSE...
I COULDN'T FIGURE OUT WHY SHE WANTED US TO DIG HOLES, THEN FILL THEM BACK UP, BUT...
HARUHI HAD BEEN THINKING ABOUT THIS ALL ALONG...
...HOW SHE WOULD GIVE US CHOCOLATES.
SHE SURE ISN'T BEING VERY STRAIGHTFORWARD.
HOW TWISTED DO YOU HAVE TO BE TO COME UP WITH THIS...?

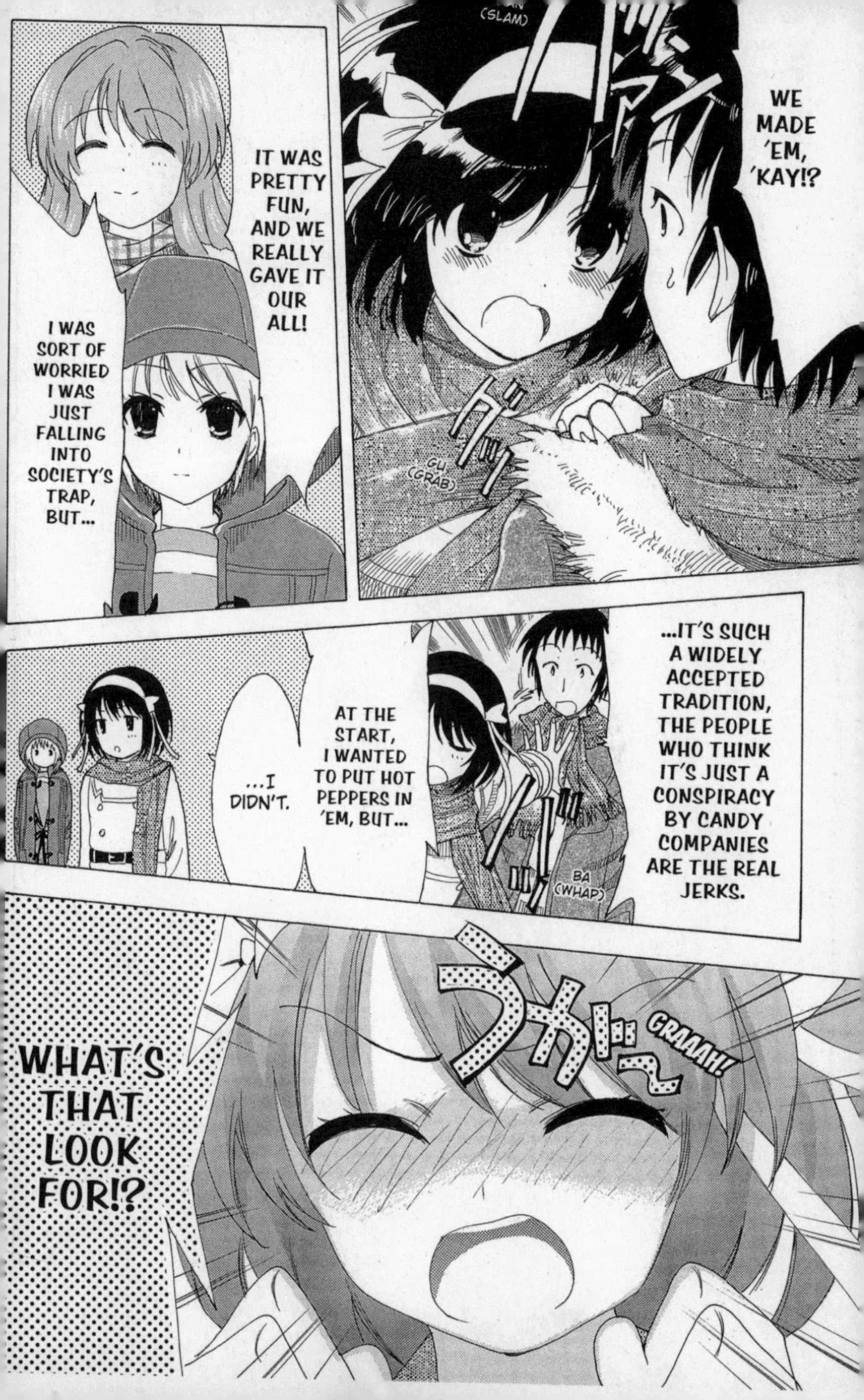

(SLAM)
WE MADE 'EM, 'KAY!?
GU (GRAB)
IT WAS PRETTY FUN, AND WE REALLY GAVE IT OUR ALL!
I WAS SORT OF WORRIED I WAS JUST FALLING INTO SOCIETY'S TRAP, BUT...
...IT'S SUCH A WIDELY ACCEPTED TRADITION, THE PEOPLE WHO THINK IT'S JUST A CONSPIRACY BY CANDY COMPANIES ARE THE REAL JERKS.
BA (WHAP)
AT THE START, I WANTED TO PUT HOT PEPPERS IN 'EM, BUT...
...I DIDN'T.
GRAAAH!
WHAT'S THAT LOOK FOR!?

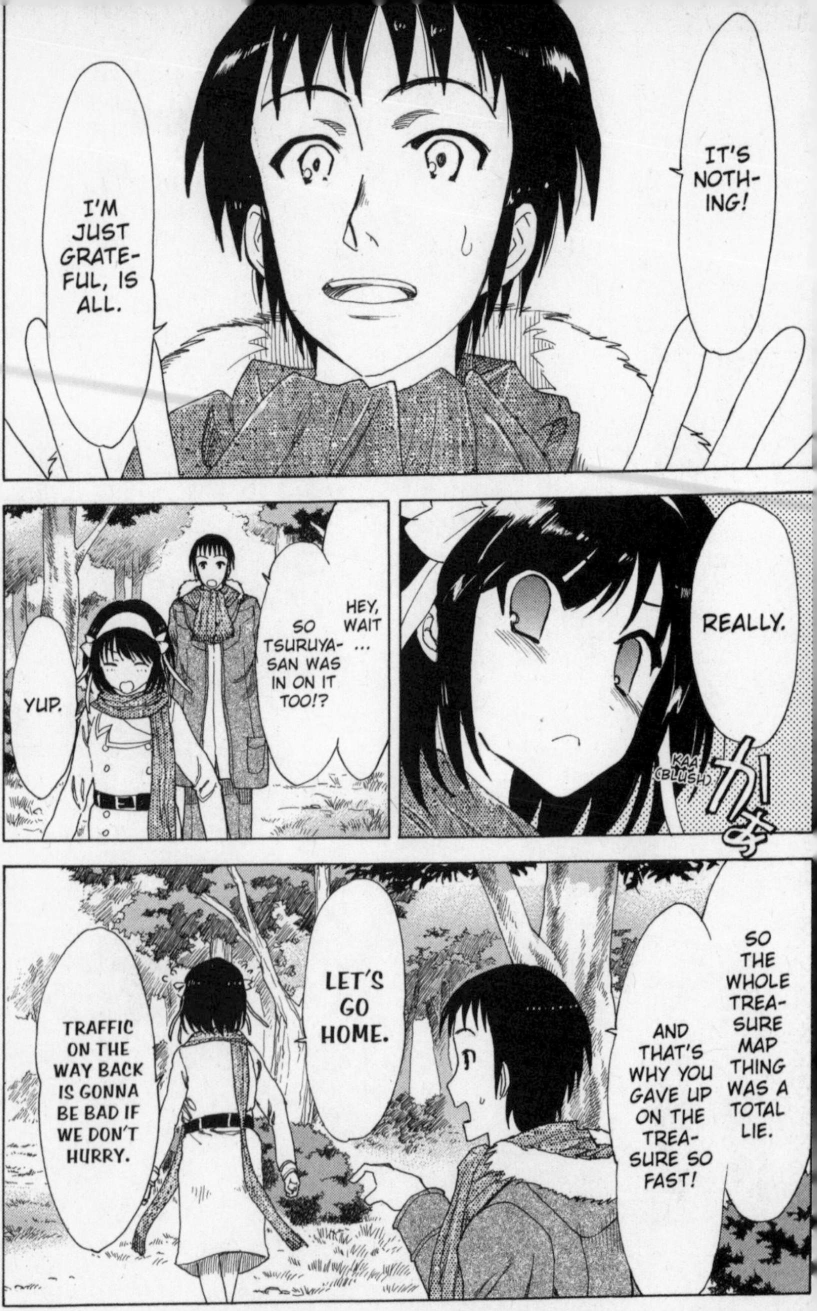
IT'S NOTH-ING!
I'M JUST GRATE-FUL, IS ALL.
REALLY.
KAA (BLUSH)
かぁ
HEY, WAIT ...
SO TSURUYA-SAN WAS IN ON IT TOO!?
YUP.
SO THE WHOLE TREA-SURE MAP THING WAS A TOTAL LIE.
AND THAT'S WHY YOU GAVE UP ON THE TREA-SURE SO FAST!
LET'S GO HOME.
TRAFFIC ON THE WAY BACK IS GONNA BE BAD IF WE DON'T HURRY.

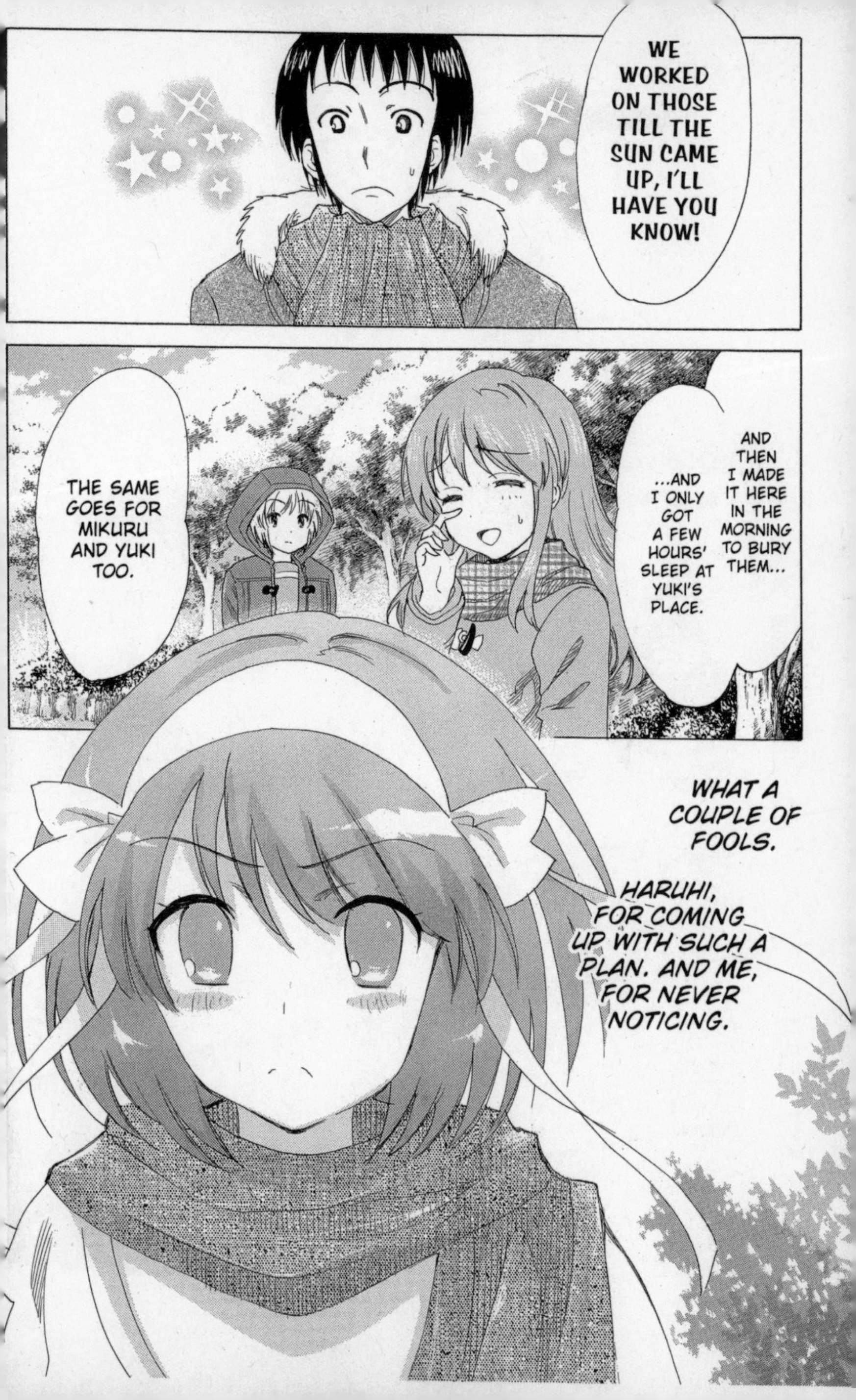
WE WORKED ON THOSE TILL THE SUN CAME UP, I'LL HAVE YOU KNOW!
...AND I ONLY GOT A FEW HOURS' SLEEP AT YUKI'S PLACE.
AND THEN I MADE IT HERE IN THE MORNING TO BURY THEM...
THE SAME GOES FOR MIKURU AND YUKI TOO.
WHAT A COUPLE OF FOOLS.
HARUHI, FOR COMING UP WITH SUCH A PLAN. AND ME, FOR NEVER NOTICING.

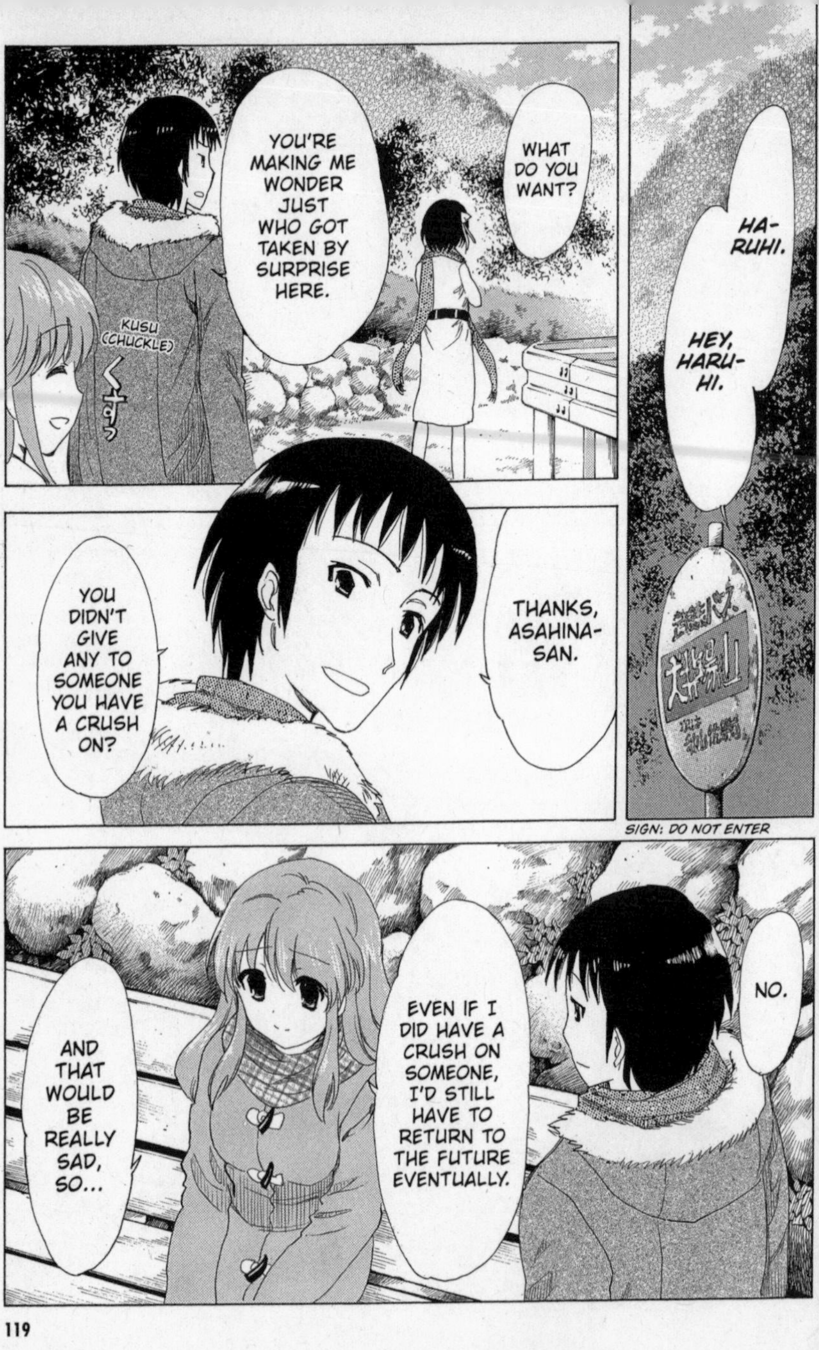
HA-RUHI.
HEY, HARU-HI.
WHAT DO YOU WANT?
YOU'RE MAKING ME WONDER JUST WHO GOT TAKEN BY SURPRISE HERE.
KUSU (CHUCKLE)
くすっ
THANKS, ASAHINA-SAN.
YOU DIDN'T GIVE ANY TO SOMEONE YOU HAVE A CRUSH ON?
NO.
EVEN IF I DID HAVE A CRUSH ON SOMEONE, I'D STILL HAVE TO RETURN TO THE FUTURE EVENTUALLY.
AND THAT WOULD BE REALLY SAD, SO...
SIGN: DO NOT ENTER

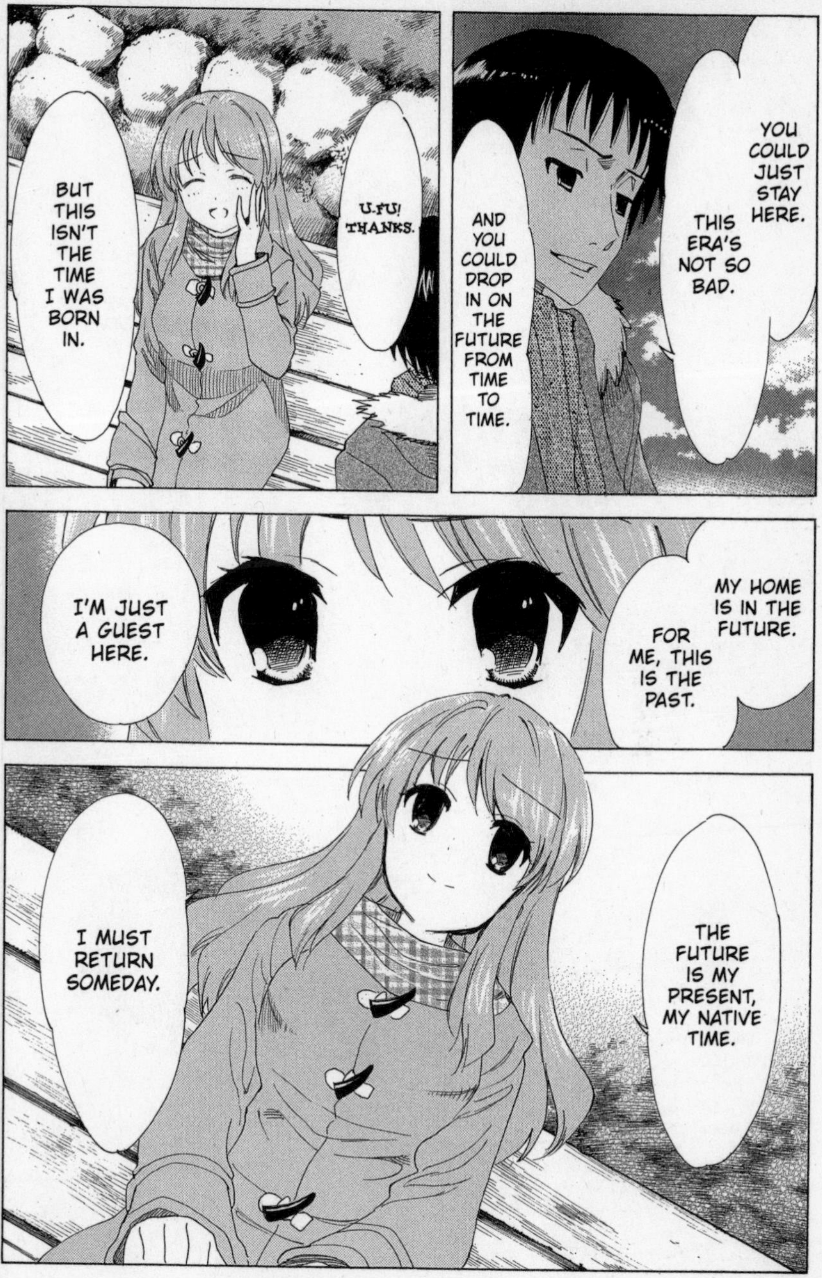
YOU COULD JUST STAY HERE.
THIS ERA'S NOT SO BAD.
AND YOU COULD DROP IN ON THE FUTURE FROM TIME TO TIME.
U-FU! THANKS.
BUT THIS ISN'T THE TIME I WAS BORN IN.
MY HOME IS IN THE FUTURE.
FOR ME, THIS IS THE PAST.
I'M JUST A GUEST HERE.
THE FUTURE IS MY PRESENT, MY NATIVE TIME.
I MUST RETURN SOMEDAY.

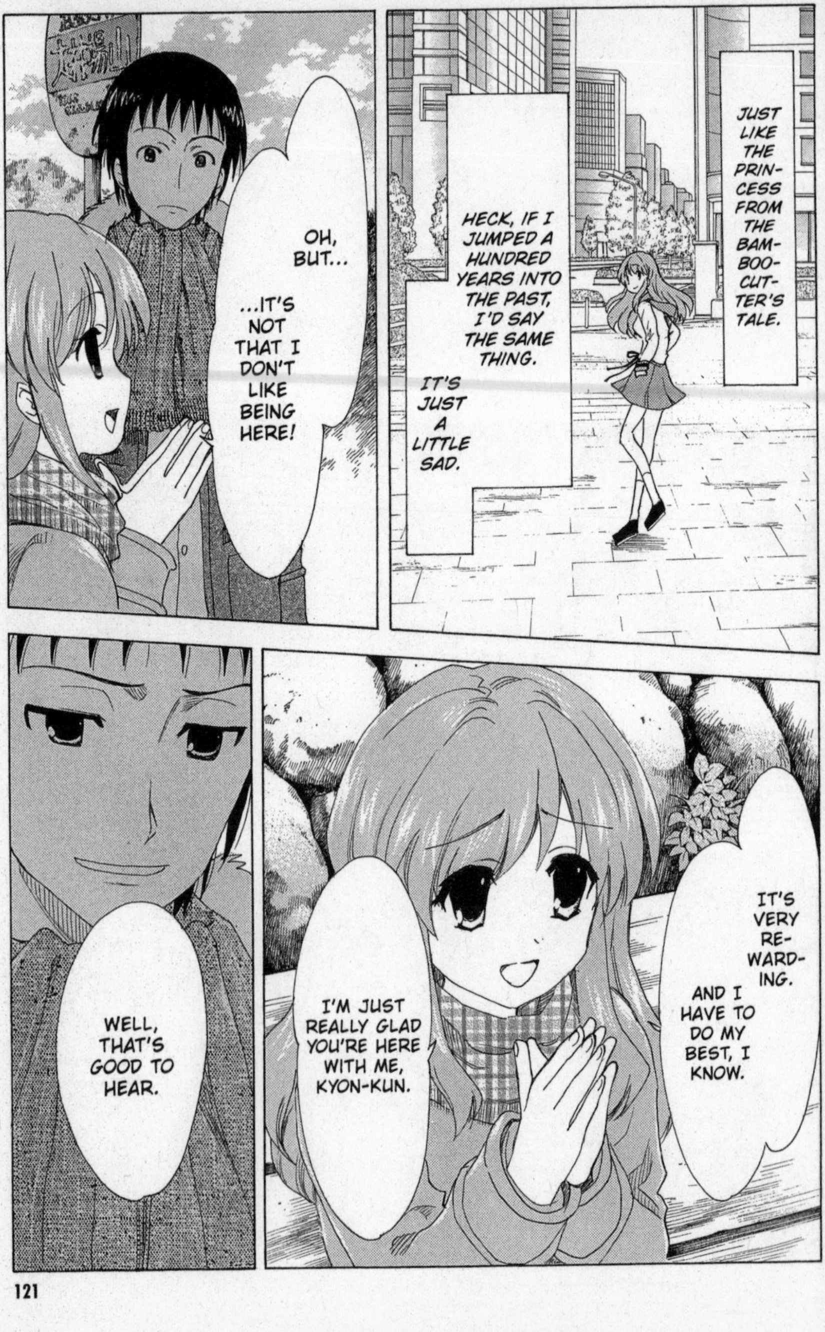
JUST LIKE THE PRIN-CESS FROM THE BAM-BOO-CUT-TER'S TALE.
HECK, IF I JUMPED A HUNDRED YEARS INTO THE PAST, I'D SAY THE SAME THING.
IT'S JUST A LITTLE SAD.
OH, BUT...
...IT'S NOT THAT I DON'T LIKE BEING HERE!
IT'S VERY RE-WARD-ING.
AND I HAVE TO DO MY BEST, I KNOW.
I'M JUST REALLY GLAD YOU'RE HERE WITH ME, KYON-KUN.
WELL, THAT'S GOOD TO HEAR.

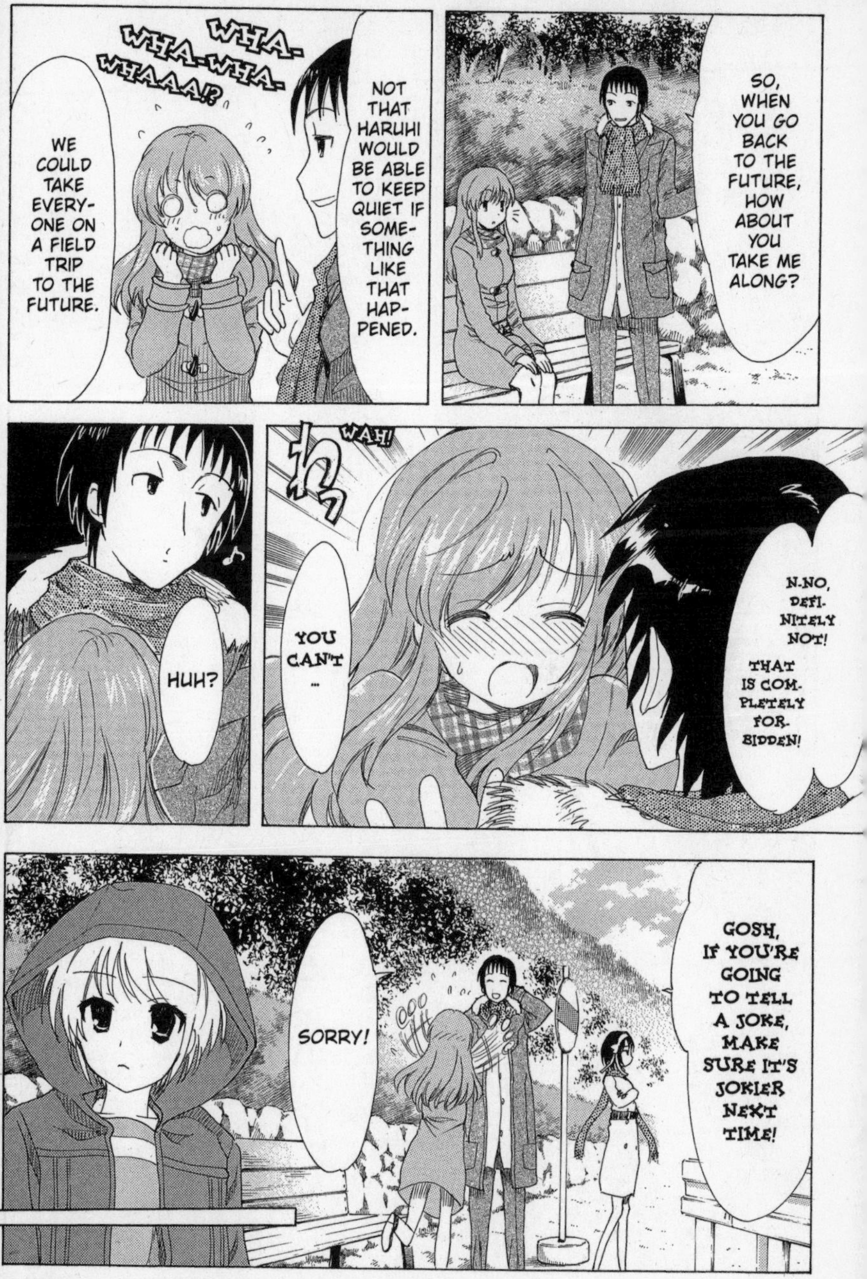
SO, WHEN YOU GO BACK TO THE FUTURE, HOW ABOUT YOU TAKE ME ALONG?
NOT THAT HARUHI WOULD BE ABLE TO KEEP QUIET IF SOMETHING LIKE THAT HAPPENED.
WHA-WHA-WHAAAA!?
WE COULD TAKE EVERYONE ON A FIELD TRIP TO THE FUTURE.
WAH!
N-NO, DEFINITELY NOT!
THAT IS COMPLETELY FORBIDDEN!
YOU CAN'T ...
HUH?
GOSH, IF YOU'RE GOING TO TELL A JOKE, MAKE SURE IT'S JOKIER NEXT TIME!
SORRY!

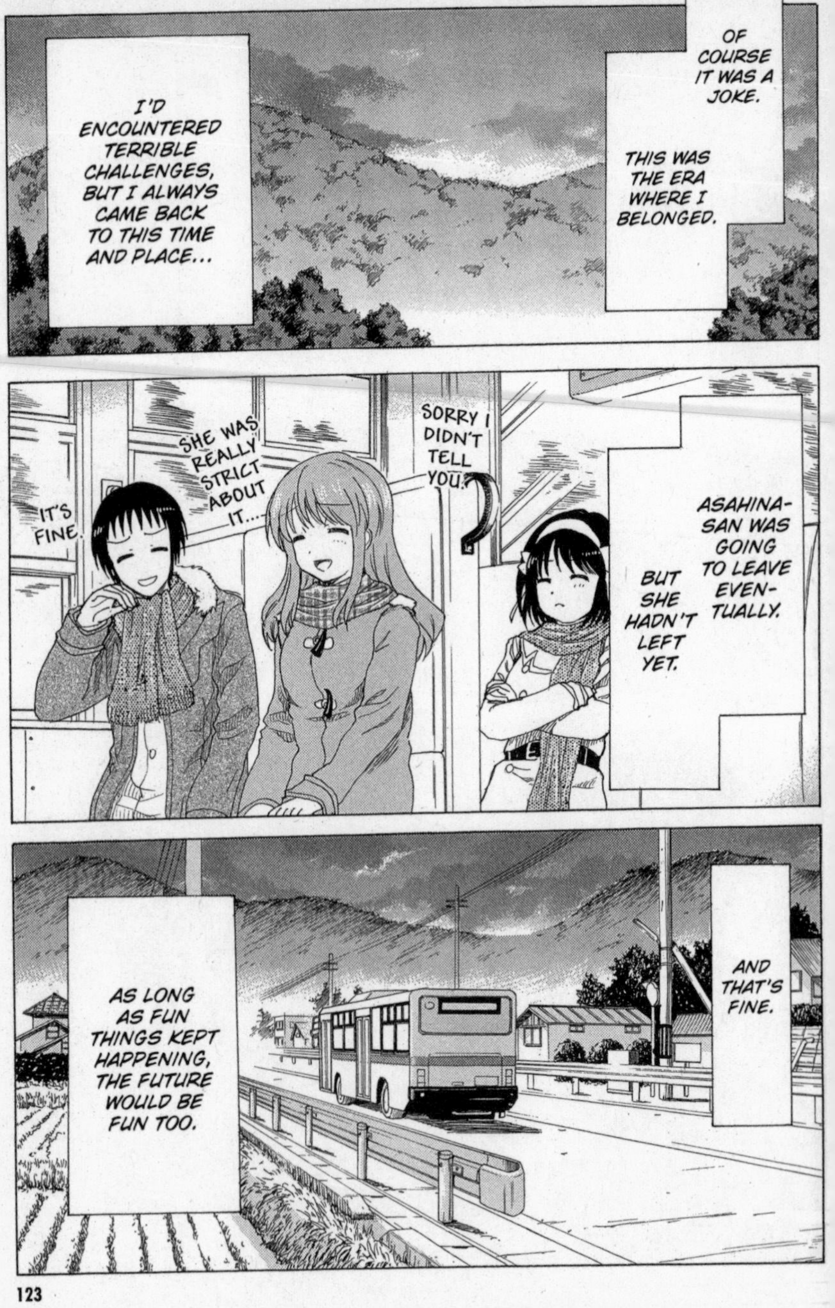
OF COURSE IT WAS A JOKE.
THIS WAS THE ERA WHERE I BELONGED.
I'D ENCOUNTERED TERRIBLE CHALLENGES, BUT I ALWAYS CAME BACK TO THIS TIME AND PLACE...
ASAHINA-SAN WAS GOING TO LEAVE EVEN-TUALLY.
BUT SHE HADN'T LEFT YET.
SORRY I DIDN'T TELL YOU.
SHE WAS REALLY STRICT ABOUT IT...
IT'S FINE.
AND THAT'S FINE.
AS LONG AS FUN THINGS KEPT HAPPENING, THE FUTURE WOULD BE FUN TOO.

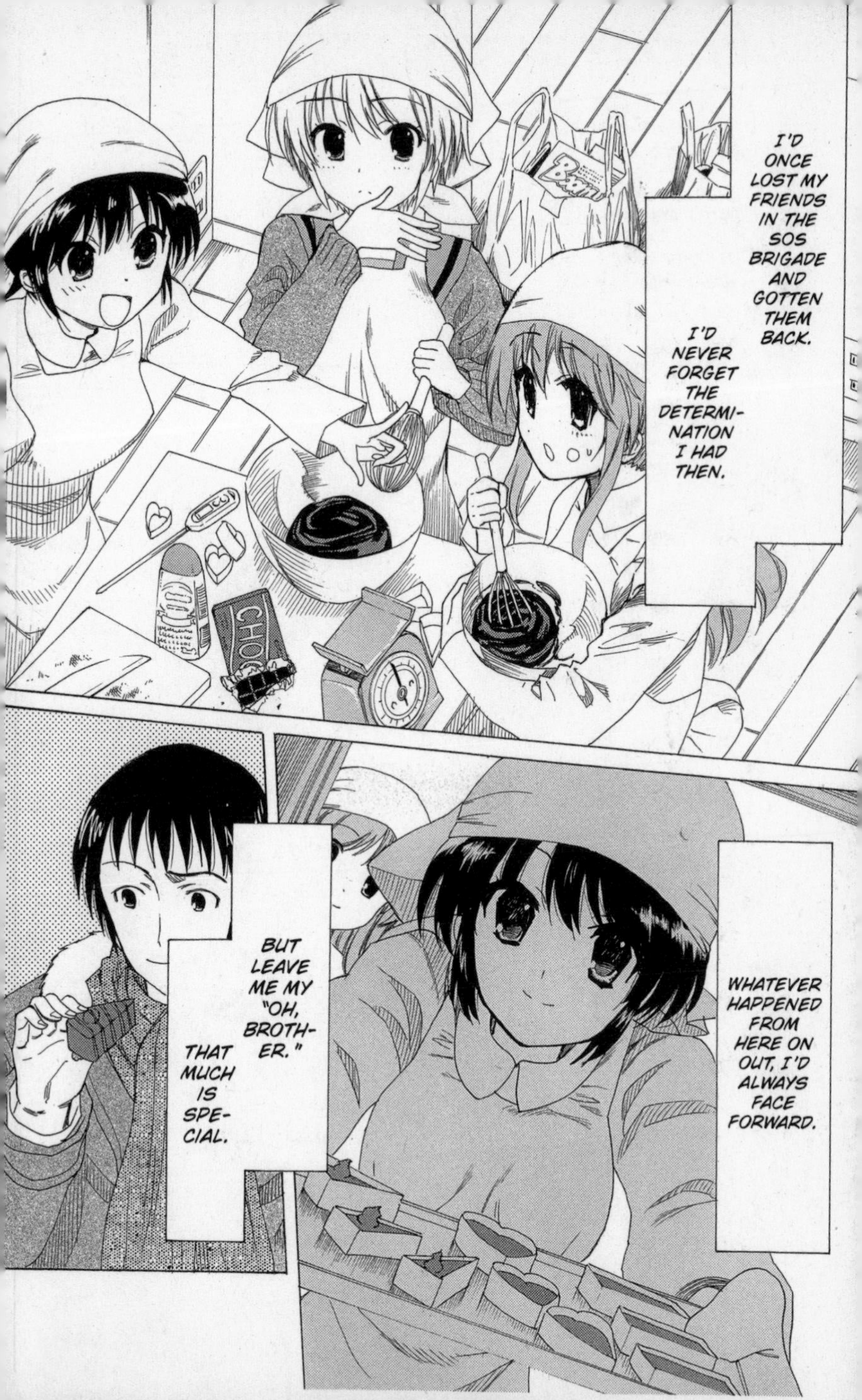
I'D ONCE LOST MY FRIENDS IN THE SOS BRIGADE AND GOTTEN THEM BACK.
I'D NEVER FORGET THE DETERMINATION I HAD THEN.
CHOC
WHATEVER HAPPENED FROM HERE ON OUT, I'D ALWAYS FACE FORWARD.
BUT LEAVE ME MY "OH, BROTHER."
THAT MUCH IS SPECIAL.

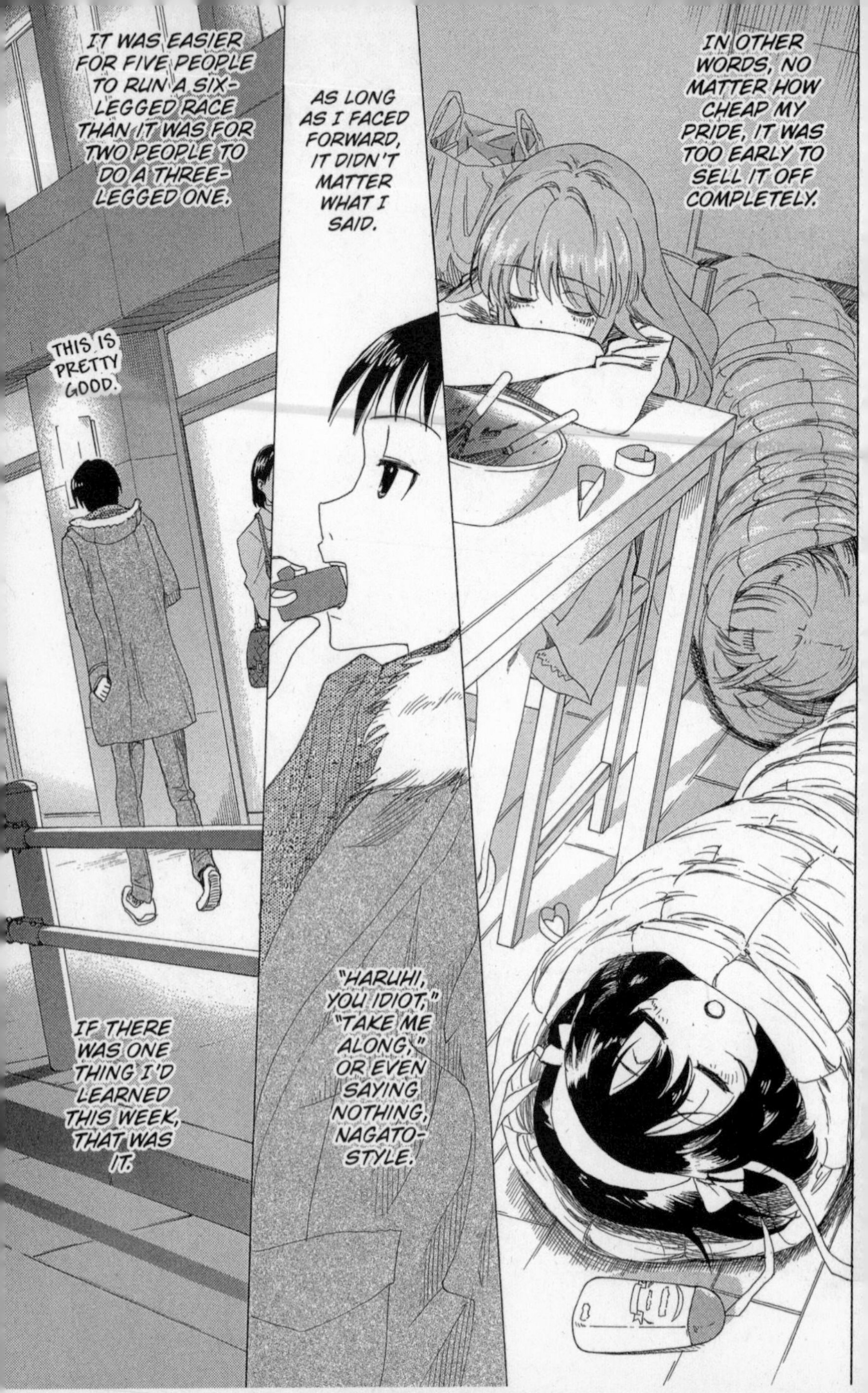
IN OTHER WORDS, NO MATTER HOW CHEAP MY PRIDE, IT WAS TOO EARLY TO SELL IT OFF COMPLETELY.
AS LONG AS I FACED FORWARD, IT DIDN'T MATTER WHAT I SAID.
"HARUHI, YOU IDIOT," "TAKE ME ALONG," OR EVEN SAYING NOTHING, NAGATO-STYLE.
IT WAS EASIER FOR FIVE PEOPLE TO RUN A SIX-LEGGED RACE THAN IT WAS FOR TWO PEOPLE TO DO A THREE-LEGGED ONE.
THIS IS PRETTY GOOD.
IF THERE WAS ONE THING I'D LEARNED THIS WEEK, THAT WAS IT.

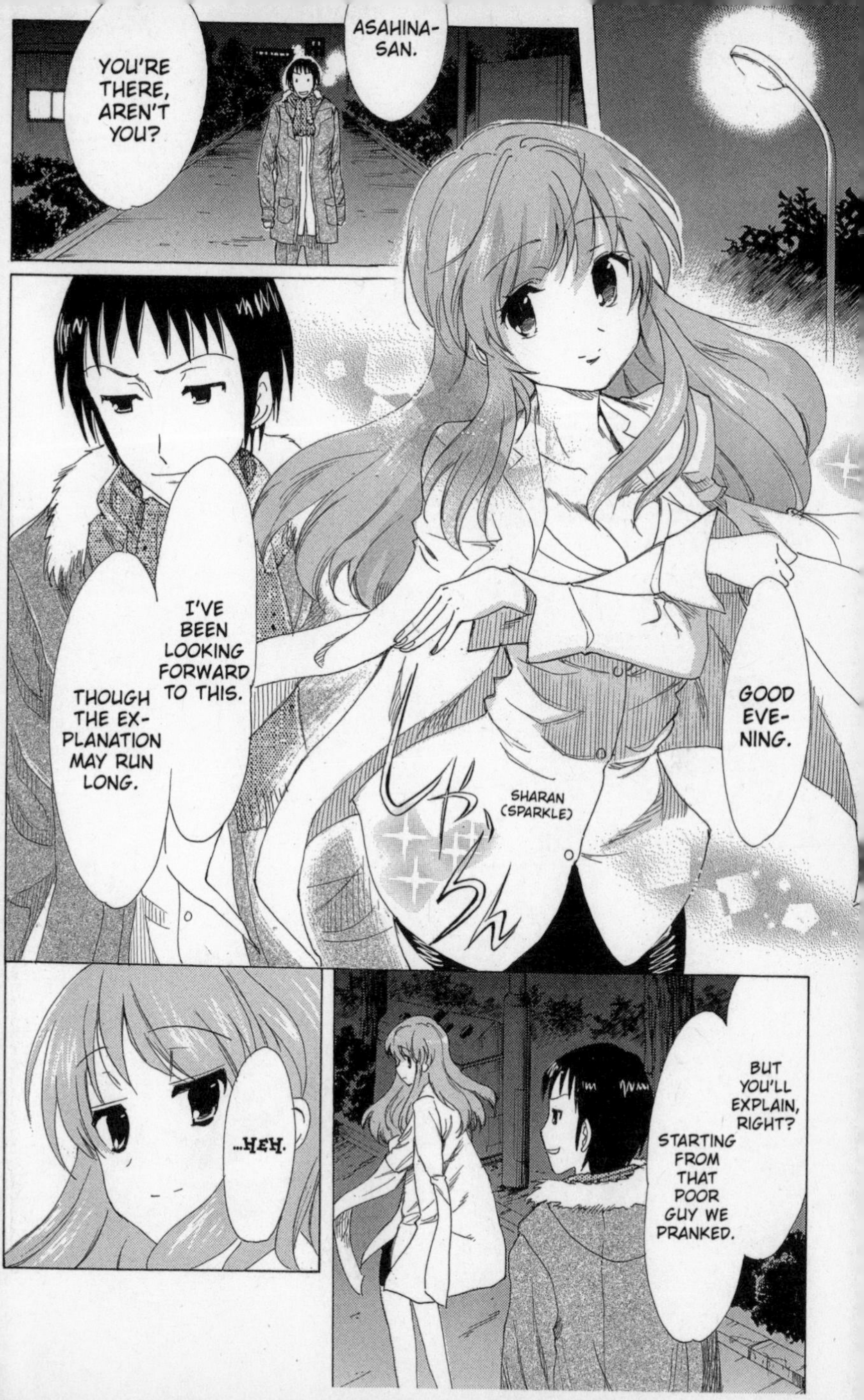
ASAHINA-SAN.
YOU'RE THERE, AREN'T YOU?
GOOD EVE-NING.
SHARAN (SPARKLE)
I'VE BEEN LOOKING FORWARD TO THIS.
THOUGH THE EX-PLANATION MAY RUN LONG.
BUT YOU'LL EXPLAIN, RIGHT?
STARTING FROM THAT POOR GUY WE PRANKED.
...HEH.

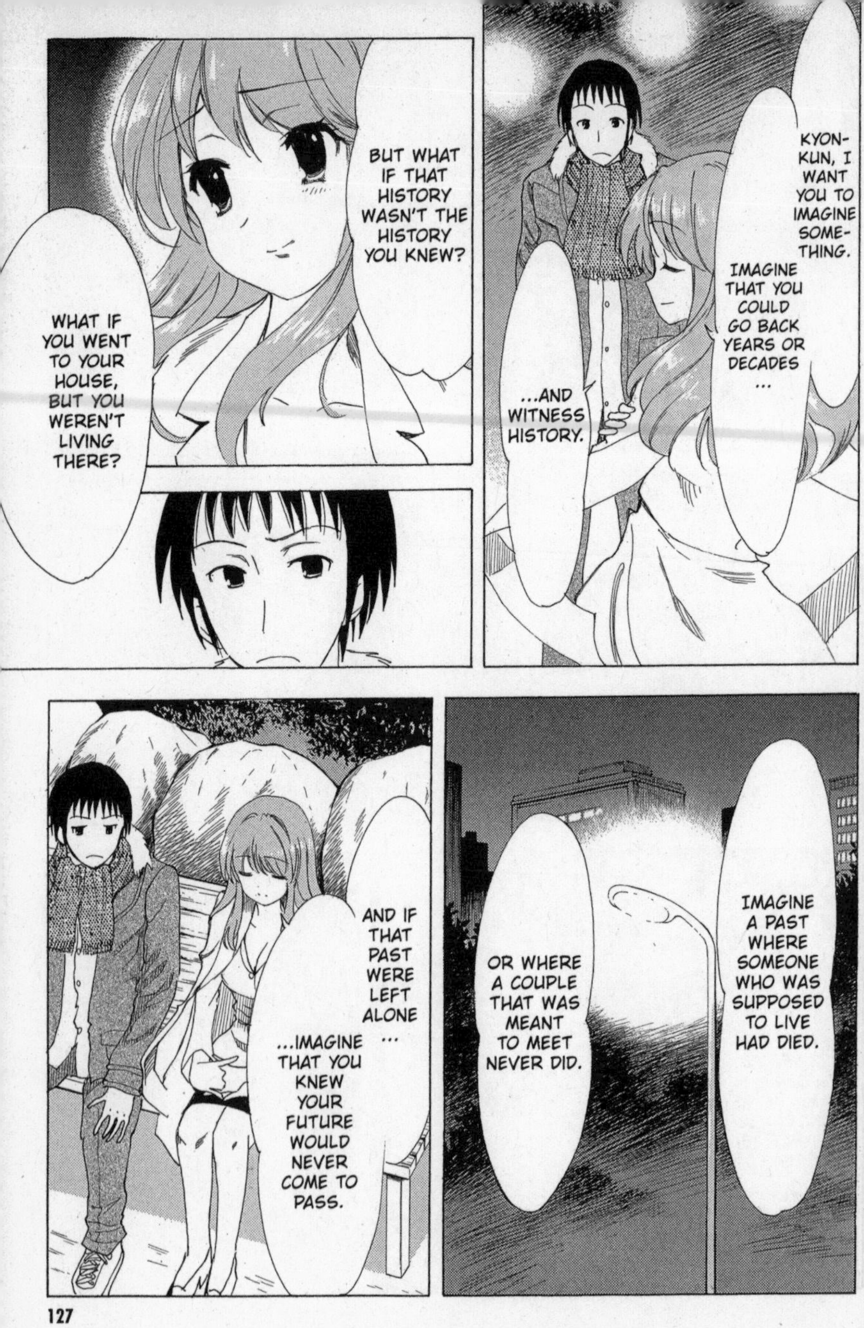
KYON-KUN, I WANT YOU TO IMAGINE SOMETHING.
IMAGINE THAT YOU COULD GO BACK YEARS OR DECADES...
...AND WITNESS HISTORY.
BUT WHAT IF THAT HISTORY WASN'T THE HISTORY YOU KNEW?
WHAT IF YOU WENT TO YOUR HOUSE, BUT YOU WEREN'T LIVING THERE?
IMAGINE A PAST WHERE SOMEONE WHO WAS SUPPOSED TO LIVE HAD DIED.
OR WHERE A COUPLE THAT WAS MEANT TO MEET NEVER DID.
AND IF THAT PAST WERE LEFT ALONE...
...IMAGINE THAT YOU KNEW YOUR FUTURE WOULD NEVER COME TO PASS.

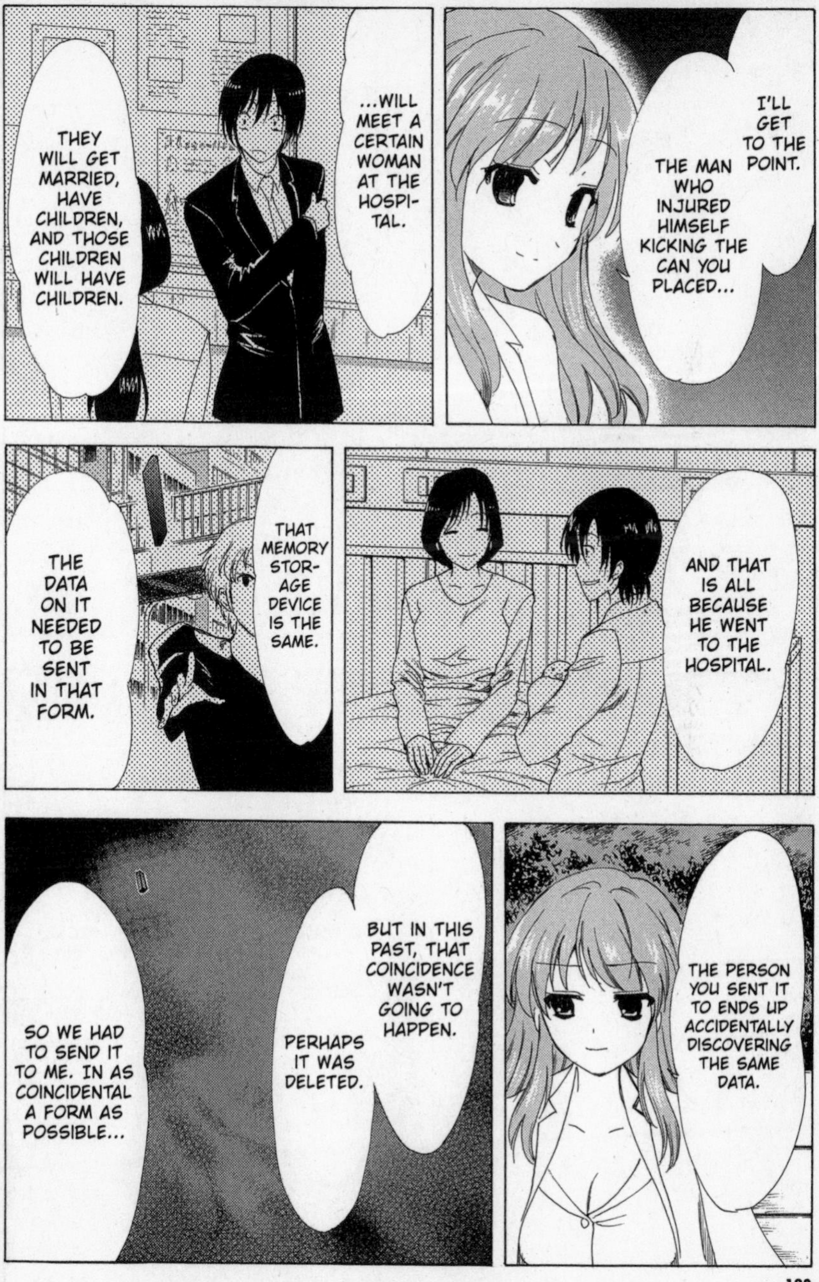
I'LL GET TO THE POINT.
THE MAN WHO INJURED HIMSELF KICKING THE CAN YOU PLACED...
...WILL MEET A CERTAIN WOMAN AT THE HOSPI-TAL.
THEY WILL GET MARRIED, HAVE CHILDREN, AND THOSE CHILDREN WILL HAVE CHILDREN.
AND THAT IS ALL BECAUSE HE WENT TO THE HOSPITAL.
THAT MEMORY STOR-AGE DEVICE IS THE SAME.
THE DATA ON IT NEEDED TO BE SENT IN THAT FORM.
THE PERSON YOU SENT IT TO ENDS UP ACCIDENTALLY DISCOVERING THE SAME DATA.
BUT IN THIS PAST, THAT COINCIDENCE WASN'T GOING TO HAPPEN.
PERHAPS IT WAS DELETED.
SO WE HAD TO SEND IT TO ME. IN AS COINCIDENTAL A FORM AS POSSIBLE...

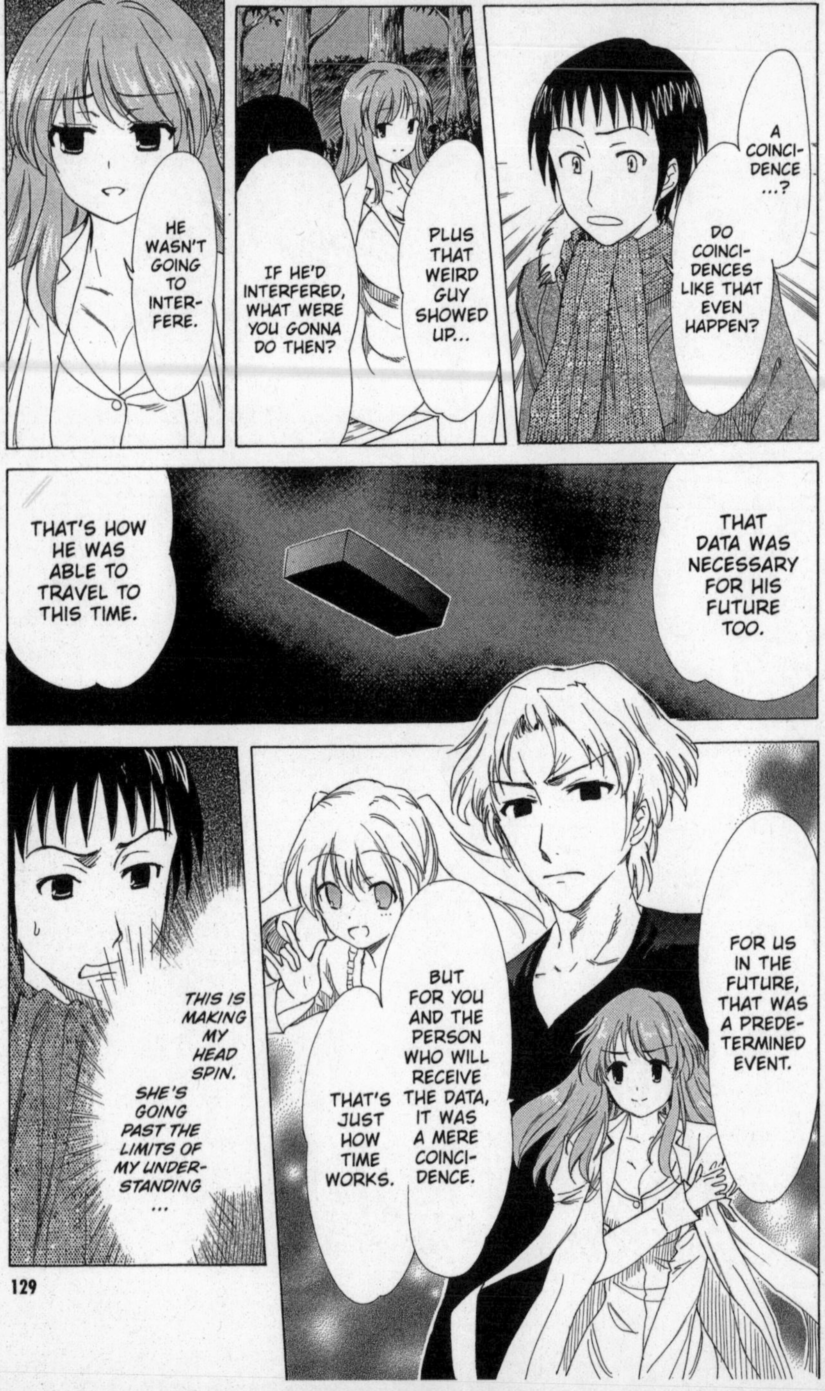
A COINCIDENCE...?
DO COINCIDENCES LIKE THAT EVEN HAPPEN?
PLUS THAT WEIRD GUY SHOWED UP...
IF HE'D INTERFERED, WHAT WERE YOU GONNA DO THEN?
HE WASN'T GOING TO INTERFERE.
THAT DATA WAS NECESSARY FOR HIS FUTURE TOO.
THAT'S HOW HE WAS ABLE TO TRAVEL TO THIS TIME.
FOR US IN THE FUTURE, THAT WAS A PREDETERMINED EVENT.
BUT FOR YOU AND THE PERSON WHO WILL RECEIVE THE DATA, IT WAS A MERE COINCIDENCE.
THAT'S JUST HOW TIME WORKS.
THIS IS MAKING MY HEAD SPIN.
SHE'S GOING PAST THE LIMITS OF MY UNDERSTANDING...

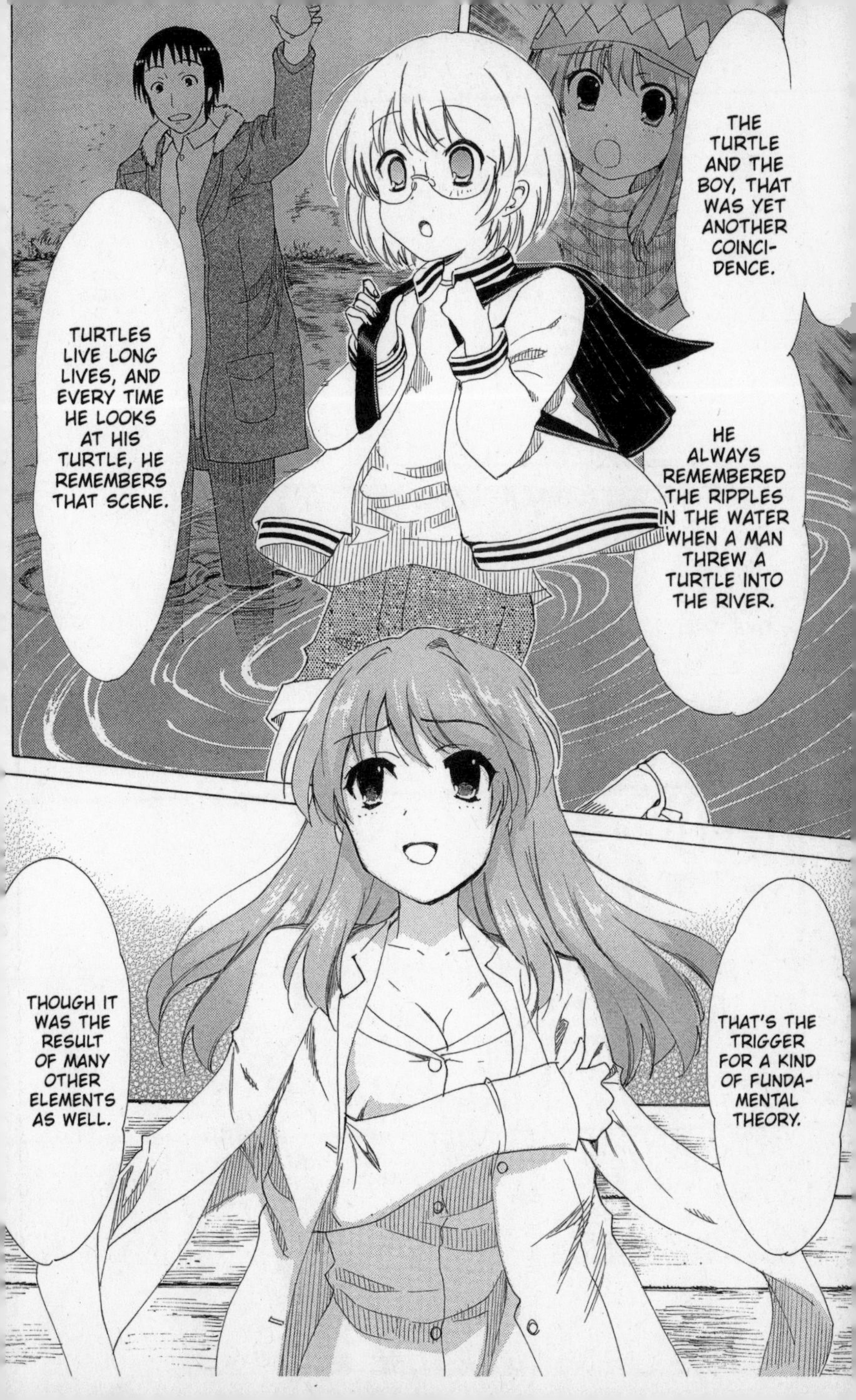
THE TURTLE AND THE BOY, THAT WAS YET ANOTHER COINCI-DENCE.
HE ALWAYS REMEMBERED THE RIPPLES IN THE WATER WHEN A MAN THREW A TURTLE INTO THE RIVER.
TURTLES LIVE LONG LIVES, AND EVERY TIME HE LOOKS AT HIS TURTLE, HE REMEMBERS THAT SCENE.
THAT'S THE TRIGGER FOR A KIND OF FUNDA-MENTAL THEORY.
THOUGH IT WAS THE RESULT OF MANY OTHER ELEMENTS AS WELL.

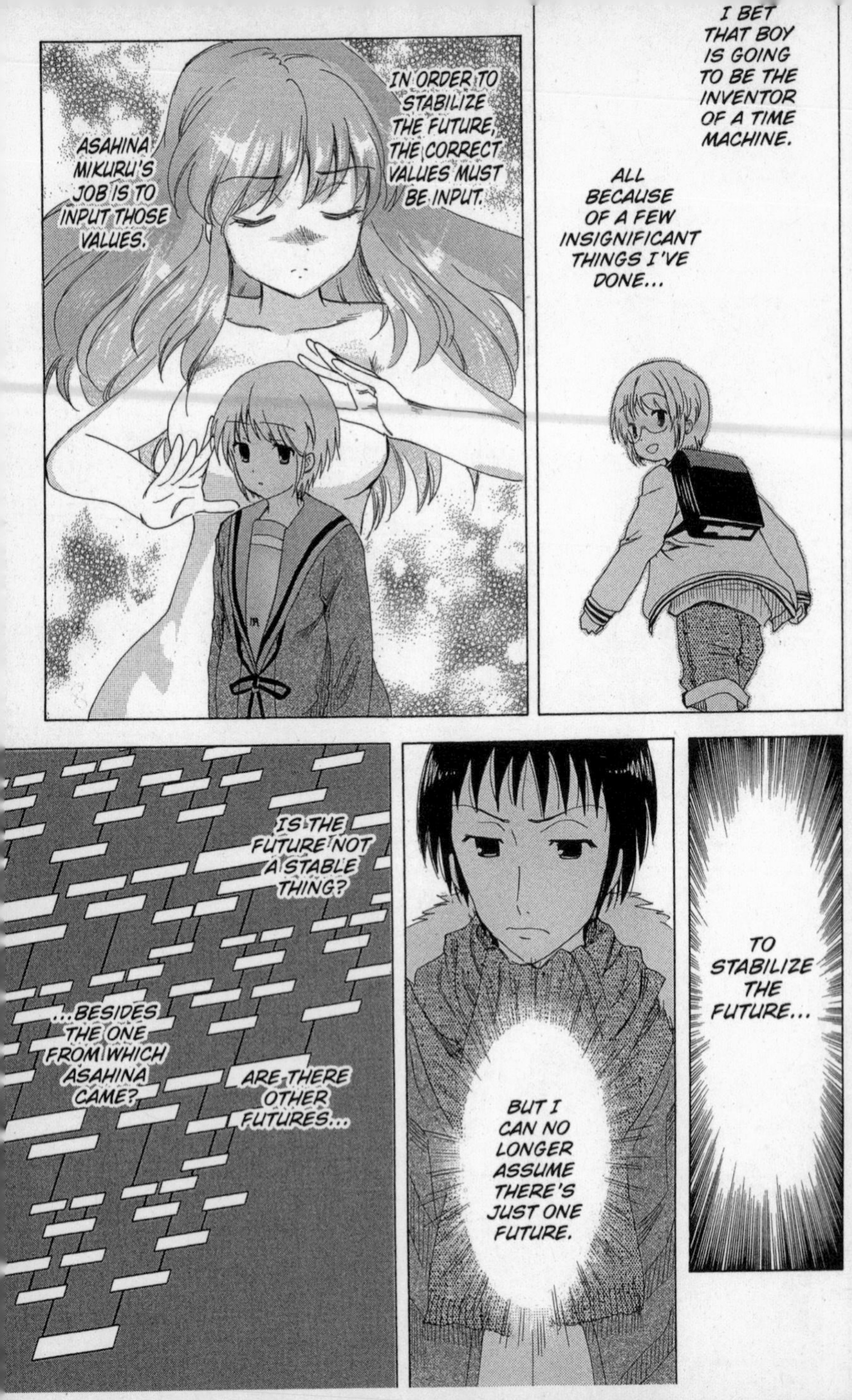
I BET THAT BOY IS GOING TO BE THE INVENTOR OF A TIME MACHINE.
ALL BECAUSE OF A FEW INSIGNIFICANT THINGS I'VE DONE...
IN ORDER TO STABILIZE THE FUTURE, THE CORRECT VALUES MUST BE INPUT.
ASAHINA MIKURU'S JOB IS TO INPUT THOSE VALUES.
TO STABILIZE THE FUTURE...
BUT I CAN NO LONGER ASSUME THERE'S JUST ONE FUTURE.
IS THE FUTURE NOT A STABLE THING?
ARE THERE OTHER FUTURES...
...BESIDES THE ONE FROM WHICH ASAHINA CAME?

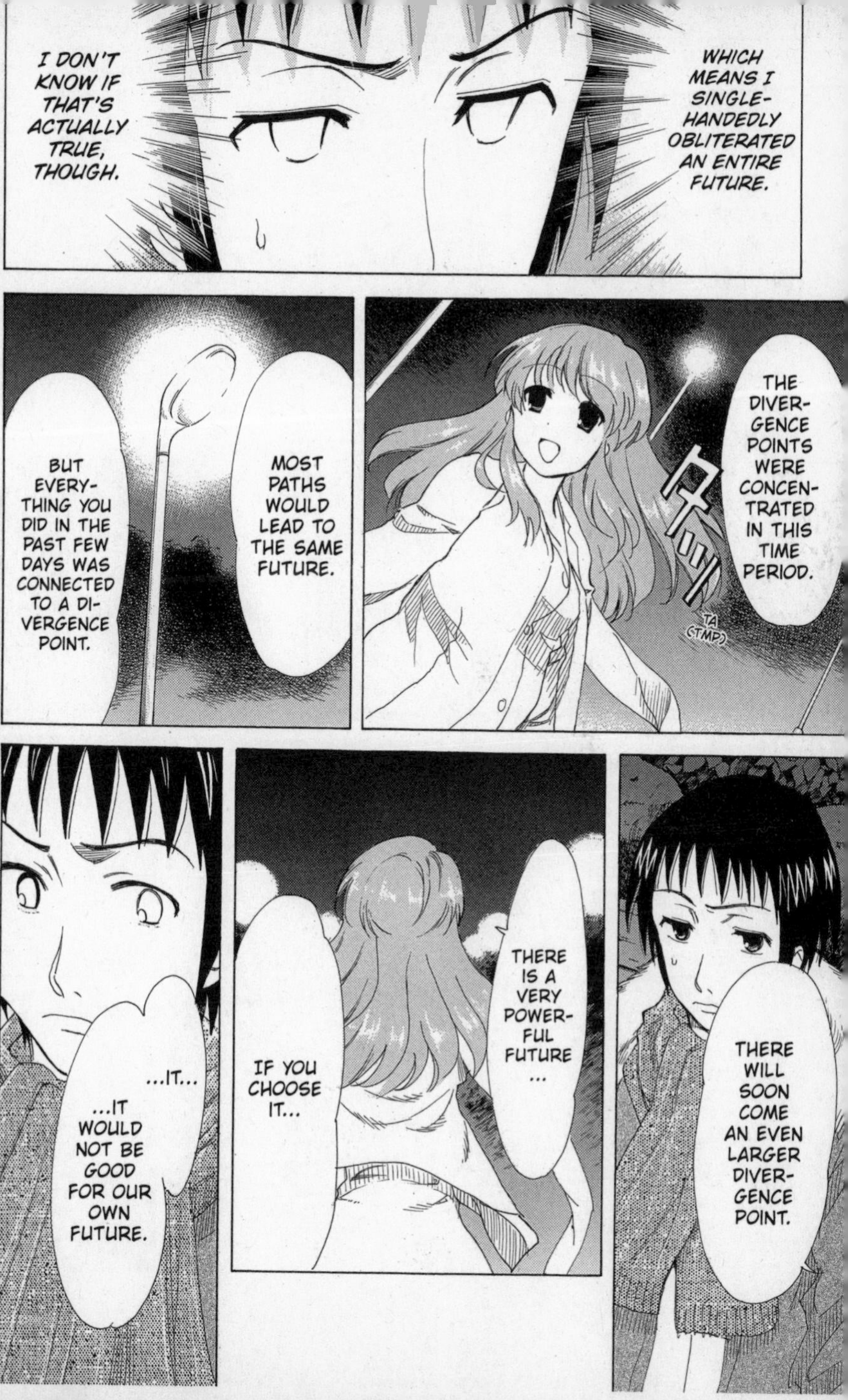
WHICH MEANS I SINGLE-HANDEDLY OBLITERATED AN ENTIRE FUTURE.
I DON'T KNOW IF THAT'S ACTUALLY TRUE, THOUGH.
THE DIVERGENCE POINTS WERE CONCENTRATED IN THIS TIME PERIOD.
TA (TMP)
MOST PATHS WOULD LEAD TO THE SAME FUTURE.
BUT EVERYTHING YOU DID IN THE PAST FEW DAYS WAS CONNECTED TO A DIVERGENCE POINT.
THERE WILL SOON COME AN EVEN LARGER DIVERGENCE POINT.
THERE IS A VERY POWERFUL FUTURE...
IF YOU CHOOSE IT...
...IT...
...IT WOULD NOT BE GOOD FOR OUR OWN FUTURE.

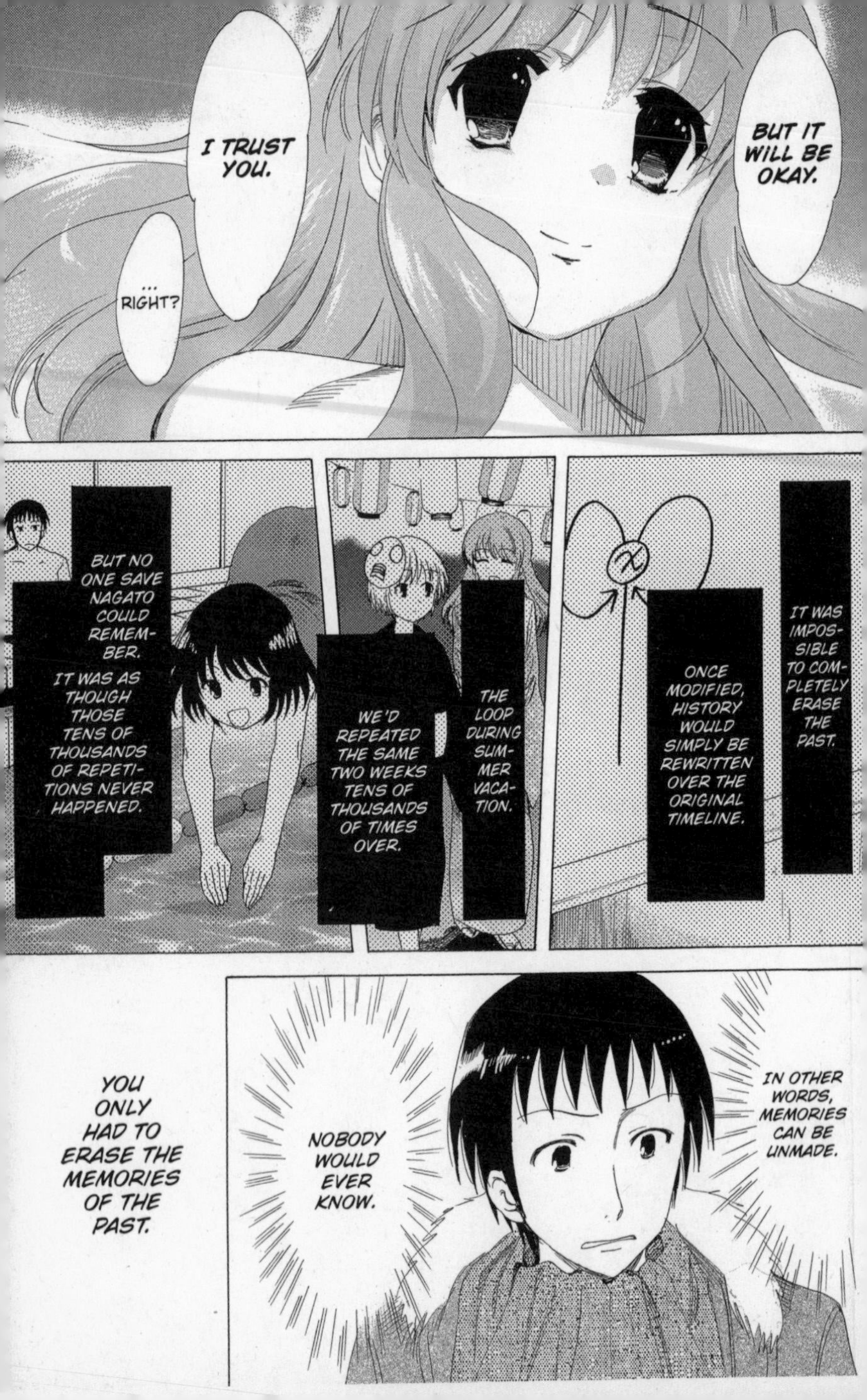
BUT IT WILL BE OKAY.
I TRUST YOU.
... RIGHT?
IT WAS IMPOSSIBLE TO COMPLETELY ERASE THE PAST.
ONCE MODIFIED, HISTORY WOULD SIMPLY BE REWRITTEN OVER THE ORIGINAL TIMELINE.
THE LOOP DURING SUMMER VACATION.
WE'D REPEATED THE SAME TWO WEEKS TENS OF THOUSANDS OF TIMES OVER.
BUT NO ONE SAVE NAGATO COULD REMEMBER.
IT WAS AS THOUGH THOSE TENS OF THOUSANDS OF REPETITIONS NEVER HAPPENED.
IN OTHER WORDS, MEMORIES CAN BE UNMADE.
NOBODY WOULD EVER KNOW.
YOU ONLY HAD TO ERASE THE MEMORIES OF THE PAST.

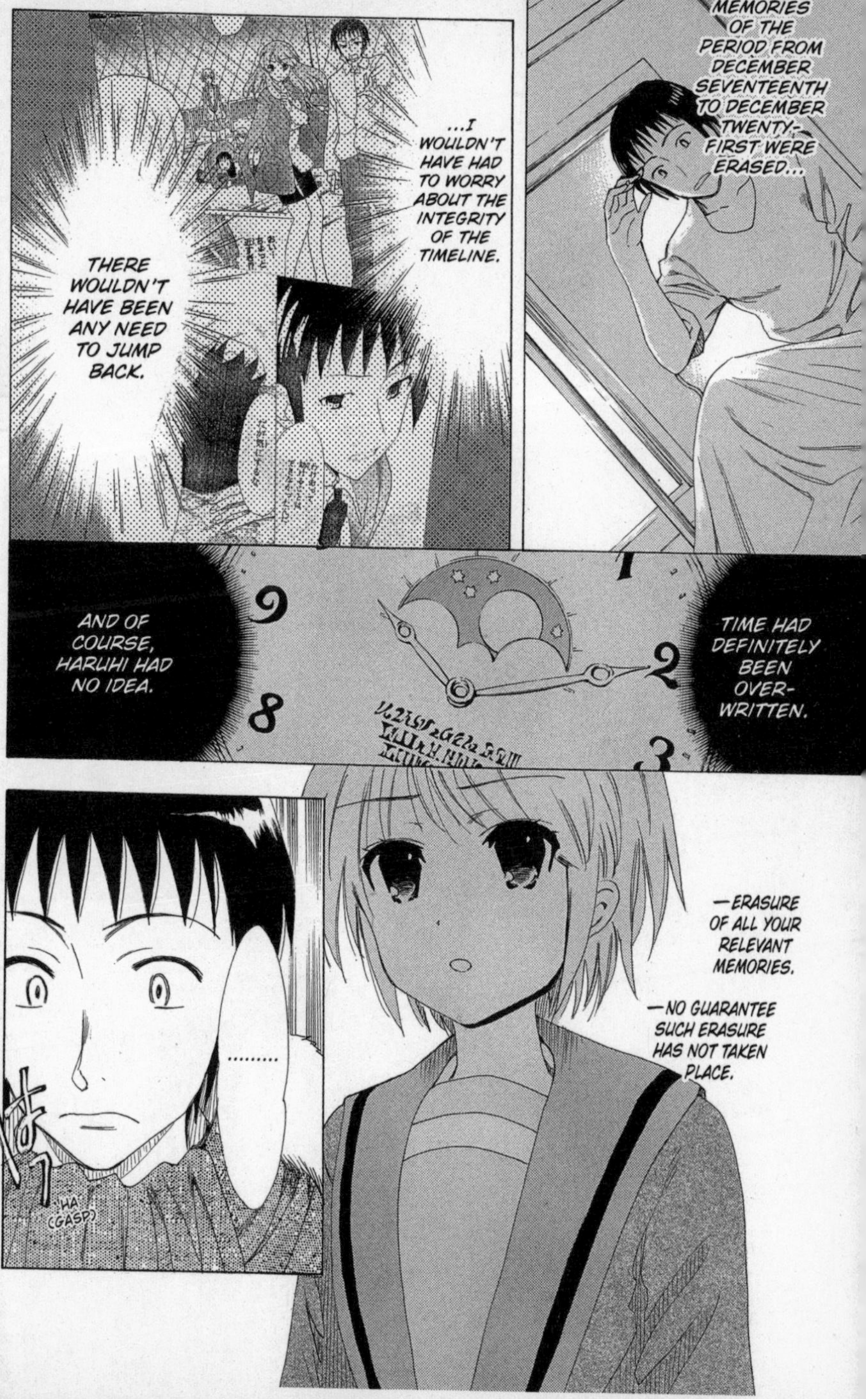
MEMORIES OF THE PERIOD FROM DECEMBER SEVENTEENTH TO DECEMBER TWENTY-FIRST WERE ERASED...
...I WOULDN'T HAVE HAD TO WORRY ABOUT THE INTEGRITY OF THE TIMELINE.
THERE WOULDN'T HAVE BEEN ANY NEED TO JUMP BACK.
TIME HAD DEFINITELY BEEN OVER-WRITTEN.
AND OF COURSE, HARUHI HAD NO IDEA.
—ERASURE OF ALL YOUR RELEVANT MEMORIES.
—NO GUARANTEE SUCH ERASURE HAS NOT TAKEN PLACE.
....
HA (GASP)

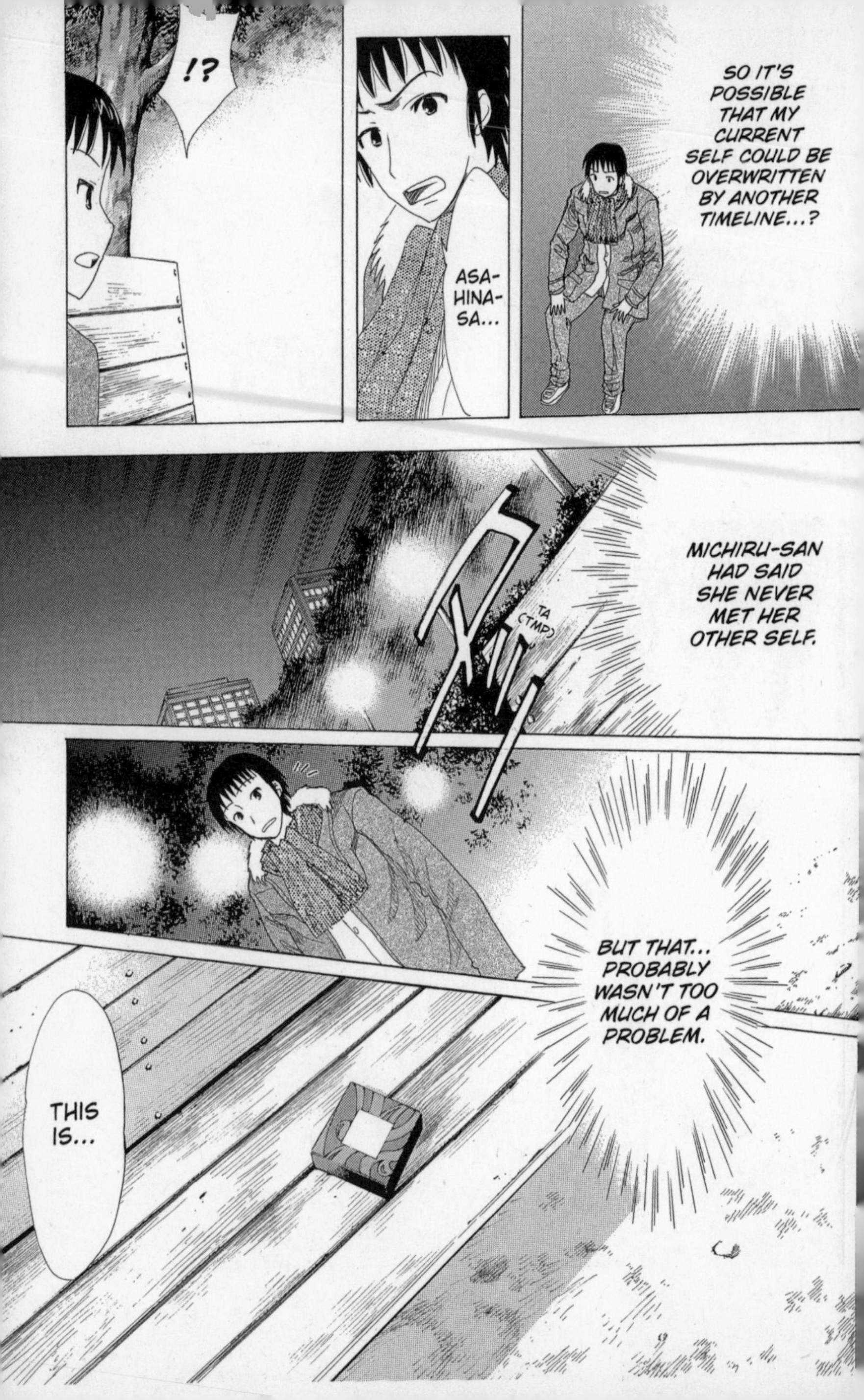
SO IT'S POSSIBLE THAT MY CURRENT SELF COULD BE OVERWRITTEN BY ANOTHER TIMELINE...?
ASA-HINA-SA...
!?
MICHIRU-SAN HAD SAID SHE NEVER MET HER OTHER SELF.
TA (TMP)
BUT THAT... PROBABLY WASN'T TOO MUCH OF A PROBLEM.
THIS IS...

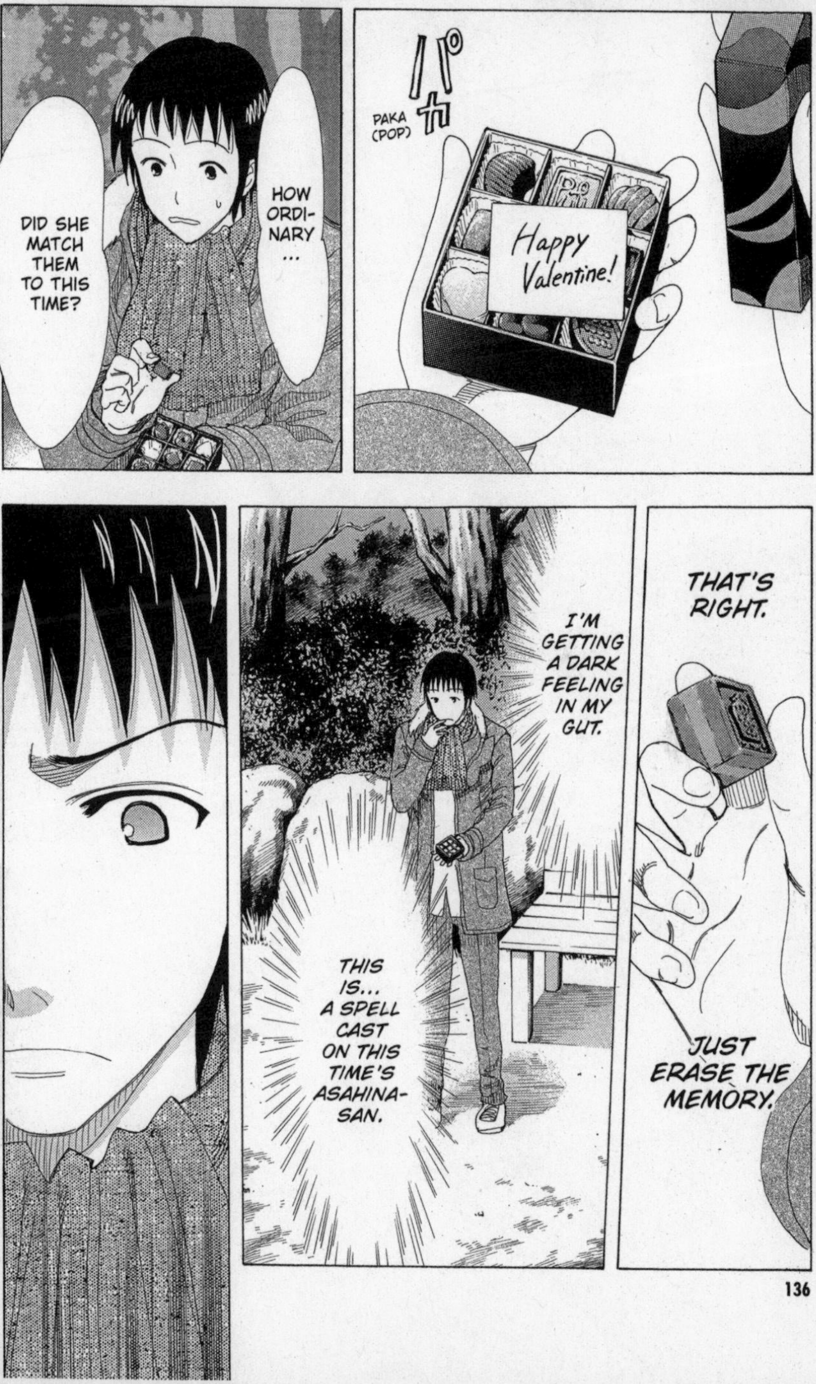
パカ
PAKA (POP)
Happy Valentine!
HOW ORDINARY...
DID SHE MATCH THEM TO THIS TIME?
THAT'S RIGHT.
JUST ERASE THE MEMORY.
I'M GETTING A DARK FEELING IN MY GUT.
THIS IS... A SPELL CAST ON THIS TIME'S ASAHINA-SAN.

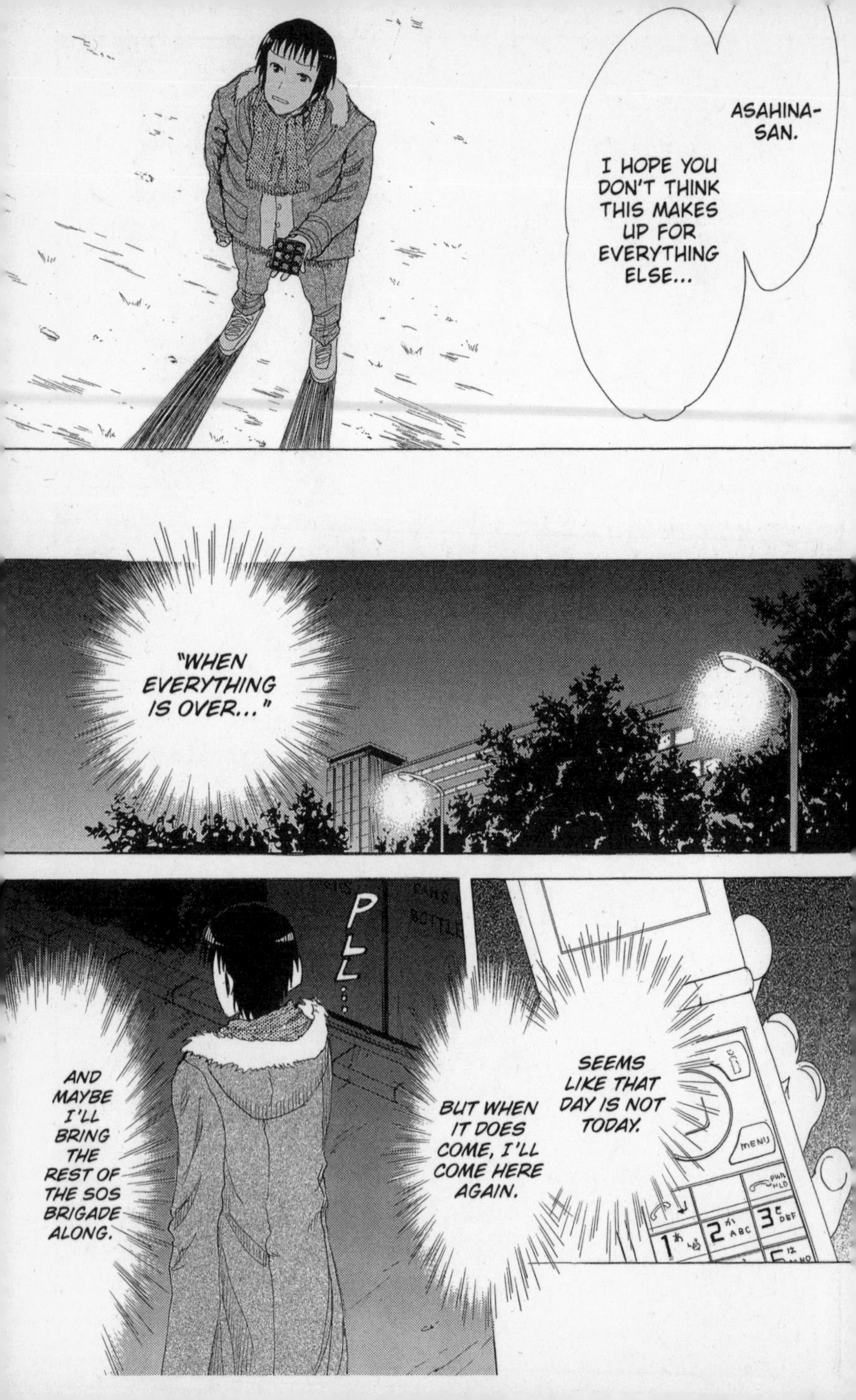
ASAHINA-SAN.
I HOPE YOU DON'T THINK THIS MAKES UP FOR EVERYTHING ELSE...
"WHEN EVERYTHING IS OVER..."
SEEMS LIKE THAT DAY IS NOT TODAY.
BUT WHEN IT DOES COME, I'LL COME HERE AGAIN.
PLL...
AND MAYBE I'LL BRING THE REST OF THE SOS BRIGADE ALONG.

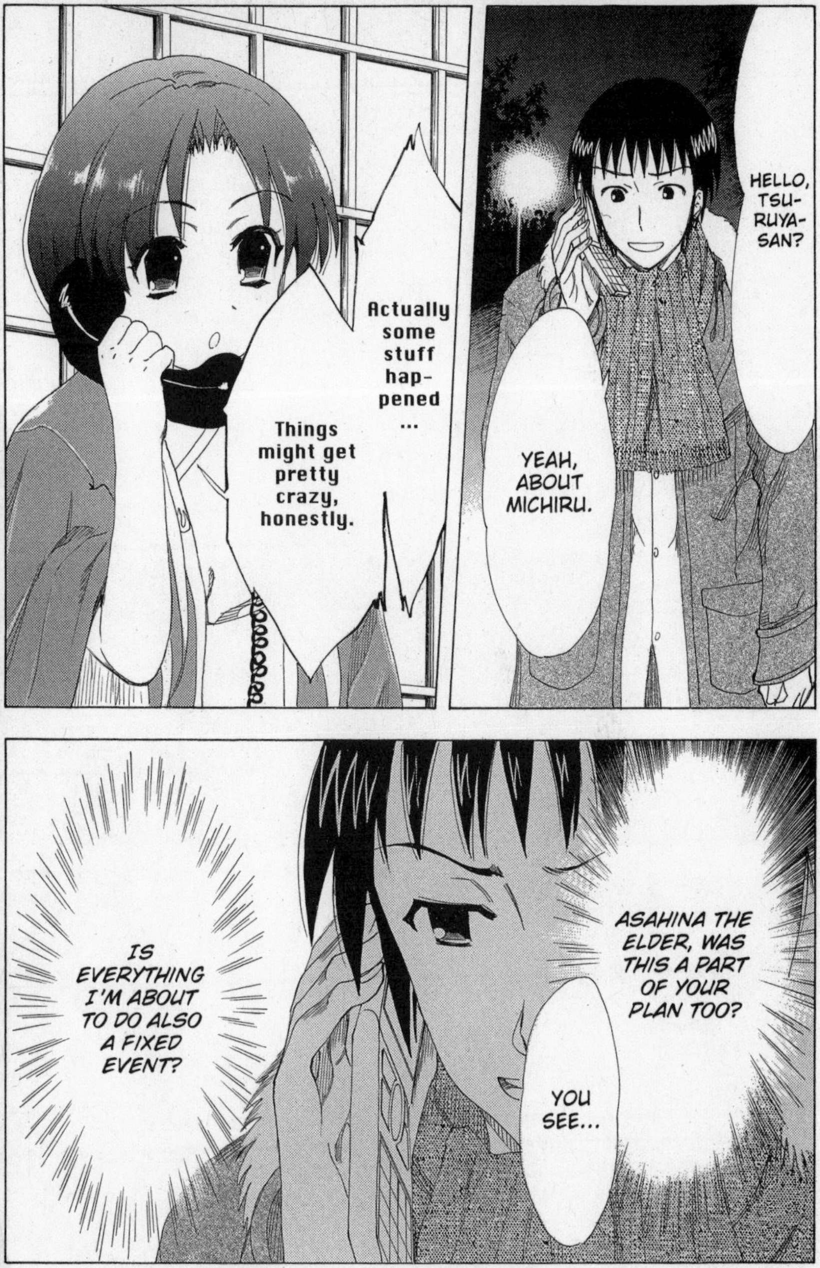
HELLO, TSU-RUYA-SAN?
YEAH, ABOUT MICHIRU.
Actually some stuff hap-pened ...
Things might get pretty crazy, honestly.
ASAHINA THE ELDER, WAS THIS A PART OF YOUR PLAN TOO?
IS EVERYTHING I'M ABOUT TO DO ALSO A FIXED EVENT?
YOU SEE...

THE INTRIGUES OF HARUHI SUZUMIYA X : END

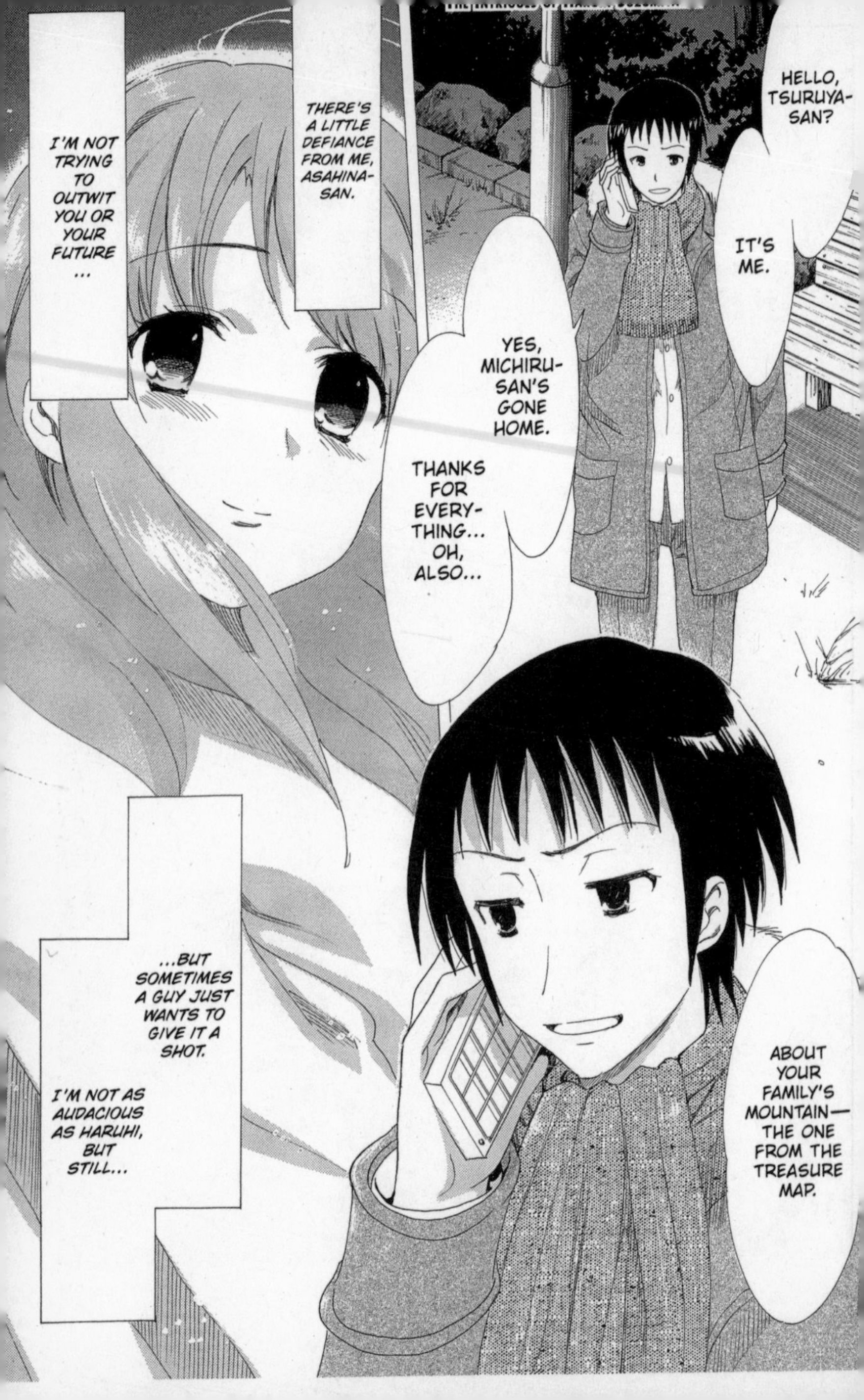
HELLO, TSURUYA-SAN?
IT'S ME.
YES, MICHIRU-SAN'S GONE HOME.
THANKS FOR EVERYTHING... OH, ALSO...
THERE'S A LITTLE DEFIANCE FROM ME, ASAHINA-SAN.
I'M NOT TRYING TO OUTWIT YOU OR YOUR FUTURE...
ABOUT YOUR FAMILY'S MOUNTAIN—THE ONE FROM THE TREASURE MAP.
...BUT SOMETIMES A GUY JUST WANTS TO GIVE IT A SHOT.
I'M NOT AS AUDACIOUS AS HARUHI, BUT STILL...

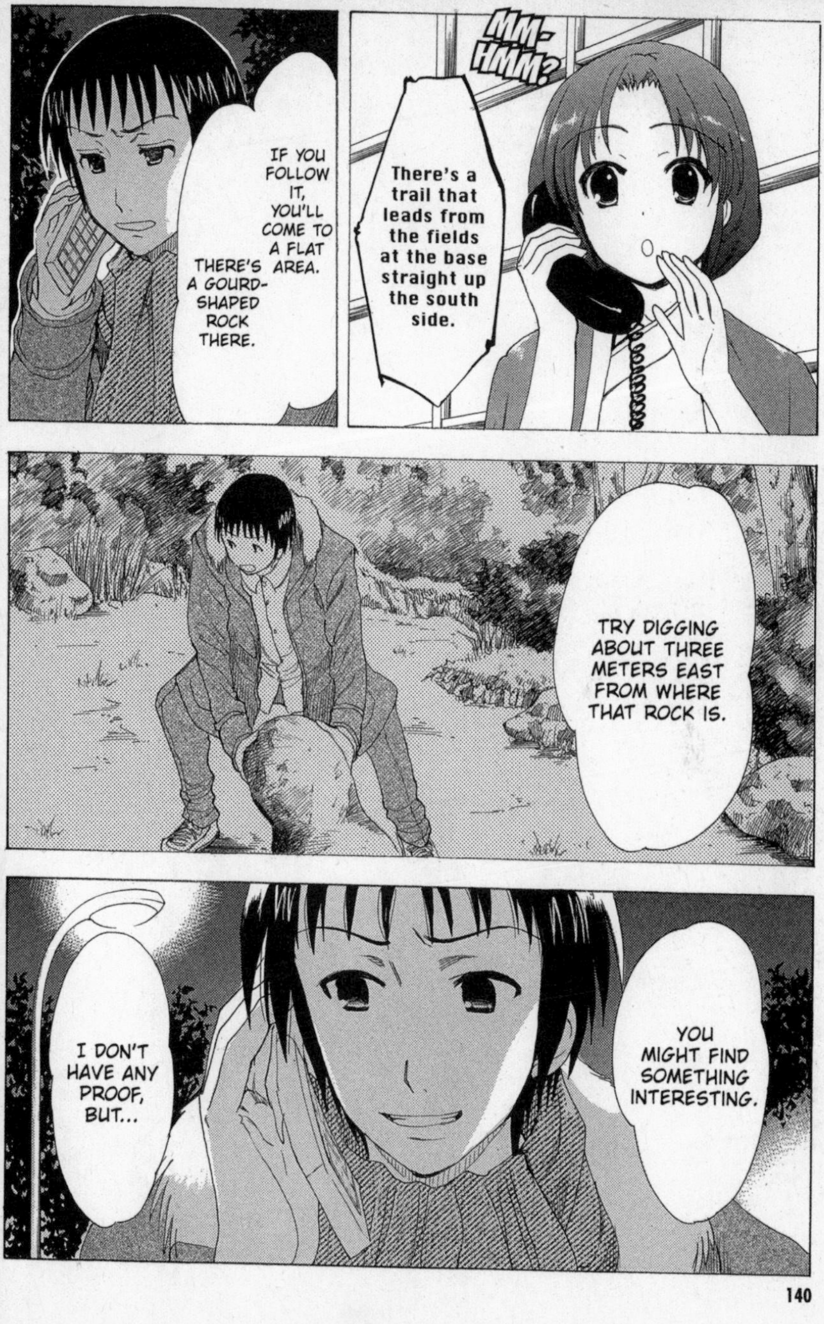
MM-HMM?
There's a trail that leads from the fields at the base straight up the south side.
IF YOU FOLLOW IT, YOU'LL COME TO A FLAT AREA.
THERE'S A GOURD-SHAPED ROCK THERE.
TRY DIGGING ABOUT THREE METERS EAST FROM WHERE THAT ROCK IS.
YOU MIGHT FIND SOMETHING INTERESTING.
I DON'T HAVE ANY PROOF, BUT...

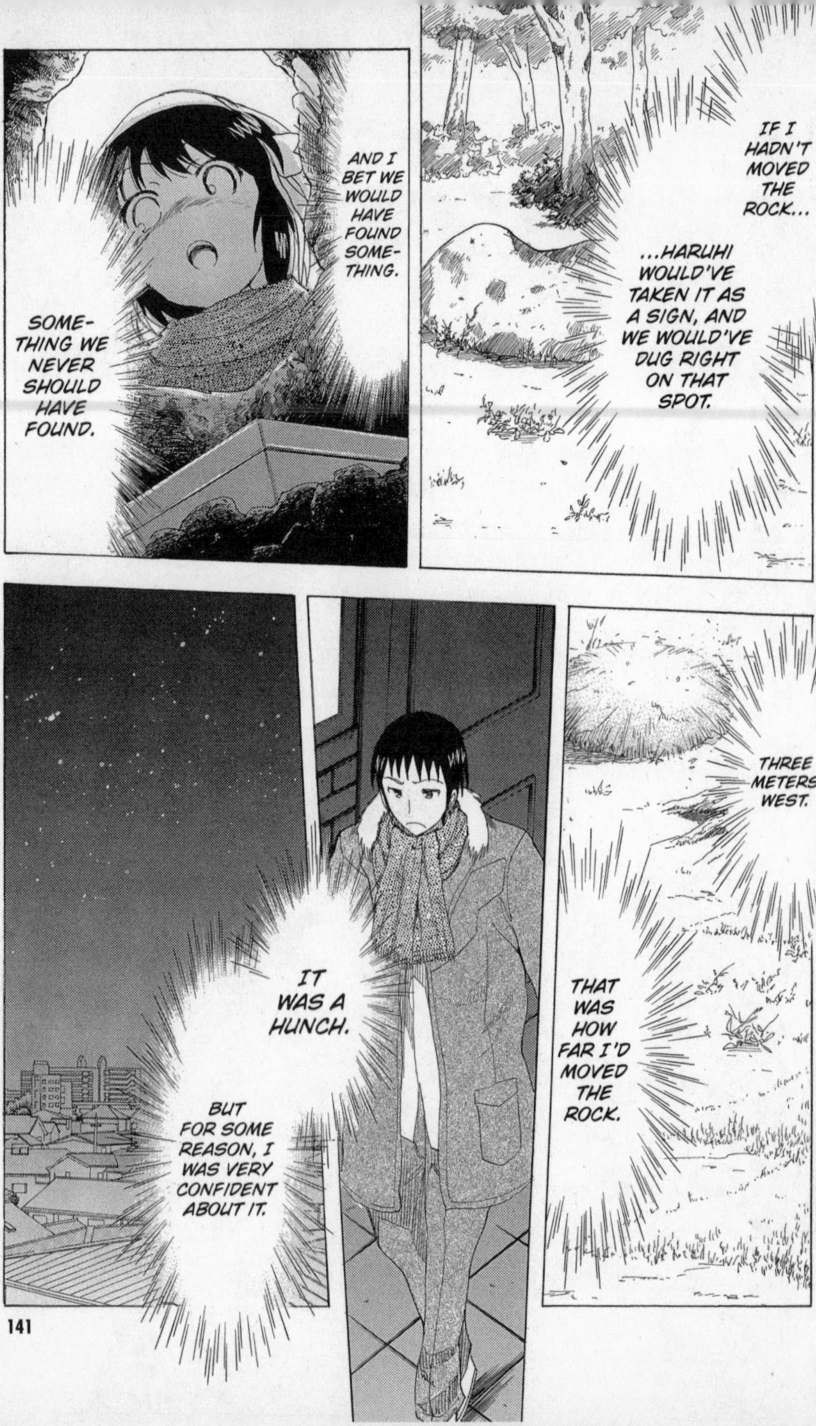
IF I HADN'T MOVED THE ROCK...
...HARUHI WOULD'VE TAKEN IT AS A SIGN, AND WE WOULD'VE DUG RIGHT ON THAT SPOT.
AND I BET WE WOULD HAVE FOUND SOME-THING.
SOME-THING WE NEVER SHOULD HAVE FOUND.
THREE METERS WEST.
THAT WAS HOW FAR I'D MOVED THE ROCK.
IT WAS A HUNCH.
BUT FOR SOME REASON, I WAS VERY CONFIDENT ABOUT IT.

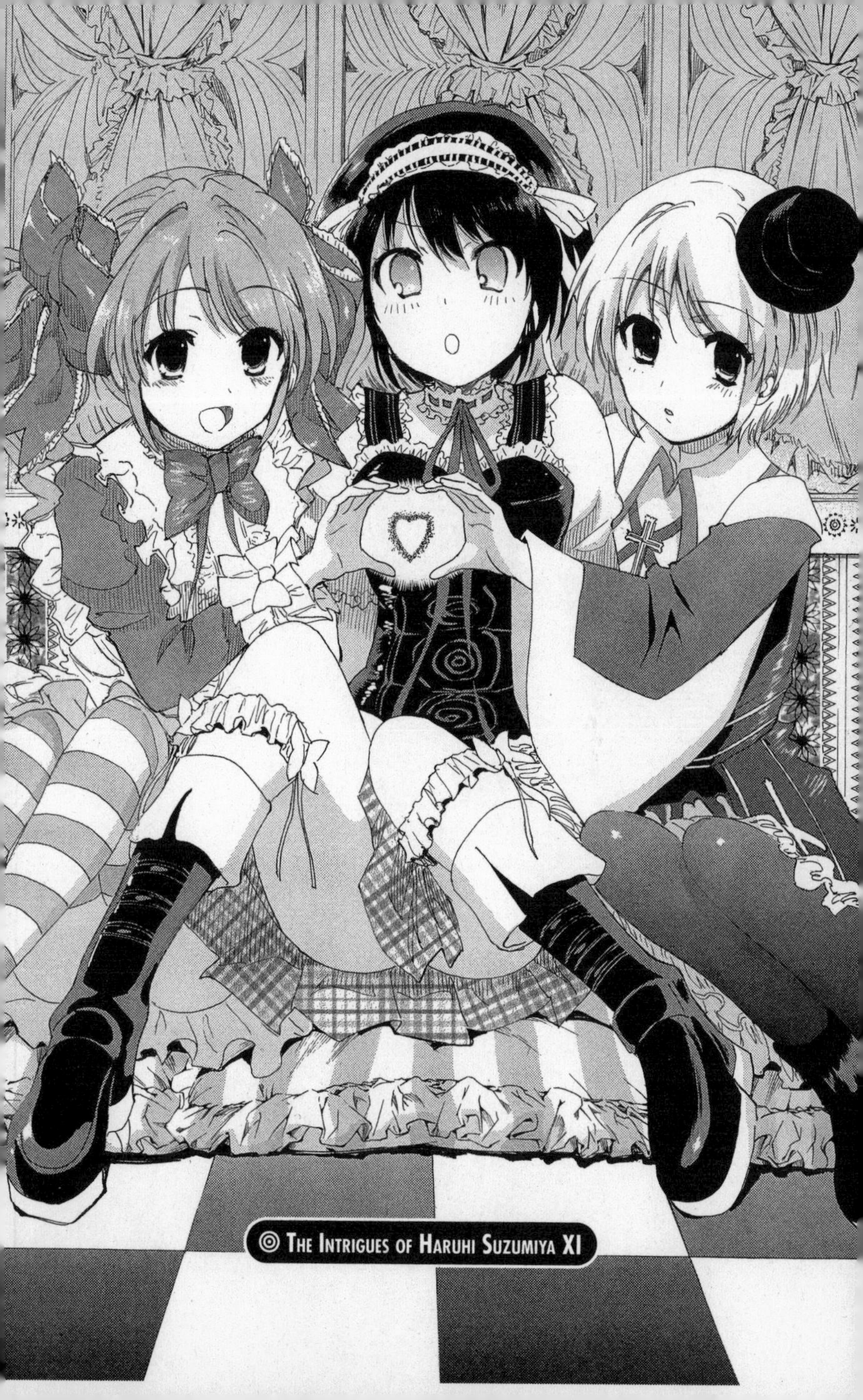

◎ The Intrigues of Haruhi Suzumiya XI

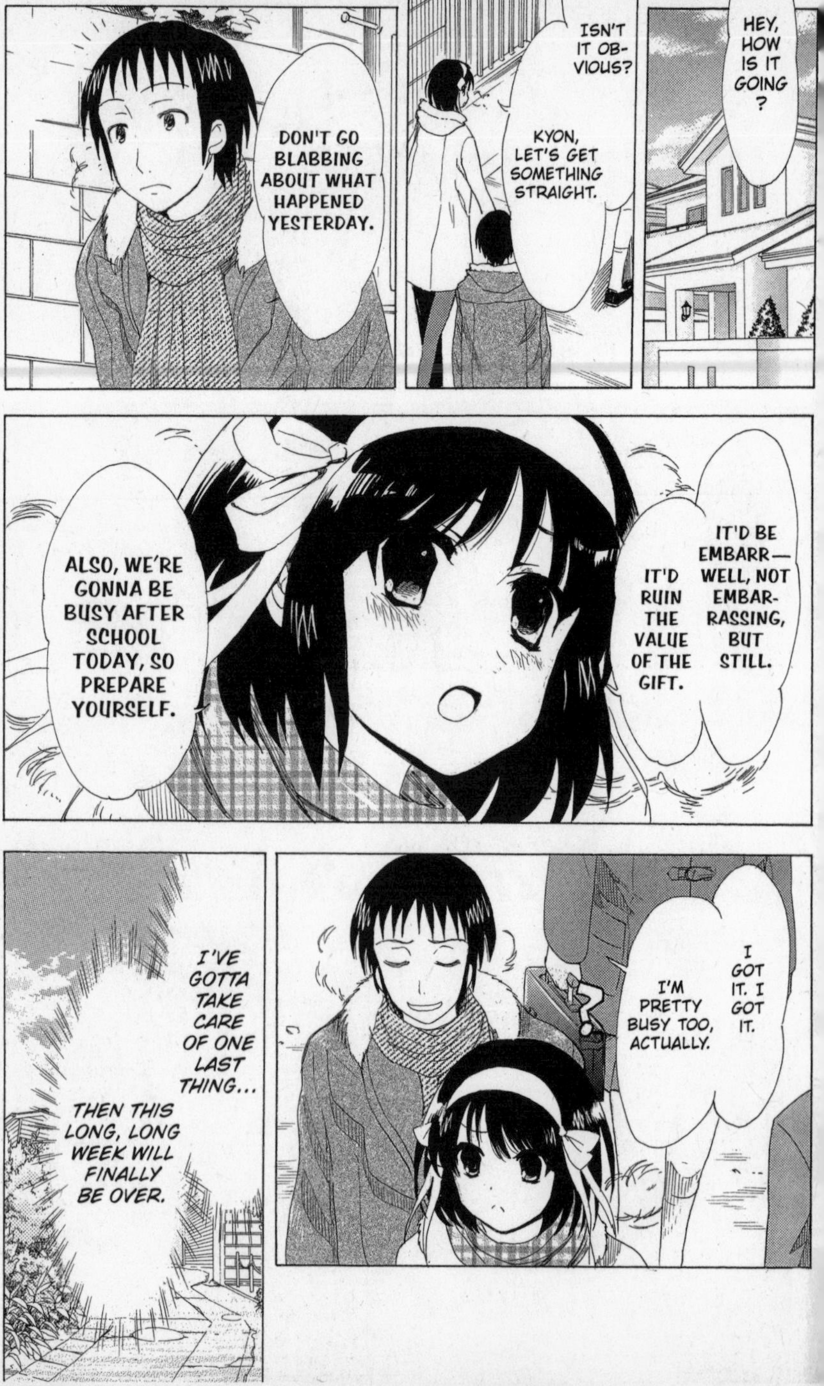
HEY, HOW IS IT GOING?
ISN'T IT OBVIOUS?
KYON, LET'S GET SOMETHING STRAIGHT.
DON'T GO BLABBING ABOUT WHAT HAPPENED YESTERDAY.
IT'D BE EMBARR— WELL, NOT EMBARRASSING, BUT STILL.
IT'D RUIN THE VALUE OF THE GIFT.
ALSO, WE'RE GONNA BE BUSY AFTER SCHOOL TODAY, SO PREPARE YOURSELF.
I GOT IT. I GOT IT.
I'M PRETTY BUSY TOO, ACTUALLY.
I'VE GOTTA TAKE CARE OF ONE LAST THING...
THEN THIS LONG, LONG WEEK WILL FINALLY BE OVER.

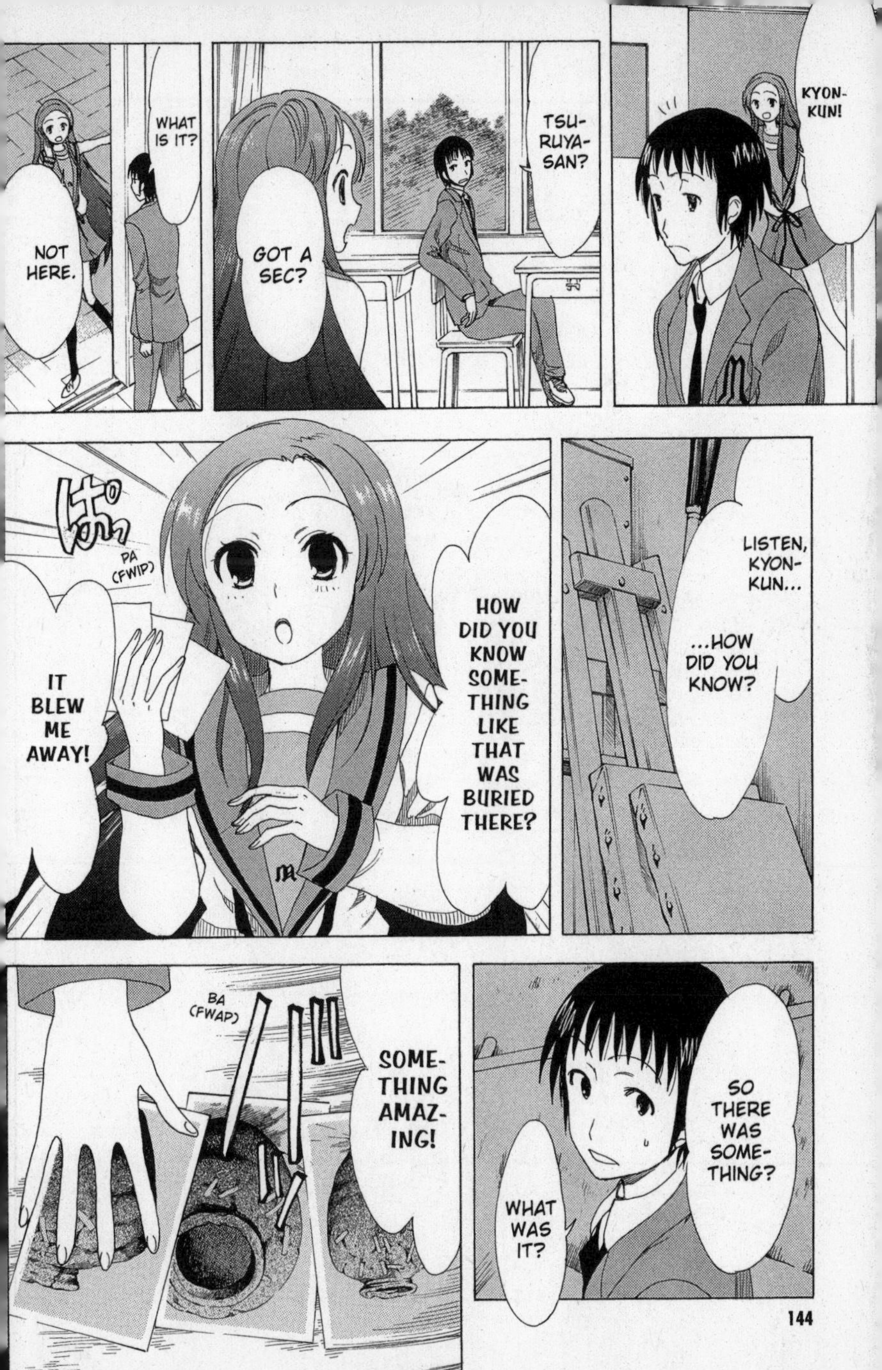
KYON-KUN!
TSU-RUYA-SAN?
GOT A SEC?
WHAT IS IT?
NOT HERE.
LISTEN, KYON-KUN...
...HOW DID YOU KNOW?
HOW DID YOU KNOW SOME-THING LIKE THAT WAS BURIED THERE?
ぱっ
PA (FWIP)
IT BLEW ME AWAY!
SO THERE WAS SOME-THING?
WHAT WAS IT?
SOME-THING AMAZ-ING!
BA (FWAP)

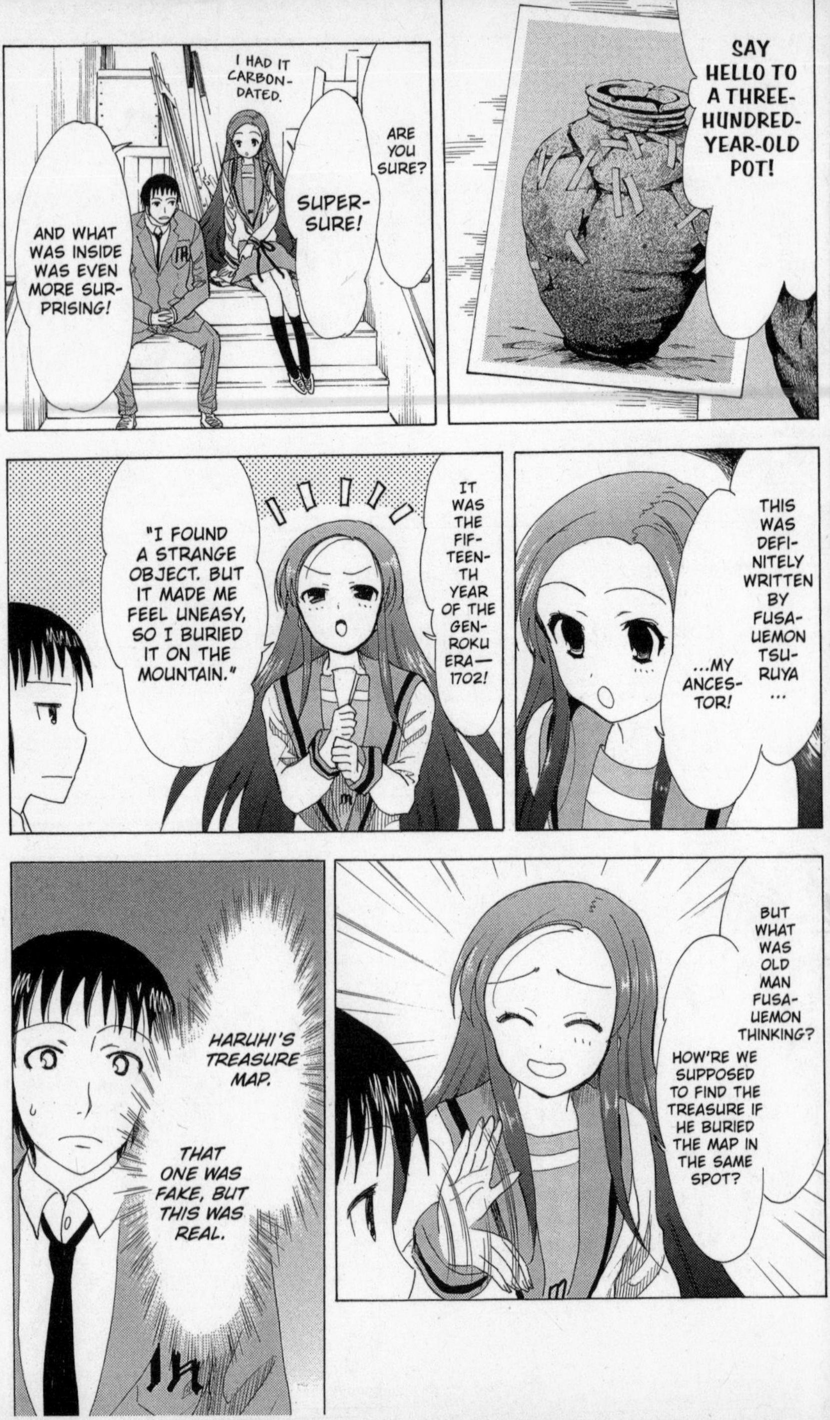
SAY HELLO TO A THREE-HUNDRED-YEAR-OLD POT!
I HAD IT CARBON-DATED.
ARE YOU SURE?
SUPER-SURE!
AND WHAT WAS INSIDE WAS EVEN MORE SURPRISING!
THIS WAS DEFINITELY WRITTEN BY FUSAUEMON TSURUYA ...
...MY ANCESTOR!
IT WAS THE FIFTEENTH YEAR OF THE GENROKU ERA—1702!
"I FOUND A STRANGE OBJECT. BUT IT MADE ME FEEL UNEASY, SO I BURIED IT ON THE MOUNTAIN."
BUT WHAT WAS OLD MAN FUSAUEMON THINKING?
HOW'RE WE SUPPOSED TO FIND THE TREASURE IF HE BURIED THE MAP IN THE SAME SPOT?
HARUHI'S TREASURE MAP.
THAT ONE WAS FAKE, BUT THIS WAS REAL.

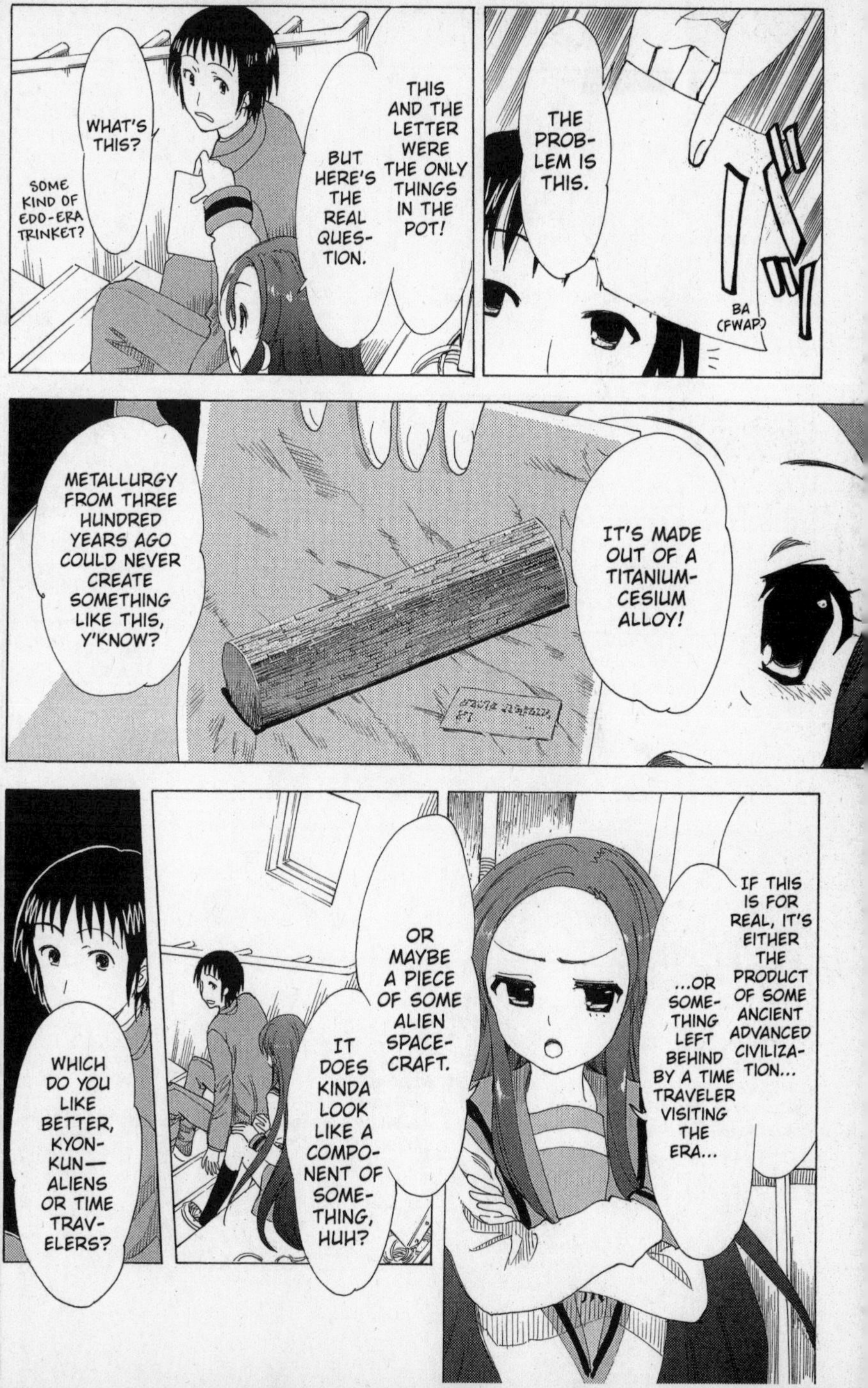
THE PROBLEM IS THIS.
BA (FWAP)
THIS AND THE LETTER WERE THE ONLY THINGS IN THE POT!
BUT HERE'S THE REAL QUESTION.
WHAT'S THIS?
SOME KIND OF EDO-ERA TRINKET?
IT'S MADE OUT OF A TITANIUM-CESIUM ALLOY!
METALLURGY FROM THREE HUNDRED YEARS AGO COULD NEVER CREATE SOMETHING LIKE THIS, Y'KNOW?
IF THIS IS FOR REAL, IT'S EITHER THE PRODUCT OF SOME ANCIENT ADVANCED CIVILIZATION...
...OR SOMETHING LEFT BEHIND BY A TIME TRAVELER VISITING THE ERA...
OR MAYBE A PIECE OF SOME ALIEN SPACECRAFT.
IT DOES KINDA LOOK LIKE A COMPONENT OF SOMETHING, HUH?
WHICH DO YOU LIKE BETTER, KYON-KUN—ALIENS OR TIME TRAVELERS?

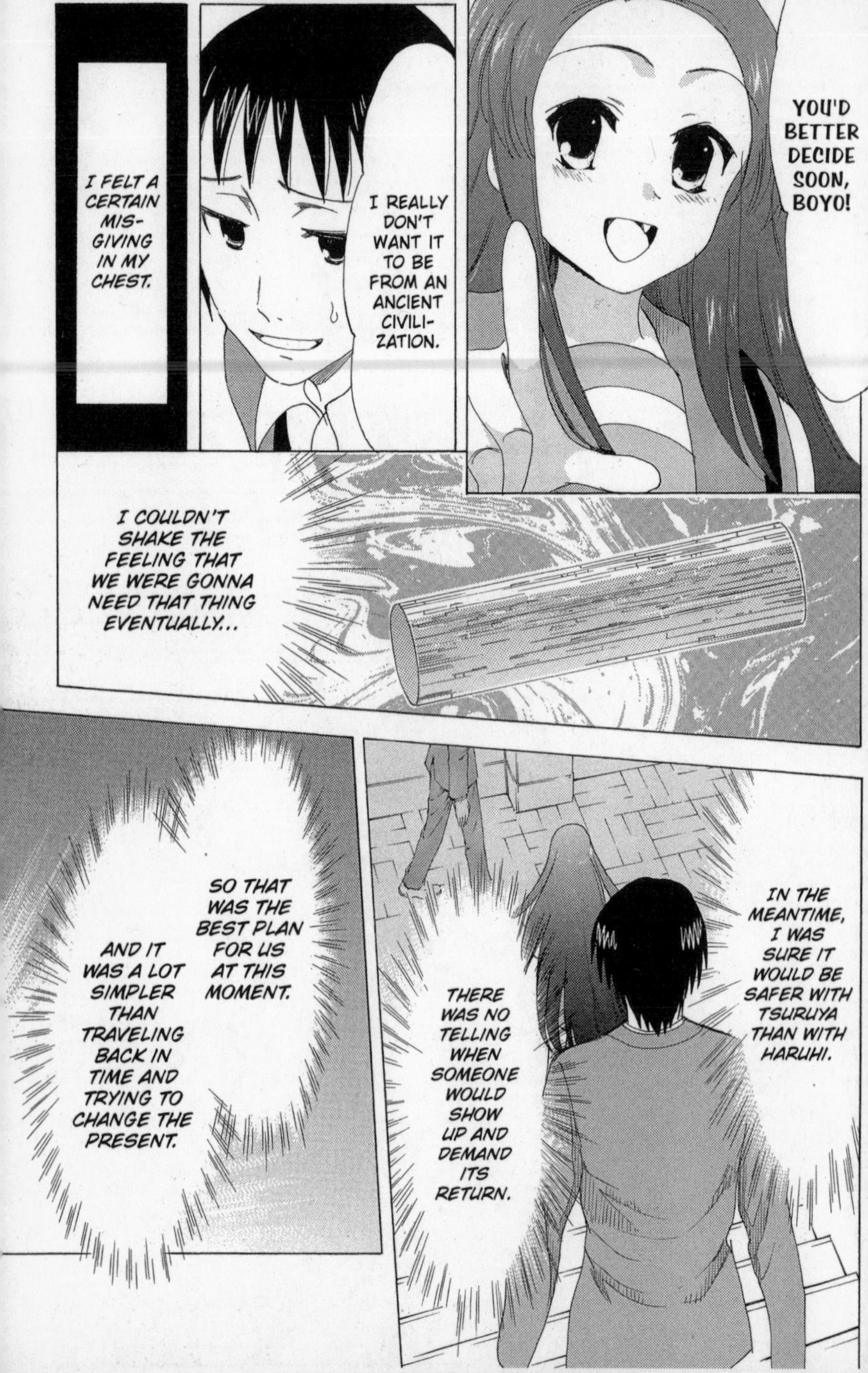
YOU'D BETTER DECIDE SOON, BOYO!
I REALLY DON'T WANT IT TO BE FROM AN ANCIENT CIVILI-ZATION.
I FELT A CERTAIN MIS-GIVING IN MY CHEST.
I COULDN'T SHAKE THE FEELING THAT WE WERE GONNA NEED THAT THING EVENTUALLY...
IN THE MEANTIME, I WAS SURE IT WOULD BE SAFER WITH TSURUYA THAN WITH HARUHI.
THERE WAS NO TELLING WHEN SOMEONE WOULD SHOW UP AND DEMAND ITS RETURN.
SO THAT WAS THE BEST PLAN FOR US AT THIS MOMENT.
AND IT WAS A LOT SIMPLER THAN TRAVELING BACK IN TIME AND TRYING TO CHANGE THE PRESENT.

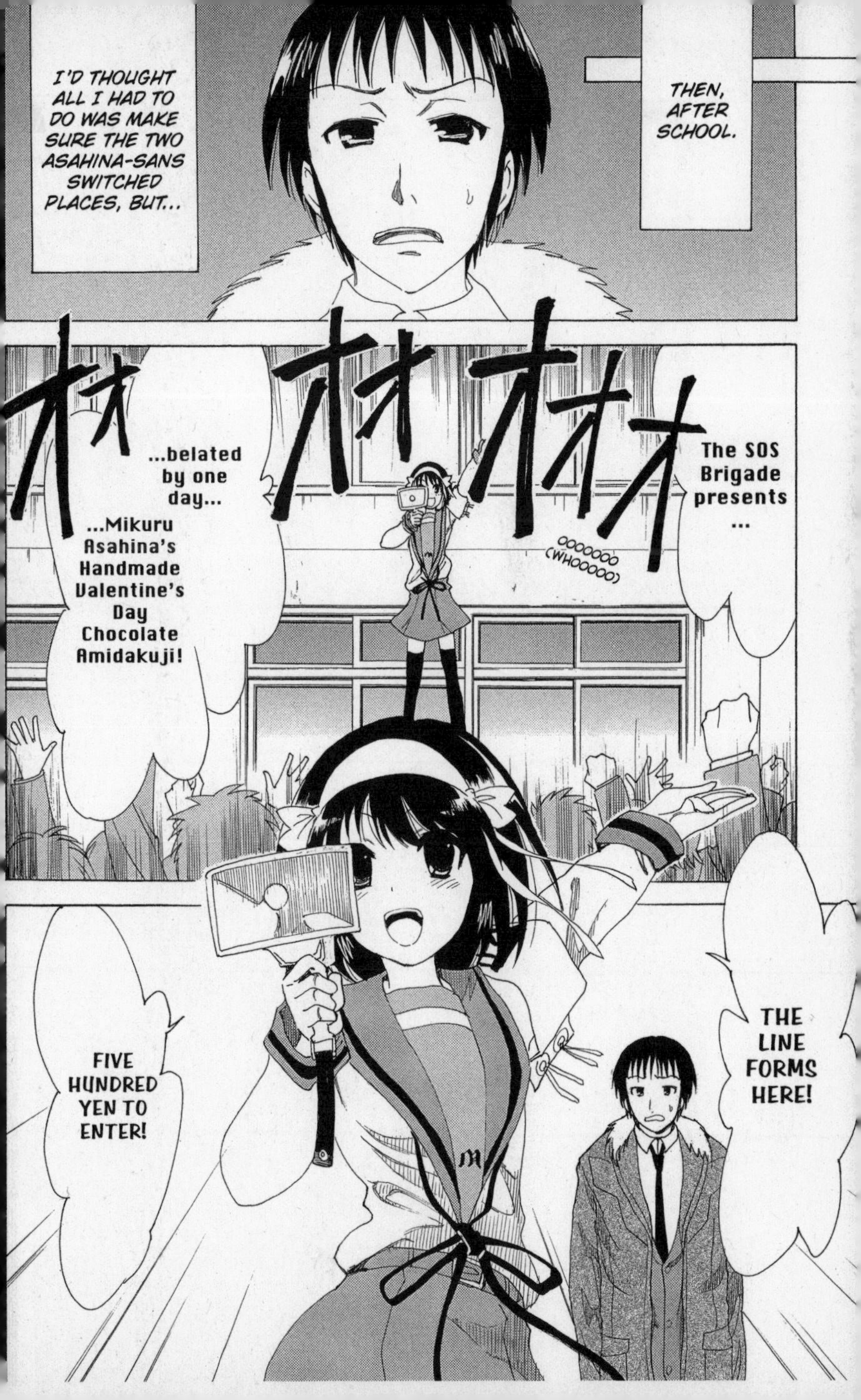
THEN, AFTER SCHOOL.
I'D THOUGHT ALL I HAD TO DO WAS MAKE SURE THE TWO ASAHINA-SANS SWITCHED PLACES, BUT...
The SOS Brigade presents...
...belated by one day...
...Mikuru Asahina's Handmade Valentine's Day Chocolate Amidakuji!
オオオオオオ
OOOOOOO (WHOOOOO)
THE LINE FORMS HERE!
FIVE HUNDRED YEN TO ENTER!

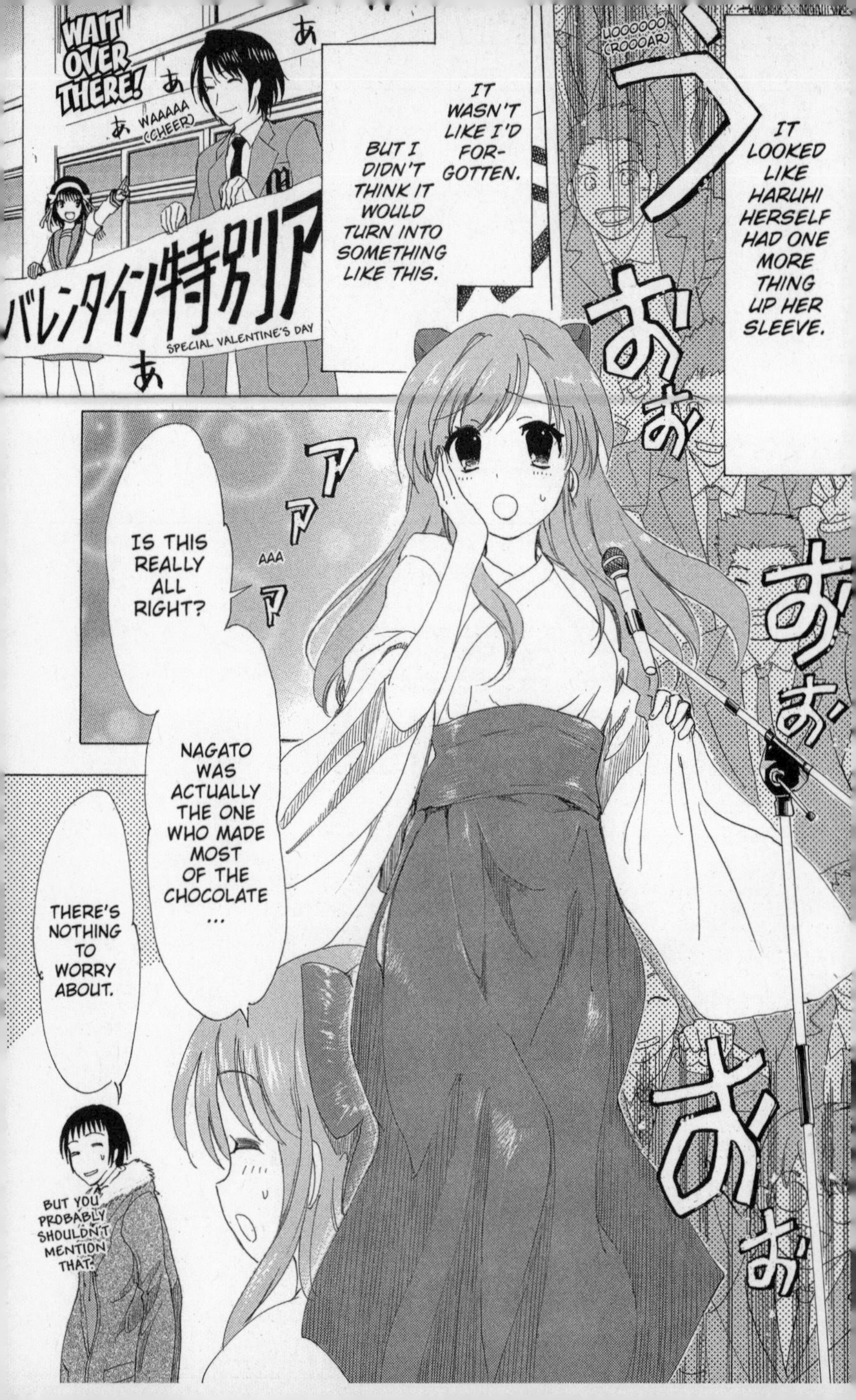

UOOOOOO (ROOOAR)
うおおおおおお
IT LOOKED LIKE HARUHI HERSELF HAD ONE MORE THING UP HER SLEEVE.
IT WASN'T LIKE I'D FORGOTTEN.
BUT I DIDN'T THINK IT WOULD TURN INTO SOMETHING LIKE THIS.
あ
WAIT OVER THERE!
あ
あ WAAAAA (CHEER)
SPECIAL VALENTINE'S DAY
あ
アアア
AAA
IS THIS REALLY ALL RIGHT?
NAGATO WAS ACTUALLY THE ONE WHO MADE MOST OF THE CHOCOLATE ...
THERE'S NOTHING TO WORRY ABOUT.
BUT YOU PROBABLY SHOULDN'T MENTION THAT.

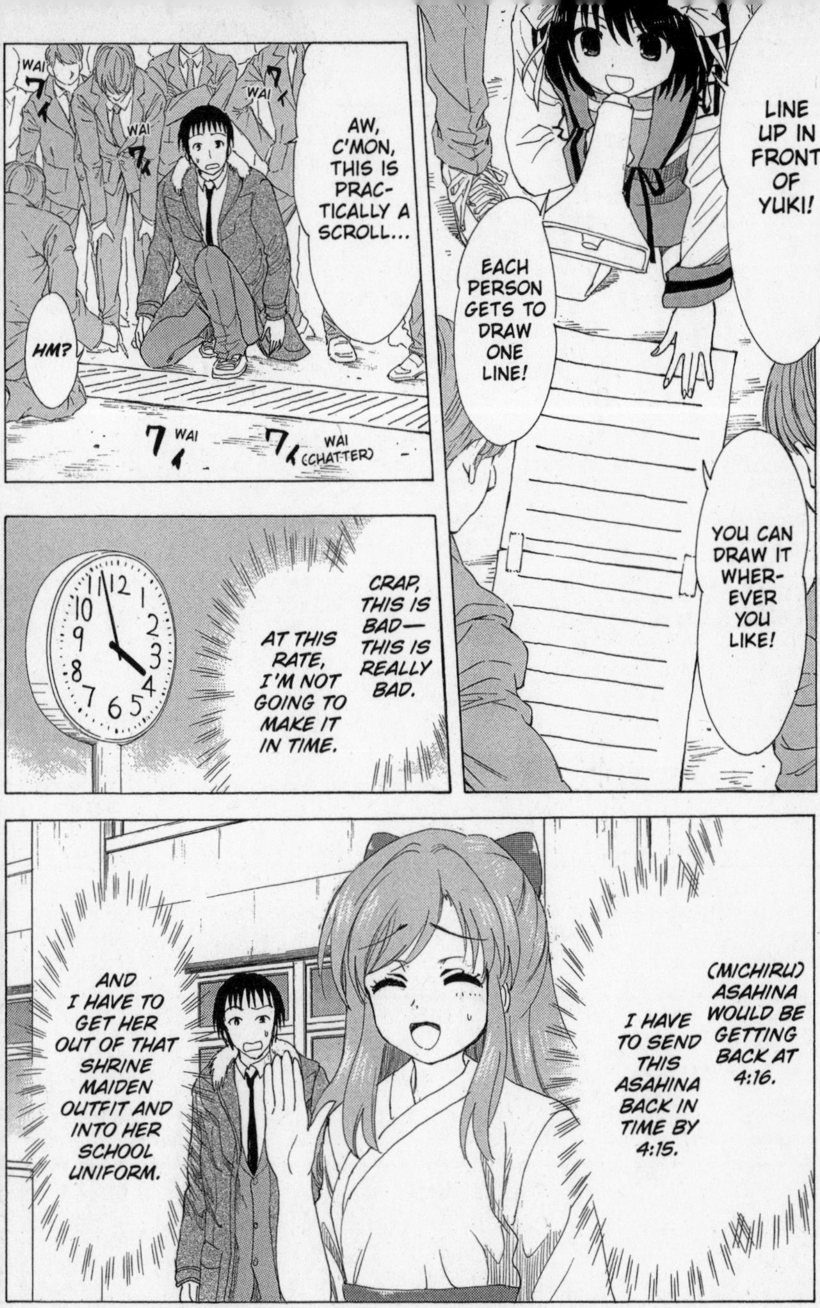
LINE UP IN FRONT OF YUKI!
EACH PERSON GETS TO DRAW ONE LINE!
YOU CAN DRAW IT WHEREVER YOU LIKE!
WAI WAI WAI
AW, C'MON, THIS IS PRACTICALLY A SCROLL...
HM?
WAI WAI (CHATTER)
CRAP, THIS IS BAD—THIS IS REALLY BAD.
AT THIS RATE, I'M NOT GOING TO MAKE IT IN TIME.
(MICHIRU) ASAHINA WOULD BE GETTING BACK AT 4:16.
I HAVE TO SEND THIS ASAHINA BACK IN TIME BY 4:15.
AND I HAVE TO GET HER OUT OF THAT SHRINE MAIDEN OUTFIT AND INTO HER SCHOOL UNIFORM.

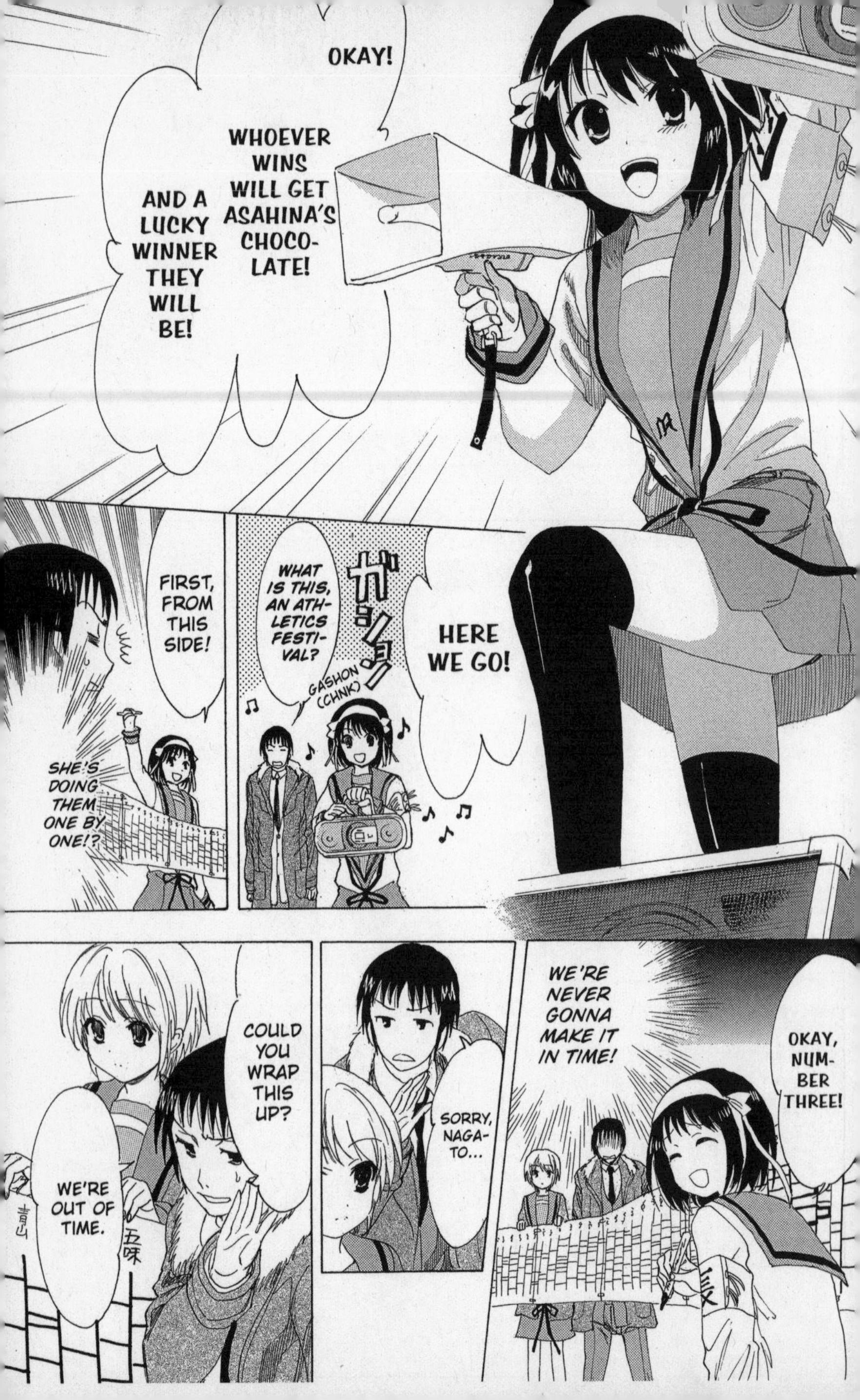
OKAY!
WHOEVER WINS WILL GET ASAHINA'S CHOCO-LATE!
AND A LUCKY WINNER THEY WILL BE!
HERE WE GO!
ガショ
GASHON (CHNK)
WHAT IS THIS, AN ATH-LETICS FESTI-VAL?
FIRST, FROM THIS SIDE!
SHE'S DOING THEM ONE BY ONE!?
OKAY, NUM-BER THREE!
WE'RE NEVER GONNA MAKE IT IN TIME!
SORRY, NAGA-TO...
COULD YOU WRAP THIS UP?
五味
青山
WE'RE OUT OF TIME.

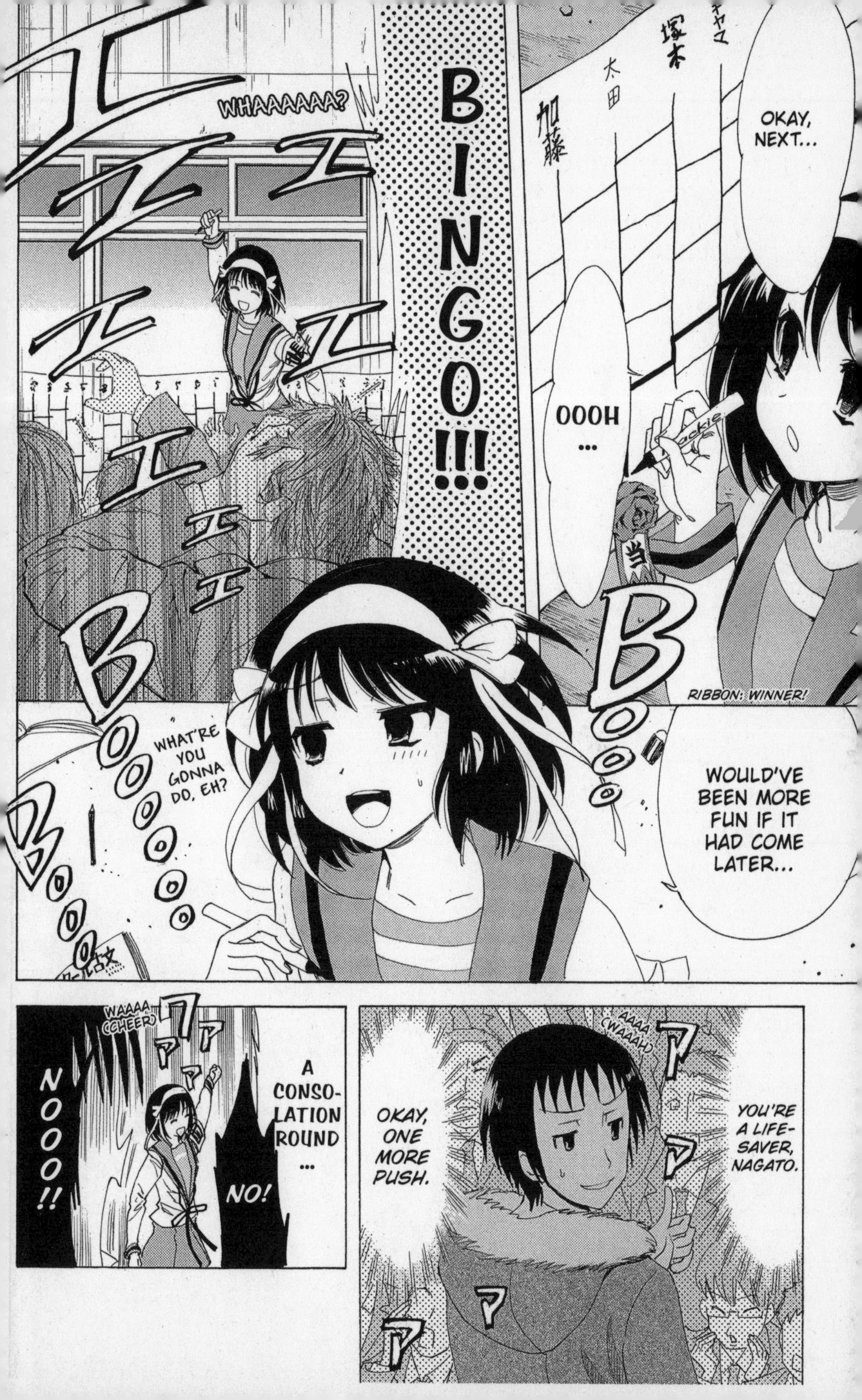

OKAY, NEXT...
OOOH ...
RIBBON: WINNER!
WHAAAAAAA?
BINGO!!!
WOULD'VE BEEN MORE FUN IF IT HAD COME LATER...
WHAT'RE YOU GONNA DO, EH?
AAAA (WAAAH)
YOU'RE A LIFE-SAVER, NAGATO.
OKAY, ONE MORE PUSH.
A CONSOLATION ROUND ...
NO!
WAAAA (CHEER)
NOOOO!!

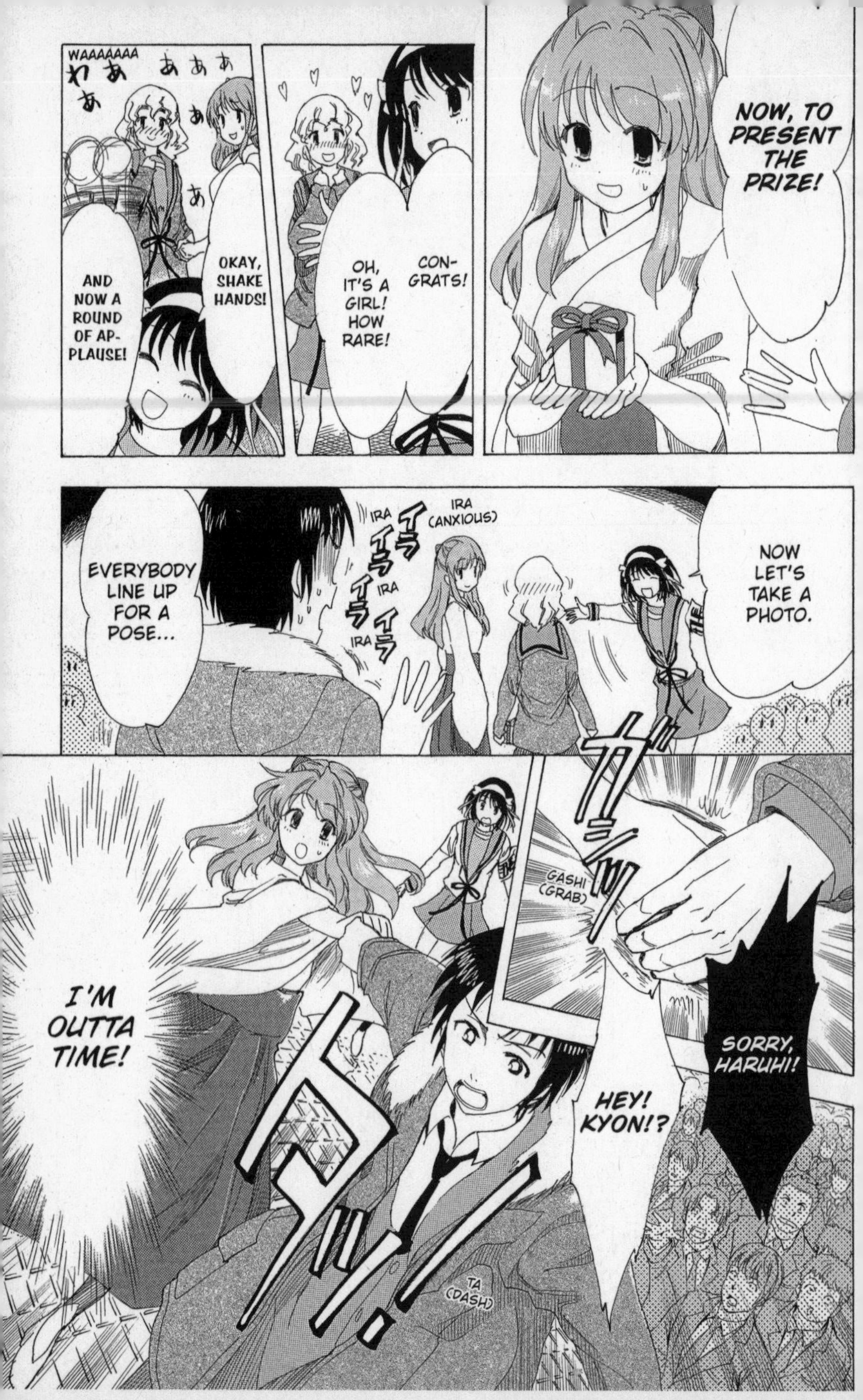
NOW, TO PRESENT THE PRIZE!
CON-GRATS!
OH, IT'S A GIRL! HOW RARE!
WAAAAAAA
わあああああ
OKAY, SHAKE HANDS!
AND NOW A ROUND OF AP-PLAUSE!
NOW LET'S TAKE A PHOTO.
IRA (ANXIOUS)
イライラ
IRA
イライラ
IRA
IRA
EVERYBODY LINE UP FOR A POSE...
ガシッ
GASHI (GRAB)
SORRY, HARUHI!
HEY! KYON!?
I'M OUTTA TIME!
タッ
TA (DASH)

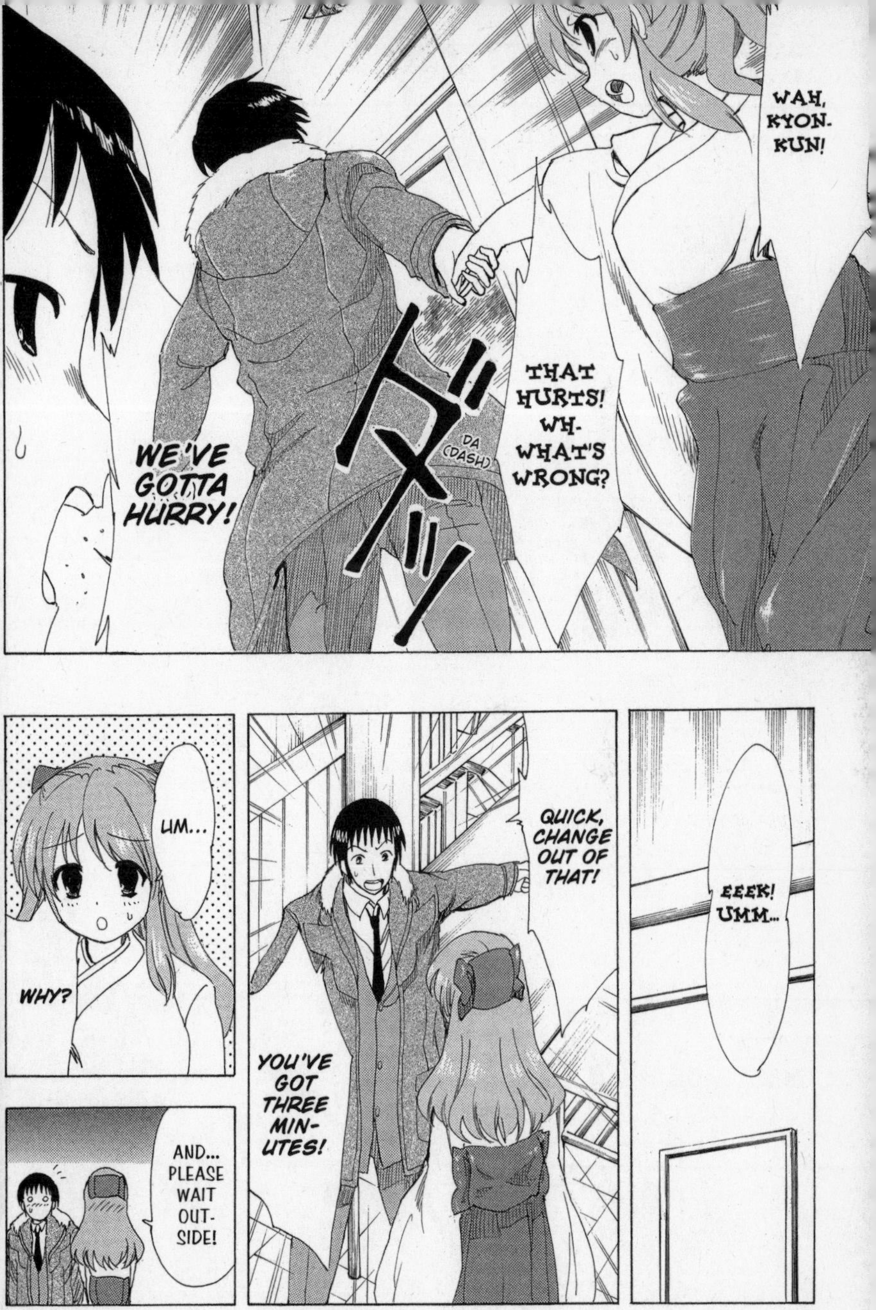
WAH, KYON-KUN!
THAT HURTS! WH-WHAT'S WRONG?
ダッ
DA (DASH)
WE'VE GOTTA HURRY!
EEEK! UMM...
QUICK, CHANGE OUT OF THAT!
YOU'VE GOT THREE MIN-UTES!
UM...
WHY?
AND... PLEASE WAIT OUT-SIDE!

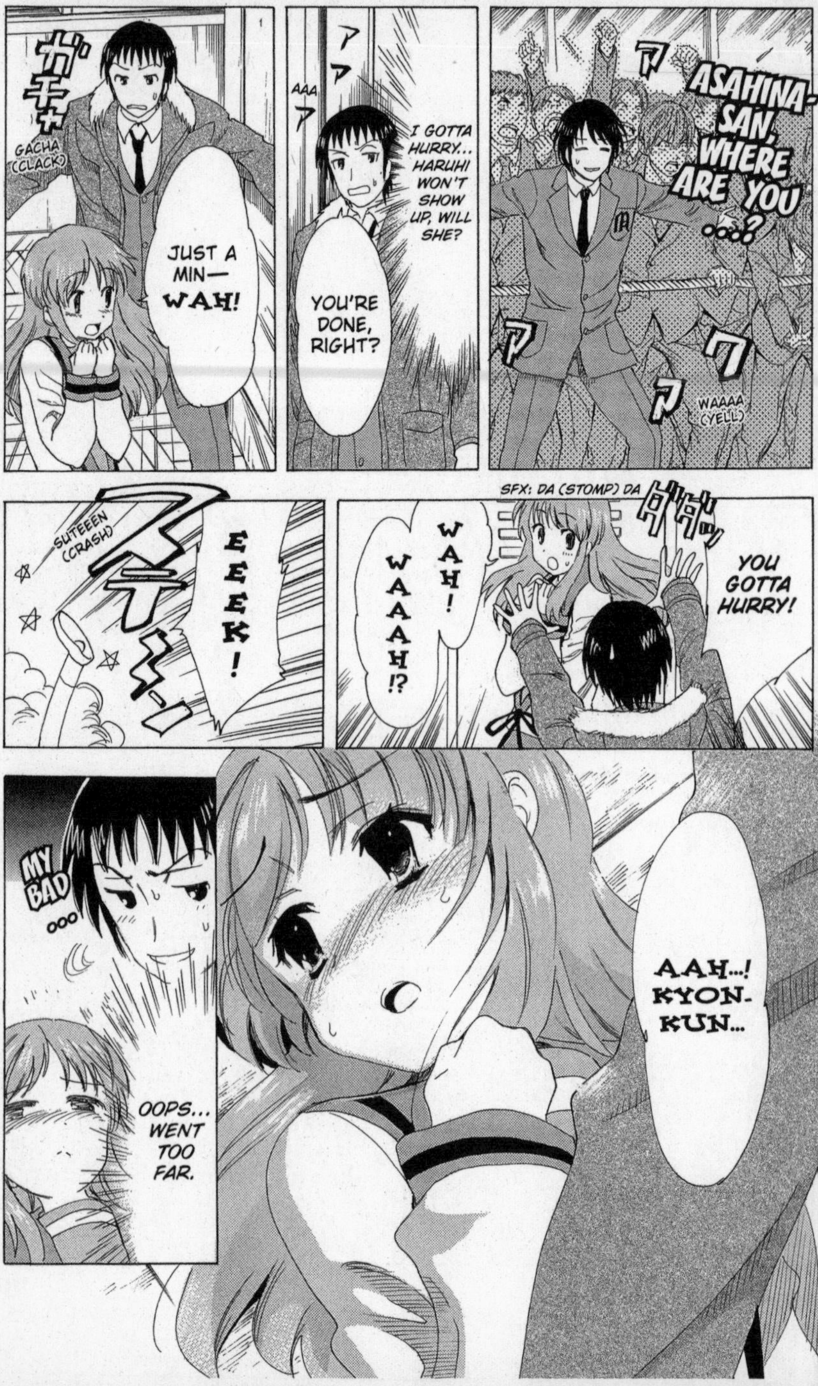
ASAHINA-SAN, WHERE ARE YOU...?
WAAAA (YELL)
AAA
I GOTTA HURRY... HARUHI WON'T SHOW UP, WILL SHE?
YOU'RE DONE, RIGHT?
GACHA (CLACK)
JUST A MIN— WAH!
SFX: DA (STOMP) DA
YOU GOTTA HURRY!
WAH! WAAAAH!?
SUTEEEN (CRASH)
EEEEK!
AAH...! KYON-KUN...
MY BAD
OOPS... WENT TOO FAR.

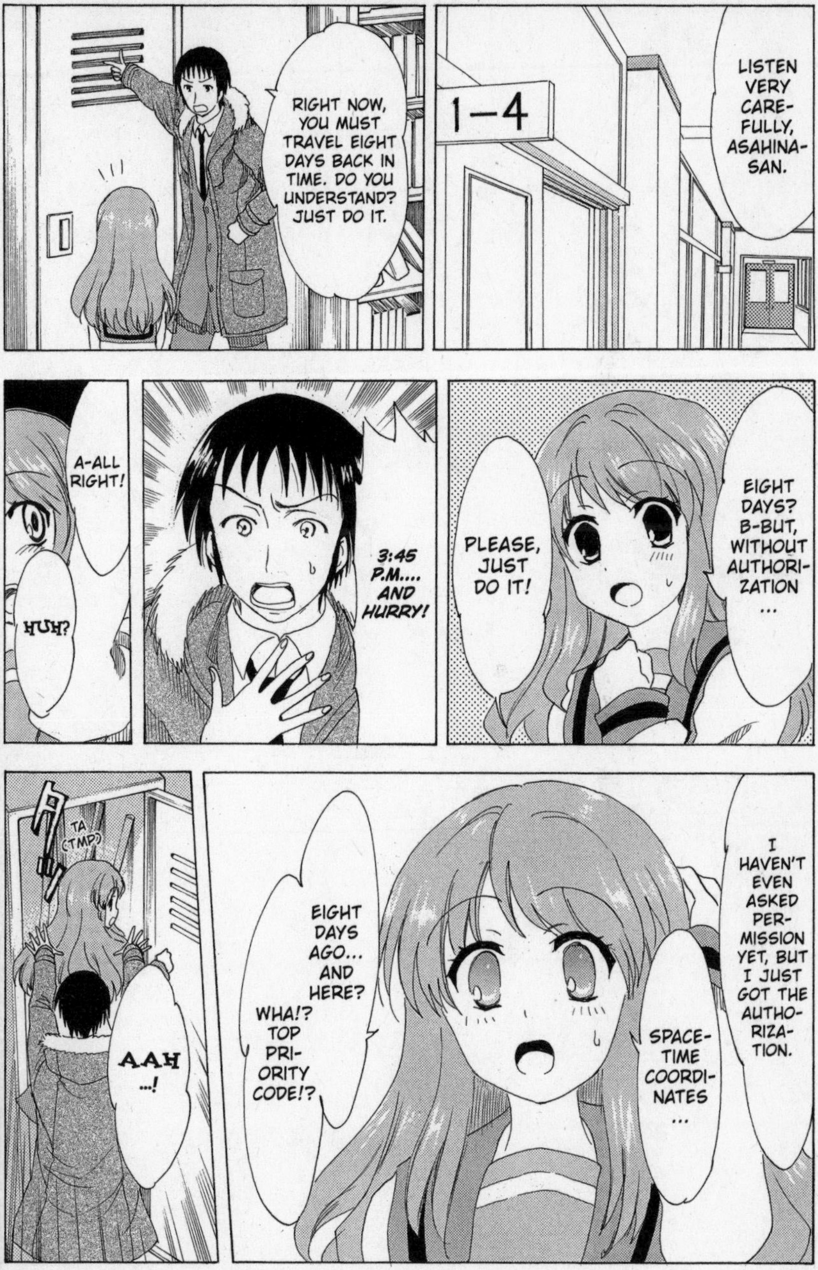
LISTEN VERY CARE-FULLY, ASAHINA-SAN.
1-4
RIGHT NOW, YOU MUST TRAVEL EIGHT DAYS BACK IN TIME. DO YOU UNDERSTAND? JUST DO IT.
EIGHT DAYS? B-BUT, WITHOUT AUTHORI-ZATION ...
PLEASE, JUST DO IT!
3:45 P.M.... AND HURRY!
A-ALL RIGHT!
HUH?
I HAVEN'T EVEN ASKED PER-MISSION YET, BUT I JUST GOT THE AUTHO-RIZA-TION.
SPACE-TIME COORDI-NATES ...
EIGHT DAYS AGO... AND HERE?
WHA!? TOP PRI-ORITY CODE!?
TA (TMP)
AAH ...!

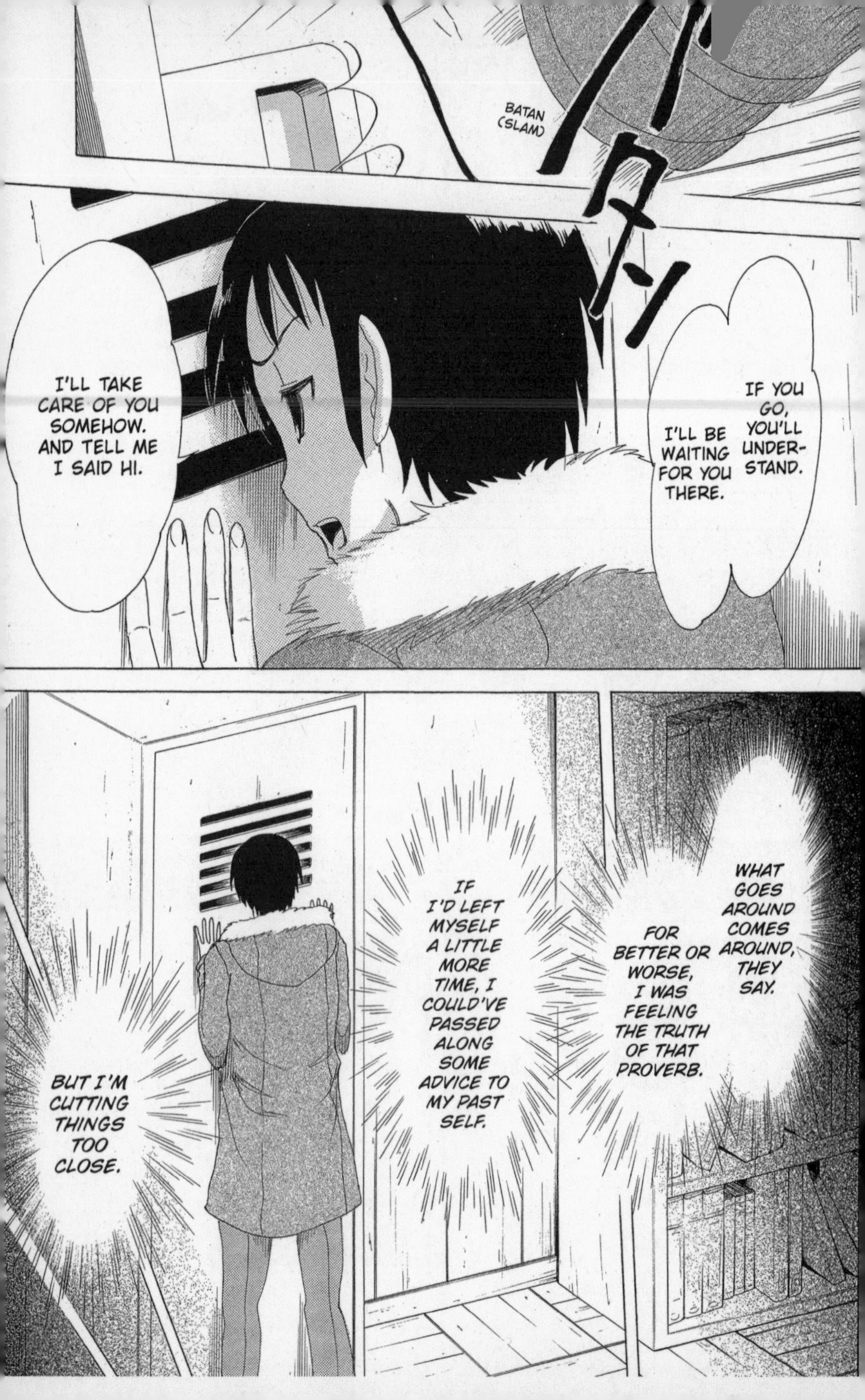
BATAN (SLAM)
IF YOU GO, YOU'LL UNDERSTAND.
I'LL BE WAITING FOR YOU THERE.
I'LL TAKE CARE OF YOU SOMEHOW. AND TELL ME I SAID HI.
WHAT GOES AROUND COMES AROUND, THEY SAY.
FOR BETTER OR WORSE, I WAS FEELING THE TRUTH OF THAT PROVERB.
IF I'D LEFT MYSELF A LITTLE MORE TIME, I COULD'VE PASSED ALONG SOME ADVICE TO MY PAST SELF.
BUT I'M CUTTING THINGS TOO CLOSE.

SFX: KON (KNOCK) KON

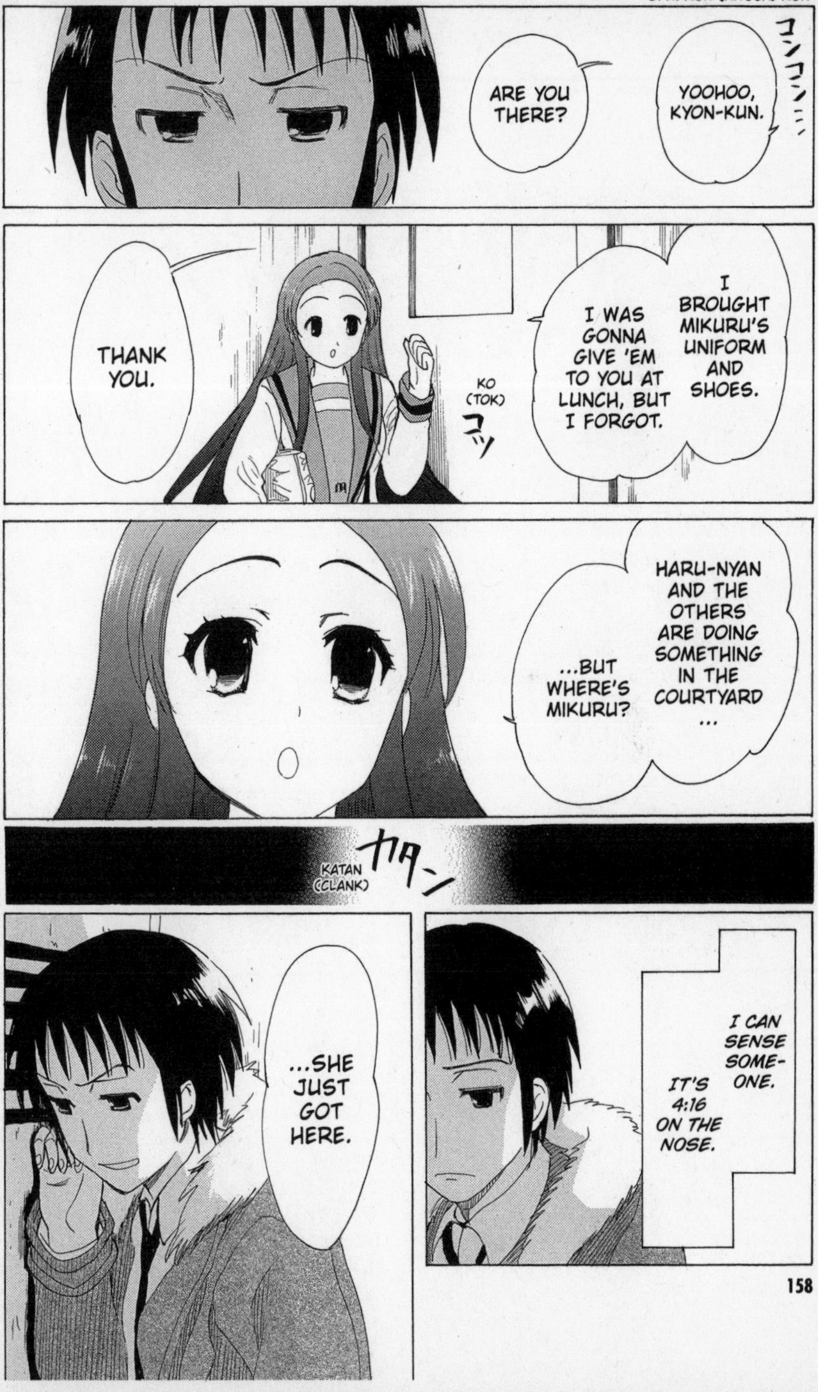
YOOHOO, KYON-KUN.
ARE YOU THERE?
I BROUGHT MIKURU'S UNIFORM AND SHOES.
I WAS GONNA GIVE 'EM TO YOU AT LUNCH, BUT I FORGOT.
KO (TOK)
THANK YOU.
HARU-NYAN AND THE OTHERS ARE DOING SOMETHING IN THE COURTYARD ...
...BUT WHERE'S MIKURU?
KATAN (CLANK)
I CAN SENSE SOME-ONE.
IT'S 4:16 ON THE NOSE.
...SHE JUST GOT HERE.

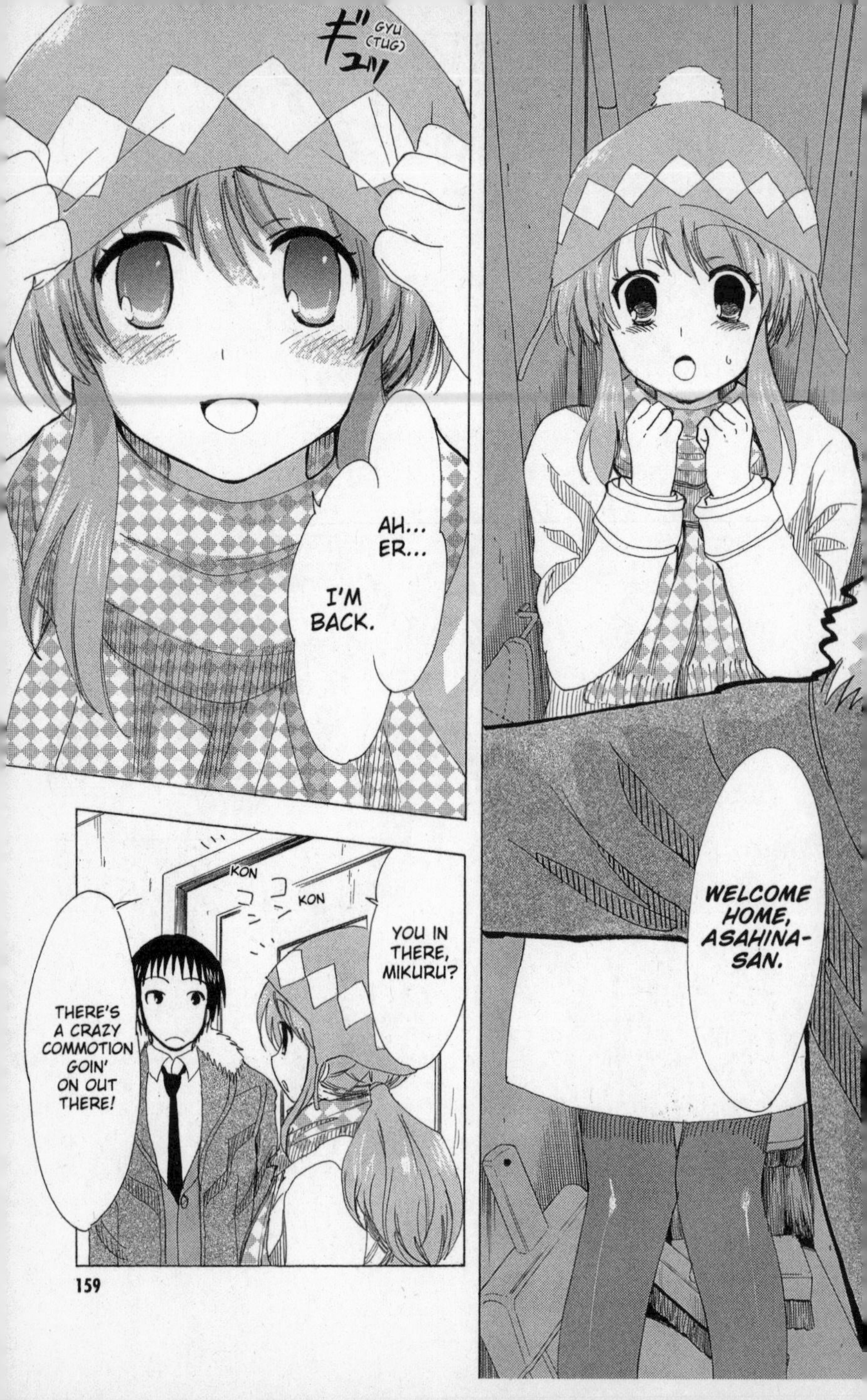
WELCOME HOME, ASAHINA-SAN.
ギュッ GYU (TUG)
AH... ER...
I'M BACK.
KON
KON
YOU IN THERE, MIKURU?
THERE'S A CRAZY COMMOTION GOIN' ON OUT THERE!

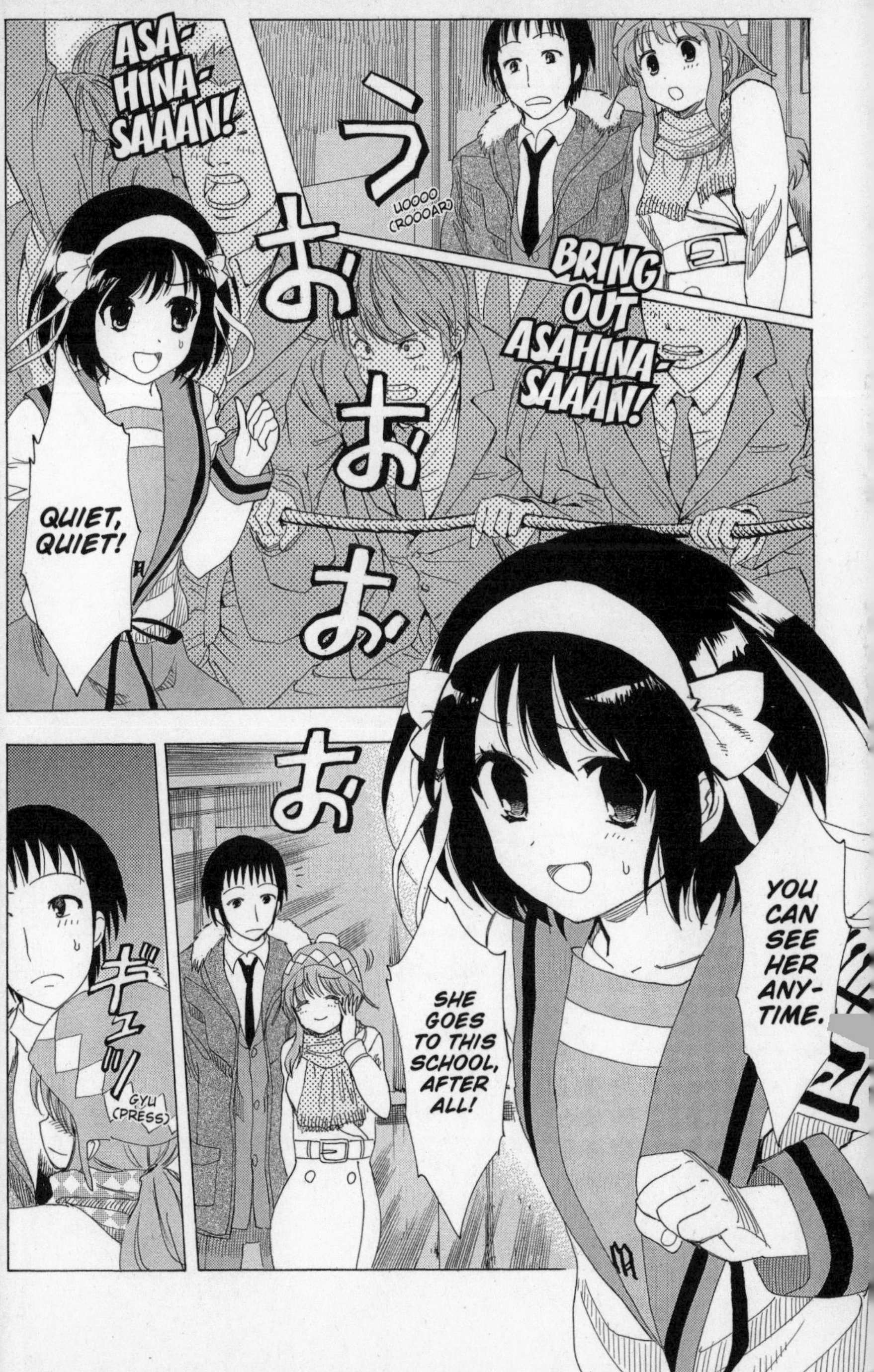
うおおおお
UOOOO
(ROOOAR)
ASA-
HINA-
SAAAN!
BRING
OUT
ASAHINA-
SAAAN!
QUIET,
QUIET!
YOU
CAN
SEE
HER
ANY-
TIME.
SHE
GOES
TO THIS
SCHOOL,
AFTER
ALL!
ギュッ
GYU
(PRESS)

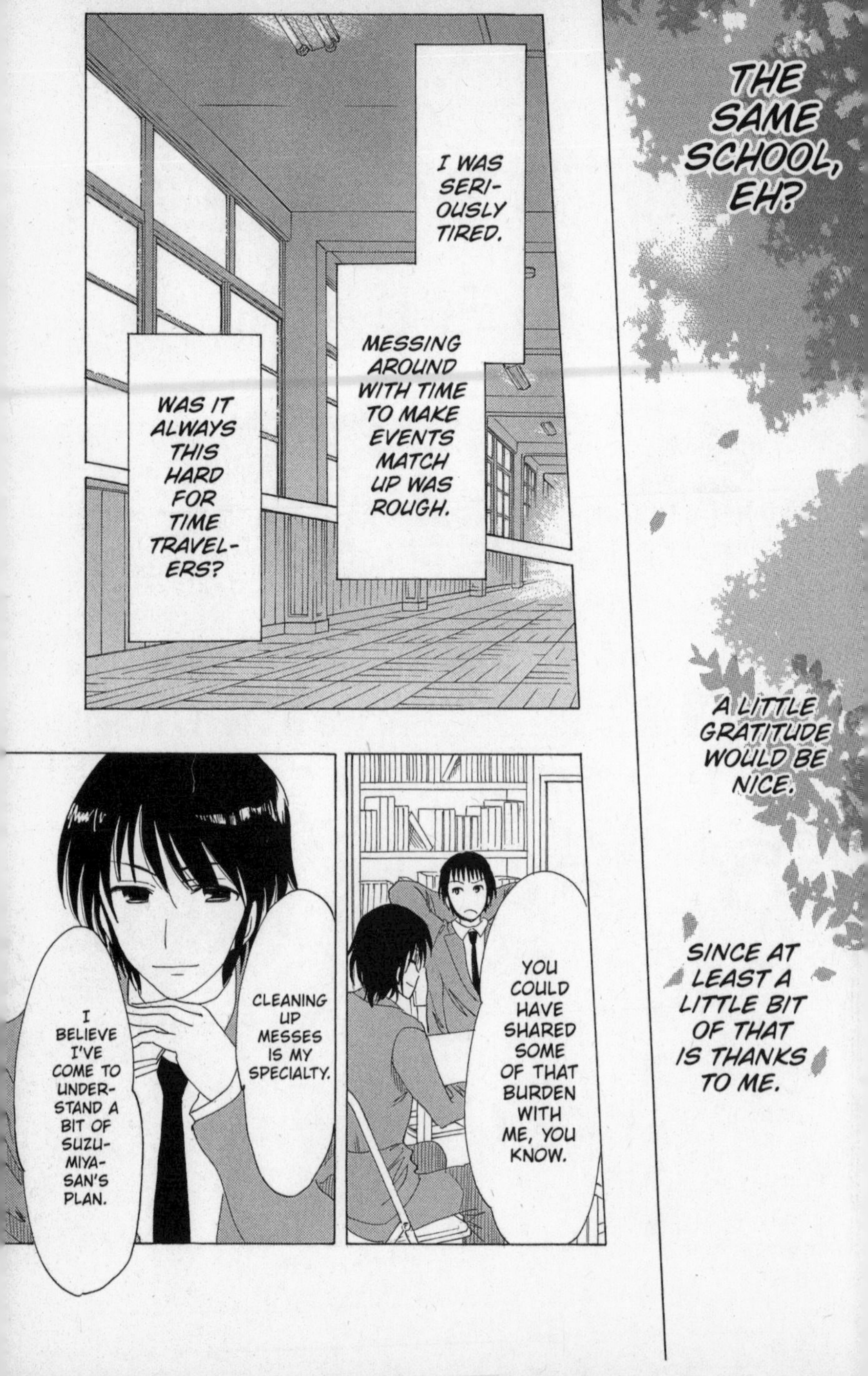
THE SAME SCHOOL, EH?
A LITTLE GRATITUDE WOULD BE NICE.
SINCE AT LEAST A LITTLE BIT OF THAT IS THANKS TO ME.
I WAS SERI-OUSLY TIRED.
MESSING AROUND WITH TIME TO MAKE EVENTS MATCH UP WAS ROUGH.
WAS IT ALWAYS THIS HARD FOR TIME TRAVEL-ERS?
YOU COULD HAVE SHARED SOME OF THAT BURDEN WITH ME, YOU KNOW.
CLEANING UP MESSES IS MY SPECIALTY.
I BELIEVE I'VE COME TO UNDER-STAND A BIT OF SUZU-MIYA-SAN'S PLAN.

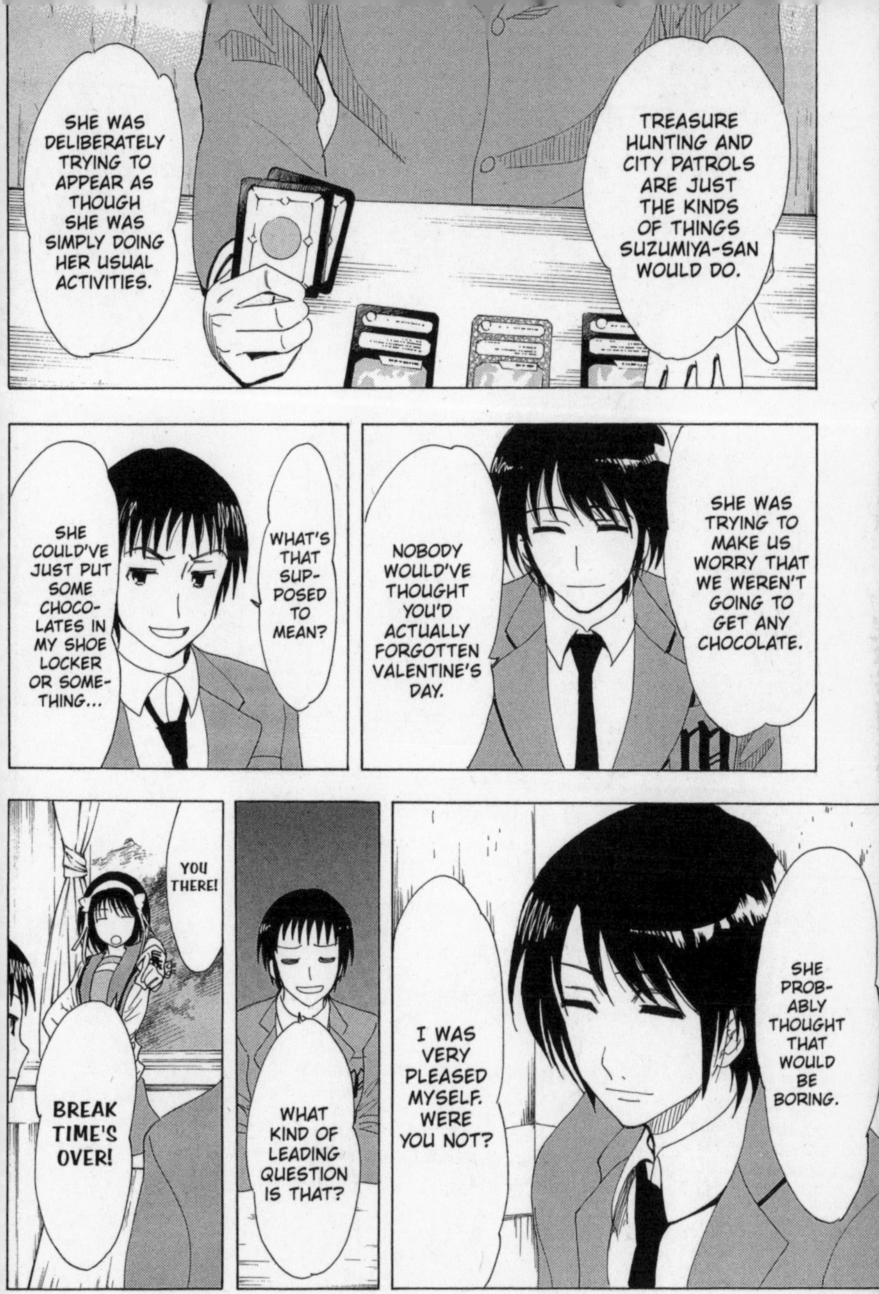
TREASURE HUNTING AND CITY PATROLS ARE JUST THE KINDS OF THINGS SUZUMIYA-SAN WOULD DO.
SHE WAS DELIBERATELY TRYING TO APPEAR AS THOUGH SHE WAS SIMPLY DOING HER USUAL ACTIVITIES.
SHE WAS TRYING TO MAKE US WORRY THAT WE WEREN'T GOING TO GET ANY CHOCOLATE.
NOBODY WOULD'VE THOUGHT YOU'D ACTUALLY FORGOTTEN VALENTINE'S DAY.
WHAT'S THAT SUP-POSED TO MEAN?
SHE COULD'VE JUST PUT SOME CHOCO-LATES IN MY SHOE LOCKER OR SOME-THING...
SHE PROB-ABLY THOUGHT THAT WOULD BE BORING.
I WAS VERY PLEASED MYSELF. WERE YOU NOT?
WHAT KIND OF LEADING QUESTION IS THAT?
YOU THERE!
BREAK TIME'S OVER!

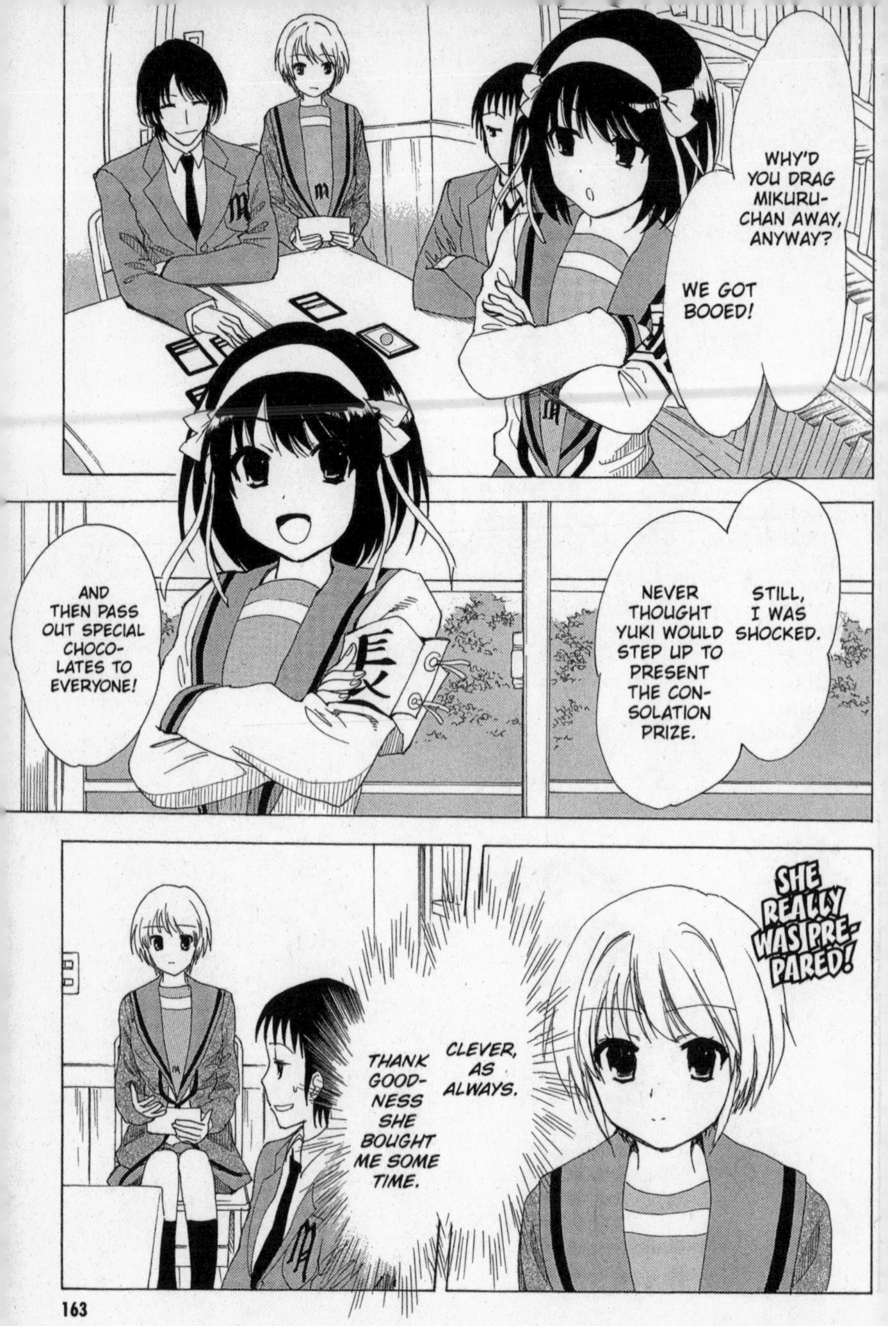
WHY'D YOU DRAG MIKURU-CHAN AWAY, ANYWAY?
WE GOT BOOED!
STILL, I WAS SHOCKED.
NEVER THOUGHT YUKI WOULD STEP UP TO PRESENT THE CON-SOLATION PRIZE.
AND THEN PASS OUT SPECIAL CHOCO-LATES TO EVERYONE!
SHE REALLY WAS PRE-PARED!
CLEVER, AS ALWAYS.
THANK GOOD-NESS SHE BOUGHT ME SOME TIME.

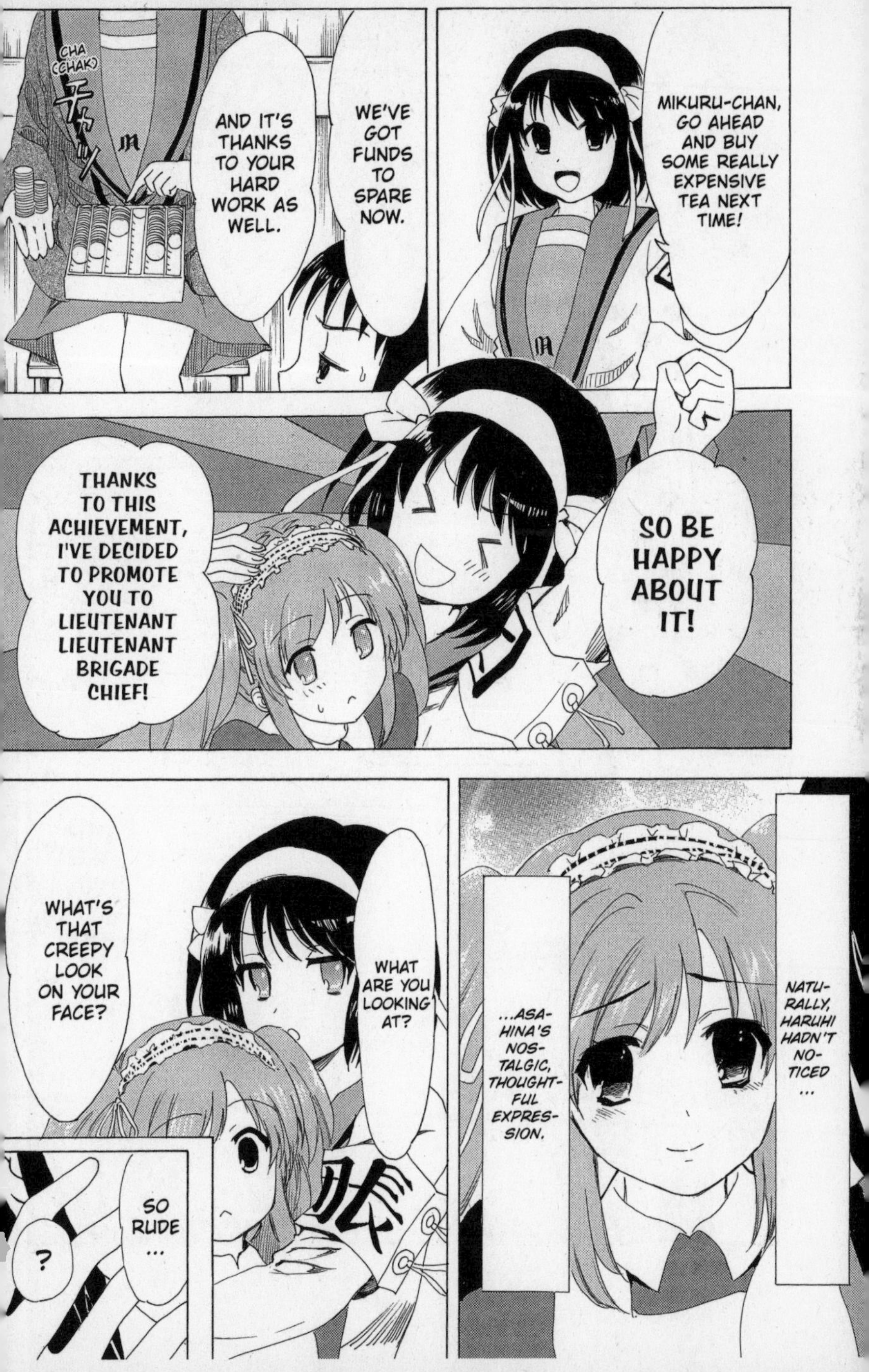
MIKURU-CHAN, GO AHEAD AND BUY SOME REALLY EXPENSIVE TEA NEXT TIME!
WE'VE GOT FUNDS TO SPARE NOW.
AND IT'S THANKS TO YOUR HARD WORK AS WELL.
CHA (CHAK)
SO BE HAPPY ABOUT IT!
THANKS TO THIS ACHIEVEMENT, I'VE DECIDED TO PROMOTE YOU TO LIEUTENANT LIEUTENANT BRIGADE CHIEF!
NATU-RALLY, HARUHI HADN'T NO-TICED ...
...ASA-HINA'S NOS-TALGIC, THOUGHT-FUL EXPRES-SION.
WHAT ARE YOU LOOKING AT?
WHAT'S THAT CREEPY LOOK ON YOUR FACE?
SO RUDE ...
?

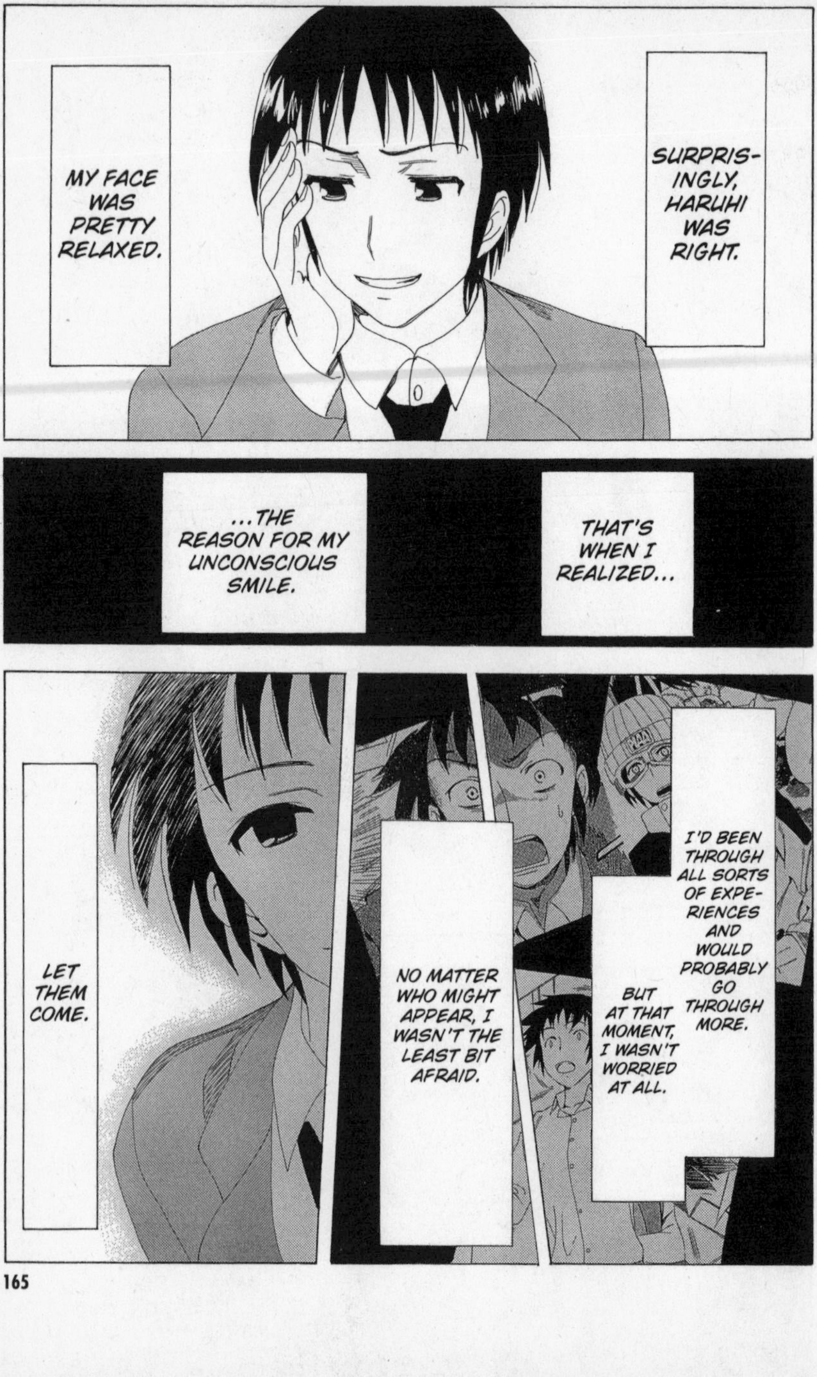
SURPRIS-
INGLY,
HARUHI
WAS
RIGHT.
MY FACE WAS PRETTY RELAXED.
THAT'S WHEN I REALIZED...
...THE REASON FOR MY UNCONSCIOUS SMILE.
I'D BEEN THROUGH ALL SORTS OF EXPE-
RIENCES AND WOULD PROBABLY GO THROUGH MORE.
BUT AT THAT MOMENT, I WASN'T WORRIED AT ALL.
NO MATTER WHO MIGHT APPEAR, I WASN'T THE LEAST BIT AFRAID.
LET THEM COME.

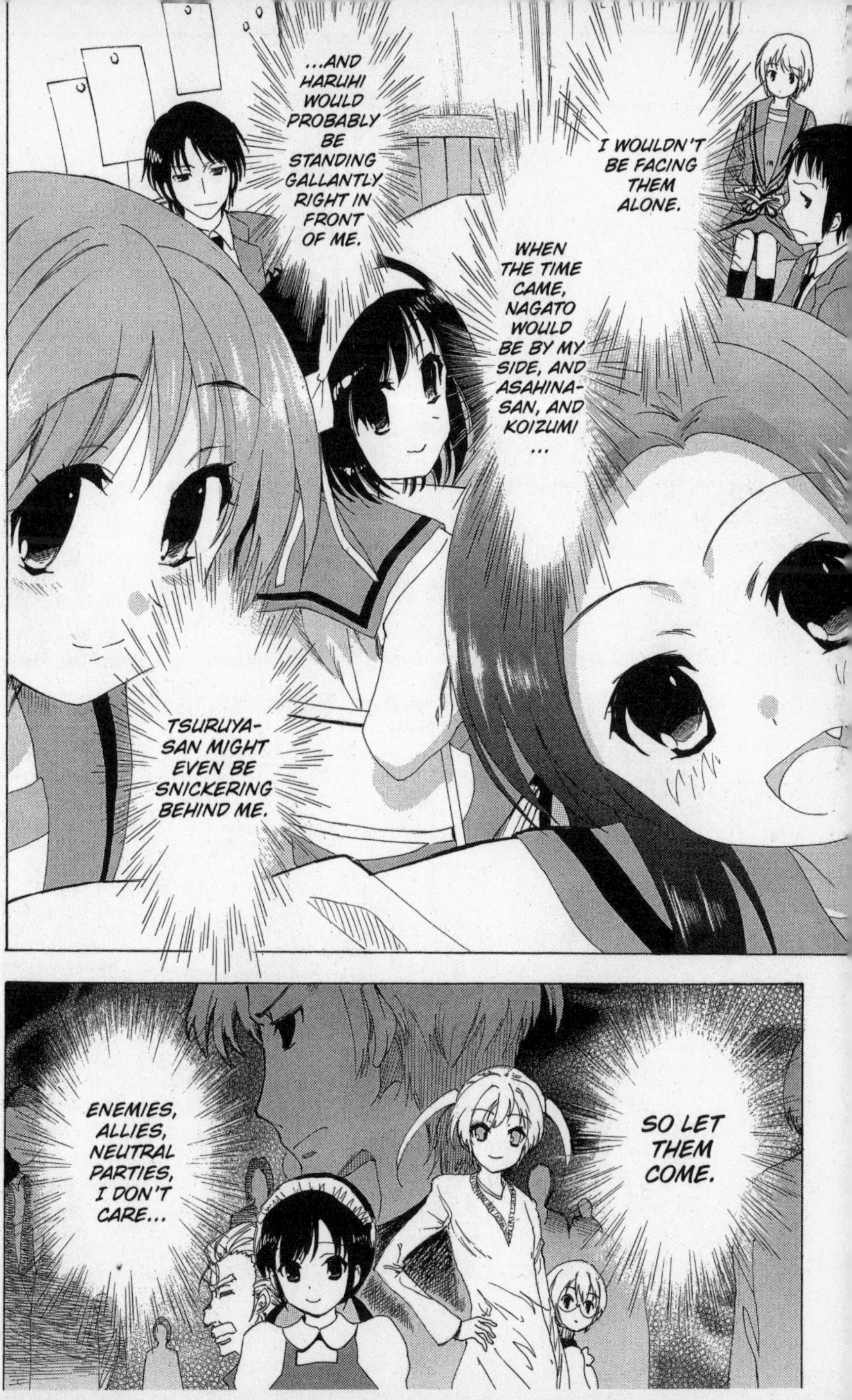
I WOULDN'T BE FACING THEM ALONE.
WHEN THE TIME CAME, NAGATO WOULD BE BY MY SIDE, AND ASAHINA-SAN, AND KOIZUMI ...
...AND HARUHI WOULD PROBABLY BE STANDING GALLANTLY RIGHT IN FRONT OF ME.
TSURUYA-SAN MIGHT EVEN BE SNICKERING BEHIND ME.
ENEMIES, ALLIES, NEUTRAL PARTIES, I DON'T CARE...
SO LET THEM COME.

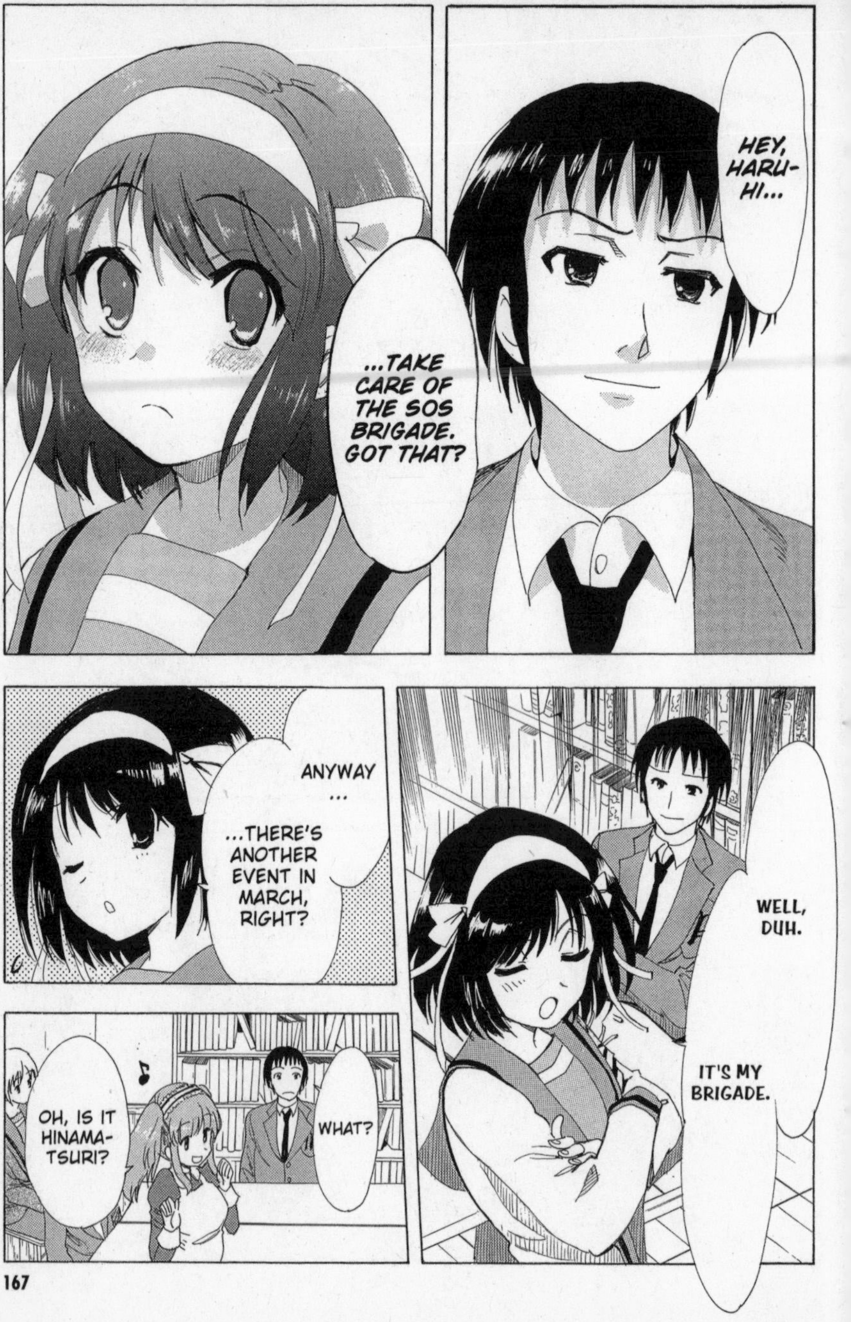
HEY, HARU-HI...
...TAKE CARE OF THE SOS BRIGADE. GOT THAT?
WELL, DUH.
IT'S MY BRIGADE.
ANYWAY ...
...THERE'S ANOTHER EVENT IN MARCH, RIGHT?
WHAT?
OH, IS IT HINAMA-TSURI?

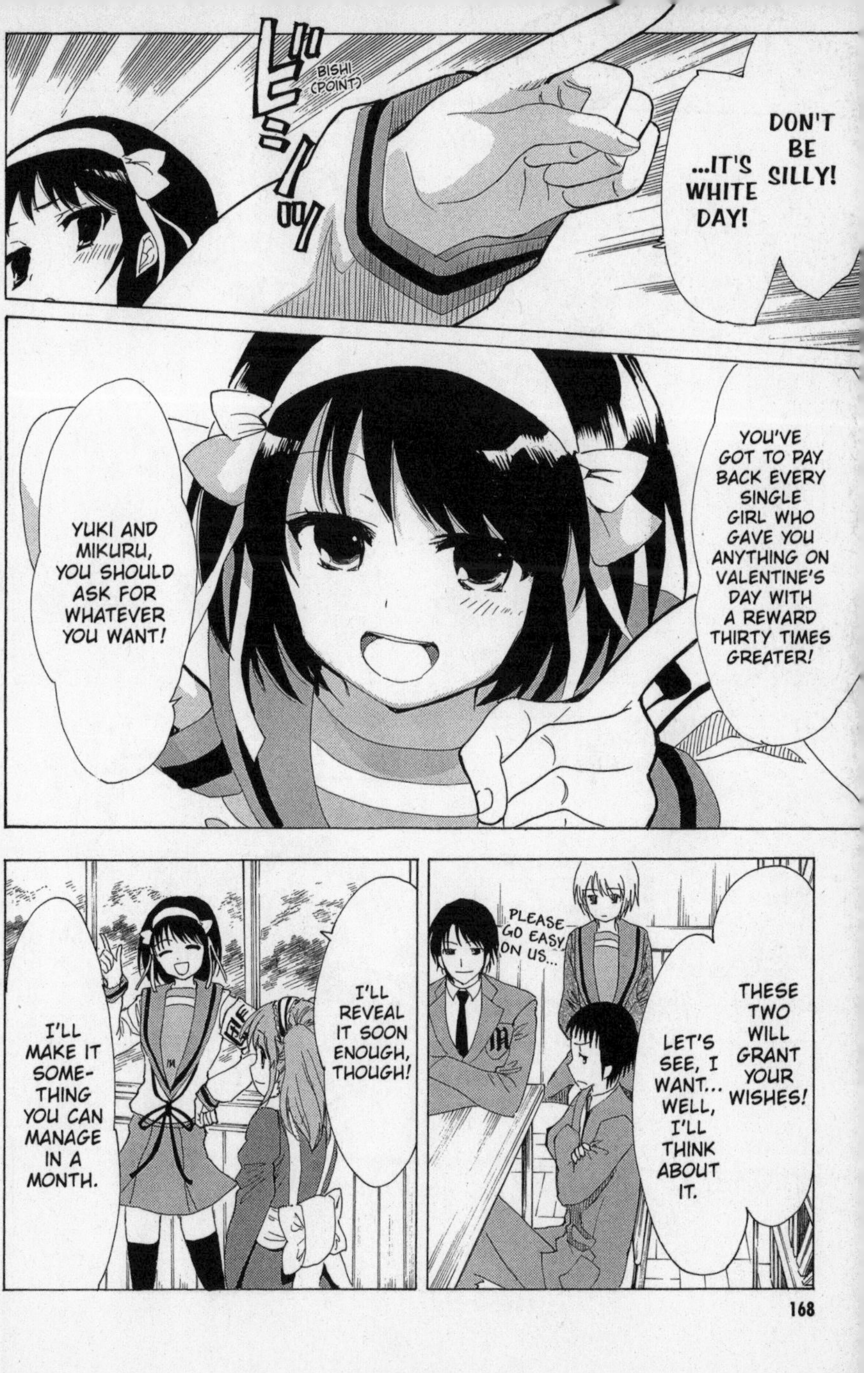
DON'T BE SILLY!
...IT'S WHITE DAY!
BISHI (POINT)
YOU'VE GOT TO PAY BACK EVERY SINGLE GIRL WHO GAVE YOU ANYTHING ON VALENTINE'S DAY WITH A REWARD THIRTY TIMES GREATER!
YUKI AND MIKURU, YOU SHOULD ASK FOR WHATEVER YOU WANT!
THESE TWO WILL GRANT YOUR WISHES!
LET'S SEE, I WANT... WELL, I'LL THINK ABOUT IT.
PLEASE GO EASY ON US...
I'LL REVEAL IT SOON ENOUGH, THOUGH!
I'LL MAKE IT SOME-THING YOU CAN MANAGE IN A MONTH.

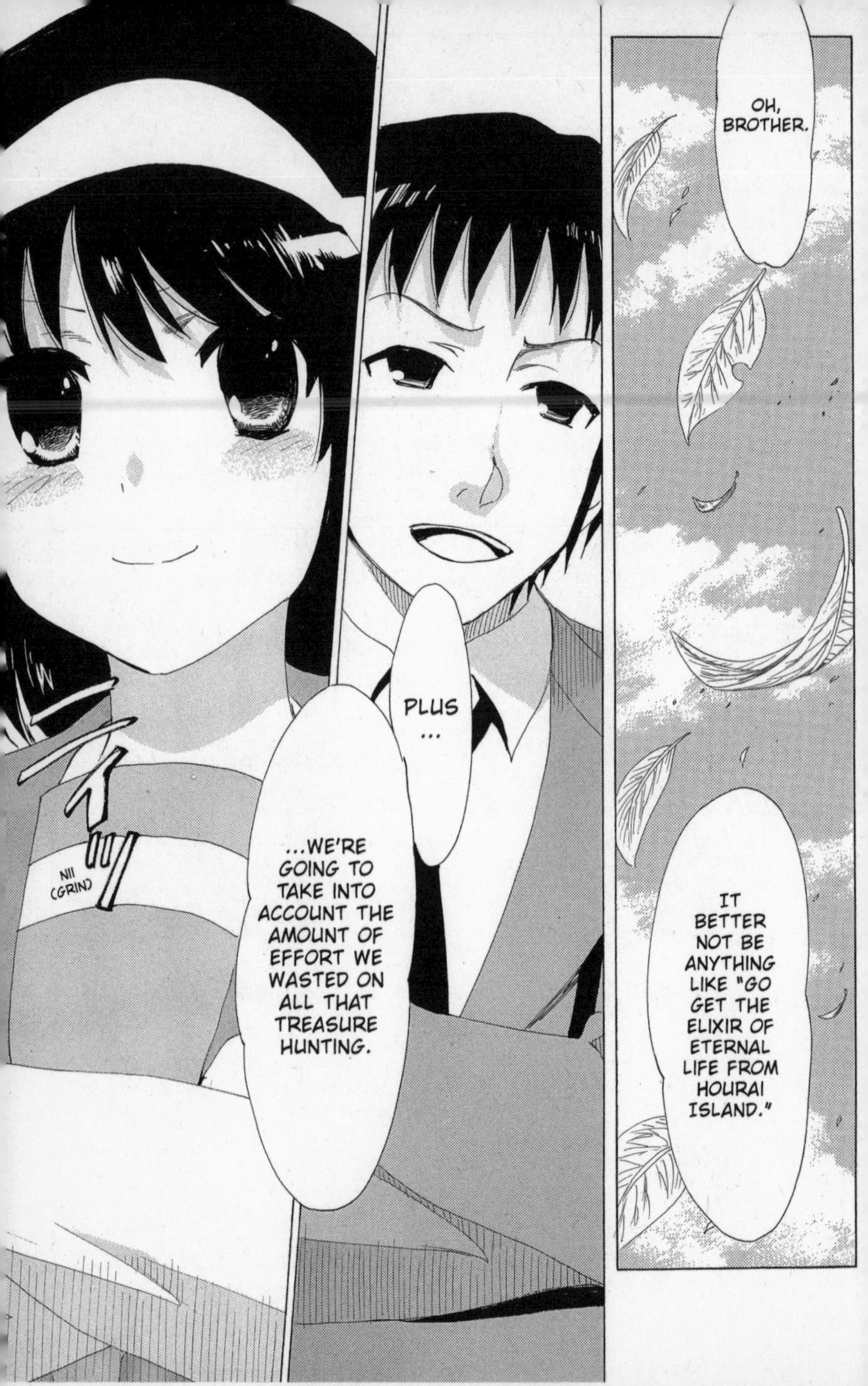
OH, BROTHER.
IT BETTER NOT BE ANYTHING LIKE "GO GET THE ELIXIR OF ETERNAL LIFE FROM HOURAI ISLAND."
PLUS ...
...WE'RE GOING TO TAKE INTO ACCOUNT THE AMOUNT OF EFFORT WE WASTED ON ALL THAT TREASURE HUNTING.
NII (GRIN)

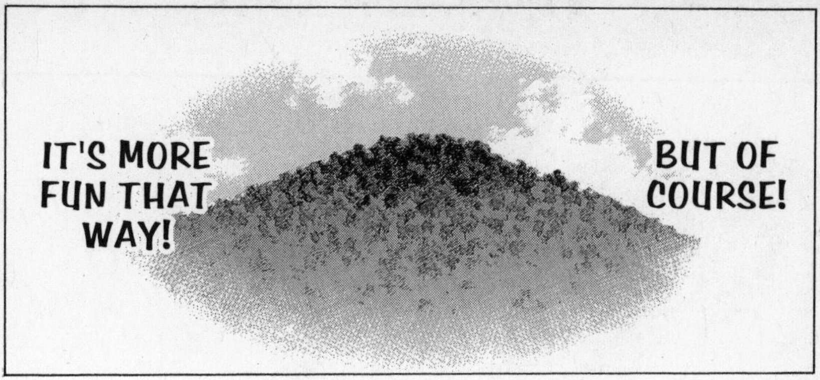
BUT OF COURSE!
IT'S MORE FUN THAT WAY!

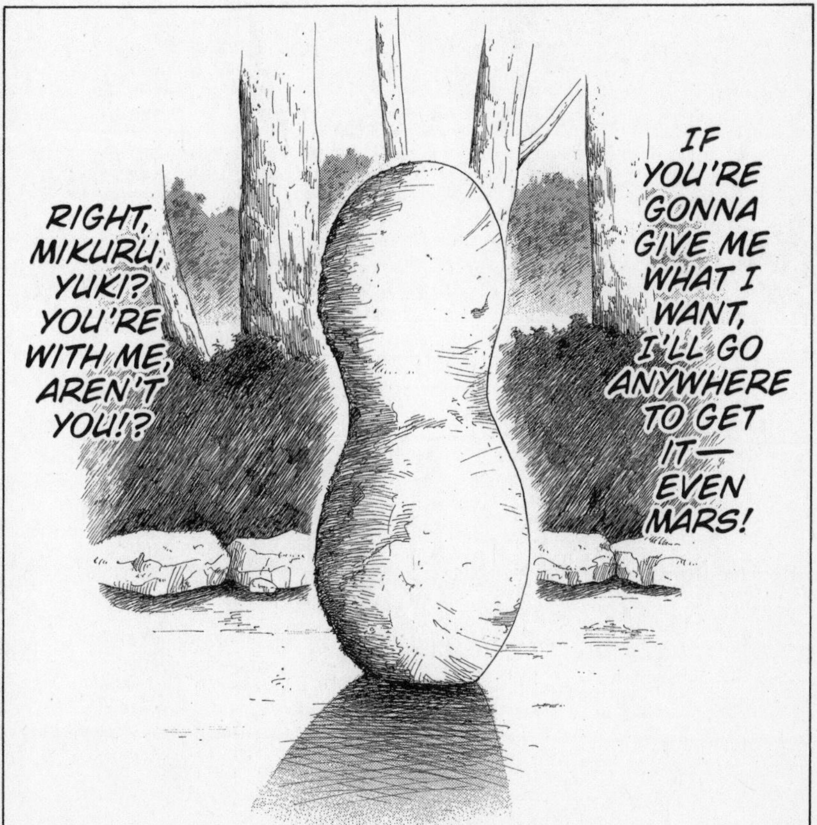
IF YOU'RE GONNA GIVE ME WHAT I WANT, I'LL GO ANYWHERE TO GET IT— EVEN MARS!
RIGHT, MIKURU, YUKI? YOU'RE WITH ME, AREN'T YOU!?

THE INTRIGUES OF HARUHI SUZUMIYA XI : END

TRANSLATION NOTES

Page 21
Doria is a common Italian dish in Japan. It is a kind of baked casserole made of ketchup fried rice, meat or seafood, tomato sauce, white sauce, and cheese.

Page 113
The Genroku era (1688 to 1704) is considered the "golden age" of the Edo Period.

Page 121
The Bamboo Cutter's Tale, or *Princess Kaguya*, is a Japanese folktale that describes the life of Kaguya-hime. Discovered as a baby within a stalk of bamboo by an elderly bamboo cutter, the little girl brings incredible wealth to her adoptive parents and eventually attracts the attention of five princes who come to her home seeking her hand in marriage. Unwilling to marry any one of them, Kaguya-hime assigns each prince an impossible task that none manages to complete. Some time afterward, the Emperor of Japan visits Kaguya-hime to ask for her hand in marriage, a request she rebuffs many times. Later, Kaguya-hime reveals that she is actually from the Capital of the Moon and must return to her people. Despite the efforts of the Emperor to keep the Moon dwellers from taking Kaguya-hime, the beautiful woman returns to her place among her countrymen on the Moon.

Page 148
Amidakuji or Ghost Leg is a common lottery method in Japan. A series of vertical lines are drawn with the prizes at the bottom. These lines are connected by randomly-drawn horizontal bars. The player chooses a vertical line and, starting from the top, moves downward, turning left or right whenever he or she encounters a horizontal bar. Whichever vertical line they finally reach the bottom of determines the outcome.

Page 167
Hinamatsuri, the Japanese Doll Festival, or Girls' Day is held annually on March 3. Customarily, a display of ornamental dolls are put up for the occasion, featuring the court of an Emperor and Empress.

Page 169
Hourai Island and Mount Hourai are taken from Chinese mythology, where the mountain is referred to as Mount Panglai, a land of riches and plenty where there is no pain and suffering and whose fruits are said to have healing powers and grant eternal life. Despite many attempts, the island and its elixer of life was never found.

Page 175 (Preview)
"Kanjizai bosatsugyo?" Mikuru is attempting to recite one of the best known texts of Buddhism, the Heart Sutra, which is sometimes used as an exorcism chant.

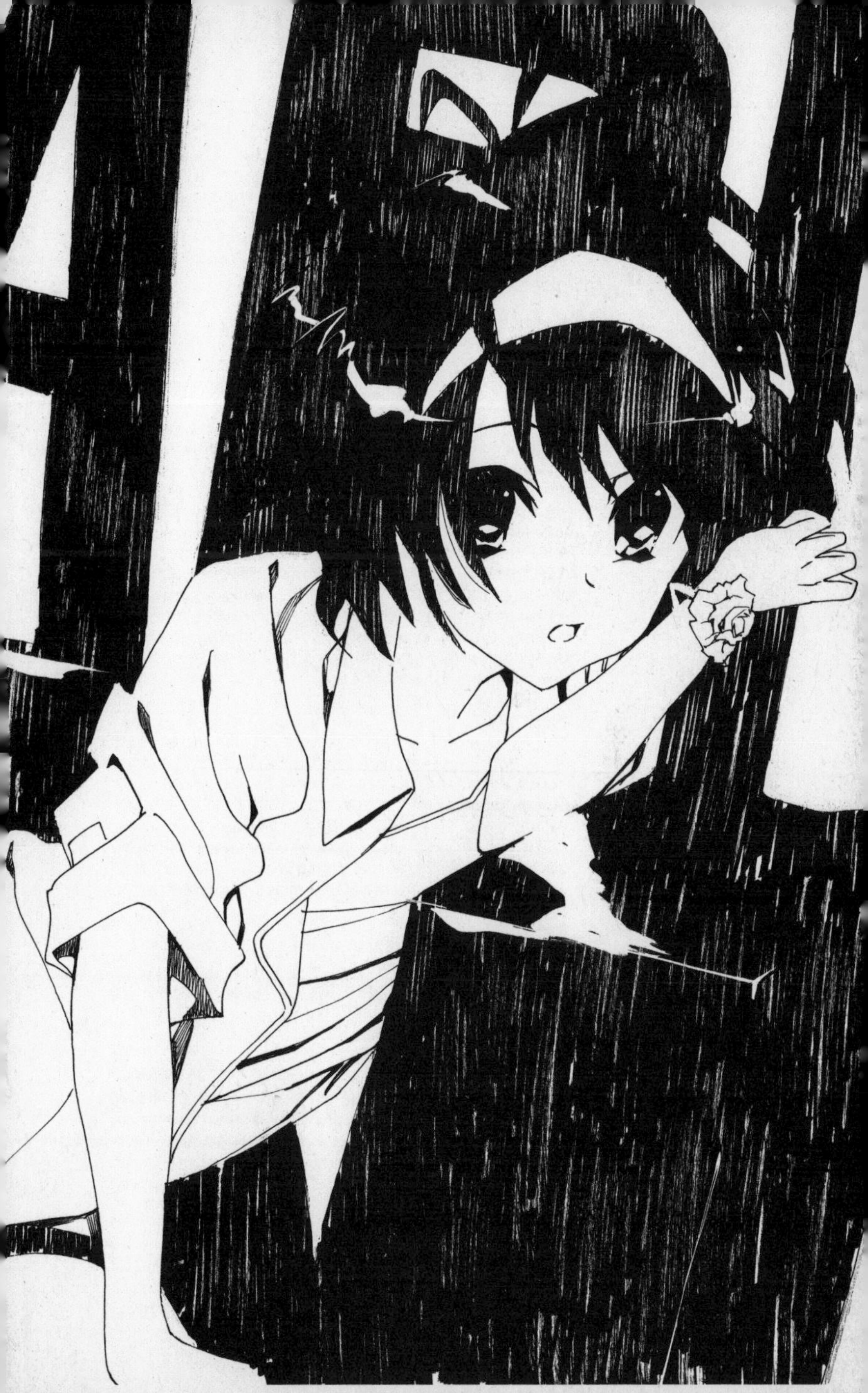

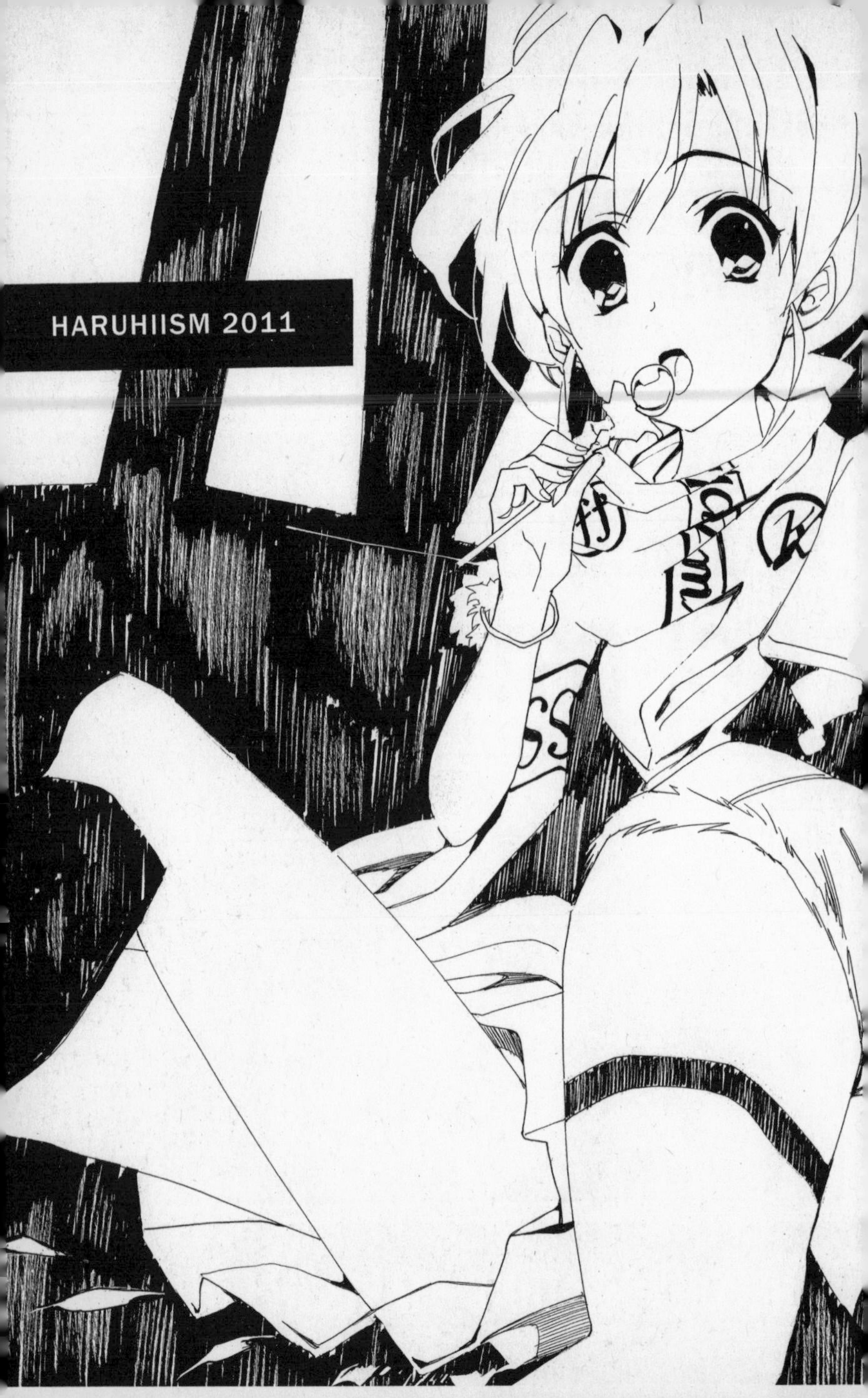
HARUHIISM 2011

BEFORE SPRING BREAK, THE SOS BRIGADE RECEIVES

A SUDDEN CLIENT!

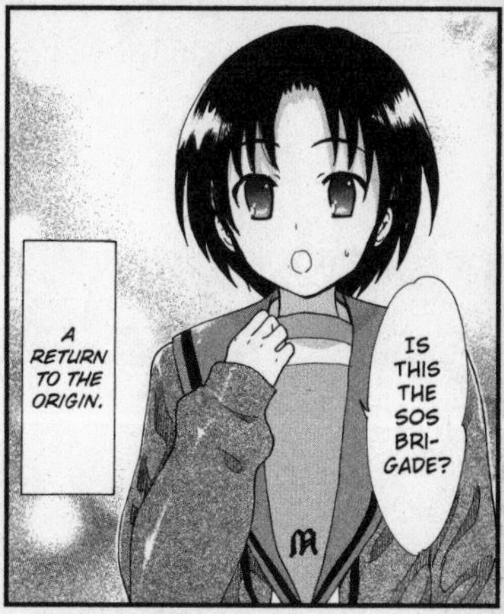

IS THIS THE SOS BRI-GADE?
A RETURN TO THE ORIGIN.

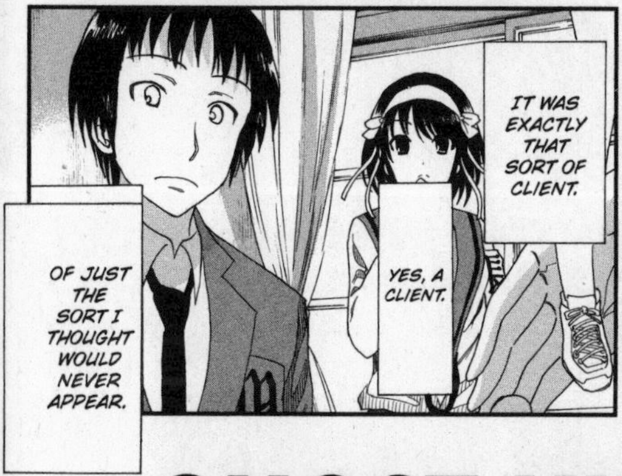

IT WAS EXACTLY THAT SORT OF CLIENT.
YES, A CLIENT.
OF JUST THE SORT I THOUGHT WOULD NEVER APPEAR.

AND THE MISSION IS...

GHOST HUNTING!?

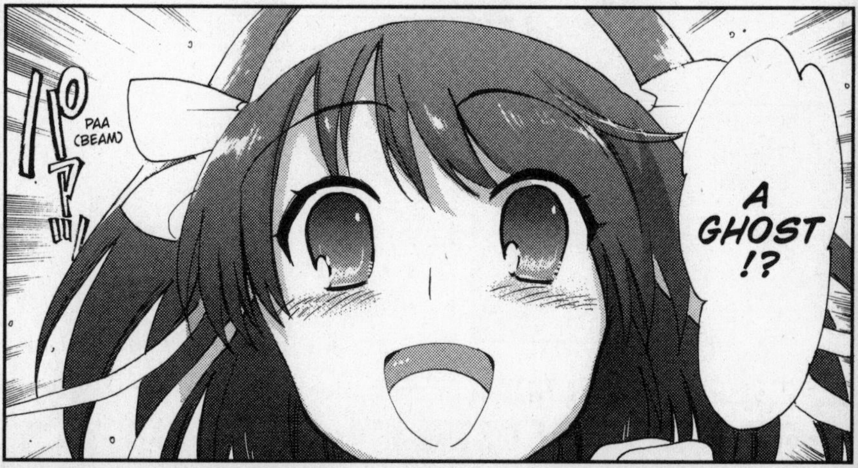

A GHOST!?
PAA (BEAM)

THE "DISSOCIATION" STARTS IN VOLUME 16!

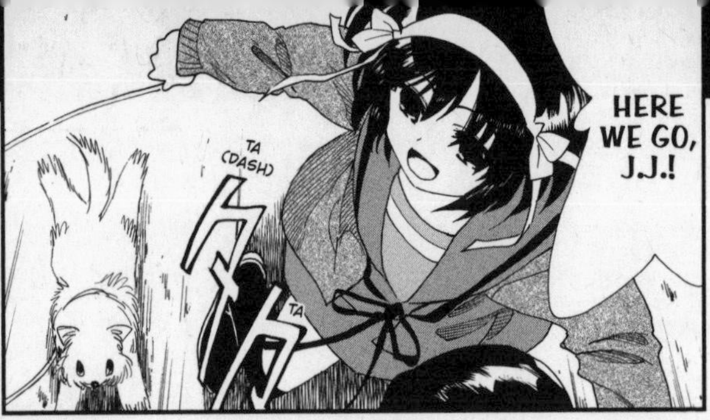
HERE WE GO, J.J.!
TA (DASH)
TA

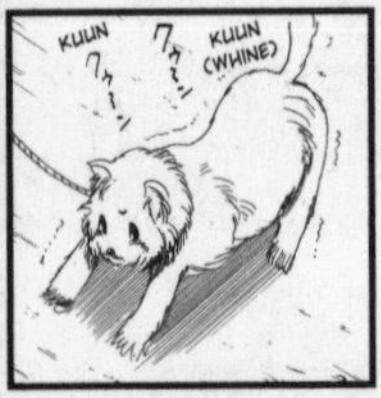
KUUN (WHINE)
KUUN

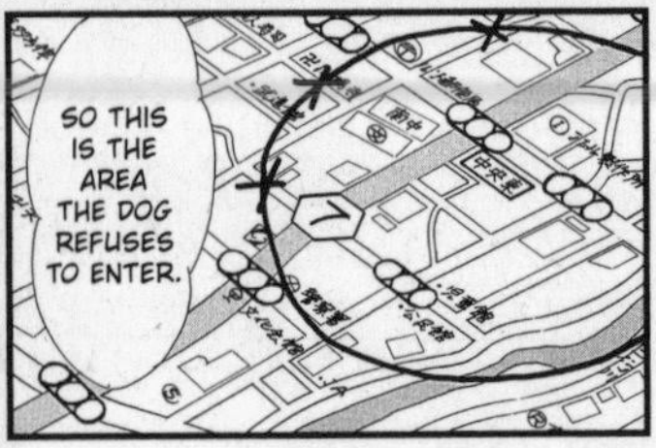
SO THIS IS THE AREA THE DOG REFUSES TO ENTER.

SPECTRAL PHENOMENA

THAT ONLY ANIMALS CAN SENSE!?

THE SOS BRIGADE HEADS TO THE SCENE, BUT...!

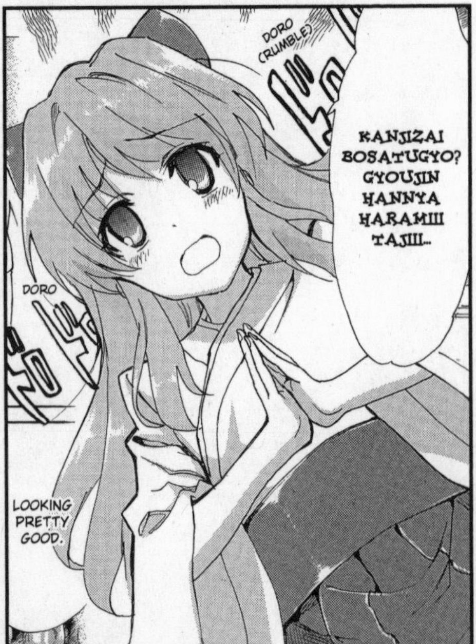
KANJIZAI BOSATUGYO? GYOUJIN HANNYA HARAMIII TAJIII...
DORO (RUMBLE)
DORO
LOOKING PRETTY GOOD.

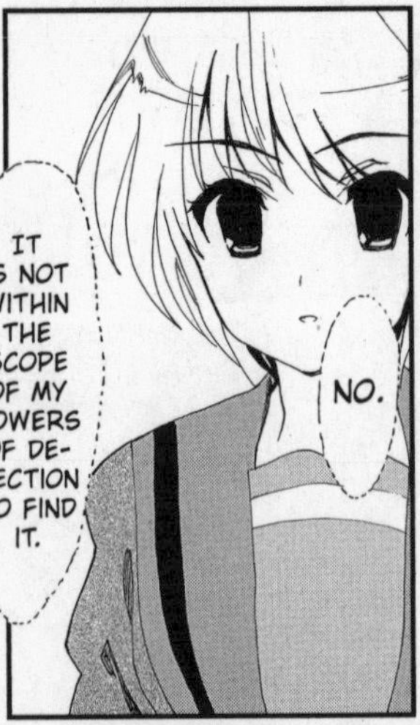
NO.
IT IS NOT WITHIN THE SCOPE OF MY POWERS OF DE-TECTION TO FIND IT.

WHAT WILL BE THE TRUTH BEHIND THE RIDDLE OF THE WANDERING SHADOW...!?

THE NEW SEMESTER HAS FINALLY BEGUN!

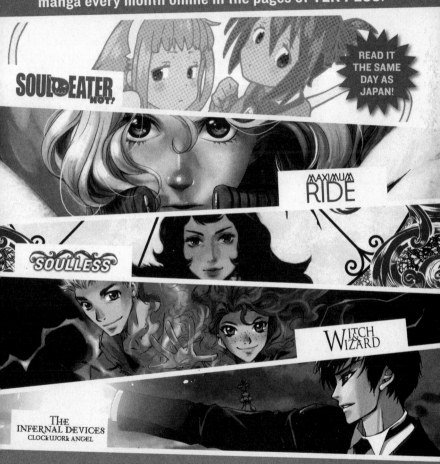
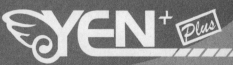

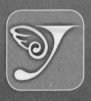
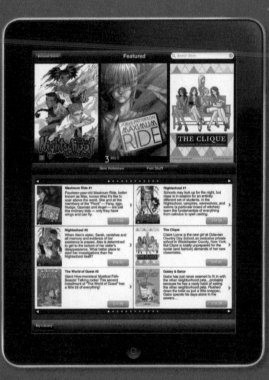
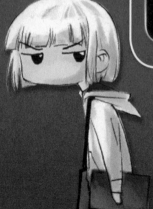

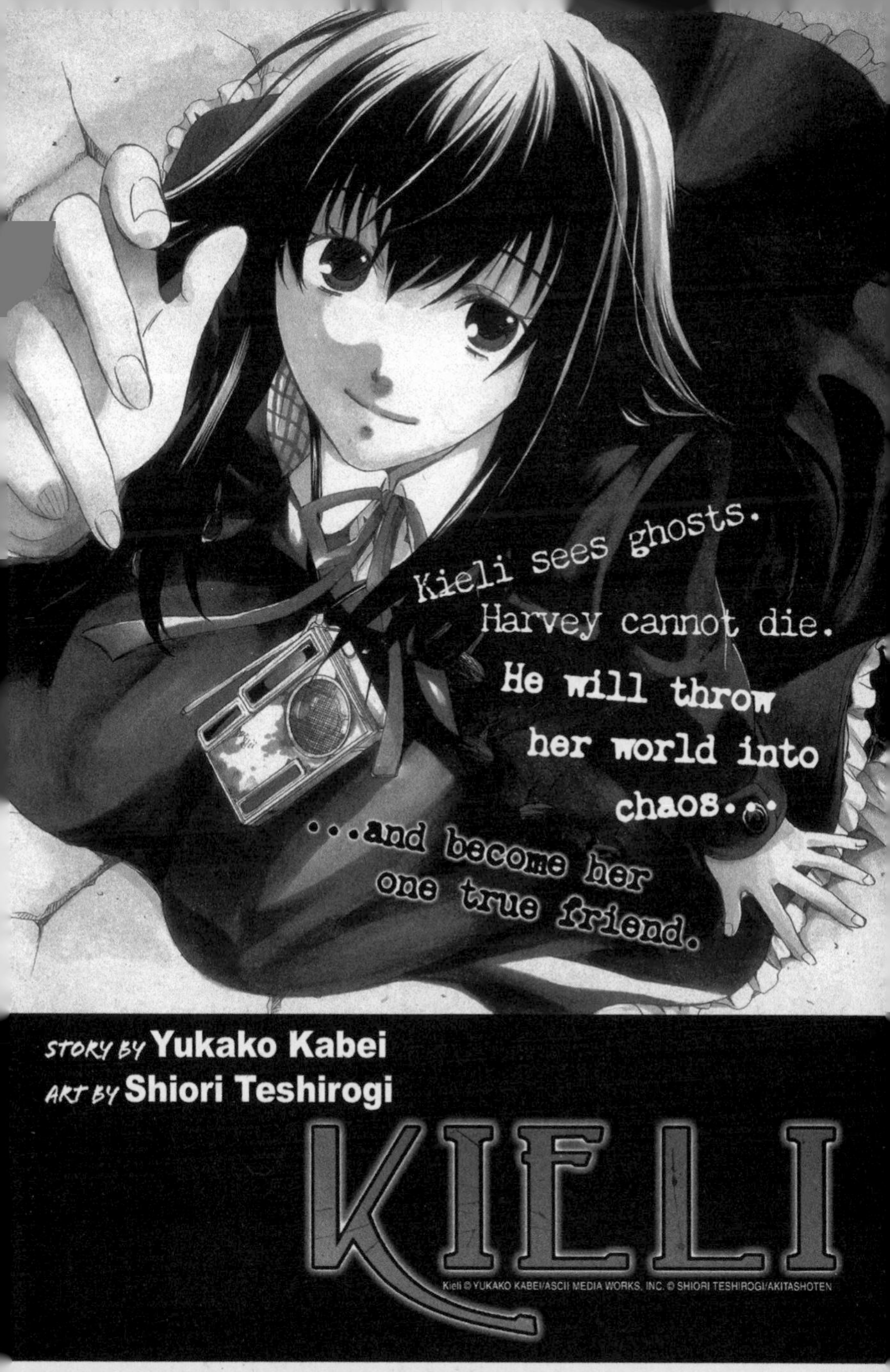
Kieli sees ghosts.
Harvey cannot die.
He will throw her world into chaos...
...and become her one true friend.
STORY BY Yukako Kabei
ART BY Shiori Teshirogi
KIELI
Kieli © YUKAKO KABEI/ASCII MEDIA WORKS, INC. © SHIORI TESHIROGI/AKITASHOTEN

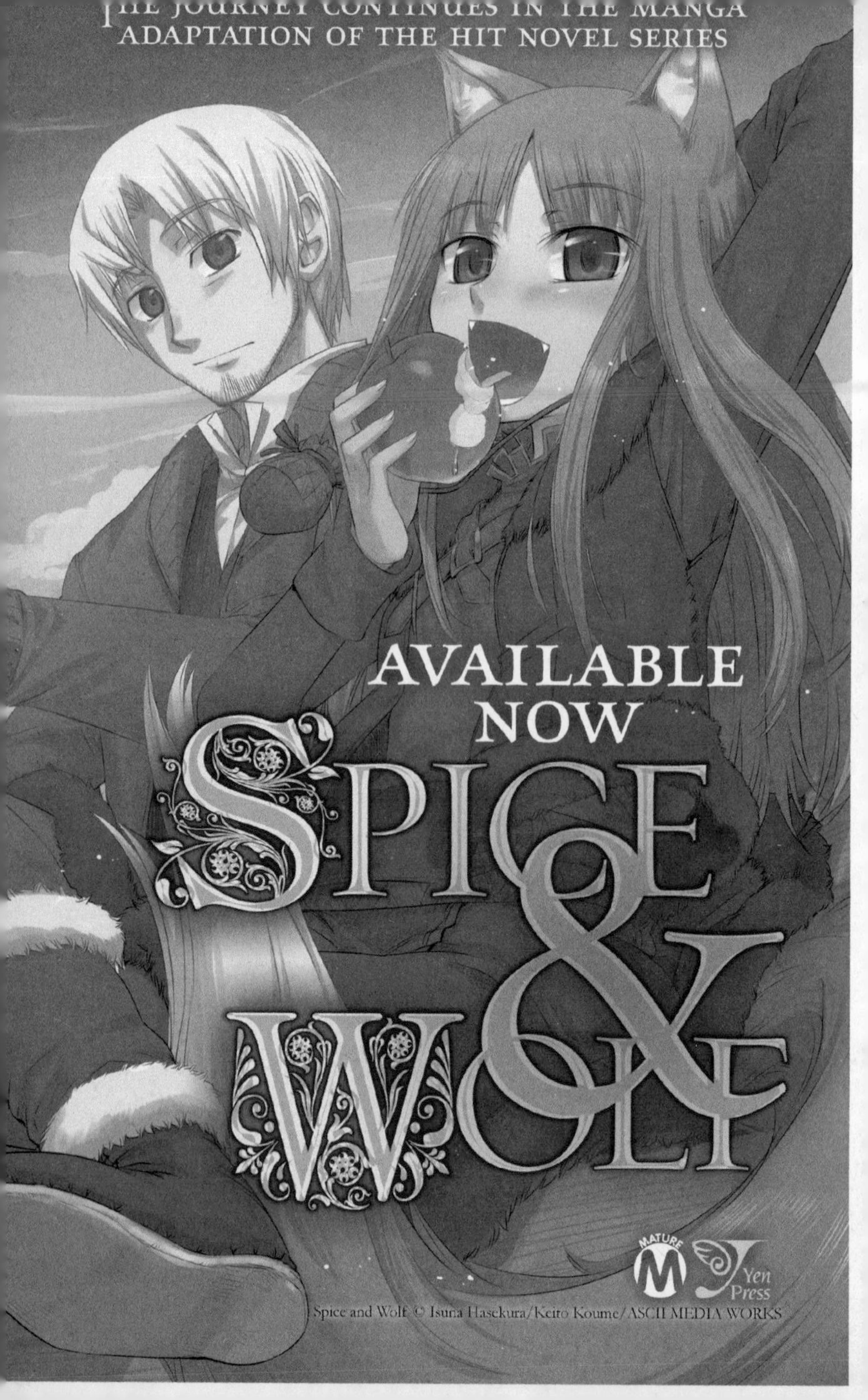
THE JOURNEY CONTINUES IN THE MANGA
ADAPTATION OF THE HIT NOVEL SERIES
AVAILABLE NOW
SPICE & WOLF
MATURE
Yen Press
Spice and Wolf © Isuna Hasekura/Keito Koume/ASCII MEDIA WORKS

THE MELANCHOLY OF HARUHI SUZUMIYA

Original Story: Nagaru Tanigawa
Manga: Gaku Tsugano
Character Design: Noizi Ito

Translation: Paul Starr
Lettering: Alexis Eckerman

This book is a work of fiction. Names, characters, places, and incidents are the product of the author's imagination or are used fictitiously. Any resemblance to actual events, locales, or persons, living or dead, is coincidental.

SUZUMIYA HARUHI NO YUUTSU Volume 15 © Nagaru TANIGAWA • Noizi ITO 2011 © Gaku TSUGANO 2011. First published in Japan in 2011 by KADOKAWA SHOTEN CO., LTD., Tokyo. English translation rights arranged with KADOKAWA SHOTEN CO., LTD., Tokyo through Tuttle-Mori Agency, Inc., Tokyo.

English translation © 2013 by Hachette Book Group, Inc.

Yen Press
Hachette Book Group
237 Park Avenue, New York, NY 10017

www.HachetteBookGroup.com
www.YenPress.com

Yen Press is an imprint of Hachette Book Group, Inc. The Yen Press name and logo are trademarks of Hachette Book Group, Inc.

First Yen Press Edition: April 2013

ISBN: 978-0-316-23230-2

10 9 8 7 6 5 4 3 2 1

BVG

Printed in the United States of America